Sexuality Counseling

Sexuality Counseling

Theory, Research, and Practice

Christine Murray
University of North Carolina at Greensboro

Amber Pope
Hodges University

Ben Willis
University of Scranton

Los Angeles | London | New Delhi
Singapore | Washington DC

Los Angeles | London | New Delhi
Singapore | Washington DC

FOR INFORMATION:

SAGE Publications, Inc.
2455 Teller Road
Thousand Oaks, California 91320
E-mail: order@sagepub.com

SAGE Publications Ltd.
1 Oliver's Yard
55 City Road
London EC1Y 1SP
United Kingdom

SAGE Publications India Pvt. Ltd.
B 1/I 1 Mohan Cooperative Industrial Area
Mathura Road, New Delhi 110 044
India

SAGE Publications Asia-Pacific Pte. Ltd.
3 Church Street
#10-04 Samsung Hub
Singapore 049483

Acquisitions Editor: Kassie Graves
Editorial Assistant: Carrie Montoya
Production Editor: Jane Haenel
Copy Editor: Grace Kluck
Typesetter: Hurix Systems Pvt. Ltd.
Proofreader: Susan Schon
Indexer: Terri Morrissey
Cover Designer: Candice Harman
Marketing Manager: Shari Countryman

Copyright © 2017 by SAGE Publications, Inc.

Printed in the United States of America

Library of Congress Cataloging-in-Publication Data

Murray, Christine E., author.

Sexuality counseling : theory, research, and practice / Christine Murray, University of North Carolina at Greensboro, Amber Pope, Hodges University, Ben Willis, University of Scranton.

pages cm. – (Counseling and Professional Identity in the 21st Century)

Includes bibliographical references and index.

ISBN 978-1-4833-4372-3 (pbk. : acid-free paper)
1. Sex counseling. 2. Sexual orientation. 3. Sexual attraction. 4. Sex. I. Pope, Amber L. II. Willis, Benjamin T. III. Title.

HQ60.5.M87 2017

306.7–dc23   2015029673

This book is printed on acid-free paper.

SFI Certified Sourcing
www.sfiprogram.org
SFI-00453

16 17 18 19 20 10 9 8 7 6 5 4 3 2 1

Brief Contents

Detailed Contents

Introduction to the Series
Counseling and Professional Identity in the 21st Century

Sexuality counseling is a unique specialty in counseling through which counselors help clients understand their sexuality, their sexual feelings and attractions toward others, and issues arising from these feelings along with sexual activities. As a result of counseling, the clients will overcome the issues and develop positive sexuality. To achieve this goal and work effectively with clients facing issues affecting their sexuality and sexual relationships, the counselors must possess knowledge and skills that are unique and specific to sexuality counseling and intervention strategies. As counselor educators, we often face a number of unique challenges when attempting to facilitate our students' understanding of the issues surrounding sexuality counseling. Beyond the specific knowledge and skills to be taught, counselor educators must also do the following: help students manage their discomfort in talking about sensitive topics related to sexuality and sexuality counseling, help students reflect on their personal biases regarding many of the topics surrounding sexuality, ground the content of sexuality in a strong basis of theory and research, and find appropriate instructional materials. *Sexuality Counseling: Research, Theory, and Practice* is a text that assists both teachers and students in addressing these issues. We are excited to present *Sexuality Counseling: Research, Theory, and Practice* which is truly a unique and effective tool that will help you on your way to become effective and competent as an emerging sexuality counseling professional.

Sexuality Counseling: Research, Theory, and Practice is a blueprint for both counselor educators and counselors-in-training. This book is grounded in an integrative, multi-level conceptual framework that addresses the various levels at which individuals experience sexuality. These levels include physiological, developmental, psychological, gender identity and sexual orientation, relational, cultural or contextual, and positive sexuality. Through addressing all these important concepts and their relevance to sexuality counseling, the book provides a unique perspective for counseling students to see how sexuality is embedded in many other mental health issues and human behaviors.

Sexuality Counseling: Research, Theory, and Practice is a text grounded in sound theory and is research based. The book emphasizes practical strategies for clinical practice that are grounded in sexuality counseling theory and research. Particularly the book addresses strategies for assessment and interventions that are not only practical but also evidence based. In addition, the book uses practical exercises, case illustrations, ethics discussions, and guided reflections. With these unique characteristics the book will assist counseling students to develop their professional competency needed for professional growth as an effective counselor in sexuality counseling.

Finally, *Sexuality Counseling: Research, Theory, and Practice* is a book that assists both counseling trainees and professionals to develop their professional identity in their practice. The text clearly defines the nature of professional identity, its value to the profession and the professional, and ways to further develop one's professional identity during professional practice.

While we are proud of the content and topics covered within this text, we are more than aware that one text, one learning experience, will not be sufficient for the development of a counselor's professional competency. The formation of both your professional identity and practice will be a lifelong process. It is a process that we hope to facilitate through the presentation of this text and the creation of our series: *Counseling and Professional Identity in the 21st Century.*

Counseling and Professional Identity in the 21st Century is a new, fresh, pedagogically sound series of texts targeting counselors in training. This series is NOT simply a compilation of isolated books matching those already in the market. Rather each book, with its targeted knowledge and skills, will be presented as but a part of a larger whole. The focus and content of each text serves as a single lens through which a counselor can view his or her clients, engage in his or her practice, and articulate his or her own professional identity.

Counseling and Professional Identity in the 21st Century is unique not just in the fact that it 'packaged' a series of traditional texts but that it provides an *integrated* curriculum targeting the formation of the readers' professional identity and efficient, ethical practice. Each book, within the series, is structured to facilitate the ongoing professional formation of the reader. The materials found within each text are organized in order to move the reader to higher levels of cognitive, affective, and psychomotor functioning, resulting in his or her assimilation of the materials presented into both his or her professional identity and approach to professional practice. While each text targets a specific set of core competencies (cognates and skills), competencies identified by professional organizations and accreditation bodies, each book in the series will emphasize each of the following:

a. The assimilation of concepts and constructs provided across the text found within the series, thus fostering the reader's ongoing development as a competent professional
b. The blending of contemporary theory with current research and empirical support
c. A focus on the development of procedural knowledge with each text employing case illustrations and guided practice exercises to facilitate the reader's ability to translate the theory and research discussed into professional decision-making and application
d. The emphasis on the need for and means of demonstrating accountability
e. The fostering of the reader's professional identity and with it the assimilation of the ethics and standards of practice guiding the counseling profession

We are proud to have served as co-editors of this series feeling sure that all of the texts included, just like *Sexuality Counseling: Research, Theory, and Practice,* will serve as a significant resource to you and your development as a professional counselor.

Richard Parsons, PhD
Naijian Zhang, PhD

Acknowledgments

I am extremely thankful to have had the opportunity to write this book, and I express my deep gratitude to Sage Publications for the opportunity and especially to the editors of this series, Naijian Zhang and Rick Parsons. My co-authors, Amber Pope and Ben Willis, exceeded all of my (already high!) expectations in the quality of their work, as well as their commitment to our collaboration on this book. It was truly a pleasure to work with you both, and I know you will continue to make me proud with all of your future accomplishments, just as you did with your work on this book. I also express my thanks to my colleagues in the University of North Carolina at Greensboro Department of Counseling and Educational Development, as well as to my current and former students, especially for all of the ways they have helped me to understand the sexuality-related concerns that clients bring to counseling and the ways that counselors can best support those clients. I also extend my gratitude to the friends and family who consistently encourage me and support me in my work. Finally, I am eternally grateful to my two sons for always challenging me to answer the most difficult questions in the simplest ways possible.

~Christine Murray

First and foremost, I would like to thank Christine Murray for inviting me to work as a co-author on this book. I am incredibly grateful for your mentorship over the past decade and hope that we will collaborate on many more projects in the future. I also extend my gratitude to all of the great counselors and educators who have contributed to my development, including my co-author Ben Willis and many others from the University of North Carolina at Greensboro (UNCG) Department of Counseling and Educational Development. Thank you to Craig Cashwell for your steady presence in my professional journey and to Keith Mobley for deepening my interest and skills in working with LGBTIQQA communities. A huge thanks to Shāna G. Cole and Jennifer P. Rosenbluth, co-owners of Tree of Life Counseling, PLLC, for their input on best practices in working with transgender clients and for offering me a home base to enhance my clinical skills in couples and sexuality counseling for two years while writing this book. To Jason and my family-of-choice, thank you for making sure I do not work too hard and for the love and enjoyment that you bring to my life. I have the best writing companion in my dog, Buster, who spent many patient hours curled by my side as I worked on this book. I feel blessed every day to work in a profession where I am constantly learning, and I am ever grateful for all the clients and students who have touched my life over the years, making me a better counselor, educator, and most importantly, a stronger person.

~Amber Pope

I would like to first off thank Christine Murray and Amber Pope for inviting me to write this book with them! I am glad for the encouragement throughout the writing process. I would also like to thank my professional mentors, teachers, and colleagues, particularly Craig Cashwell, Amy Banner, Keith Mobley, Scott Young, Kelly Wester, Todd Lewis, and Patty Von Steen. I use things that I have learned working with you in my teaching, writing, and counseling, and my experiences with you have benefited me and this book. My clients have also added to this book, and I appreciate your openness about your genuine experiences and to me. I have learned a lot about positive sexuality, development, and health by working with you; thank you. Thank you also to my doctoral studies colleagues, Ed Wahesh, Ryan Reese, Janeé Avent, Lucy Pergason, Myra Jordan, Missy Wheeler, and Laura Jones, for your support and talks through and about scholarship and writing. Thanks to the Giver of Good Gifts and to my families. Also, I am extremely grateful for Meghan, Brady, and Tessa who have supported me through it all, put up with me through all of the time away from you while writing, and taught me so much about myself, life, and sexuality. You all make my life brighter and have made my contributions to this book better.

~Ben Willis

About the Authors

Christine Murray is an associate professor and coordinator of the couple and family counseling track in the University of North Carolina at Greensboro (UNCG) Department of Counseling and Educational Development. Dr. Murray received her PhD in counselor education, with a specialization in marriage and family counseling, from the University of Florida. She completed her undergraduate degree in psychology and sociology at Duke University. She teaches graduate-level courses in family counseling, family violence, sexuality counseling, and counseling research. Dr. Murray is a licensed professional counselor and a licensed marriage and family therapist in North Carolina. She has worked as a therapist in the adult outpatient department in a community mental health agency, where she worked primarily with adults who experienced chronic, mental health disorders. She also has provided counseling in a variety of other settings, including a school for at-risk adolescents, a children's outpatient mental health treatment department, a juvenile delinquency diversion program, and churches.

Dr. Murray's primary research interest relates to bridging the gap between research and practice in the area of domestic violence. In addition, she has published in the areas of sexuality counseling, counselor education, premarital counseling, and the role of resources in couple relationships. Dr. Murray has authored over 50 published or "in press" articles in peer-reviewed scholarly journals. Dr. Murray is the lead author of *Responding to Family Violence*, a book on conducting psychotherapy with clients impacted by various forms of family violence, which was released in September 2012 by Routledge Mental Health. In addition, Dr. Murray wrote a popular press book, *Just Engaged: Prepare for Your Marriage Before You Say "I Do,"* which was based on her dissertation research and was published by Adams Media in 2008. She is also the co-founder of the See the Triumph campaign (www.seethetriumph.org), which aims to end the stigma surrounding intimate-partner violence.

Amber Pope is an associate professor and the program chair of the Clinical Mental Health Counseling program at Hodges University in Fort Myers, Florida. Dr. Pope received a PhD in counselor education and her MS in community counseling (now clinical mental health counseling) from the University of North Carolina at Greensboro. She received her undergraduate degree at UNC Chapel Hill in Psychology. She is a licensed professional counselor in North Carolina (currently pursuing licensure as a licensed mental health counselor [LMHC] in Florida) and a national certified counselor (NCC). Dr. Pope stays involved in professional development and leadership as an active member of the American Counseling Association (ACA), Association for Lesbian, Gay, Bisexual, and Transgender Issues in Counseling (ALGBTIC), Association for Counseling Education and Supervision (ACES), and other professional organizations at the state, regional, and national level. Dr. Pope currently serves as an editorial board member of the Journal of LGBT Issues in Counseling.

Dr. Pope specializes in the areas of couples counseling, sexuality concerns, gender and sexuality development, and LGBTQ-related counseling. She has experience working with transgender persons to support them through the transitioning process and conducting cross-sex hormone and gender-reassignment surgery assessments. She has worked in various clinical, mental health settings including private practice, college-campus counseling centers, outpatient mental health at community agencies, and hospitals treating a variety of presenting issues. She is trained in emotionally focused couples therapy and dialectical behavior therapy, and also utilizes solution-focused, mindfulness training, and interpersonal process techniques in therapy.

Ben Willis is an assistant professor and co-program director of the Clinical Mental Health Counseling Program at the University of Scranton in Pennsylvania. He regularly teaches and supervises Masters' in counseling students in research methods, assessment and diagnosis, group process and practice, professional issues, practicum, and internship. Dr. Willis received his MS with a specialization in couples and family counseling and his PhD in counselor education from the University of North Carolina at Greensboro. He received his bachelor's degree in biology from the University of North Carolina Chapel Hill. He is a licensed professional counselor associate in North Carolina as well as a national certified counselor and approved clinical supervisor. He has experience counseling in community agency, private practice, and college university settings working with a variety of presenting concerns including mood, anxiety, identity, relationship, development and adjustment, sexuality, substance issues, child abuse or neglect, and health concerns. He has completed an externship in emotionally focused couples therapy and utilizes a developmental and wellness approach in working with clients and students. His research is focused around how people develop and change their self-conceptualization of specific identities as well as their general sense of self.

I dedicate this book to all of my current and former students in the Sexuality Counseling class. As my students, you are also always my greatest teachers.
~Christine Murray

To Drs. Gülşah Kemer, Allison Pow, and Ali Wolf: It is a privilege to know you, learn beside you, and laugh with you.
~Amber Pope

To my clients and students: my work with you has enriched the content of this book, and may your openness and genuineness be rewarding to the readers and those that they work with! Thank you, and keep up the good work.
~Ben Willis

Chapter 1

Addressing Sexuality in Professional Counseling

What is sexuality?
What is your understanding of sexuality?
To what extent does sexuality define people's lives and intimate relationships?

We would wager a guess that if we asked the questions above to ten people, we would hear ten very different responses. We've grown accustomed to the interesting looks and responses we get when we tell people we address the topic of sexuality in our teaching, research, and clinical practice, and the responses were similar when we shared the news with our friends and family that we were writing this book. We need to look no further than these responses to know that sexuality is a topic to which people ascribe a lot of meaning, which gives rise to a range of emotional and attitudinal responses.

We can see the confusion about sexuality at a cultural level as well. On the one hand, sex is virtually everywhere—such as in popular music, advertising, movies, and television. On the other hand, many people are very uncomfortable with even the idea of discussing sex in their most personal relationships, including with their romantic partners and their children. Further, in many geographic areas, there is very limited education about sexuality in school settings (Denehy, 2007). From a family systems perspective, the issue of sex in society is a classic "double bind," in that there are conflicting social messages of "Have a lot of sex" and "Don't have sex or at least not unless you are in a committed or marriage relationship," along with the third message of "Please, *please* don't talk about it!"

Despite their professional training, counselors are not immune to the discomfort surrounding sexuality (Binik & Meana, 2009; Harris & Hays, 2008). Training in sexuality counseling is not required for many mental health professionals (Binik & Meana, 2009; Harris & Hays, 2008; Juergens, Smedema, & Berven, 2009; Kazukauskas & Lam,

2009; Miller & Byers, 2010; Southern & Cade, 2011), so unfortunately, many counselors enter their professional careers without having any formal education on how to address sexuality-related issues with their clients. Counselors are, of course, human first and as such, they are products of their social and cultural environments, and therefore often experience a good deal of anxiety discussing sexuality (Juergens, Smedema, & Berven, 2009; Kazukauskas & Lam, 2009; Kleinplatz, 2009; Nasserzadeh, 2009). Even counselors who feel generally comfortable discussing the topic often have certain sexuality-related topics that are more anxiety-provoking than others. And yet, how can counselors expect their clients to be comfortable discussing their sexuality-related concerns when they themselves are not comfortable with these topics?

Clients often seek counseling for concerns related to their sexuality, whether as their primary concern or as a secondary concern to more pressing issues (Miller & Byers, 2010; Southern & Cade, 2011). However, many counselors likely do not view sexuality concerns as being within the scope of their professional identities or competence. In many cases, clients' sexuality-related concerns are never addressed or are addressed inadequately. The reasons for this may include that their counselors fail to ask about their sexuality-related concerns, that clients do raise the issues but counselors move on prematurely to discussing other concerns, and/or that clients and counselors fumble through discussing these issues at a surface level but fail to address them with enough depth to produce meaningful change.

For all of these reasons, we believe that sexuality is an essential topic for counselors to become competent enough to address in their work. The scope of the topics included in this book demonstrates the broad range of sexuality-related concerns that clients may bring to counseling. We cannot imagine a clinical setting in which counselors would not have the potential to work with clients experiencing sexuality-related concerns. Therefore, we believe that counselors with any and all specialized backgrounds must have at least a basic understanding of how to address sexuality concerns, either themselves or through referrals to other specialized clinicians.

Our goal in this book is to provide readers with an understanding of these concerns, as well as research- and theory-based interventions for addressing them. This first chapter provides the foundation for the remaining chapters, and we begin this chapter by defining sexuality and providing an overview of the aspects of sexuality addressed later in this book. Then, we discuss key professional issues, including credentialing, the history of sexuality counseling and sex therapy, and important professional competencies. Later in the chapter, we introduce the unique ethical context for sexuality counseling. The chapter concludes with an overview of the remainder of the book. After reading this chapter, readers will be able to do the following:

a. Describe the Contextualized Sexuality Model
b. Understand the historical context surrounding sexuality counseling

   c. Delineate the distinctions between sexuality counseling and sex therapy

   d. Discuss key ethical considerations for doing sexuality counseling

DEFINING SEXUALITY

One of the most comprehensive and widely cited definitions of sexuality is the following one put forward by the World Health Organization (WHO; World Health Organization, 2010):

> Sexuality is "a central aspect of being human throughout life (that) encompasses sex, gender identities and roles, sexual orientation, eroticism, pleasure, intimacy and reproduction. Sexuality is experienced and expressed in thoughts, fantasies, desires, beliefs, attitudes, values, behaviours, practices, roles and relationships. While sexuality can include all of these dimensions, not all of them are always experienced or expressed. Sexuality is influenced by the interaction of biological, psychological, social, economic, political, cultural, legal, historical, religious and spiritual factors." (p. 4)

This definition shows that sexuality is far broader than many people initially assume. Further, the term *sexuality* is inclusive of, but not limited to, the physical act of sex and sexual orientation. The WHO (2010) definition of sexuality also emphasizes that sexuality is a very individual aspect of people's lives. Given all of the varying influences upon sexuality, each and every person expresses his or her sexuality in a unique and personalized manner.

A COMPREHENSIVE, CONTEXTUAL FRAMEWORK FOR UNDERSTANDING SEXUALITY

Several scholars advocate for a comprehensive, integrative, multidisciplinary approach to understanding human sexuality (e.g., Bitzer, Platano, Tschudin, & Alder, 2008; Levine, 2009). As such, this book is grounded in the comprehensive, contextual conceptualization of human sexuality that is presented in Figure 1.1. We refer throughout this book to this framework, which we call the *Contextualized Sexuality Model*, as an organizational framework for understanding the diverse influences on the sexuality-related issues that clients bring to counseling. This model holds that sexuality is a core component of human life, and it is embedded within numerous contextual influences. As shown in Figure 1.1, the contextual influences on human sexuality that will be discussed through the rest of the book include physiology, developmental influences, psychology, gender identity and sexual orientation, intimate relationships, cultural

Figure 1.1   The Contextualized Sexuality Model

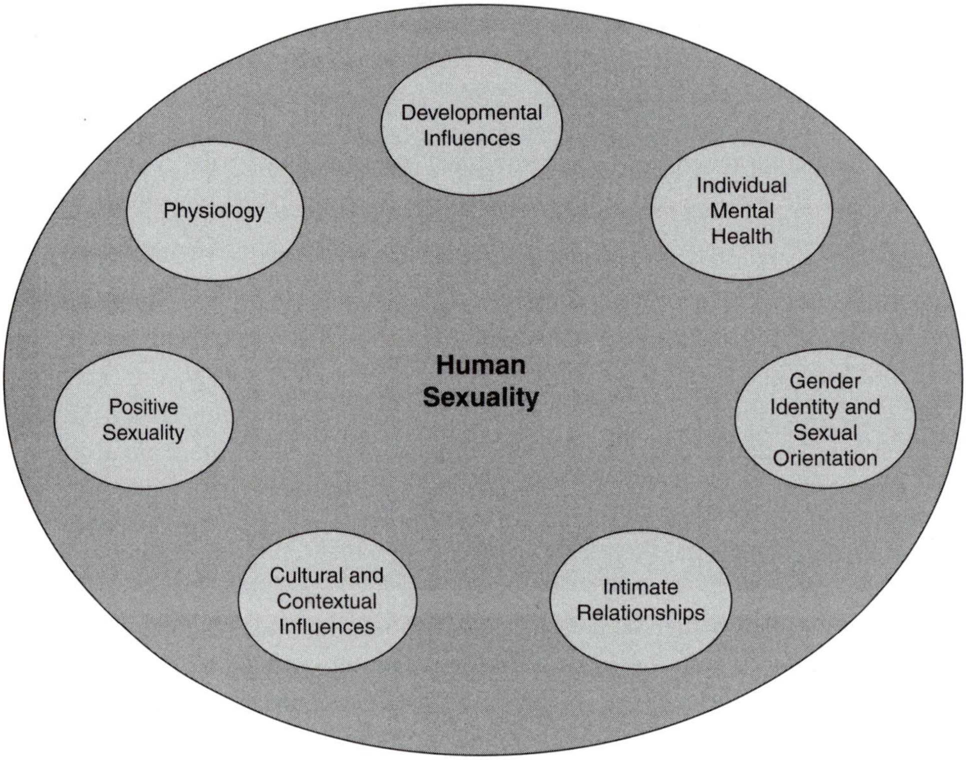

and contextual influences, and positive sexuality. These influences are reciprocal, in that each one impacts a person's sexuality, and likewise, one's views of and experiences with sexuality can impact growth and development in the contextual areas.

Although we depict each contextual influence as an independent entity, the influences are interactive and are combined in unique ways for each person. For example, one's sexual orientation cannot be understood fully without consideration of such other influences as how that sexual orientation is viewed within the client's significant cultural and social relationships or how the person expresses his or her sexual orientation within intimate relationships. We developed the Contextualized Sexuality Model to be adaptable to clients' unique needs and circumstances. We assume that clients will vary in the extent to which each contextual influence is at play in the sexuality-related concerns that they bring to counseling. For example, consider the following three case examples, all depicting scenarios of couples presenting for counseling related to conflict over disparate levels of sexual desire between partners.[*]

*All case illustrations in this book are fictional and not based on any real individuals. They were imagined to illustrate the points being made in the text.

CASE ILLUSTRATION 1.1

THE CASE OF SUSAN AND KENT

Susan (age 32) and Kent (age 33) recently had their third child. The pregnancy and delivery were difficult for Susan, and she feels overwhelmed by the responsibilities of caring full-time as a stay-at-home mom to the couple's three children. Kent works long hours as an emergency room physician. Now that the baby is 2 months old, Kent was hoping the couple would be enjoying sexual intimacy again, but Susan admits that she has no desire for sex because she is too exhausted from her parenting responsibilities. She says, "I just don't have anything left for Kent."

CASE ILLUSTRATION 1.2

THE CASE OF JOANNA AND STEVE

Joanna (age 48) and Steve (age 45) have been married for five years, and it is the second marriage for each partner. They have no children, and both enjoy busy and fulfilling jobs. However, Steve is currently being treated for depression, and his treatment includes monthly meetings with a counselor and an antidepressant medication. Steve reports that, since he was diagnosed with depression and began the medication, he has lost any interest in sex. Joanna reports that she is frustrated and would like to have a sexual relationship, but she says that she just turns her focus to her work to keep her mind off of her frustrations while Steve is being treated.

CASE ILLUSTRATION 1.3

THE CASE OF ELENA AND SOPHIA

Elena (age 65) and Sophia (age 64) are a lesbian couple who have been together for 20 years. The couple reports that they share a loving, stable relationship and feel supported and loved by their network of family and friends. They are seeking counseling because they are both nearing retirement and are concerned about the stress this transition may bring to their relationship. They indicate that one of their major concerns is the impact that this transition will have upon their sexual relationship. Both partners state that they view the physical, sexual intimacy they share as an important avenue for growing their relationship and fostering personal growth. However, because for the past several years Elena's level of sexual desire has grown increasingly greater than Sophia's, they are concerned that this will be an area for conflict once they end their careers and have more free time available.

Although each of these couples in the cases above are presenting for counseling with a similar underlying issue—one partner has a higher level of sexual desire than the other partner—the dynamics of their relationships and concerns in counseling are very different. Although all of the influences in the Contextualized Sexuality Model are likely at play to some degree in each couple's situation, certain themes are likely to be more prominent for each couple. For Susan and Kent, the most prominent influences are likely the developmental transition to expanding their family, the physiological effects of pregnancy and childbirth for Susan, and the dynamics of their intimate relationship. For Steve and Joanna, Steve's mental health appears to be a primary influence, as well as likely the physiological impacts of his antidepressant medication. And finally, for Elena and Sophia, their intimate relationship patterns over the past several years are likely interplaying with their views of the importance of sexuality for promoting positive relationships and personal growth as they figure out how to adapt their sexual relationship to their new phase of life in retirement. Of course, if we knew more details about each couple, it is likely that we would find other influences at play as well. Nonetheless, these cases demonstrate how the complexity of clients' sexuality concerns can be understood best within the broader framework of contextual influences. Before we move on to addressing professional considerations for sexuality counseling, we provide a brief introduction to each of the categories of influences in the Contextualized Sexuality Model.

Physiology

Sex and sexuality have their origins within the body, from the anatomical body parts that determine one's biological sex, to the physical touching and connections involved in intimacy with another person, and further to the physiological requirements of human reproduction (Althof, 2010; Bitzer et al., 2008; Levine, 2009). Many counselors lack intensive training in biology and anatomy, and therefore, this aspect of sexuality can be intimidating to many counselors and counselors-in-training. Nonetheless, physiological components are essential for understanding human sexuality, and therefore, counselors should equip themselves with a basic understanding of the physiological underpinnings of human sexuality. For example, a counselor working with a female concerned about her ability to become aroused to orgasm would need to understand the basic physiology surrounding female sexual functioning, as well as be comfortable discussing this client's functioning and attitudes toward that functioning as part of the counseling process.

Developmental Influences

Human sexuality can be viewed as a lifelong process that grows and evolves as people move through various developmental phases in their lives and relationships. Expectations surrounding people's sexuality often begin even while in the womb—such as through the gender expectations that arise when parents learn their baby's sex and through comments that people often jokingly make about the possibilities for the baby's future (e.g., "Someday your daughter can marry my son so we can be family!"). Sexuality in childhood often takes the form of curiosity, exploration, and many, many questions. Parents and educators often struggle with how best to talk with children about their emerging sexuality. Sadly, rates of childhood sexual abuse remain high, and therefore, some children's experiences with sexuality are impacted by their experiences of abuse.

As individuals progress through adolescence and young adulthood, their emerging sense of themselves as sexual beings continues to evolve as they navigate dating, intimate relationships, and realities about the potential consequences of sexual activities (e.g., sexually transmitted infections [STIs] and unplanned pregnancies). Throughout all of adulthood, people grow and change in their sexuality in unique and individualized ways. Although older adults are often stereotyped as being nonsexual, many adults continue to enjoy a healthy sense of sexuality throughout their entire lives. Overall, then, it is important for sexuality counselors to understand common sexuality-related developmental transitions, challenges, and opportunities that people face and how these impact clients' concerns in counseling (Althof, 2010).

Individual Mental Health

A person's overall mental health is closely intertwined with his or her sexuality (Bitzer et al., 2008; Levine, 2009). Sexuality is one avenue through which people express their beliefs, values, feelings about themselves, and body image (Juergens, Smedema, & Berven, 2009). Therefore, one's sexuality can impact one's mental health, and one's mental health can impact one's sexuality. For example, a client presenting with depressive symptoms may report a loss of interest in sexual activities, and this loss of interest in sex may also bring about anxieties about one's sexuality and relationships. Indeed, researchers have demonstrated common links between mental health disorders and sexual functioning. In addition, the Diagnostic and Statistical Manual of Mental Disorders (DSM-V; American Psychiatric Association, 2013a) contains sections on sexual dysfunctions and gender dysphoria, and therefore, a category of mental disorders relates directly to sexuality-related concerns. Further, there is growing recognition of the links between addiction and sexuality, including sexually compulsive and addictive behaviors. In addition, the mental health consequences of trauma, whether related to sexual abuse or other forms of trauma, can impact clients' sexuality. Therefore, individual mental health functioning is an important contextual area for understanding human sexuality.

Gender Identity and Sexual Orientation

Sexuality is undoubtedly impacted by how people view their gender and sexual orientation. Gender identity encompasses not only whether one views him- or herself to be male, female, and/or transgender but also the meanings the person ascribes to that gender role (Juergens, Smedema, & Berven, 2009). Therefore, counselors can make no assumptions about what it means for someone to be a woman, man, or transgender person in society today. Likewise, sexual orientation is a more complicated construct than a categorical view (i.e., straight, gay, lesbian, or bisexual) that this construct implies. For example, Holden and Holden (1995) described the Sexual Identity Profile (SIP), which demonstrates that people's sexual identities are far more multidimensional than commonly thought. The SIP suggests that people define their sexual identities along five continuums, falling somewhere between homosexual and heterosexual on the following five dimensions: (a) sexual orientation (i.e., toward which sex one is erotically attracted), (b) sexual attitudes (i.e., one's beliefs about which sexual orientations are acceptable or unacceptable), (c) erotic behaviors (i.e., the sex or sexes with which the person engages in sexual behaviors), (d) public image (i.e., how others perceive one's sexual orientation), and (e) nonerotic behaviors (i.e., the sex or sexes with which the person uses non-sexual forms of interaction and touch, such as handshakes). Holden and Holden asserted that the ideal profile, meaning the one that would most likely lead the person to feel a sense of congruence about his or her sexual identity, is one in which the person falls at similar points along the first four dimensions and falls near the center along the fifth continuum. In other words, a person with a congruent profile would understand the sex(es) that are erotically attractive, believe that this sexual orientation is acceptable, engage appropriately in sexual behaviors that are consistent with his or her sexual orientation, and be accepted by others as having that sexual orientation, and yet they would feel comfortable interacting and engaging with others regardless of gender. Therefore, it is important for counselors to understand not only the labels that clients ascribe to their gender and sexual orientation but also how their gender identity and sexual orientation fit within the broader social and individual context (Bitzer et al., 2008; Levine, 2009).

Intimate Relationships

Relationship functioning is an important aspect of sexuality (Althof, 2010; Bitzer et al., 2008; Levine, 2009). Sexual activity often occurs within the context of an intimate relationship, and so the health and dynamics of that relationship contribute to how sexual and relationship partners experience sex and sexuality. Common folklore holds that "Sex is the glue that holds partners together," and also that "Sex is a barometer of how things are in other areas of a couple's relationship." Although there may be some truth to these statements for some couples, counselors must set aside the assumptions that they hold about the role of sex in intimate relationships, as clients will vary widely in their sexual attitudes, behaviors, and practices within their relationships. For some couples, sexual intimacy is a primary vehicle for connection, but other couples place a much lower value on physical intimacy and may achieve intimacy in various other ways. Further, some couples cannot engage in sexual behaviors, such as when physical health conditions or disabilities prohibit this form of sexual expression. Relationships can come in many forms, from casual dating relationships to monogamous partners, to marriage and domestic partnerships, to open and polyamorous relationships. The meaning and functions of sexuality within clients' intimate relationships are important for understanding how clients express and view their sexuality.

Cultural and Contextual Influences

Tiefer (2009) defined sexuality as

> a socially constructed realm of human experience composed of interpersonal conduct, psychomotor learning, cultural attitudes and values, and physical function. Because of its connections to social location, reproduction, and pleasure, sexuality is first and foremost political, as witness the history of monitoring and regulation in all cultures. (p. 1046)

Tiefer's (2009) perspective on sexuality contrasts with many common assumptions that sexuality begins with the physical components and our goal is not to determine which perspective holds the most truth. However, Tiefer's commentary on the political nature of sexuality provides an important reminder that sexuality always occurs within social contexts, and those social contexts influence the norms and rules that determine how clients express their sexuality. These contextual influences include ethnicity and culture, but they also extend to religion and spirituality, socioeconomic factors, geographic influences, and the influences of the media (Althof, 2010; Bitzer et al., 2008; Levine, 2009; Juergens, Smedema, & Berven, 2009).

Positive Sexuality

The notion of positive sexuality suggests that sexuality can provide an important avenue for personal and relational growth and that healthy sexuality is not merely the absence of sexual problems and dysfunctions. Although positive sexuality is inherently linked to all of the other areas discussed above, we believe it is important to consider it as a unique context for understanding human sexuality. Historically, much of the emphasis on sexuality within the mental health professions has focused on the treatment of sexual dysfunctions and other problematic areas of clients' expression of their sexuality. However, as we discuss in Chapter 10, a new view is emerging that provides a more positive lens for understanding the roles that sexuality can play in people's lives. Clients need not be experiencing sexual difficulties to benefit from addressing their sexuality within counseling. Rather, clients' expressions of their sexuality can provide insights and opportunities for enhancing their personal development and achieving greater connectedness and fulfillment within their intimate relationships.

PROFESSIONAL ISSUES IN SEXUALITY COUNSELING

The area of sexuality counseling raises many questions for counselors, including how sexuality counseling differs from sex therapy, whether additional credentials are required, and what constitutes professional behaviors and competence when practicing in this area. These issues can best be understood within a historical context, and we begin this section by reviewing key historical developments that impact sexuality counseling practice today.

The Historical Context

Perspectives on human sexuality within the mental health professions have shifted significantly over time. Some of the earliest views on sexuality were proposed by Freud, who viewed sexual feelings as reflective of internal psychological conflicts (Goodwach, 2005a; Southern & Cade, 2011). However, sexuality remained relatively under-studied until Alfred Kinsey began his high-profile research in the 1940s and 1950s (Goodwach, 2005a; Southern & Cade, 2011), which challenged many predominant norms about sexuality and especially female sexuality. Following this and led by the work of William Masters and Virginia Johnson, sex therapy was predominantly focused on behavioral approaches to address sexual dysfunction (Goodwach, 2005a; Southern & Cade, 2011). The term *sex therapy* was first used in the 1950s by Masters and Johnson, although it was not used widely until the 1970s (Binik & Meana, 2009). Around this same time (i.e., from the late 1950s to the 1970s), the American culture at large also experienced a significant period of sexual exploration and experimentation (Goodwach, 2005a). This resulted in a range of humanistic approaches (e.g., surrogate partners, nudism, mind-body approaches, and counselors using sexual touch with clients) (Tiefer, 2006), many of which are no longer accepted as professional or ethical today.

Early sex therapy in the 1970s focused on dysfunction-specific treatments that typically integrated educational approaches combined with behavioral and communication-based interventions (Binik & Meana, 2009). In particular, Dr. Helen Singer Kaplan's approach in the 1970s integrated medical and psychological approaches with sex therapy (Southern & Cade, 2011). A new category of sexual dysfunctions first appeared in the DSMIII in 1980 (Binik & Meana, 2009). Sexuality moved further into the mainstream of social dialogue in the United States in the 1980s with the publication of several high-profile sexual self-help books and numerous TV personalities (e.g., Dr. Ruth) emerging on different media platforms (Binik & Meana, 2009; Southern & Cade, 2011).

Moving further into the 1980s and 1990s, the field of sex therapy experienced a shift toward medical approaches to treating sexual dysfunction, especially with a series of highly publicized medications designed to treat erectile dysfunction (Goodwach, 2005a; Tiefer, 2006). By and large, conceptualizations of sexual dysfunctions were grounded in heterosexual sexuality (Marshall, 2002). The focus on medical aspects of sexuality has received some pushback from sex therapists and feminist scholars (Tiefer, 2001). In particular, advocates have raised concerns that the pharmaceutical industry will do to female sexuality what they perceived occurred to male sexuality, which is reducing it to problems that are solvable simply by popping a pill (Tiefer, 2001). Further, advocates argue that the full scope of human sexuality and eroticism is difficult to capture in empirical medical approaches to research (Tiefer, 2001).

In response to the increasing medicalization of sexual problems, a feminist working group convened to develop the New View Campaign to present an alternative framework for understanding women's sexual concerns (Nicholls, 2008; Southern & Cade, 2011). Rather than adopting a view of sexual problems that is based in Masters and Johnson's conceptualization of the sexual response cycle, the New View focused on the multiple contexts that influence women's sexuality, including their physiology, psychology, and social relationships (Nicholls, 2008). The fundamental tenet of the New View is that women's sexual functioning can best be understood within their relational context. The New View suggests that women's sexual problems generally fall into the following four categories, with additional subcategories falling within each broader category: (a) sexual problems due to sociocultural, political, or economic factors (e.g., lack of sex education or health care and problematic social norms); (b) sexual problems relating to partner or relationship (e.g., abuse, different levels of desire, and communication problems); (c) sexual problems due to psychological problems (e.g., sexual aversion and fear); and (d) sexual problems due to medical factors (e.g., pregnancy, medication side effects, and medical conditions) (Southern & Cade, 2011). Nicholls conducted a qualitative study to determine the extent to which the New View aligned with women's lived experiences of their sexuality. Approximately 70% of the women's sexual concerns corresponded with the subcategories of the broader categories outlined in the New View framework, and Nicholls suggested that the other concerns were aligned with the framework with some modifications.

More recently, the sex therapy field has shifted to a more comprehensive, systemic approach to understanding and treating sexual concerns (Goodwach, 2005a). This has included a greater acceptance of varying sexual orientations, an increased treatment focus on family-of-origin issues, and more emphasis on sexual education for clients (Goodwach, 2005a). In addition, Althof (2010) noted that four major, recent advances in the sex therapy field include advances in combined medical and psychotherapeutic approaches, the use of mindfulness-based approaches, therapy that integrates the use of the Internet, and new approaches to understanding and treating female genital pain disorders. Another important development in more recent decades was the proliferation of Internet use among the general population, which provided both positive advances—such as greater availability of sexual health information—and potential pitfalls—such as easier access to compulsive sexual behaviors (Southern & Cade, 2011).

Clients today still may seek help for sexual concerns and desire behavioral and/or medical solutions (Goodwach, 2005b; Marshall, 2002). Indeed, the medical aspects of sexual treatment have outpaced new psychotherapy advances in the new millennium (Althof, 2010). Some sex therapists view the focus on medical advancements as a detriment to the field because of the preferred emphasis on medical treatments as compared to psychotherapeutic ones (Binik & Meana, 2009). However, psychotherapy can be integrated into medical treatment (Binik & Meana, 2009) and may even offer benefits and growth for the sex therapy field (Binik & Meana, 2009). Pukall and Reissing (2007) suggested that advancements in medicine related to human sexuality will not harm, but rather help, the non-medical professional approaches to sexuality. In particular, they suggested that medical advancements offer new opportunities for sex therapists to train medical professionals about sexuality and relationships. Medical advances also raise the public profile of the topic of sexuality, such that members of the general population may become more inclined to seek all forms of treatment for their sexual concerns.

Within the past 20 years, the field of sex therapy and counseling has been criticized for failing to advance and innovate (Althof, 2010; Binik & Meana, 2009). However, the research base surrounding the treatment of sexual problems has continued to grow and encompass more rigorous methods (Althof, 2010). Within the relatively short history of this area of practice, there have been numerous and significant changes in the practices and assumptions within the field. At the same time, there has been a growing emphasis on the professionalism of the field, as evidenced by the current availability of the professional credentials discussed in the next section.

Credentialing and Professional Identity Issues

Professional organizations and credentialing help to ensure that a profession maintains high standards and protects client welfare (Guldner, 1995). In addition, credentialing requires that professionals meet minimum training and experiential requirements specific to sexuality, and professionals without credentials have no such guaranteed minimal requirements (Kleinplatz, 2009). Although there are credentials available for sexuality counselors and sex therapists (Binik & Meana, 2009), these areas of practice generally are not regulated by state licensure bodies, and therefore, there is less oversight of practice in these areas than in general mental health professional licensure (Binik & Meana, 2009).

Distinguishing Between Sexuality Counseling and Sex Therapy

Before describing the main credentialing options available, it is important to begin with definitions that can help to clarify the difference between *sexuality counseling* and *sex therapy*. The American Association of Sexuality Educators, Counselors, and Therapists (AASECT) is the primary credentialing organization in the United States. AASECT (2013) offers the following definitions of sexuality counselors as compared to sex therapists:

> Sexuality counselors . . . assist the client to realistically resolve concerns through the introduction of problem solving techniques of communication as well as providing accurate information and relevant suggestions of specific exercises and techniques in sexual expression. Sexuality counseling is generally short term and client centered, focusing on the immediate concern or problem. (para. 2)

> Sex therapists are licensed mental health professionals, trained to provide in-depth psychotherapy, who have specialized in treating clients with sexual issues and concerns. . . . Sex therapists work with simple sexual concerns also, but in addition, where appropriate, are prepared to provide comprehensive and intensive psychotherapy over an extended period of time in more complex cases. (para. 3)

Therefore, according to AASECT (2013), the main distinctions between sexuality counselors and sex therapists are the degrees of the intensity of the treatment and the complexity of the cases. Southern and Cade (2011) stated that sexuality counseling incorporates a focus on developmental influences on individual and relational sexual functioning, and it also integrates general counseling theories, current research-based approaches, collaborations with medical professionals, and postmodern thinking. Sex therapy is considered to be much more specialized than sexuality counseling, as reflected in Althof's (2010) statement that sex therapy is "a specialized form of psychotherapy that draws upon an array of technical interventions known to effectively treat male and female sexual dysfunctions" (p. 6). Later in this chapter, we will discuss the PLISSIT model, which is a useful tool for helping practitioners determine which cases require the more intensive therapy provided by sex therapists (American Association of Sexuality Educators, Counselors, and Therapists, 2013).

Is Sexuality a True Specialty Area?

The specialized credentialing of sexuality counselors and sex therapists has not been without controversy, and there has been some professional dialogue regarding whether sex therapy is justifiably considered a unique specialization. For example, Binik and Meana (2009) suggested that sex therapy lacks many of the basic foundations needed for a psychotherapy practice to be considered a unique specialty, including a strong underlying theoretical basis, a distinct approach to clinical practice, and a strong empirical basis to show the effectiveness of treatment. Binik and Meana argue that the view of sex therapy as a distinct specialty has had the effect of marginalizing sexual treatment within the broader field of psychotherapy. As a result, many counselors view sexuality-focused treatment as falling outside the scope of their practice (Binik & Meana, 2009).

In response to Binik and Meana (2009), Kleinplatz (2009) wrote that credentialing in the area of sex therapy and sexuality counseling serves the primary and important function of protecting clients. In particular, due to the general lack of training in sexuality among most mental health professionals, in combination with the proliferation of inaccurate and biased information that exists in society, there is a high potential for harm when clients seek treatment related to sexuality from inadequately trained professionals (Kleinplatz, 2009). Kleinplatz cited anecdotal evidence that credentialed therapists often work with clients who have been harmed by other, inadequately prepared professionals when they practiced outside of the bounds of their competence. Kleinplatz goes on to suggest that until all mental health and other healthcare professionals receive adequate training in sexuality as part of their professional preparation, specialized credentials are needed. Tiefer (2009) also responded to Binik and Meana (2009) and suggested that a specialization related to sexuality is necessary because sexuality is an inherently and extensively complicated issue that faces unique contexts—especially related to the social, political, and relational contexts—as compared to other areas of mental health practice.

Despite the dialogue regarding whether sexuality counseling and sex therapy are justified as being considered unique specialization areas, both professionals and the general public now view sex therapy as a specialized discipline (Binik & Meana, 2009). The availability of professional training programs for professionals interested in working as sex therapists or sexologists, as well as specialized professional journals (Binik & Meana, 2009), add to the general view that these areas require specialized training and educational experiences.

Credentialing Options

AASECT (2013) offers certification as a certified sexuality counselor and as a certified sex therapist, in addition to their certified sexuality educator credential for those who do teaching and training about sex and sexuality. Both of the sexuality counselor and sex therapist certifications require a combination of professional requirements (e.g., membership in AASECT and adherence to the AASECT Code of Ethics), educational requirements, direct practice (i.e., clinical work) under appropriate supervision, and training experiences addressing personal attitudes and values related to sexuality (American Association of Sexuality Educators, Counselors, and Therapists, 2013). Mental health professionals who hold at least a master's degree and are licensed in their states are not eligible for the certified sexuality counselor credential, as they are only eligible for credentialing as a certified sex therapist once they meet the requirements (American Association of Sexuality Educators, Counselors, and Therapists, 2013). Readers interested in these credentialing options are encouraged to consult the AASECT website (www.aasect.org) for the most current information regarding credentialing requirements.

Relevant Professional Organizations

Counselors interested in gaining additional information and professional networking opportunities may wish to become involved with AASECT and/or other professional associations related to sexuality. Beyond AASECT, which holds an annual conference and offers other such benefits as a referral service, list-serv, and advocacy, two other relevant organizations are the Society for Sex Therapy and Research (SSTAR; http://www.sstarnet.org/) and the Sexuality Information and Education Council of the United States (SEICUS; www.seicus.org). All of these organizations are very interdisciplinary (Binik & Meana, 2009) and provide potentially valuable resources for sexuality counseling.

PROFESSIONAL COMPETENCE IN SEXUALITY COUNSELING

Ethically, professionals must always practice within the bounds of their professional competence. Therefore, professionals must understand their own level of competence to address sexuality-related issues in their work. Whether or not they seek a specialized credential in this area, all counselors should be equipped with a basic understanding of sexuality issues, as well as where they can refer clients for issues that extend beyond the scope of their own competence. Again, clients in any clinical setting may experience sexuality-related problems or other concerns that impact their sexual functioning. However, existing research suggests that most mental health professionals lack the basic competence to address sexuality issues in counseling (Harris & Hays, 2008). This is problematic for a number of reasons because when counselors fail to address sexuality-related issues with their clients, issues that are important to clients may be ignored and clients remain ill-equipped to process the misinformation about sexuality that they receive from others and social messaging (Harris & Hays, 2008).

Training related to sexuality is sorely lacking in many mental health, professional training programs. For example, Miller and Byers (2010) surveyed 162 practicing clinical and counseling psychologists in the United States and Canada. They found that although less than one-third (31%) of the psychologists they surveyed had taken a graduate-level course in sexuality and less than 70% of them had received any other form of observational learning related to sexuality during their graduate training, most participants had provided psychotherapy to clients whose concerns related to sexuality. Training in certain areas, such as masturbation, STIs, and working with sex offenders, was especially limited. Many of the participants in Miller and Byers had sought out other forms of education (e.g., reading books and attending workshops). Of course, the quality and content of these informal resources can vary widely.

We cannot understate the importance of counselors seeking out training and experience to foster their competence in the area of sexuality counseling. Two surveys of mental health professionals underscore the importance of knowledge in this area. First, Juergens, Smedema, and Berven (2009) surveyed 116 students in master's degree programs for rehabilitation counseling in the United States. They found that students who had greater levels of knowledge about sexuality, as well as more comfort with sexuality, were more willing to discuss sexuality-related issues with their clients. Second, in a survey of clinical members of the American Association for Marriage and Family Therapy, Harris and Hays (2008) found that therapists who had specific training and who had received supervision related to sexuality counseling issues were most likely to feel comfortable raising the topic of sexuality with their clients. In addition, therapists who were more comfortable themselves with the subject of sexuality were, perhaps not surprisingly, more comfortable raising the topic with their clients. To assist readers in determining their current level of competence for sexuality counseling and in identifying areas for further growth, we provide the following checklist of the core components of competence to address sexuality in counseling (Kazukauskas & Lam, 2009; Southern & Cade, 2011).

Exercise 1.1

WHAT IS YOUR CURRENT LEVEL OF COMPETENCE IN SEXUALITY COUNSELING?

Consider the following questions that reflect different aspects of competence in sexuality counseling. Circle "Yes" or "No" in response to each question. The questions for which you answered "No" are indicators of areas in which you may benefit from seeing additional training, experience, and/or information about local and national resources.

1. Are you comfortable talking about sexuality with clients? Yes/No

2. Do you understand the impact that common sexual health problems (e.g., STIs, infertility, sexual dysfunctions, relational conflict about sexual intimacy, and high-risk sexual behaviors) can have on clients? Yes/No

3. Are you knowledgeable about appropriate assessment strategies to assess the sexual health problems described in question 2? Yes/No

4. Are you knowledgeable about appropriate treatment strategies to use in counseling to address the sexual health problems described in question 2? Yes/No

5. Do you understand the basics of human anatomy and physiology related to sex and sexuality, such that you could describe these to clients? Yes/No

6. Do you have the training and experience to be competent to address related client concerns, such as body image and relationship issues? Yes/No

7. Are you knowledgeable of and connected to referral sources for clients whose sexuality-related concerns are beyond your competence? Yes/No

8. When addressing sexuality issues in counseling, are you able to maintain appropriate boundaries and address boundary crossings, such as a client expressing romantic interest in you? Yes/No

Readers likely vary in their levels of competence in each of the items included on the checklist above (Southern & Cade, 2011). To help counselors further determine those sexuality-related issues they are competent to address and those for which they should refer clients to specialized treatment, Juergens, Smedema, and Berven (2009) and Southern and Cade (2011) provided an overview of Annon's PLISSIT Model. This model's name stands for Permission – Limited Information – Specific Suggestions – Intensive Therapy. This model provides a framework for helping counselors decide if and when to refer clients for help that reaches beyond the scope of their competence. At the first level of Permission, clients receive the opportunity and support to discuss their sexuality concerns. Second, the Limited Information level involves counselors offering clients accurate sex information and the chance to explore the social messages surrounding clients' concerns. The third level of Specific Suggestions involves specific interventions that are designed to meet the clients' needs, and these may integrate interventions focusing on physiology, mental health, and/or relationships. At the final level of Intensive Therapy, clients receive in-depth treatment to address the full complexity of their concerns. Counselors must consider which of these levels their training and experience have adequately equipped them to provide to clients (Southern & Cade, 2011).

The question of when counselors should refer clients for specialized treatment (e.g., to a certified sex therapist) is a complicated one. Counselors must consider carefully whether they are referring out of personal discomfort rather than based on what is in the best interest of the client (Binik & Meana, 2009). Clients may feel that their concerns are being dismissed by the original therapist if they are immediately referred for specialized sex therapy treatment (Binik & Meana, 2009). When a counselor refers a client to a specialized sex therapist for specific treatment of a sexual dysfunction, she or he runs the risk that the client's sexual dysfunction may be treated outside of the broader context surrounding the client's sexual concerns, including relational, other psychological, and broader social context issues (Binik & Meana, 2009). When a client's sexual concerns fall clearly outside of the counselor's level of professional competence, a referral for specialized sex therapy may indeed be warranted. However, these referrals must be handled with care to ensure that the client's needs are considered during the transfer process.

There is a critical need for more training in sexuality for counselors (Harris & Hays, 2008). Until this is widely done, however, many counselors will be left to their own devices to seek out the knowledge, skills, and personal comfort to address these issues with their clients. Counselors should be up front with their clients if they are venturing into an area around which the counselor has limited competence and/or training (Corley & Schneider, 2002). We also suggest clinical supervision in areas where counselors are developing new areas of competence.

Competence and Personal Values: The Importance of Self-Reflection

In the realm of sexuality, counselors must be careful to avoid confusing personal values that conflict with clients' choices for a lack of competence. Counselors are ethically bound to provide services without discriminating against clients based on their ethnic backgrounds, nationality, gender, sexual orientation, and other personal characteristics (e.g., American Counseling Association, 2014). This can certainly present challenges to counselors if they hold personal beliefs that conflict with clients' sexual orientations, culturally derived sexual norms, or other sexual practices. In light of a string of recent court cases, the issue as to whether religious counselors may refuse to work with homosexual clients on the grounds of their religious beliefs has recently received a good deal of professional attention (Priest & Wickel, 2011). These cases have shown that when someone enters a training program and profession that ascribes to a Code of Ethics that contains such a nondiscrimination policy, they are required to be able to provide counseling services to clients without discrimination, regardless of their personal beliefs (Rudow, 2012; 2013).

Simply referring clients whose sexual orientations or practices are uncomfortable to counselors has a great potential for harming clients (Priest & Wickel, 2011). Certain client populations, such as lesbian, gay, bisexual, and transgender (LGBT) clients, have historically felt marginalized from psychotherapy, and so it may be valuable for counselors to make extra efforts to make their treatment settings welcoming and responsive to these clients' needs (Safren, 2005; Sobocinski, 1990). Beyond sexual orientation, counselors should consider other sexual concerns or practices that may lead them to have potentially harmful reactions to clients. For example, consider a counselor who believes that sexual intercourse should occur only in the context of a committed, heterosexual marriage. How might this counselor react when a client shares experiences of swinging or engaging in a ménage a trois? This counselor may have an internal reaction (e.g., anxiety, judgmental thoughts, or disgust), as well as a nonverbal response, such as raised eyebrows, a facial expression of shock, or a change in tone of speech (e.g., talking quickly or with a shaky voice). Managing internal reactions is part of an ongoing process of self-reflection for counselors, and if managed effectively, these reactions can be prevented from negatively impacting the counseling relationship. However, the likely impacts of negative non-verbal responses include clients feeling judged or condemned, losing trust in the counselor, and choosing to not disclose additional personal information. Therefore, counselors must be aware of possible biases that they bring to the counseling relationship (Goodwach, 2005b; Priest & Wickel, 2011). Through personal reflection, clinical supervision, and consultation, counselors should examine their biases and the extent to which these may impact their competence in treating certain client populations (Goodwach, 2005b; Sobocinski, 1990).

The Ability to Talk Professionally and Comfortably About Sexuality as a Counselor

Sex and sexuality are often very difficult topics to discuss, whether personally or in a professional context. Binik and Meana (2009) suggested that although many mental health professionals lack comfort in talking about sexuality-related issues with clients, sexuality is a significant and natural part of life that all counselors must strive to develop comfort and competence to address in their work. Binik and Meana even said, "If sex, the very activity that perpetuates human life, is a source of paralyzing anxiety for a would-be mental health practitioner, then something is wrong with our professional training" (p. 1023).

A more valuable question to ask than, "Are you comfortable talking about sexuality with your clients?" is "Which aspects of sexuality are you more and less comfortable discussing?" Given all of the conflicting societal messages and lack of education on sexuality, it is likely that every single person has certain sexuality-related topics that they would be at least somewhat anxious to talk about with others. Some counselors may feel wholly uncomfortable with the topic, while others may experience discomfort in just a few specific topic areas. Nonetheless, existing research suggests that feeling comfortable talking about sexuality may be even more important than knowledge in counselors' ability to raise the issue of sexuality with their clients (Harris & Hays, 2008).

Counselors therefore should strive to increase their comfort in talking about sexuality in a professional context. Several activities can help to promote this comfort. First, counselors can practice engaging in these discussions during training exercises, clinical supervision, and professional consultation. Second, counselors can develop an extensive vocabulary to use when discussing sexuality issues. As will be discussed later in this book, it is important for counselors to use language that is in line with clients' worldviews. Overly clinical and technical language can decrease the emotional aspects of clients' experiences, whereas overly informal language may be interpreted as crude or offensive by clients. Third, when addressing sexuality concerns with clients, counselors must strike a balance between the professional boundaries in place and the personal impact of this work (Nijs, 2006). Counselors of course cannot deny their humanity and are likely to be impacted personally by their work related to sexuality, especially when working with clients impacted by sexual trauma (Nijs, 2006). Therefore, to continue to develop increasing comfort in addressing sexuality in counseling, counselors should engage in self-care when working with clients on sexuality-related issues (Nijs, 2006). Finally, counselors can engage in ongoing reflection to examine their personal barriers to becoming comfortable discussing sexuality, as well as strategies to overcome these barriers. To help counselors start with this final activity, we provide sample reflection questions in Exercise 1.2.

Exercise 1.2

GUIDED REFLECTION EXERCISE: BARRIERS TO PERSONAL COMFORT IN TALKING ABOUT SEXUALITY

Take time to consider your reactions to the following questions. You can write in a journal about your responses or discuss your responses with a trusted colleague or supervisor.

1. Growing up, how comfortable was your family in talking about sex and sexuality?

2. What messages did you receive when talking about sexuality when you were a child?

3. Thinking back to the earliest questions about sexuality that you asked adults during your childhood, what responses did you get to these questions?

4. With which types of clients do you believe you would be most and least comfortable talking about sexuality? What factors make you more or less comfortable with each population?

5. Which sexual practices might clients discuss that would be most shocking to you? How do you think you would respond if a client talked about his or her experiences with these practices?

6. Imagine if a client asked you to give him or her specific advice on sexual technique (e.g., how to make a partner orgasm or how to masturbate). What would your response be?

7. Think through the clinical, informal, and slang terms you know to describe sex and sexual parts of males' and females' bodies. What reactions do you have to these words? Now imagine saying those words to a client or supervisor. What emotional reactions might you have to saying those words?

ETHICAL CONSIDERATIONS FOR SEXUALITY COUNSELING

Sexuality counseling presents counselors with unique ethical considerations that reflect the sensitive and personal nature of the subject of sexuality. In this section, we draw upon two primary ethical codes, that of the American Counseling Association (ACA; American Counseling Association, 2014) and the American Association of Sexuality Educators, Counselors, and Therapists (AASECT; American

Association of Sexuality Educators, Counselors, and Therapists, 2004). Mental health professionals from other disciplines must be sure that they are following the ethical guidelines of their professional associations, as well as all relevant legal regulations. In addition to the ethics of the competence issues already reviewed above, the ethical issues reviewed in this section are as follows: the ethics of sexual relationships and client vulnerability, client confidentiality and secrets, so-called reparative therapies for clients with a same-sex orientation, and sexual attractions or relationships within client-counselor and counselor-supervisor relationships. Additional ethical considerations are discussed throughout this book in the relevant chapters. Counselors are advised to seek additional training through continuing education programs to maintain an ongoing focus on addressing these ethical concerns throughout their careers (Hoffman, 1995).

The Ethics of Sexual Relationships and Client Vulnerability

Sexual relationships bring inherent ethical dimensions. Darling and Mabe (1989) suggested that there are four main principles for determining whether sexual relationships are ethical. The first principle is *noncoercion,* in that people should have full ability to choose for themselves whether, when, and how they wish to engage in sexual activities. Second, the principle of *nondeceit* holds that people should have full information available to them when deciding whether to engage in sexual activities. The third principle suggests that *people should not treat others solely as means to an end,* namely that they should not be used merely for another person's personal sexual gratification. The final principle of *respect for beliefs* holds that people should respect their partners' beliefs about sex and not set out to change those beliefs. Counselors must consider all of these dimensions as they help their clients navigate the sexuality concerns they bring to counseling.

Because each of these dimensions is extremely complex and open to different interpretations, sexuality is an inherently sensitive aspect of people's lives and relationships. This sensitivity can contribute to a unique level of vulnerability for clients seeking counseling related to their sexuality. The AASECT (2004) Code of Ethics even states, "The member shall bear a heavy social responsibility because society deems the services as representing specialized expertise and because the consumers using the services are vulnerable" (para. 2). Sexuality is perhaps one of the most private areas of people's lives, and for a variety of reasons, many people carry a lot of shame and discomfort about their sexual practices, histories, and experiences. To begin to understand the nature of the vulnerability of clients in counseling discussing their sexual concerns, we encourage readers to pause reading in order to do the following guided reflection exercise on client vulnerability.

Exercise 1.3

GUIDED REFLECTION EXERCISE: CLIENT VULNERABILITY IN SEXUALITY COUNSELING

First, think about some aspect of your own sexuality—such as a past experience, a preference you have for types of sexual activity, or some physical characteristic—that may lead you to feel uncomfortable, upset, or embarrassed.

Second, think through some of the reasons that this issue brings up an emotional response for you. Perhaps you've been teased about this issue by someone else. Maybe you fear what people would think about you if they knew that you did this or think this way. It could be that you view this issue as going against your or your community's religious or cultural values.

Third, consider how you would feel speaking about this issue with a professional counselor. Ask yourself, "If I were to tell my counselor about this issue, what would I be feeling, and what would I be looking for in how my counselor reacts to me?"

Counselors must be proactive in creating a counseling environment in which clients can feel safe and supported in discussing some of their most personal thoughts, feelings, and experiences. In addition to working to build a strong rapport with clients, three fundamental ethical principles can guide counselors in creating this supportive environment. First, it is important for counselors to maintain professional boundaries at all times when engaging in sexuality counseling (American Association of Sexuality Educators, Counselors, and Therapists, 2004; Principle 3.4). A clear professional boundary can help assure the client that the counselor is competent and prepared to address the client's sexuality concerns in an ethical and professional manner. Second, sexuality counselors must avoid imposing their values on their clients (American Counseling Association, 2014, A.4.b). Sex is an extremely value-laden issue. Because counselors have a powerful position with regard to their level of influence on their clients, they must be extremely careful to ensure that they do not use this privileged position to sway clients toward their own personal value systems. Third, counselors should respect clients' autonomy for their own lives and decisions. The ACA (2014) Code of Ethics states that counselors' primary ethical responsibility is "to respect the dignity and to promote the welfare of clients" (A.1.a). Therefore, on the one hand, clients in sexuality counseling can be considered vulnerable because of the sensitive nature of the topic of sexuality. However, counselors must bear in mind that their role is to help their clients make decisions and behavioral changes that support their own life goals, even if the counselor has reason to believe that behavior may have negative consequences. Exceptions to confidentiality in issues such as this are discussed below.

Client Confidentiality and Secrets

Client confidentiality issues are especially relevant for sexuality counseling, given the sensitive nature of the subject. When there are possible legal implications of the clinical work (e.g., when working with sex offenders; Aubrey & Dougher, 1990; Priest & Wilcox, 1988), counselors should be especially mindful of client confidentiality issues. As in all counseling, the limitations to confidentiality should be discussed clearly with clients at the outset of therapy (Priest & Wickel, 2011). As discussed above, counselors must respect clients' autonomy. However, there may be cases in which counselors view clients' decisions as having potentially harmful consequences for themselves or for others. The decision whether to break confidentiality in such cases must be made carefully and through consultation with other professionals (American Counseling Association, 2014), including possibly seeking legal advice. When there is a risk of severe harm, as in a threat of suicide or homicide, breaking confidentiality is ethically justifiable (American Association for Sexuality Educators, Counselors, and Therapists, 2004; American Counseling Association, 2014). However, the ethical response to some sexual issues is less clear. For example, a client may disclose that he intends to coerce a partner into sexual activity. Disclosing this information to the partner (especially when the partner is not a client in conjoint treatment) is a more ambiguous issue. The AASECT (2004) Code of Ethics states that confidential information may be disclosed "when there is clear and imminent danger of bodily harm or to the life or safety of the consumer or another person" (Principle 3.D.2). This client's counselor will need to gather additional information and consult with colleagues to determine if a disclosure is warranted. Sexually transmitted diseases are another related concern, and the ACA (2014) Code of Ethics says the following:

> When clients disclose that they have a disease commonly known to be both communicable and life threatening, counselors *may* [emphasis added] be justified in disclosing information to identifiable third parties, if they are known to be at demonstrable and high risk of contracting the disease. (B.2.b)

The use of the word "may" in the standard above indicates that there is substantial room for interpretation in these cases. Counselors in this situation must weigh the following factors: the severity of the diagnosis and disease, the ability to identify the third party at risk of contracting the disease, and all relevant laws in their jurisdiction.

Another ethical consideration that may arise when working with clients around sexuality issues is whether and how counselors should keep secrets for clients in conjoint couple treatment, as Corley and Schneider (2002) discussed. According to these authors, secrets may be especially prominent when working with clients in which one partner has a sex addiction. In general, keeping secrets for clients can be difficult for therapists and damaging to the therapeutic relationship. Keeping a secret may be warranted in some situations, however, such as when disclosing the secret could lead to physical violence. When appropriate, therapists can work toward disclosure of the secret by the client during a session to facilitate appropriate processing of the disclosure and a supportive context for the revelation of the previously undisclosed information (Corley & Schneider, 2002).

Reparative Therapies

When counselors have the opportunity to work with clients exploring their sexual orientation, additional ethical considerations may arise. One particularly controversial area is the topic of reparative therapies (also referred to as *conversion therapies*) that aim to assist clients in getting rid of their same-sex sexual attractions (Drescher, 2001; Forstein, 2001; Morrow & Beckstead, 2004; Safren, 2005; Schroeder & Shidlo, 2001; Throckmorton, 1998; Yarhouse & Throckmorton, 2002). Proponents for the availability of reparative therapy suggest that clients should have the right to work toward changing their sexual orientations, especially if their career situations and/or religious beliefs penalize them for same-sex attractions (Drescher, 2001; Morrow & Beckstead, 2004; Throckmorton, 1998; Yarhouse & Throckmorton, 2002). However, these approaches are reflective of social stigmatization of homosexuality and can have damaging and blaming effects for clients (Drescher, 2001). Further, historically many of the clients who have entered reparative therapies have not done so under full free will, but rather, they were forced or coerced into treatment by their family members or religious organizations (Drescher, 2002). In addition, reparative therapies are unproven and are largely based on political and religious dialogue rather than on sound scientific evidence (Forstein, 2001). For these reasons, reparative therapies violate many basic principles of counseling ethics, including "competence, integrity, respect for people's rights and dignity, and social responsibility" (Morrow & Beckstead, 2004, p. 648). Thus, reparative therapies have been denounced by most major mental health professional organizations (Just the Facts Coalition, 2008).

In contrast to reparative therapies, "identity therapists" are those who believe that sexual orientation is but one aspect of a person's human development and believe that counselors should not attempt to change clients' sexual orientations (Drescher, 2002). When working with clients questioning their sexual orientations, it is important for counselors to avoid pushing their clients toward one sexual orientation or another (Drescher, 2002). During this process, counselors may feel compelled to disclose their personal sexual orientations with their clients (Drescher, 2002), but this and all forms of self-disclosure should be done carefully and with ultimate respect for the clients' welfare.

Sexual Attractions or Relationships With Clients or Supervisees

An ethical issue on which there is clear consensus is that sexual relationships with clients are harmful to clients and are unethical (Avery & Gressard, 2000; Larrabee & Miller, 1993; Plaut, 2008; Seto, 1995). Sexual misconduct is one of the more frequent ethical violations reported to state professional credentialing agencies (Avery & Gressard, 2000; Hoffman, 1995). Sexual relationships with clients are a violation of the trust that clients place in their counselors (Cummings & Sobel, 1985). These relationships can have many negative impacts on clients, including shame, anger, being afraid to seek additional counseling in the future, depression, confusion, and fear (Schoener, Milgrom, & Gonsiorek, 1984; Seto, 1995). Research suggests that sexual misconduct with clients is more likely among male therapists but does not differ based on professional discipline (Seto, 1995). Sexual relationships may arise if either or both the counselor and/or client are especially vulnerable, such as after a divorce (Edelwich & Brodsky, 1984). Counselors who engage in sexual relationships with their clients often rationalize this behavior (Edelwich & Brodsky, 1984), such as by viewing the counseling relationship as complete and separate or by claiming that their connection transcends professional boundaries. Counselor-client sexual relationships can develop through a number of pathways, including the client taking on a role of wanting to help the counselor and the proverbial case of 'one thing leading to another' (Hoffman, 1995). Clients who have previously been exploited by a former counselor may require additional sensitivity to ensure that the client has the opportunity to work through the negative impacts of those experiences (Schoener, Milgrom, & Gonsiorek, 1984).

Although sexual relationships with current clients are viewed as clearly unethical, some related issues, such as sexual relationships with former clients or with supervisees, are less clear (Avery & Gressard, 2000; Hoffman, 1995; Larrabee & Miller, 1993). Some states do prescribe time limits on how long after the counseling relationship terminates counselors and former clients are not allowed to engage in a sexual relationship, although some states have no such limits (Avery & Gressard, 2000). The range of timelines varies widely. Avery and Gressard (2000) reported ranges from six months to three years, with some states providing for extensions on the timeline if the client remains vulnerable beyond the set timeline. The question of how long after treatment ends a client remains vulnerable to the power differential inherent in the counselor-client relationship remains uncertain, although there is growing recognition that some forms of counseling creates a greater sense of vulnerability than others, such as the contrast between brief career counseling and intensive, long-term psychotherapy (Hoffman, 1995).

Some state statutes also prohibit counselors from engaging in sexual relationships with supervisees, and sexual harassment regulations also may come into play in these situations (Avery & Gressard, 2000). A counseling supervisor holds power over his or her supervisees, and supervisors can use sexual relationships to coerce and manipulate their supervisees (Larrabee & Miller, 1993; Plaut, 2008). Sexual relationships between supervisors and supervisees also likely cloud the supervisor's ability to effectively serve in a gatekeeping role for the profession (Larrabee & Miller, 1993). Counselors should consult their local jurisdiction's regulations when considering sexual relationships with former clients and/or current or former supervisors or supervisees to ensure that they are not violating any legal statutes. If readers are not currently familiar with regulations in their local jurisdiction regarding these matters, we suggest they pause reading to seek out relevant regulations before proceeding to read further in this chapter.

Heiden (1993) advocated for increased efforts to implement counselors-in-training strategies for preventing counselor-client sexual relationships. The following examples of Heiden's recommendations offer valuable guidance to both trainees and practicing counselors. First, counselors should monitor whether they are providing differential treatment to clients and whether that reflects that they are attempting to meet their own needs for intimacy with certain clients. Second, counselors should gain a greater understanding of the dangers involved in counselor-client sexual relationships, and these dangers should be kept at the forefront of counselors' minds when such possibilities arise. Third, counselors should take preventive steps to ensure that they do not find themselves in situations in which they would be tempted to engage in sexual activities with clients. These steps may include discussing the situation with others, seeking professional therapy oneself, and identifying and addressing issues of possible transference and countertransference early. Training programs also can promote ethical behavior in this regard by modeling clear professional boundaries and adequate training on sexuality-related issues that impact the counseling process (Hoffman, 1995; Plaut, 2008).

Although sexual relationships between counselors and clients are clearly unethical, sexual attractions certainly may arise between the counselor and client, whether one-sided or mutual (Edelwich & Brodsky, 1984; Hoffman, 1995; Rodgers, 2011). Such attractions may be especially likely to develop when sexuality-related topics are discussed in session. Clients may be especially likely to experience these feelings if they are being treated for sex addictions (Griffin-Shelley, 2009). These attractions may reflect natural human attraction processes and/or transference and countertransference (Edelwich & Brodsky, 1984). Edelwich and Brodsky (1984) suggested that clients who are attracted to their counselors may engage in various behaviors that push the limits of the professional boundary that defines their relationship with their counselor. These behaviors may include enhancing their appearance for sessions, asking the counselor intimate questions about the details of their lives, and making frequent unscheduled contacts, both in and out of the office, with the counselor. Clients also may seduce their counselors to avoid working on their presenting concerns (Edelwich & Brodsky, 1984). When a client discloses attraction toward a counselor or the counselor suspects that the attraction has developed, the counselor must address this issue in a therapeutic and ethical manner.

Countertransference reflects counselors' reactions and feelings that they develop toward their clients (Griffin-Shelley, 2009). When countertransferential reactions arise, counselors should monitor these carefully and examine the impact they have on the therapeutic relationship (Griffin-Shelley, 2009; Rodgers, 2011). When counselors do not manage these reactions effectively, the result can be a negative impact on the clients (Griffin-Shelley, 2009). If therapists experience sexual feelings toward their clients, they must consider carefully whether to disclose these to the clients (Fisher, 2004). Processing these feelings with a clinical supervisor, colleagues, or one's own therapist can provide valuable insights as to the reasons for these attractions (Fisher, 2004; Rodgers, 2011). These feelings can then be normalized, and in and of themselves, they do not constitute sexual misconduct (Fisher, 2004; Hoffman, 1995). However, many therapists feel ashamed when these attraction feelings arise (Rodgers, 2011). For a therapist to disclose these feelings to a client is more likely to be harmful to the client than it is to offer them any therapeutic benefits, and it can also expose the therapist to a potential slippery slope toward sexual misconduct (Fisher, 2004).

INTERDISCIPLINARY COLLABORATIONS FOR SEXUALITY COUNSELING

Sexuality is an interdisciplinary topic that can be addressed on many different levels. Counselors working with clients on sexuality-related concerns should consider other community resources that may help clients make further progress toward their treatment goals. A first step for virtually any possible sexual dysfunction is for clients to have a physical examination by a qualified health care professional to determine if physiological causes are contributing to clients' concerns (Goodwach, 2005b). Medical interventions—such as medications—may be useful for clients when there is a physiological basis for their concerns. There is growing recognition of the importance of integrated mental health and medical treatment for sexual problems, often referred to as combination therapy (Althof, 2010). The integration of both approaches can help to capitalize on the benefits that clients may achieve through each approach and help clients achieve their treatment goals more quickly and efficiently (Althof, 2010).

Further, combination therapies can help to ensure that the medical, psychological, and relational implications of clients' sexual concerns are all addressed adequately (Althof, 2010). The diverse group of medical professionals with whom sexuality counselors may work includes the following: urologists, gynecologists, endocrinologists, family practice physicians, internists, cardiologists, neurologists, nurse practitioners, physician assistants, and physical therapists (Althof, 2010).

Beyond collaborations with medical professionals, counselors can assist their clients in accessing other potentially helpful resources, and counselors can work with professionals involved with these resources to promote clients' treatment progress. For example, clients may benefit from resources that provide information about sexual health and any specific concerns the client is facing. Therefore, counselors should become familiar with sources of credible sexual health information in their communities, as well as other sources available online and in print media (e.g., books, magazines). Counselors also can provide clients with information about support groups in their communities for people facing similar issues, such as infertility and sex addiction. Many communities also offer centers or groups for the LGBT population, as well as groups for family members of these people (e.g., PFLAG: Parents, Families, Friends, and Allies United with LGBT People). Some clients may need assistance with finding legal advice, such as if they have experienced a sexual assault. Other community-based programs that may be relevant for some clients include support programs for teenage parents, agencies that provide free or reduced-cost contraception, sex trafficking recovery organizations, couple relationship-education workshops, parenting education programs, and culture-specific organizations. We encourage counselors to think beyond the therapy room and consider how sexuality counseling can be enhanced through connections within the broader community context.

OVERVIEW OF THE REMAINDER OF THIS BOOK

The rest of the chapters in this book will delve deeper into the various sexuality-related concerns that can impact clients. We begin by focusing on general strategies for clinical assessment and interventions in Chapters 2 and 3, respectively. The remaining chapters each cover the different levels in the Contextualized Sexuality Model, in order to provide readers with an understanding of unique considerations at each level. Throughout the book, our aim is to present a comprehensive, in-depth, practice-focused overview of sexuality counseling to equip counselors and trainees with the information and intervention strategies needed to effectively work with clients who are facing sexuality-related issues. We hope that readers will find this book to be a useful resource in helping clients navigate the complexity of the sexuality-related concerns they face.

KEYSTONES

- Despite their professional training, counselors are not immune to the discomfort surrounding sexuality.
- Clients often seek counseling for concerns related to their sexuality, whether as their primary concern or as a secondary concern to more pressing issues.
- Sexuality is an essential topic for counselors to become competent to address in their work.
- Based on the Contextualized Sexuality Model, the contextual influences on human sexuality include physiology, developmental influences, psychology, gender identity and sexual orientation, intimate relationships, cultural and contextual influences, and positive sexuality.
- Recently, the sex-therapy field has shifted to a more comprehensive, systemic approach to understanding and treating sexual concerns.
- The main distinctions between sexuality counselors and sex therapists are the degrees of the intensity of the treatment and the complexity of the cases.
- Professionals must understand their own level of competence to address sexuality-related issues in their work.
- Counselors should strive to increase their comfort in talking about sexuality in a professional context.
- Sexuality counseling presents counselors with unique ethical considerations that reflect the sensitive and personal nature of the subject of sexuality.
- Sexuality is an interdisciplinary topic that can be addressed on many different levels. Counselors working with clients on sexuality-related concerns should consider other community resources that may help clients make further progress toward their treatment goals.

ADDITIONAL RESOURCES

- American Association of Sexuality Educators, Counselors, and Therapists (AASECT; http://www.aasect.org/)
- American Counseling Association *2014 Code of Ethics* (ACA; http://www.counseling.org/docs/ethics/2014-aca-code-of-ethics.pdf?sfvrsn=4)
- Sexuality Information and Education Council of the United States (SEICUS; www.seicus.org)
- Society for Sex Therapy and Research (SSTAR; http://www.sstarnet.org/)

Chapter 2

Assessment in Sexuality Counseling

Sex is a natural function. You can't make it happen,
but you can teach people to let it happen.

—William Masters (Brody, 1984)

Including the assessment of sexuality as part of the overall biopsychosocial assessment of clients' functioning during the intake interview is important for several reasons. First, sexuality is a central component of the human experience that impacts our overall psychological well-being (Barratt & Rand, 2009). Sexual problems may impact and/or be impacted by clients' presenting issues, and thus, counselors may overlook major symptoms if they do not assess sexual concerns early in therapy. Secondly, as sexuality is a topic that is influenced by cultural norms, many of which serve to diminish and/or limit the experience of sexuality for individuals, clients may never have experienced open conversations about sexuality, may feel conflicted about sexuality, and may have internalized messages that impact their sexuality negatively and elicit anxiety, guilt, or shame. Many cultures do not actively promote a positive sexuality, which can create harmful consequences for individuals, including effects on their mental (e.g., low self-esteem, anxiety), interpersonal (e.g., sexual difficulties in intimate relationships), and physical (e.g., not practicing safe sex) health. By inquiring about sexuality in the assessment process, counselors can create spaces to educate and support clients in developing a positive sexuality.

Finally, the culture of silence around sex leads many individuals to engage in risky behaviors during sexual experiences, and the spread of sexually transmitted infections (STIs) and the occurrence of unwanted pregnancies remain major public health concerns in the United States and beyond. Indeed, it is estimated that almost half of Americans will contract a STI at some point during their lifetimes (Planned Parenthood, 2014a). In a time in which many medical professionals are finding themselves battling time constraints that do not allow for a holistic evaluation of their clients or patients (Barratt & Rand, 2009), counselors do have the ability to engage individuals in a thorough biopsychosocial evaluation. Even more important, counselors can build a therapeutic alliance so that clients feel comfortable opening up about matters as personal as sex. Thus, counselors are well-situated to evaluate individuals' sexual health and to promote safe sex practices through their counseling services. To ignore sexuality and not include it as part of the assessment process is to do a disservice not only to the individual clients that we are working with but also to the larger public, as open dialogues about sexuality are necessary to advance healthy sexual experiences.

We start this chapter with Case Illustrations 2.1, 2.2, and 2.3 for you to reflect on as you learn about the assessment of sexuality. As you read the rest of the chapter, consider what areas you would want to assess more in-depth with each of the following cases, the interview questions would be relevant to ask, and instruments that would be appropriate to administer.

CASE ILLUSTRATION 2.1

CASE OF JASON AND AMANDA

Jason (age 30) and Amanda (age 28) present to couples counseling with their main complaint being difficulties with sexual intimacy. They have been married five years and had their first child almost two years ago. Jason reports that up until having their child, he was satisfied with their sex life and that they were having sex several times a week. The frequency of their sexual activity has diminished to about once a month, and Jason says he feels like sex has become a "chore" for Amanda and that she does not want him to touch her anymore. Amanda says that she knows sex is important to Jason but that her sexual desire has diminished since the birth of their son. Amanda also reports that she has struggled with postpartum depression and sought individual counseling, although she discontinued her therapy a few months ago because she no longer felt it was helping.

CASE ILLUSTRATION 2.2

CASE OF CARSON

Carson (age 14) is brought to counseling by his dad, Don (age 45), and stepmom, Sarah (age 50). Don and Sarah report that Carson came out as gay to them approximately eight months ago. They say that they were initially shocked but have been trying to learn more about how to support Carson in his development as a gay male and "love him no matter what" as their son. Don and Sarah are concerned because Carson has stopped talking to them like he used to about school and his friends, and they describe him as "sullen" and "quick-tempered" around the house over the past few months. Carson seems unwilling to talk to you in front of his parents, so you ask to meet with him individually for further assessment. As you meet with him alone, Carson starts to open up and begins to answer the intake questions from his perspective.

CASE ILLUSTRATION 2.3

CASE OF LENA

Lena (age 64) is a Latina woman who was referred by her oncologist to counseling. She was diagnosed with breast cancer approximately three years ago and went through chemotherapy, radiation, and a double mastectomy, which eliminated the cancer at that time. A few months ago, it was discovered that her cancer had returned in her lymph nodes during a physical checkup. Her oncologist is recommending more surgery to remove the affected lymph nodes, as well as follow-up chemotherapy and radiation, but Lena is currently refusing to have the treatment. Lena has been married for 42 years and has three children. Lena reports that she has missed several big events in her family, has been unable to care for her grandchildren, and has had difficulties being sexually intimate with her husband due to the side effects of the treatments over the past few years. She says that she is tired of having her quality of life diminished by the medical treatments and wants to put her health "in God's hands" moving forward.

This chapter will begin by discussing skills for introducing sexuality-related topics into the intake interview with clients. Next, we will discuss how to assess how clients' presenting concerns may be impacting and/or impacted by their sexuality. The chapter will then outline informal and formal assessment tools related to each of the areas within the Contextualized Sexuality Model, as well as strategies for counselors to use informal assessment strategies to aid in defining clients' sexuality concerns, setting related goals, and informing treatment planning in counseling. Finally, an appendix is included to review instruments that can enhance the assessment and treatment of clients' sexuality concerns in counseling. After reading the chapter, the reader will be able to do the following:

a. Describe general assessment strategies for sexuality counseling
b. Understand formal and informal strategies for assessing clients' functioning across the different domains of the Contextualized Sexuality Model

GENERAL ASSESSMENT STRATEGIES

We begin with general recommendations on how to incorporate sexuality considerations into the initial assessment process with clients.

1. *Include questions related to sexuality as a part of the intake interview process you use with all clients.* Clients typically will not initiate conversations about sexuality unless prompted to do so by their health care providers, including counselors, particularly if their presenting concern is not directly linked to sexuality. Of more concern is that counselors themselves may be reluctant to bring up the topic of sexuality during the initial session with clients (Harris & Hays, 2008; Dune, 2012). This hesitancy may occur because counselors are not used to talking about sex in their own lives, worry that they may embarrass or make their clients uncomfortable, and/or feel like they do not know what to ask or how to respond, and thus may appear incompetent (Risen, 2010). Unless a client is presenting in a crisis or therapy is extremely time-limited, counselors should ask *every* client about sexuality-related questions and concerns, including couples, older adults, adolescents, and the family members of younger children.

Immediately asking questions about sexuality may be abrupt and off-putting. However, gathering information about sex and sexuality can be integrated into the initial psychosocial assessment and be comfortably addressed as you build rapport with the client, even within the first session. Including general questions about sexuality in your initial paperwork and/or intake interview can help prompt clients to speak up about any sexuality-related concerns. Further, by including questions

Table 2.1	Sample Interview Questions for the General Assessment of Sexuality-Related Topics

- What is your gender identity?

- What is your sexual/affectional orientation?

- Are you currently in an intimate relationship? How would you describe your relationship at this time?

- Are you sexually active? If so, how would you describe your sexual activity (e.g., how often, with whom, etc.)? With women, men, or both?

- Do you have any general medical conditions? If so, how have these medical conditions impacted your overall functioning and interpersonal relationships?

- Have you ever sought counseling previously or sought help for mental health problems? If so, how have your mental health problems impacted your overall functioning and interpersonal relationships?

- Do you have any sexuality-related concerns that you would like to discuss in counseling?

as part of the intake interview, counselors can offer a simple clarification if clients seem unsettled by the questions about sexuality, such as,

> The intake includes questions about sexuality because it is an integral part of the human experience, and our sexual development and functioning, including our sexual thoughts, feelings, and behaviors, contributes to our overall well-being as individuals and our satisfaction in intimate relationships. I would like for this to be a space where you can feel comfortable addressing any questions or concerns about sexuality as you feel it is relevant to your counseling goals.

Addressing the relevance of your questions and inviting clients to speak openly about sexual topics can directly confront any awkwardness or embarrassment that clients may experience when sharing about their sexual health (Risen, 2010). In Table 2.1 we provide you with some sample interview questions, and we encourage you to add any questions that you think are relevant to your counseling situation.

After asking these general questions, counselors can follow up with more specific questions based on clients' presenting concerns, which are reviewed in the Dimensions of Assessment in Sexuality Counseling section.

2. *Be matter-of-fact and objective as you discuss sexuality-related topics with clients, and utilize process skills and immediacy to address clients' discomfort in*

session. As sexuality remains a taboo topic and one that is not openly discussed or even acknowledged at times, do not be surprised if clients are uncomfortable discussing their sexuality, particularly in the initial few sessions (Risen, 2010). Some clients may have never had an in-depth or honest discussion about sex or their sexuality with anyone in their lives before coming to counseling, so they may be unsure of how to talk about sex or how much to disclose in counseling. As individuals tend to internalize messages that frame sex, their sexuality, and their body images in a negative light from their families, peers, culture, religion, and/or the media, the topic of sexuality may elicit feelings of anxiety, guilt, or shame for many clients. Anxiety, guilt, and shame tend to be emotions that people want to avoid experiencing, and thus, some clients may be reluctant to talk about sexuality-related topics to avoid facing those emotions.

Thus, it is important that you can remain matter-of-fact, objective, and comfortable as a counselor in discussing sexuality with clients so that your personal values and biases do not interfere with clients' openness to share sexual concerns (Barratt & Rand, 2009). If you demonstrate your own discomfort, clients may interpret this as it not being okay to talk about sexuality in counseling. At an extreme, showing uneasiness could be misconstrued as judgment of what clients are saying, which could cause harm by eliciting or reinforcing guilt and shame around their sexuality. Counselors, however, are subject to many of the same conflicting messages about sexuality that our clients receive, and thus, it is not uncommon for counselors-in-training to feel uncomfortable discussing sex in an open and straightforward manner (Harris & Hays, 2008). Counselors may avoid topics due to their inexperience with the sexual material being presented, difficulties imagining the experience their client is discussing, or because the material may elicit their own internal conflict due to past sexual experiences (Risen, 2010).

To practice asking questions related to sexuality similar to those you may use during an intake interview and to experience being asked questions about your sexuality in order to increase empathy for your clients, readers are invited to complete Exercise 2.1 in small groups. Readers who experience uneasiness during this activity may want to take other steps to practice talking about sexuality, such as initiating conversations about sex with a trusted partner, family member, or friend. Anyone who feels an intense amount of discomfort may want to seek individual counseling to increase their ability to discuss sex more openly with clients.

3. *Develop a sexuality vocabulary, recognizing that sometimes clients' words may be unfamiliar to you and that your words may be unknown to clients.* Another area that counselors can struggle with when assessing sexuality with clients is the language to use to describe sexual experiences, typically due to discomfort with saying the words out loud or worries about offending their clients (Risen, 2010).

Exercise 2.1

SEXUALITY INTERVIEW

Directions: Working with a colleague, take turns being an interviewer and interviewee. Together, spend approximately 30 minutes with each person being interviewed. As interviewer, base your interview on the questions listed below, although you do not have to go through each question specifically. To increase the safety in this activity, **the interviewee should be reminded that they do not have to answer any question(s) that she or he does not want to answer.** Once the interviews are complete, process what it was like in each of the roles as interviewer and interviewee, reflecting on the following two questions: (1) What did you learn through this activity? and (2) How does this interview connect to your thoughts about your work with clients in counseling?

SUGGESTED QUESTIONS FOR SEXUALITY INTERVIEW:

- What are your earliest memories of learning about sex? What emotions do you remember experiencing when you were first learning about sex?
- What kind of communication did you have with your parents about sex? Were there any adults in your life that you felt comfortable talking about sex with while growing up?
- What kinds of messages and/or "rules" did you get from your parents about sex?
- As a child, what kinds of questions did you have about sex? To whom did you ask these questions? Did you feel that your questions got answered?
- What kinds of messages did you receive about gender (including gender roles and expression) from your family?
- What were the attitudes toward the body in your family (e.g., was the body considered natural or provocative, messages about nudity and covering up the body, etc.)?
- What were your feelings toward your body as a child and as an adolescent?
- Did you talk about sex with your friends growing up? If so, how was sex talked about among your friends?
- How did your friends and peers influence your views about sex while growing up?
- What types of messages about sex did you receive from the media as a child and/or adolescent? Do you think you have internalized any of these messages?

(Continued)

(Continued)

During the activity, you may modify these questions or add other related questions. Other topics to ask about may include messages and/or experiences with sexual play as a child, sexual education in schools, masturbation, contraception, and early sexual feelings and experiences. Asking about how others reacted to the disclosure of these experiences may also be relevant to understanding your own beliefs about sex and sexuality.

* Note: This activity has been adapted from Dr. Peter Sherrard's Sexuality and Mental Health course that was offered in the University of Florida Department of Counselor Education.

It is important that counselors develop an ease in saying words related to sex and sexuality, as well as skills for how to handle language discrepancies that will inevitably come up during session. Counselors need to get comfortable with sex-related terminology, as it is up to us to introduce the words into counseling so that clients feel allowed to use sexual language as well. Exercise 2.2 invites you to generate sexuality-related terms in a group setting and to practice saying the terms out loud in front of others.

At times, clients may seem uncomfortable with a term that a counselor uses during session. If you notice clients' discomfort, perhaps they are appearing uneasy or are avoiding using the term themselves, you can bring that to the forefront by saying, "It seems that when I describe your concerns as 'erectile difficulties' that it is

Exercise 2.2

SEXUALITY-RELATED LANGUAGE

In a group, generate a list of at least 30 words related to sex, sexuality, or sexual intercourse. Everyone in the group should add at least one term to the list, and try not to censor the terms that you contribute. Once you have constructed a list of terms, each person will pick out the five words in which they would feel the most uncomfortable saying out loud in front of others. Break into smaller groups or pairs, and practice saying the five words out loud at least three times. Try to stay aware of your thoughts, feelings, and behaviors while vocalizing the words to another person, as well as being in tune with your experience in hearing others say the words they selected. Briefly process your experience: What was it like for you the first time that you vocalized the terms that you selected? What was it like for you by the last time that you stated the words? What was it like listening to others verbalize the words?

not quite fitting with your experience. Can you tell me how you would describe your concerns in your own words?" The language around sexuality is constantly evolving to reflect our sexual understanding, so clients may use terms that are foreign to us. People use many different words, including cultural slang, to describe sexual experiences, and it is not necessary for counselors to know every sexuality-related term in our vernacular. What is more important is for counselors to inquire about unfamiliar expressions with clients so that they understand what the client is presenting during sessions (Risen, 2010), which can be done by simply asking, "Can you tell me what the term [insert expression] means? It's not one I've heard before."

4. *Focus your assessment on clients' current sexual health and the holistic experience of sex, including satisfaction and pleasure.* Rather than taking an unnecessary history of sexual behaviors that often is not extremely relevant to current sexual health behaviors (Barratt & Rand, 2009), counselors should stay focused on clients' recent sexual experiences and present sexuality-related concerns during their assessment. Further, our experiences of sexuality are impacted by sociocultural and relational factors (Nicholls, 2008; Southern & Cade, 2011), so history-taking in regard to sexuality assessment should focus more on the impact of contextual factors (e.g., family of origin messages, cultural values, and political contexts) instead of obtaining specific information related to past sexual activities. For example, in Case 1 with Jason and Amanda, it may be useful for a counselor to inquire about their positive experiences with sex prior to their baby being born and ask about their beliefs and values in taking on their new role as parents. However, it likely would not be pertinent to explore specific details about their sexual activity in other relationships unless it seems experiences from those previous relationships are impacting their current functioning. Thus, counselors should assess clients' sexual history as it is relevant to their existing concerns, but be aware when a line of questioning does not seem significant to understanding clients' presenting issues.

DIMENSIONS OF ASSESSMENT IN SEXUALITY COUNSELING

If clients identify any sexuality-related concerns during the general assessment process, counselors will want to follow-up with more specific questions based on their presenting concerns. Counselors should use their clinical judgment to decide which areas require more in-depth assessment with clients. As discussed in Chapter 1, human sexuality is complex and shaped by multiple, interacting influences. Familiarity with assessment strategies for each of these influences is important for counselors to evaluate clients' functioning across the various levels of sexuality and to identify a starting point for interventions. In the following section, assessment guidelines are reviewed for each influence within the Contextualized Sexuality Model.

Informal and formal assessment strategies will be reviewed in this chapter. Each section includes a list of open-ended questions that can be utilized during the clinical interview. These questions are meant to serve as a starting point to guide the assessment process, and thus, counselors may need to add other questions to gather more specific information from their clients. Further, these questions are meant to serve as guidelines, so the wording should be tailored to fit each counselor's personal style as well as the needs of each client. This chapter concludes with an appendix that contains a Directory of Selected Instruments for Assessing Sexuality, which describes assessments that correspond to each influence within the Contextualized Sexuality Model. Basic information including the number of questions, reliability, and validity about each instrument is presented, and strengths and limitations of the instruments are reviewed to give counselors an idea of how to best utilize each instrument. Before using these instruments, readers should consult the original sources listed in the directory for more information about administration of the assessments with clients. Some of the instruments listed may need to be purchased for clinical use, while others are publicly available for free administration. All of the available instruments for assessing sexuality are not included given space limitations, but the directory serves as a good starting point for counselors wishing to utilize more formal assessment strategies within therapy. For a comprehensive resource on sexuality assessments, refer to the *Handbook of Sexuality-Related Measures* (Fisher, Davis, Yarber, & Davis, 2010).

PHYSIOLOGY

Historically, sexuality assessment focused on physiological sexual functioning in the mental health and medical fields. As discussed in Chapters 1 and 4, the biomedical approaches to sexuality have been critiqued for their narrow definitions of sexuality that do not address the social and psychological factors which also influence sexual functioning (Nicholls, 2008). Although the other influences in the Contextualized Sexuality Model also are likely to be impacting your clients' sexual concerns, it is still important to begin the assessment of their sexual functioning by ruling out medical factors or physiological causes that could be contributing to their issues (Southern & Cade, 2011). Thus, it is important for counselors to ask clients about their medical history including their last visit to their physician, current medical conditions or physical limitations, current medications, and substance use. If clients have not had a recent physical checkup and/or have not talked with their health care providers about their problems with sexual functioning, counselors should recommend a basic medical screening for clients early on during the therapeutic process to rule out organic contributing factors. It is also recommended that counselors obtain an authorization for release of health information so that counselors can collaborate directly with their health care providers, particularly if any physical problems are identified as contributing to their sexual concerns (Southern, 1999).

Counselors may find it useful to incorporate instruments in addition to open-ended questions to gather more specific information on clients' sexual functioning as related to their sexual-response cycle and physical health, such as the Changes in Sexual Functioning Questionnaire Short-Form (CSFQ-14; Keller, McGarvey, & Clayton, 2006) and the Derogatis Interview for Sexual Functioning (DISF; Derogatis, 1997). We provide you some sample interview questions to assess physiological issues impacting sexuality in Table 2.2.

Table 2.2   Sample Interview Questions for Assessing Physiological Issues Impacting Sexuality

- Have you had any difficulties in your sexual response (e.g., lack of desire, difficulties with arousal such as lack of lubrication for women and erectile dysfunction for men, or inability to reach orgasm) during sexual encounters? If so, assess for concrete details with the following questions:

  o How often does the difficulty occur?

  o When did it start? Has it happened with multiple partners (if client has had sex with more than one person since the start of the difficulty)?

  o What are the contextual factors surrounding its occurrence (e.g., does it only happen during sex with a partner or during masturbation too)?

  o To assess if the difficulty could be anxiety-related, ask the following: Do you feel relaxed or tense during sexual encounters? If tense, when does the tension start and where do you feel it in your body? What types of thoughts are going through your head during sexual encounters?

  o How does this difficulty impact your sexual pleasure?

  o How does this difficulty impact your sexual self-image and your intimate relationships?

  o What have you done to try to cope with this difficulty, both individually and within your relationships?

- How do you feel about your body? Do you like your physical characteristics and/or do you feel comfortable within your body?

(Continued)

Table 2.2 (Continued)

- Has sex ever been painful or not pleasurable for you?

- How are you using protection during sexual encounters, including oral sex, to protect yourself against sexually transmitted infections and/or unwanted pregnancies (if the client is engaging in sexual activity with the opposite sex)?

- Have you ever been tested for STIs and HIV, and when was the last time you were tested?

- Do you have any medical conditions or physical limitations? If so, ask more specific questions about the medical condition. Did the sexual concern you are experiencing start before or after the onset of the medical condition?

- Have you talked with your physician about the sexual functioning concerns you are experiencing to see if they could be related to your medical condition?

- When is the last time you had a general checkup from a physician? If it has been over a year, the counselor may want to refer the client to their primary care physician for a medical screening or to their gynecologist for women.

- Do you have any reproductive concerns at this time?

- Are you taking any medications at this time? Have you talked with the prescribing physician about potential sexual side effects of these medications?

- Have you ever stopped taking medications because of concerns about how they were impacting your sexual functioning?

Developmental Issues

Healthy sexual development occurs throughout the lifespan, from the time we are in the womb until the end of our lives. Early childhood experiences shape our sexuality and can impact us well into adulthood in our sexual health, sexual satisfaction, and in creating quality intimate relationships. Thus, it is important that counselors incorporate at least basic questions assessing sexuality into intake interviews with *all* clients, including the parents or caregivers of young children to older adults. Assessing what clients know about sex that is appropriate for their current stage of life as well as what information they feel they are lacking is necessary for counselors to support healthy sexual development, which may be impacted by a lack of sex education and inadequate knowledge about sexual biology and changes over the lifespan (Nicholls, 2008). Counseling is a space where clients can access information that will improve their sexual health and pleasure throughout their lives.

Counselors should assess for sexual abuse in all clients regardless of age, as abuse greatly impacts sexual development, with examples of age-appropriate questions for children provided in Table 2.3. Counselors should include questions about sexual development in the assessment of children when meeting with their parents or caregivers alone and should discuss with the parents any questions that are appropriate to ask young clients about sexuality before addressing these inquiries directly with the child. Depending on the presenting issue, talking about sex directly with the child may be beneficial, but it is even more important to support the child's caregivers in handling any sexual communication and/or concerns with their child. As clients enter adolescence, counselors should start asking the client directly about sexual

Table 2.3 Sample Interview Questions for Assessing Developmental Issues
For Parents or Caregivers
• How do you communicate with your children about sex and sexuality?
• What values and beliefs about sexuality do you want to communicate to your children?
• How do you teach your child what is sexually appropriate behavior? Have you ever talked to your child about "good touch/bad touch"?
• What does your child know about sex? Where did he or she learn about sex?
• Has your child ever demonstrated any sexual behavior that is concerning to you? If so, describe what occurred. How did you respond?
• What else would you like to know about healthy sexual development in children and/or adolescents and what to expect as your child gets older?
• How can I help you in supporting your child's healthy sexual development?
For Individuals
• Questions for children: What do you know about "good touch/bad touch"? What would you do if anyone ever touched you in a way that made you uncomfortable? Is there someone you would feel safe telling?
• Questions for adolescents: What do you know about sex? Where did you learn about sex? Are you engaging in any sexual activities? Have you felt comfortable with these activities? Were they good experiences?
• Questions for adults: How have your sexual desire and preferences changed as you aged? How have you responded to these changes?
• Are you going through any current transitions or life challenges that may be impacting your sexuality, such as your sexual satisfaction or sexual health?
• What else would you like to know about healthy sexual development and what to expect at your current age and/or as you get older?

experiences. Counselors may want to re-ask questions about sexuality when meeting with adolescents alone after interviewing the clients with their family, as many adolescents may not be openly sharing their sexual experiences or concerns with their caregivers but may feel safe talking about sex within therapy. Past adolescence, counselors should incorporate basic questions assessing sexuality in order to introduce the topic into counseling and allow for clients to provide information about sexual concerns that can be addressed through treatment planning.

Formal assessments may be particularly useful for incorporating the subject of sexuality into counseling, particularly for populations in which society renders sexuality invisible, such as children, adolescents, and older adults. The Child Sexual Behavior Inventory (CSBI; Friedrich et al., 1992; Friedrich et al., 2001) assesses children's sexual behavior and can be useful in identifying children with sexual-behavior problems. The Adolescent Clinical Sexual Behavior Inventory-Self Report (ACSBI; Friedrich, Lysne, Sim, & Shamos, 2004) is appropriate to assess for sexual risk-taking behaviors in adolescents, and the Geriatric Sexuality Inventory (GSI; Kazer, Grossman, Kerins, Kris, & Tocchi, 2013) can be useful to identify areas of intervention with older adults. In Table 2.3, there is a list of interview questions that can be useful when counselors make an assessment of developmental issues for parents or caregivers and other individuals.

Mental Health

Sexuality concerns and mental health issues often co-occur (DeFronzo Dobkin, Leiblum, Rosen, Menza, & Marin, 2006; Quinn & Browne, 2009), and clients' concerns in one area often impact the other, which can make the assessment of psychological effects on sexuality a complex and tricky process. As such, it can be helpful to view the relationship between mental health and sexuality as circular rather than linear. For example, clients with depression may experience sexual difficulties, which could be related to the depression itself or taking psychotropic medications to manage the depression. Experiencing sexual difficulties may impact a client's self-image and intimate relationships, all of which can compound their depressive state (DeFronzo Dobkin et al., 2006). Counselors should ask clients during the intake how the changes in their mental health impacted their sexual functioning, as well as assess if their sexual functioning altered prior to the onset of their mental health difficulties. Counselors also need to consider how clients' sexual functioning, including their decision-making and activity, may be impacted by history of trauma, substance use, and psychotropic medications during the assessment process (Quinn & Browne, 2009). At times, psychoeducation may be warranted to help clients understand the relationship between mental health and healthy sexuality.

Counselors also need to be prepared for evaluation when the primary concern of clients is linked to sexuality. Counselors should have basic knowledge of the sexuality-related disorders within the DSM, which is covered more in depth in Chapter 6, in order to evaluate clients for an accurate diagnosis and/or referral to appropriate services. Although many clients will seek out a sexuality counselor for specific services, any counselor may run across a client whose primary difficulty is related to sexuality during the assessment process. The sexuality-related disorders often get little attention in diagnosis training as the education is focused on the more common mental health disorders such as mood and anxiety, but desire, arousal, and orgasmic dysfunctions are still classified as mental health disorders in the DSM, along with paraphilias (American Psychiatric Association, 2013a). Although not specified in the DSM-5, sexual compulsions, sexual addiction, or hypersexuality is receiving increased attention as patterns of behavior that interfere with individuals' daily functioning, and these patterns may present along with other mental health disorders (Riemersma & Sytsma, 2013). Diagnosing is a skill that is developed along with experience in clinical settings, so counselors should seek supervision and consultation when making diagnoses that they are unfamiliar with to prevent inaccurately labeling clients' presenting issues.

The Garos Sexual Behavior Inventory (GSBI; Garos, 2009) is a lengthier yet versatile assessment of sexual adjustment that can be used in a wide range of clinical settings. The Sexual Arousal and Desire Inventory (SADI; Toledano & Pfaus, 2006) assesses for the subjective experiences of sexual arousal and desire that may be impacting sexual functioning. Counselors can use the Sexual Addiction Screening Test-Revised (SAST-R; Carnes, Green, & Carnes, 2010) to help identify clients with sexual addiction, and the Early Sexual Experiences Checklist (ESEC; Miller, Johnson, & Johnson, 1991) as a brief assessment for adolescents and adults to identify unwanted sexual experiences in childhood. Table 2.4 contains some interview questions when counselors make assessment of mental health issues impacting sexuality.

Gender Identity and Sexual/Affectional Orientation

An essential part of the sexuality assessment process with clients is to allow clients to define their own sexual identities, particularly when it comes to gender identity and sexual/affectional orientation. Presuming that a client is heterosexual or cisgender can potentially harm lesbian, gay, bisexual, transgender, intersex, queer, questioning, and ally (LGBTIQQA) clients through (typically subtly) communicating the message that their identities are "less than" or outside of the normal spectrum of human sexuality and gender expression. As discussed in the general strategies section, counselors should use gender-neutral language when assessing

Table 2.4	Sample Interview Questions for Assessing Mental Health Issues Impacting Sexuality

- Have you ever experienced aversion or mistrust during sexual activities?

- Have you ever felt inhibited in experiencing or expressing sexual pleasure?

- Has anyone ever touched you in a way that made you feel uncomfortable? If so, how do you feel this experience is impacting your sexuality and sexual activities currently?

- Do you ever worry about possible consequences of sexual activities (e.g., pregnancy, STIs/HIV, rejection by or loss of partner, embarrassment, impact on reputation, etc.)?

- Have you ever experienced pain during intercourse that cannot be attributed to physiological factors (e.g., have seen a physician and no medical cause can be identified to explain the pain)?

- When did you first notice your difficulties with [insert mental health issue—e.g., depression, anxiety, etc.] and when did you first notice difficulties with your [insert sexuality concern]?

- Do you feel that your [insert mental health issue] impacts your sexuality and intimate relationships, and if so, how?

- Do you ever feel unable to control your sexual desires and/or behaviors?

- Are you currently taking any medications for your mental health difficulties? If so, have you talked with your prescribing physician about the potential sexual side effects of these medications?

- Have you ever stopped taking mental health medications because of concerns about how they were impacting your sexual functioning?

- Do you drink alcohol or use other drugs? Are you using when experiencing difficulties in your sexual functioning?

persons' current and past relationships in order to not make assumptions about clients' sexual/affectional orientation or gender identity.

Gender dysphoria (formally gender identity disorder) is included as a diagnosis in the DSM-5 (American Psychiatric Association, 2013b), which provides counselors with a useful outline for assessing gender incongruence and dysphoria. Whether or not gender dysphoria should be included as a diagnosis in the DSM remains under debate in medical and psychological communities, as the inclusion perpetuates the stigma attached to gender variance by labeling it as a disorder or disease (Knudson, De Cuypere, & Bockting, 2010). The World Professional Association for Transgender Health (WPATH), does not consider gender dysphoria to be pathological nor a mental disorder (Knudson et al., 2010). We, the authors, agree with their assertion and the belief that gender variance and noncomformity is normal, healthy, and can be integrated into a positive sexuality. The inclusion of gender dysphoria in the DSM, however, can still be useful to counselors in assessing clients' gender identity and gives the mental health and medical communities a common language for understanding transgenderism and to support those seeking to transition.

The criteria for a diagnosis of gender dysphoria are the strictest for children presenting with incongruence, given that the persistence of gender dysphoria from childhood into adulthood is inconsistent (Coleman et al., 2011). Further, diversity and flexibility in gender roles and expression is more common in children, making gender dysphoria harder to diagnose. The criteria for gender dysphoria in children includes consistent statements or expressions of the desire to be the other sex, preference for wearing clothes of the opposite sex and cross-sex roles during play and fantasies, strong rejection of the typical toys and play associated with one's sex, and a strong preference for playing with children of the opposite sex over at least a 6-month period. Children may also present a strong dislike of their sexual anatomy and indicate a strong desire for the sex characteristics (e.g., penis, vagina) of the opposite gender (American Psychiatric Association, 2013b).

Gender dysphoria that lasts into or presents in adolescence typically persists long-term. Thus, the criteria to diagnose gender dysphoria in adolescents or adults are more broad and rely more on their self-report rather than behavioral indicators. Adolescents and adults who present with an incongruence between their experienced and/or expressed gender and their assigned gender (i.e., primary and secondary sex characteristics) also typically indicate a strong desire to prevent development or be rid of sex characteristics associated with one's assigned gender. Further, there is usually a strong desire to have the sex characteristics of the opposite gender, to be treated as the other gender (or an alternative gender other than one's assigned gender), and a strong conviction that one experiences the feelings and reactions typically associated with the other gender (American Psychiatric Association, 2013a). Refer to the DSM-5 for the full criteria of gender dysphoria.

The Gender Identity/Gender Dysphoria Questionnaire for Adolescents and Adults (Deogracias, Johnson, Meyer-Bahlburg, Kessler, Schober, & Zucker, 2007; Singh, Deogracias et al., 2010) is a useful instrument to help corroborate the diagnosis of gender dysphoria, particularly in clients who may not be experiencing distress related to their gender incongruence or for those who are subthreshold for a complete DSM diagnosis. The Social Roles Questionnaire (SRQ; Baber & Tucker, 2006) may be utilized to assess clients' attitudes toward gender and could be particularly useful to identify areas of intervention with clients who are struggling with more general gender variance or family members of gender variant clients. In Table 2.5, we provide a list of sample interview questions for assessing gender identity concerns.

Table 2.5 Sample Interview Questions for Assessing Gender-Identity Concerns

- What is your preferred name? What are your preferred pronouns to describe your gender identity?

- At what age was your first memory of gender incongruence and what was the memory?

- Have you ever dressed in attire of the opposite gender? In private, public, or both?

- Have you told anyone about your feelings of gender incongruence? At what age did you tell this person(s), and what reaction did you receive?

- (If client has came out to family) How is your family supportive or not supportive of your gender identity? How are their reactions impacting your current level of distress?

- Who is supportive in your life regarding your gender identity and/or transitioning or where do you get that support (e.g., friends, religious affiliations, support groups, counseling, etc.)?

- Are you employed or in school? Has your employer and/or school been supportive of your preferred gender identity?

- (If deciding to transition) Who have you informed of your intended transition? What was their reaction?

- Over the course of making the decision to transition, has there been a reduction of personal distress?

Instruments such as the Lesbian, Gay, and Bisexual Identity Scale (Mohr & Kendra, 2011) may be useful for clients who are questioning and/or experiencing concerns about their sexual/affectional orientation and to assess for the impact of minority stress on their presenting issues. In Table 2.6, we provide some sample interview questions for assessing sexual/affectional orientation concerns.

Relationship Dynamics

It is essential for counselors to assess for relational and contextual factors external to the individual that may be creating and/or maintaining clients' sexual difficulties. Relationship dynamics have a major influence on individuals' sexual functioning, and sexual problems are often indicative of, and subsequently exacerbate, relationship distress (Johnson & Zuccarini, 2010). Satisfying sexual experiences with one's partner is an important factor contributing to intimacy and satisfaction within the relationship, although couples place more importance on sex (or typically, the lack thereof) as relationships become distressed. Difficulties in sexual functioning or a lack of sexual intimacy in a relationship plays a powerful role in defining the quality of intimate relationships, and sexual problems are

Table 2.6	Sample Interview Questions for Assessing Sexual/Affectional Orientation Concerns

- What is your preferred descriptor for your sexual/affectional orientation?

- Have you told anyone about your sexual/affectional orientation? At what age did you tell this person(s), and what reaction did you receive?

- Do you consider yourself out? If so, to whom and in what environments are you out?

- (If client has came out to family) How is your family supportive or not supportive of your sexual/affectional orientation? How are their reactions impacting your current level of distress?

- Who is supportive in your life regarding your sexual/affectional orientation or where do you get that support (e.g., friends, religious affiliations, support groups, counseling, etc.)?

- Are you employed or in school? Are you out in these environments? If so, has your employer and/or school been supportive of your sexual/affectional orientation?

- Are you currently in a relationship? Describe your current relationship.

- Have you ever been in a relationship that you would consider mentally, emotionally, or physically abusive?

- Do you feel that you experience any undue stress related to your sexual/affectional orientation? If so, how have you tried to cope with these stressors?

- What other identities in your life are important to you? How do they impact your sexual/affectional orientation?

named as one of the leading factors contributing to divorce (McCarthy, 2003). Moreover, the majority of sexual activity in Western countries occurs within committed intimate relationships (Diamond & Huebner, 2012). Thus, it is essential that counselors interview clients about physical and sexual intimacy, particularly when their presenting issue is related to relationship difficulties. Since sexual intimacy is closely connected to overall relationship satisfaction, the informal questions below assess for general relationship dynamics, particularly the emotional closeness and sense of security within the relationship (Johnson, 2004). Instruments such as the Dyadic Adjustment Scale (DAS; Spanier, 1976), the Personal Assessment of Intimacy in Relationships (PAIR; Schaefer & Olson, 1981), and the Relationship Intimacy Assessment (RIA; Metz, 2007) survey overall relationship dynamics and satisfaction, and include questions to assess sexual intimacy. Table 2.7 presents sample interview questions to use to assess concerns related to clients' intimate relationships.

Table 2.7   Sample Interview Questions for Assessing Relationship Dynamics

During Couples Sessions

- In general, how do you feel close and connected to each other?

- What tends to break the connection? Do you feel that the things that break the connection impact your sex life with each other?

- Describe a typical argument. What are triggers for arguments? Are there any attempts at repair after the argument? Do you feel that your arguments with each other impact your sex life, and if so, how?

- Have arguments ever escalated to physical violence? If so, assess for more details about the occurrence of the violence and the levels of safety in the relationship.

- Do either of you drink alcohol or use other drugs? If so, assess frequency and amount of use. What is the impact of alcohol or other drug use on your relationship, and do you feel that substance use has ever enhanced or diminished your physical connection?

- Are you able to comfort each other at this time? If so, how and when? If not, what is your primary source of comfort at this time?

- How do you show physical affection to each other?

- How do you feel about the overall quality of physical connection, including non-sexual touch, within your relationship?

- Do you have sex/make love? If so, how often?

- Which partner tends to initiate sex?

- Do you experience discrepancies in desire for sexual activity and/or sexual preferences?

- Do you feel close and/or connected with or distant from your partner during sex?

- Do you feel like you can communicate openly about sex with your partner?

- What keeps you in the relationship with your partner?

During Individual Sessions

- Have you ever had an affair and if so, does your partner know?

- Are there times that you feel afraid of your partner?

- Reassess substance use if reported in couples session. If partner is using ask the following: How do you feel about your partner's substance use? Do you feel that it impacts your relationship and your physical intimacy?

- Do you have a history of physical, emotional, or sexual trauma? If so, how do you see this impacting your sexual relationship with your partner?

- Have you had any past significant relationships? Did you experience similar physical intimacy concerns in those relationships?

- How comfortable do you feel when communicating your sexual interest and preferences to your partner? What inhibits your communication?

- Do you ever worry about losing your partner or being rejected by your partner before, during, or after sexual activities?

- What keeps you in the relationship with your partner at this time?

Cultural and Contextual Issues

We discuss an intersectional approach to understanding contextual influences on sexuality in Chapter 9 as our sexual development is shaped and impacted by the contexts in which we live. These contextual factors all intertwine to influence individual sexuality, and thus, clients' sexual concerns are best understood in relation to cultural and relational factors that can perpetuate sexual difficulties (Nicholls, 2008; Southern & Cade, 2011). A comprehensive sexuality assessment will include questions that emphasize the sociocultural dimensions of sexuality, invite clients to explore the messages they have internalized from contextual influences around sex, and begin to evaluate whether these messages are harmful or helpful to them at this time. Additionally, it can be empowering for clients to locate their sexual difficulties as resulting from systemic causes rather than as an internal shortcoming, and help clients feel they have more agency over their sexuality and desired changes (Southern & Cade, 2011).

Many of the instruments listed in the Appendix have been developed in Western societies and normed in samples that were not racially or ethnically diverse (i.e., the samples were largely Caucasian), and thus, their utility for clients from various backgrounds may be limited. Moreover, many of the current instruments do not account for the influence of contextual factors on the constructs they are designed to measure. Counselors should investigate the appropriateness of using these assessments with clients from diverse backgrounds before administering them and gather more information from clients about contextual factors to assist in interpreting the results from formal assessment strategies. Conducting an informal assessment through the intake interview and including open-ended questions about contextual influences such as the ones listed below can aid counselors in determining which formal assessments may be the most appropriate for their clients. Further, reviewing the results with clients and asking for their perceptions about the assessment is helpful to improve the applicability of the instrument to individuals' needs and to avoid generalizations that may not accurately reflect clients' experiences. The Brief Sexual Attitudes Scale (BSAS; Hendrick, Hendrick, & Reich, 2006) is an established instrument that can be used to survey clients' beliefs and values toward human sexual expression. You may use the sample questions in Table 2.8 to begin

Table 2.8 Sample Interview Questions for Assessing Cultural and Contextual Issues

- What messages have you received about sex throughout your life, from your family and friends? Do you view these messages as helpful or harmful to you in creating a positive sense of your sexuality?

- How did you first learn about sex and from whom did this information come?

- How was sex discussed and/or sexuality expressed within your family? Was the focus on sex as it relates to reproduction, or did you also learn about sex as it relates to pleasure?

- How are the sexual expectations and roles of men and women defined by your family?

- What are cultural expectations about sex and sexuality that you feel impact you personally? How are the sexual expectations and roles of men and women defined by your culture?

- How do your family or work obligations impact your sexual life?

- Do you have a religious or spiritual affiliation that is important to you? How does your religious or spiritual affiliation influence your beliefs about sex and sexuality?

- Do you feel you have access to adequate resources (e.g., birth control, medical care, etc.) that promote your sexual health? If not, what do you view as the barriers to accessing the sexual health resources that you would like to utilize?

- What messages have you received from the media about your body image and sexuality? How do you feel these messages impact your ability to develop a positive sexuality?

a dialogue with clients about how their cultural and other contextual backgrounds impact their current sexuality-related concerns.

Positive Sexuality

Although the pleasurable aspects of sexuality have been recognized more in research and practice in the mental health professions over recent years, much of the focus still remains on problems and deficits in sexual functioning (Diamond & Huebner, 2012). While some of the questions asked during an interview need to concentrate on problem-definition and the context in which the issue is occurring in order to establish a baseline of clients' functioning, it is important that counselors incorporate questions that emphasize clients' strengths and the positive components of sexuality. Further, counselors can phrase questions in a way that allows clients' to process and define positive sexuality for themselves, affirming their sexual identity, development, and experiences and helping clients make informed decisions about engaging in sexual activities as long as clients' choices are respectful of the sexual rights of others (Southern & Cade, 2011). The interview questions below draw on strengths-based theories, particularly Solution-Focused

Brief Therapy (SFBT; de Shazer, 1982) and can be useful to shift clients away from "problem talk" to "change talk," which highlights clients' assets and the agency that they have to influence change in their lives. Some sample questions are provided in Table 2.9 for interviewing clients about their views on positive sexuality.

Assessment is integral to collaborative goal setting and effective treatment planning in counseling. Counseling as a profession emphasizes holism, wellness, and development over the lifespan, and as sexuality is an essential part of human well-being (Diamond & Huebner, 2012), counselors need to include sexuality as a component during the assessment phase with all clients. As we conclude this chapter on assessing sexuality in counseling, think back to the case studies presented at the beginning of the chapter. What interview questions did you identify as the most relevant for each case? What instruments do you think would be helpful to either provide you more information about their presenting issue and/or to establish a baseline for each client's functioning? We invite you to practice the assessment strategies that you identified as relevant to these cases in Exercise 2.3 and to utilize

---

Table 2.9 Sample Interview Questions for Assessing and Constructing Positive Sexuality

- What questions or concerns related to your sexual health, satisfaction, and/or pleasure would you like to discuss in counseling?

- What does positive sexuality look like to you?

- On a scale of 1-10, with 10 being the highest, how would you rate your current level of sexual health?

- On a scale of 1-10, with 10 being the highest, how would you rate your current level of sexual satisfaction?

- How does your sexual health impact your sexual satisfaction and vice versa?

- What are ways in which you can promote your sexual health? What are ways in which you can promote your sexual satisfaction?

- Tell me about times when you are not experiencing [insert specific sexual concern]. That is, what are times when you have felt satisfied with your sexual experiences? What was different about those times?

- What are ways in which you wish to express your sexuality to feel congruent with your sense of self?

- Do you have any areas where you feel shame connected to your sexuality? How can you give voice to these areas and confront the feelings of "I'm not good enough" in order to construct a positive sense of your sexual self?

- If you could wake up tomorrow and have the perfect sex life, what would that look like?

Exercise 2.3

PRACTICING SEXUALITY ASSESSMENT IN COUNSELING

Directions: After you have identified relevant assessment strategies for each of the cases at the beginning of the chapter on your own, choose a case to role-play in small groups. One person should take on the role of the counselor, one to three people will take on the role of the clients in the case scenarios, and the remaining individuals in the group can observe the role-play. The individual playing the counselor should utilize the interview questions throughout this chapter in order to help the client(s) further define their presenting concern, particularly how it is impacting and/or impacted by their sexuality, and help the client(s) set 2 to 3 goals toward their desired change. Goals should be strengths based, observable, and measurable. Should the counselor feel stuck at any point, they can pause the "session" to allow the observers to provide feedback on the assessment process. Once the client(s) have generated goals, come back together in your small groups and brainstorm potential means by which the goals can be achieved. Based on your general knowledge about counseling, what are some interventions that may be effective in addressing the sexuality-related concerns of the client(s)?

---

these strategies in defining the presenting issue, establishing goals, and creating an initial treatment plan for one or all of these cases.

KEYSTONES

- It is important to include the assessment of sexuality as part of the overall biopsychosocial assessment of clients' functioning during the intake interview.
- Counselors are well-situated to evaluate individuals' sexual health and to promote safe sex practices through their counseling services.
- Clients typically will not initiate conversations about sexuality unless prompted to do so by their health care providers, including counselors and other mental health practitioners, particularly if their presenting concern is not directly linked to sexuality.
- It is important that you can be matter-of-fact, objective, and comfortable as a counselor in discussing sexuality with clients so that your personal values and biases do not interfere with clients' openness to share sexual concerns.
- It is important that counselors develop an ease in saying words related to sex and sexuality.

- Counselors should assess clients' sexual history as it is relevant to their existing concerns, but be aware when a line of questioning does not seem significant to understanding clients' presenting issues.
- If clients identify any sexuality-related concerns during the general assessment process, counselors will want to follow-up with more specific questions based on their presenting concerns.
- Counselors should use a combination of informal and formal assessment strategies and tools to assess clients' functioning at each influence within the Contextualized Sexuality Model.

ADDITIONAL RESOURCES

- Association for Assessment and Research in Counseling (http://aarc-counseling.org)
- Fisher, T. D., Davis, C. M., Yarber, W. L., & Davis, S. L. (2010). *Handbook of sexuality-related measures* (3rd ed.). New York, NY: Routledge.

APPENDIX: DIRECTORY OF SELECTED INSTRUMENTS FOR ASSESSING SEXUALITY

This directory contains an overview of instruments that counselors can include in the clinical assessment of sexuality and sexuality-related concerns of clients, which correspond to each area of the Contextualized Sexuality Model. These assessments may be useful to corroborate information obtained during open-ended interviews with clients. The sources for each assessment are included so counselors can locate directions for administration and how to obtain the instrument for clinical use. Some of the full-length instruments are published in the original sources and may be free to administer, but it is the counselor's responsibility to ensure that copyright instructions are followed when using these assessments in therapeutic practice.

Instrument Name and Source	Construct(s) Designed to Assess	Number of Items; Domains/Subscales; Sample Item(s)	Reliability and Validity Information	Strengths of Instrument for Clinical Practice	Limitations of Instrument for Clinical Practice
Physiology					
Changes in Sexual Functioning Questionnaire Short-Form (Keller et al., 2006)	The CSFQ-14 assesses sexual functioning and can be used to assess for changes in functioning following a medical or mental health diagnosis and/or start of a medication regimen.	Fourteen-item instrument with parallel male and female versions, each with five subscales: Pleasure, Desire/Frequency, Desire/Interest, Arousal/Erection, and Orgasm/Ejaculation. The following is a sample item on both versions: "How much pleasure or enjoyment do you get from your orgasms?"	Cronbach's $a = .90$ for the female version and .89 for the male version. There is evidence of construct validity.	• Short version of the full CSFQ (35 items) is quick and easy to administer • May be more comfortable for clients to fill out this form to identify problem areas than respond to open-ended interview questions • Psychometric properties tested with a large sample from clinics across the United States	• Self-report questionnaires may not yield as much valid information, so important to follow up clients' responses with interview questions • Sample was mostly Caucasian, married, and employed full-time so applicability to diverse populations needs further testing

				• Full version of the CSFQ is published in Spanish	
Derogatis Interview for Sexual Functioning (Derogatis, 1997)	The DISF is a semi-structured interview that assesses the quality of current sexual functioning with individuals. It is also available in a self-report version (DISF-SR).	Twenty-six items that evaluate five domains of sexual functioning: Sexual Cognition/ Fantasy, Sexual Arousal, Sexual Behavior/Experience, Orgasm, and Sexual/ Drive Relationship. The following is a sample item: "Your ability to have an orgasm." This can be interpreted at the item level, the domain level, or the total-score level. The DISF-SR also has 26 items that parallel the interview.	Adequate internal consistency for the subscales (Cronbach's *a* range from .74 to .80). The DISF and DISF-SR have demonstrated test-retest and inter-rater reliability. There is evidence of construct validity. Demonstrated ability to identify sexual dysfunction, and sensitivity and specificity to treatment effects.	• Available in seven languages • Can be administered in a relatively brief time frame of 15–20 minutes • Can be utilized as a pre- and posttest or across treatment • Uses gender-neutral language so appropriate for individuals of various sexual/affectional orientations • Gender norms established for instrument	• Continued research is needed to develop norms for various populations • The DISF has primarily been developed through medical clinical research trials, so more research is needed on the applicability and utility of the DISF in mental health settings • Utilized Master's & Johnson's model in the development, so may overlook important contextual factors that affect clients' sexual functioning

(Continued)

(Continued)

Instrument Name and Source	Construct(s) Designed to Assess	Number of Items; Domains/Subscales; Sample Item(s)	Reliability and Validity Information	Strengths of Instrument for Clinical Practice	Limitations of Instrument for Clinical Practice
Developmental Issues					
Child Sexual Behavior Inventory (Friedrich et al., 1992; Friedrich et al., 2001)	The CSBI assesses the frequency of specific sexual behaviors over the past 6 months through parent reports for children ages 2–12.	Thirty-eight item instrument that assesses nine domains: Boundary Problems, Exhibitionism, Gender Role Behavior, Self-Stimulation, Sexual Anxiety, Sexual Interest, Sexual Intrusiveness, Sexual Knowledge, and Voyeuristic Behavior. The following is a sample item: "Touches sex (private) parts at home."	The internal consistency (Cronbach's a) for the CSBI ranged from .72 to .92 across samples. There is a very adequate test-retest reliability and inter-rater reliability demonstrated between parents, teachers, and nurses. There is evidence of the ability to discriminate between sexually abused and non-abused children.	• Psychometric properties have been tested in racially and economically diverse samples • Useful in identifying children who are demonstrating sexual behavior problems	• Critiqued for its use to discriminate between sexually abused and non-abused children based on normative sexual behaviors, due to other confounding variables such as physical abuse, domestic violence, or neglect (Drach, Wientzen, & Ricci, 2001)

Adolescent Clinical Sexual Behavior Inventory-Self Report (Friedrich et al., 2004)	The ACSBI assesses sex-related behaviors in adolescents ages 12–18, including sexual interest, avoidance or discomfort, and sexual risk-taking and nonconforming behaviors. This includes a parent-report (ACSBI-P) and self-report (ACSBI-S) version.	Forty-five item measure with five domains: Sexual Knowledge/Interest, Sexual Risk/Misuse, Divergent Sexual Interests, Concerns about Appearance, and Fear/Discomfort. The following is a sample item: "Uses phone sex lines or computer sex chat rooms."	Adequate internal consistency (Cronbach's a for ACSBI-P/ACSBI-S) for three of the subscales: Divergent Sexual Interest (.81/.65), Sexual Knowledge/Interest (.76/.77), and Sexual Risk/Misuse (.79/.68). There is questionable internal consistency on two of the subscales: Concerns about Appearance (.65/.68) and Fear/ Discomfort (.39/.45). There is evidence of agreement between the ACSBI-P and ACSBI-S, test-retest reliability, and convergent validity.	• Designed to comprehensively assess adolescent sexual behavior • The ACSBI-P and ACSBI-S only shared a small amount of variance, suggesting that parents may have different perceptions or a lack of knowledge about their teen's sexual behavior, so administering both forms in a clinical setting may provide valuable information to enhance family counseling	• Questionable internal consistency of some of the subscales • Sample was homogeneous (predominantly White, middle-to-upper class) so more testing is needed to test its applicability in ethnically and economically diverse populations • Unstable home life and trauma correspond to risky sexual behavior in adolescents, so it is important to assess for contextual information to clarify the results of this instrument and to not pathologize a typical response to environmental stressors

(*Continued*)

Instrument Name and Source	Construct(s) Designed to Assess	Number of Items; Domains/Subscales; Sample Item(s)	Reliability and Validity Information	Strengths of Instrument for Clinical Practice	Limitations of Instrument for Clinical Practice
Geriatric Sexuality Inventory (Kazer et al., 2013)	The GSI assesses the sexual health needs of older adults.	Thirty-four item instrument that assesses eight dimensions of sexual health: Medication and Illness, Self-Concept, Sexual Satisfaction, Sexual Knowledge, Relationship with Health Care Provider, Environmental Issues, Safe Sex, and Partnership Status. It includes three open-ended questions to gather information on additional sexual concerns. The following is a sample open-ended item: "With whom do you discuss sexual concerns?"	There is adequate internal consistency (Cronbach's a = .74). There is evidence of test-retest reliability and content validity. Other forms of validity (e.g., convergent, discriminant) have not been established.	• Items were developed utilizing recent literature and expert review • Assesses physiological, psychological, relational, and contextual factors contributing to sexual health • Utilizes a yes/no format that may be an easier response format for older adults • Developed for use across various types of clinical settings in addition to research	• The psychometric properties of the GSI were tested in a small homogeneous (mostly Caucasian female) sample (N=34), so further research is needed on the reliability and validity of the instrument

Garos Sexual Behavior Inventory (Garos, 2009)	The GSBI assesses multiple areas of sexual difficulties and behaviors, including sexual adjustment and internal conflict, preoccupation with sex, attitudes and values about sex, and level of comfort with sex and sexual stimuli.	Seventy-item scale that includes four Main domains (Discordance, Permissiveness, Sexual Obsession, and Sexual Stimulation), three Masking domains (Sexual Control Difficulties, Sexual Excitability, and Sexual Insecurity), and an Inconsistent Responding Index.	The subscales demonstrated adequate internal consistency across studies: Discordance (.80–.85), Permissiveness (.66–.73), Sexual Obsession (.72–.80), Sexual Stimulation (.67–.74), and alphas > .74 for the masking scales. There is evidence of test-retest reliability and factorial, discriminant, and convergent validity. There is initial evidence of sensitivity and specificity to treatment-related effects.	• Useful for various clinical contexts, including use with couples, sexual addiction, sex offenders, and sexual or abuse trauma treatment • The Masking scales and Inconsistent Responding Index help control for defensive and random responding, which is useful in a self-report measure • Normative data is available for males and females	• The amount of time taken to administer and score the assessment may not be feasible in all clinical settings

(*Continued*)

(Continued)

Instrument Name and Source	Construct(s) Designed to Assess	Number of Items; Domains/Subscales; Sample Item(s)	Reliability and Validity Information	Strengths of Instrument for Clinical Practice	Limitations of Instrument for Clinical Practice
Sexual Arousal and Desire Inventory (Toledano & Pfaus, 2006)	The SADI assesses subjective experiences of sexual arousal and desire in both men and women.	This includes 54 descriptors of sexual arousal and desire that can be applied to normative sexual experiences or specific fantasies or erotic experiences. It includes four factors: Evaluative, Negative/Aversive, Physiological, and Motivational. The following are sample evaluative descriptors: "tempted, quivering sensations, wet/hard, and 'sensual.'"	There is excellent internal consistency for the overall scale ($a = .90$) and for three of the four subscales: Evaluative (.91), Negative/Aversive (.86), Physiological (.85), and Motivational (.72). There is evidence of convergent and divergent validity.	• Assesses for psychological experiences of desire and arousal outside of physiological and behavioral components • The SADI can be used in experimental situations (e.g., after watching an erotic film) • Utilizes gender-neutral language	• Sample for instrument development was mostly young, heterosexual, and white so further testing is needed for applicability to diverse populations • More research is needed on the application of the SADI in clinical settings

Sexual Addiction Screening Test – Revised (Carnes et al., 2010)	The SAST-R was designed to be a screening tool for sexually addictive behaviors	Fifty-two item scale that assesses four core components of sexual addiction: preoccupation, loss of control, affective disturbance, and relationship disturbance in addition to an Internet scale and gender and sexual orientation scales. The following is a sample item: "Has sex become the most important thing in your life?"	Cronbach's a for the core score ranged from .77 to .92 across populations of women and men in various settings, including outpatient counseling, clergy, and college. This demonstrated the ability to discriminate between those with sex addiction vs. those without, as well as varying levels of severity in symptoms.	• The revised version was designed to be clinically relevant across populations and to reflect societal changes that influence sexual addiction • Has scales specific to assess characteristics of sexual addiction unique to women (W-SAT) and gay men (G-SAT) • The subscales can provide useful information for treatment planning by identifying the areas in which there is the most distress for clients	• The SAST-R shows potential to be clinically useful across populations, including women and gay men, but further testing is needed in these populations, as well as contrasting non-clinical populations with those in mental health settings. • Culturally relevant to Western societies but utility outside of these cultures is unknown

(Continued)

(Continued)

Instrument Name and Source	Construct(s) Designed to Assess	Number of Items; Domains/Subscales; Sample Item(s)	Reliability and Validity Information	Strengths of Instrument for Clinical Practice	Limitations of Instrument for Clinical Practice
Early Sexual Experiences Checklist (Miller et al., 1991)	The ESEC assesses for experiences of unwanted sexual contact and childhood sexual abuse occurring before 16 years of age (the age limit can be adapted as relevant to administration) in older adolescent and adult populations.	Contains a 9-item checklist of sexual behaviors and asks additional questions about the context of the event, such as age at time of occurrence, age and identity of the other person involved, frequency and duration of the sexual behavior, and coercive experiences. The following is a checklist prompt: "When you were under the age of 16, did any of these incidents ever happen to you when you did not want them to?"	The ESEC is a checklist so internal consistency data is unavailable. Test-retest reliability (Cohen's kappa) = .92. In terms of validity, the ESEC is useful for detecting a range of unwanted sexual contact that participants may not define as "abuse" or that may not be detected by other instruments.	• Checklist is brief and can be administered quickly • Assesses for a range of unwanted sexual experiences in childhood • Asks for contextual information about the unwanted sexual experiences • May be useful in a clinical context for clients who do not label their experiences as "abuse," and for clinicians to gather valuable information that clients may not be comfortable verbalizing in session	• Empirical testing of the instrument's psychometric properties is limited due to its format

| Gender Identity/Gender Dysphoria Questionnaire for Adolescents and Adults (Deogracias et al., 2007) | The GIDYQ-AA assesses the degree to which individuals are struggling with their gender identity. | Twenty-seven item scale with versions for males and females. The following is a sample item from the female version: "In the past 12 months, have you felt more like a man than a woman?" (Deogracias et al., 2007, p. 377). | The measure demonstrated a one-factor solution with high internal consistency (Cronbach's a =.97). There is evidence of convergent and discriminant validity. | • Measure was developed using control groups of heterosexual and nonheterosexual participants
• Instrument is short and easy to administer
• Can help to corroborate diagnosis of Gender Dysphoria | • The samples with which the GIDYQ-AA was developed were largely Caucasian and the participants with gender dysphoria were recruited from hospital-based clinics, so more testing needs to be done for its cross-cultural applicability |
| Social Roles Questionnaire (Baber & Tucker, 2006) | The SRQ assesses gender role attitudes, including beliefs about social roles for men and women as well as attitudes that transcend binary categories of gender. | Thirteen item instrument with two subscales: Gender-Linked (beliefs about certain roles associated with gender) and Gender Transcendent (viewing gender as non-binary). The following is a sample item: "People should be treated the same regardless of their sex." | Adequate internal consistency for the subscales: Gender-Linked (a = .77) and Gender Transcendence (a =. 65). Subscales had adequate variability and evidence of test-retest reliability. There is evidence of construct, convergent, and discriminant validity. | • Utilized a social constructivist perspective in the development of the instrument
• Utilized statistical analysis on a longer measure to create a brief assessment | • Sample for instrument development was 98% Caucasian and mostly middle class, so applicability to diverse populations needs to be tested, as race, ethnicity, culture, and socioeconomic status may impact perceptions of gender roles. |

(Continued)

Instrument Name and Source	Construct(s) Designed to Assess	Number of Items; Domains/Subscales; Sample Item(s)	Reliability and Validity Information	Strengths of Instrument for Clinical Practice	Limitations of Instrument for Clinical Practice
Lesbian, Gay, and Bisexual Identity Scale (Mohr & Kendra, 2011)	The LGBIS assesses development of a positive LGB identity.	Twenty-seven items with 8 subscales: Acceptance Concerns, Concealment Motivation, Identity Uncertainty, Internalized Homonegativity, Difficult Process, Identity Superiority, Identity Affirmation, and Identity Centrality. The following is a sample item from the Identity Affirmation subscale: "I'm glad to be LGB" (Mohr & Kendra, 2011, p. 245)	The mean internal consistency (Cronbach's alpha) for the subscales ranged from .75 to .91 across samples. Test-retest reliability for the subscales ranged from .70 to .92. There is preliminary evidence for convergent validity of the LGBIS.	• Developed from theoretical literature on identity formation • Measure is multi-dimensional • Can be administered and scored quickly	• The samples with which the LGBIS was developed were largely white college students in the United States, so its cross-cultural applicability is not known. • Validity was established based on self-report measures administered at the same time, so the results could be inflated due to shared method variance

| Dyadic Adjustment Scale (Spanier, 1976) | The DAS assesses for marital distress, including items assessing sexual intimacy. | Thirty-two item instrument with four subscales: Dyadic Consensus, Dyadic Satisfaction, Dyadic Cohesion, and Affective Expression. The following is a sample item: "Do you kiss your mate?" | Mean Cronbach's a (Graham, Liu, & Jeziorski, 2006): Dyadic Consensus (.87), Dyadic Satisfaction (.85), Dyadic Cohesion (.79), and Affective Expression (.71). Thus, three of the four subscales have demonstrated adequate internal consistency across studies, but the Affective Expression subscale may take on different meanings in various populations. This is an effective measure to discriminate between distressed and non-distressed couples. There is evidence of predictive validity in identifying couples more likely to divorce. | • The most widely used scale in research to assess for marital distress, thus its psychometric properties have been thoroughly tested in various populations across cultures
• Has been translated into multiple languages
• Demonstrated clinical usefulness for men and women (South, Krueger, & Iacono, 2009) | • Critiqued for different response formats, which affects the variance that the items contribute to the total score
• White, married men may not respond as consistently to the Affective Expression subscale (Graham et al., 2006) |

(Continued)

(Continued)

Instrument Name and Source	Construct(s) Designed to Assess	Number of Items; Domains/Subscales; Sample Item(s)	Reliability and Validity Information	Strengths of Instrument for Clinical Practice	Limitations of Instrument for Clinical Practice
Personal Assessment of Intimacy in Relationships (Schaefer & Olson, 1981)	The PAIR was developed to assess actual and ideal levels of intimacy, including sexual intimacy, in various types of partner relationships.	Thirty-item measure that can be answered in two modes of current perceptions and ideal expectations. Includes five subscales: Emotional Intimacy, Social Intimacy, Sexual Intimacy, Intellectual Intimacy, and Recreational Intimacy. Includes a 6-item Conventionality scale to test for social-desirability bias. The following is a sample item: "I hold back my sexual interest because my partner makes me feel uncomfortable."	Adequate internal consistency for each of the subscales across studies (Cronbach's $a > .70$) except the Recreational Intimacy subscale demonstrates lower internal consistency (.55 to .70). The five-factor structure did not hold up in the confirmatory factor analysis study with participants reporting sexual dysfunction (Moore, McCabe, & Stockdale, 1998). There is evidence of convergent validity.	• Useful for clinicians to assess couples over a range of intimate areas and can provide insight for couples into their partners' needs • Developed for use in all types of intimate partnerships, including friendships, dating, and committed relationships	• Psychometric stability of the PAIR is questionable, although the measure could still provide useful information in clinical settings • Developed for opposite-sex relationships but has been used in research with lesbian couples (Eldridge & Gilbert, 1990) and demonstrated similar psychometric outcomes as in studies with opposite-sex partners. More research is needed to demonstrate applicability to same-sex partnerships

| Relationship Intimacy Assessment (Metz, 2007) | The RIA assesses the areas of intimacy including sexual intimacy that are important to each partner, as well as individuals' current satisfaction with these areas in their relationships. | Twelve items that are facets of relationship intimacy, which the individual ranks in order of importance to their experience of intimacy and then rates their satisfaction with each area on a 1–10 Likert scale. The following is a sample item: "Sexual Intimacy: sensual-emotional satisfaction; the experience of sharing and self-abandon in the physical merging of two persons' fantasies and desires." | The RIA is a value-ranking inventory so no psychometric data is available. | • Developed by a practitioner for use in clinical settings
• Asks users to assess intimacy based on their personal values, so it can be appropriately administered to clients of varying cultural backgrounds
• Can be a useful tool to open up conversation about intimacy with couples in counseling | • There is no research to support the utility of the RIA in clinical settings or to provide strategies for how the RIA can be most useful to clinicians and clients |

(Continued)

Instrument Name and Source	Construct(s) Designed to Assess	Number of Items; Domains/Subscales; Sample Item(s)	Reliability and Validity Information	Strengths of Instrument for Clinical Practice	Limitations of Instrument for Clinical Practice
		Cultural and Contextual Influences			
Brief Sexual Attitudes Scale (Hendrick et al., 2006)	The BSAS was developed from the 43-item SAS (Hendrick & Hendrick, 1987) as a multi-dimensional measure to assess attitudes toward sex in individuals or all types of partnered couples.	The BSAS is a 23-item measure with four subscales: Permissiveness (casual, open attitudes toward sex), Birth Control (attitudes toward safe-sex practices), Communion (sex as an important experience), and Instrumentality (sex as a natural and useful part of life). The following is a sample item: "Casual sex is acceptable."	Cronbach's a adequate for each of the subscales (Permissiveness = .95; Birth Control =.88; Instrumentality =.77; and Communion =.73). Inter-subscale correlations were adequate. There are test-retest correlations for the subscales ranging from .57 to .92. There is evidence of concurrent validity.	• Can be completed quickly • Measures various types of sexual attitudes that can impact sexual behavior and safe-sex practices • Useful in both individual and couples counseling and applicable to partners in varying types of intimate relationships	• Researchers have found that men tend to report higher permissive and instrumental attitudes than women, so clinicians need to consider the impact of gender on assessment results • Does not assess for all sexual attitudes, such as attitudes toward sexual coercion or gender roles

Chapter 3

General Interventions and Theoretical Approaches to Sexuality Counseling

*The way we commonly think about how intimacy and
sex work in marriage is only part of the picture.*

—Schnarch, 1997, p. 38

When considering how best to address clients' sexuality-related concerns in counseling, it is important to think more broadly about sexuality than is common in society today. As Albert Einstein is quoted saying, "Problems cannot be solved with the same mindset that created them" (Goodreads, 2015). Counselors may draw from a wide range of theory- and practice-based approaches when working with clients to address sexuality concerns. In particular, counselors may adapt sex therapy interventions, presuming they work within the bounds of their competence and training. We begin this chapter with general recommendations for competent sexuality counseling practice. Then, we review a range of intervention approaches and models, followed by treatment strategies for specific sexuality concerns. After reading this chapter, readers will be able to do the following:

a. Understand general guidelines for conducting sexuality counseling
b. Summarize a range of approaches to addressing sexuality-related concerns, including medical treatments and counseling interventions
c. Describe treatment interventions that are used to address specific sexuality-related concerns
d. Discuss research examining the effectiveness of sexuality counseling treatments

GENERAL GUIDELINES FOR SEXUALITY COUNSELING

Regardless of the treatment approach used, counselors can aim to create a supportive therapeutic environment for addressing the sensitive topics that can arise when discussing sexuality concerns. Toward that end, we offer the following eight general guidelines for sexuality counseling.

1. *Create a Safe, Private Space for Clients.* Sexuality counseling requires a supportive, cooperative context that is fostered by the counselor (Rosenbaum, 2009; Southern & Cade, 2011). It should occur in a space that is private and feels safe for the client to discuss sensitive sexuality-related topics (Juergens, Smedema, & Berven, 2009). Many clients are reluctant to seek treatment for sexual concerns, and in fact, many people with sexual problems don't seek any help at all (Stinson, 2009). Often, clients will feel too embarrassed to bring up sexual dysfunctions or may wait for a clinician to address the topic (Sadovsky et al., 2011). Because so many value-laden issues arise when addressing sexuality concerns, counselors should take steps to ensure that they establish a respectful and supportive climate for clients (van der Kwaak, Ferris, van Kats, & Dieleman, 2010). The earliest sessions of sexuality counseling should focus on building rapport, and therefore, they may not involve the client discussing their sexual concerns in great detail (Goodwach, 2005b). Because each client's perspectives and meaning systems are unique, it is important for counselors to explore and validate clients' meaning systems regarding their sexuality-related problems and experiences (Rosenbaum, 2009). One useful avenue for this exploration is to examine the social influences on those internalized meaning systems (Rosenbaum, 2009). Some other counselor practices that foster a supportive environment for sexuality counseling include demonstrating positive communication skills, conveying a professional demeanor, showing respect for the client's autonomy, providing a physically safe and private location, using active listening skills, and using culturally competent approaches (Hatzichristou et al., 2010; Southern & Cade, 2011).

2. *Incorporate Assessment Findings Into the Treatment Plan.* Sexuality counseling treatment plans should be grounded firmly in data collected through the counselor's clinical assessment of the client (Bartlik, Rosenfeld, & Beaton, 2005; Hatzichristou et al., 2010). The assessment should be comprehensive and consider the interplay between biology, psychological influences, and relational and other social factors (Basson, Wierman, van Lankveld, & Brotto, 2010). Assessment should address relationship problems, as well as other psychological symptoms that may coexist with sexual problems, such as anxiety and depression. Readers can refer to Chapter 2 for additional information about sexuality counseling assessment considerations. When establishing a treatment plan and identifying treatment

goals, it is important to ensure that those plans and goals are consistent with the clients' strengths and priorities that emerge through the clinical assessment.

3. *Consider Different Treatment Formats.* Sexuality counseling requires flexibility with regards to identifying the best treatment format. At different points in treatment, clients may benefit from individual counseling (Althof, 2010), group counseling (Althof, 2010; Basson et al., 2010), and/or conjoint couples treatment. Conjoint treatment is especially useful when sexual concerns are linked to relationship problems (Althof, Lieblum et al., 2005). Sessions may vary within the course of treatment in terms of who is included in sessions. For example, Bartlik et al. (2005) wrote that traditional sex therapy for couples typically began with a conjoint session, then moved to individual sessions for each partner, and then brought the partners back together again for subsequent sessions. Therefore, counselors should discuss treatment format options with clients and cooperatively determine the best format(s) to address the clients' presenting concerns.

4. *Refer for a Medical Evaluation as Appropriate.* Sexual problems may stem from physiological causes (e.g., anatomic or biochemical problems), psychological and relational causes, or a combination of both (Hatzichristou et al., 2010). Therefore, a physical examination should always be a precursor to clinical assessment and treatment when sexual dysfunctions are suspected (Basson et al., 2010; Goldstein, 2007; Goodwach, 2005b; Hatzichristou et al., 2010; Southern & Cade, 2011). Some physiological issues to rule out as potential causes or contributors to sexual problems include hormone levels, other physical health problems, medication side effects, drug and alcohol use, and aging (Southern & Cade, 2011).

Sexuality is an inherently interdisciplinary issue, so counselors must think beyond solely psychotherapeutic approaches to address clients' sexuality concerns (Firth & Mohamad, 2007; Hatzichristou et al., 2010; Jones, Meneses da Silva, & Soloski, 2011; Rosenbaum, 2011). Likewise, there has been a growing push for medical professionals to be more inclusive of psychotherapeutic approaches (Rosenbaum, 2011). In practice, the integration of these approaches can be difficult, so further efforts are needed to ensure that interdisciplinary models to address sexuality concerns are available to meet clients' needs (Rosenbaum, 2011). However, we urge counselors to make efforts to build collaborative relationships with medical professionals in order to provide comprehensive, coordinated treatment for their clients. Additional information about medical treatments for sexual dysfunctions is provided later in this chapter.

5. *Be Comprehensive in Your Approach.* Sexuality is a complex issue that clients experience in many areas of their lives. Clients may enter counseling with a somewhat narrow view of their sexuality concerns, such as focusing on a specific

physiological function. Counselors can help clients explore new dimensions of sexuality so that they can come to view sexuality as a more comprehensive aspect of their lives (Juergens et al., 2009). Sexuality counseling should include a consideration of multiple dimensions of functioning (e.g., medical, individual psychology, relational) (Sadovsky et al., 2011) and address a comprehensive set of topics that are relevant to clients' presenting concerns. Some of the topics that may be addressed depending on clients' unique circumstances are as follows: areas of sexual distress and sexual satisfaction, body image, cultural values, developmental history, emotional components of sexuality, family-of-origin dynamics, gender influences, intimacy issues, masturbation, mental health concerns that impact sexuality, physical health and wellness, prior abuse and other trauma, relational functioning, relationship history, sexual functioning, and spiritual beliefs (Lobitz & Lobitz, 1996; Southern & Cade, 2011; Stephenson & Meston, 2010; Tiefer, 2001; Tiefer et al., 2002). Attention also should be given to clients' readiness to make changes (Southern & Cade, 2011) and may incorporate motivational interviewing techniques. This extensive list of topics underscores the importance of counselors taking a broad view to understanding and addressing clients' sexuality-related concerns.

6. *Address Sexual Satisfaction, Not Just Problems*. Clients may present for sexuality counseling with a focus on problems. They may want those problems to be resolved, but counselors can go beyond merely aiming for problem resolution to helping clients achieve positive sexuality and greater sexual satisfaction in their lives and relationships. The Interpersonal Exchange Model of Sexual Satisfaction (Byers & Macneil, 2006) offers a useful framework for counselors to understand the dynamics of sexual satisfaction within couple relationships. This model holds that there are four main components of sexual satisfaction: (1) how balanced sexual rewards and costs are within the relationship; (2) how those *actual* rewards and costs match up with the person's *expectations* about rewards and costs; (3) how equivalent the rewards and costs are between the partners in the relationship; and (4) how satisfying other, non-sexual aspects of the couple's relationship are.

A series of research studies provides support for the validity of the Interpersonal Exchange Model in Canada and China (Byers & Macneil, 2006). Key findings from these studies have implications for counseling practice to help clients enhance their sexual satisfaction. First, when someone experiences a long-term imbalance between the sexual rewards and costs within their relationship, it's likely their sexual satisfaction will decrease. Thus, counselors can help clients examine this balance within their relationship in order to identify steps to lead to a more favorable balance of more rewards and fewer costs. Second, research suggests that sexual satisfaction is higher when both partners have higher levels of satisfaction, both sexually and within the relationship. This suggests that counselors should address power and satisfaction imbalances to promote both partners' sexual satisfaction. In other words, if only one partner is satisfied with the couple's sexual relationship, the relationship overall may suffer. Therefore, an intentional focus on enhancing clients' sexual satisfaction—rather than just mitigating distress—can foster treatment progress and enhance clients' relationship outcomes. Additional information about positive sexuality and sexual satisfaction can be found in Chapter 10 of this book.

7. *Address Sexuality Concerns Within a Developmental Context.* Sexuality is not static over time, and individual and relational development impacts how people experience sexuality and intimacy. In particular, significant developmental transitions can affect individuals' and couples' sexuality. For example, the transition to having children often signals a shift in the role of sexuality in couples' relationships (Trice-Black & Foster, 2011). Even later life brings new developmental challenges related to sexuality, such as relationships following the passing of one's spouse and accepting one's body as it ages (Seeber, 2001). At these transitional points, counselors can help clients re-evaluate and re-establish their sexual identity in relation to the context of their new phase of life (Trice-Black & Foster, 2011).

Changes in sexuality and sexual satisfaction naturally fluctuate over time. For example, up to half of all women may experience low sexual desire during their lifetimes at some time (Mintz, Balzer, Zhao, & Bush, 2012). In addition, Lobitz and Lobitz (1996) suggested that relational intimacy waxes and wanes throughout couples' relationships. Like Schnarch (1997), they suggest that greater emotional intimacy often leads people to feel less safe to take sexual risks, which ultimately may decrease sexual excitement and satisfaction. Lobitz and Lobitz also suggest that couples may go through periods of increased risk-taking, as well as periods of more safe encounters through the process of developing sexually. Sexual problems present opportunities for personal and relational growth (Kleinplatz, 2003). Counselors can help clients take advantage of these opportunities, rather than become discouraged by them. It is useful to maintain a focus on strengths at any developmental phase, so counselors also should address positive emotions and affection between partners, such as love and care (Althof et al., 2005).

8. *Apply the Common Factors Framework.* In the next section, we discuss a variety of specific sexuality-counseling treatment approaches. Although specific treatment approaches are useful for providing a framework to conceptualize and treat clients, a growing body of research suggests that specific approaches are less influential on treatment outcomes than other common factors that underlie all psychotherapy. Donahey and Miller (2000) applied the common factors approach to sex therapy, arguing that enhancing these factors is more beneficial to treatment than is developing new techniques and theoretical approaches. Donahey and Miller

apply the four common factors contributing to success in general psychotherapy, which involve extra-therapeutic factors, the therapeutic relationship, expectancy effects, and models and/or techniques. In previous research, the specific therapy models and techniques used accounted for only about 15% of the effectiveness of therapy. More influential were the extra-therapeutic factors (which accounted for 40% of change) and the therapeutic relationship (which accounted for 30%). The final 15% is accounted for by expectancy effects (i.e., a placebo).

The sizeable contribution of extra-therapeutic factors provides a reminder to counselors that much of clients' progress toward their treatment goals stems from clients' actions and experiences that occur outside of counseling sessions (Donahey & Miller, 2000). As such, counselors can support their clients in seeking out useful resources and support systems to promote progress between sessions, as well as remind clients that the changes they experience come mostly from their efforts outside of counseling. Likewise, the therapeutic relationship is an important consideration for sexuality counselors. Especially given the sensitive nature of the issues discussed, counselors must be especially mindful of building a strong alliance with their clients to address their clients' sexuality-related concerns. Regarding expectancy effects, counselors should seek to understand their clients' beliefs about what they hope and expect to receive through the sexuality counseling experience. Clients who begin counseling with negative expectations or limited hope that they will change may benefit from motivational interventions, as well as a more intentional focus on positive changes that they experience.

Further highlighting the impact of expectancy effects, Bradford and Meston (2011) studied the effect of a placebo intervention for women experiencing sexual dysfunctions. They defined a placebo as "the outcome of a richly contextualized clinical encounter in which elements other than the presumed active treatment are beneficial" (p. 191). They cited previous research that showed that placebo effects contributed to reduced sexual dysfunctions among women. One possible explanation for the benefit of placebos is that they prompt women to make behavioral changes that are consistent with the changes they desire from the placebo intervention. For example, a woman who expects to see an improvement in her sex life may set aside a greater amount of time for sexual encounters with her partner. Bradford and Meston's study included 50 women diagnosed with female sexual arousal disorder, based on DSM-IV criteria. The women were asked to take the placebo tablet before engaging in any sexual activity during a 12-week treatment time frame. A majority of the participants experienced statistically significant positive changes, and about one-third demonstrated clinically significant positive changes in sexual satisfaction as a result of experiencing the placebo. Although the researchers noted the range of individual variation in responses to the placebo, this study provides a powerful example of the impact of expectancy effects on sexuality-related interventions.

Although specific therapeutic modalities contribute a relatively small percentage to the change that clients experience through counseling, Donahey and Miller (2000) suggest that approaches remain valuable by providing a specific structure and lens for conceptualizing clients' cases and guiding interventions. Therefore, although Donahey and Miller suggest that sexuality counseling is enhanced to the greatest extent by focusing on helping clients change outside of sessions and strengthening the client-counselor relationship, specific treatment modalities are important to understand and utilize in connection with clients' treatment goals. Given the broad range of approaches to sexuality counseling, counselors have a variety of resources at their disposal to be able to incorporate different theoretical approaches and techniques to meet each client's unique needs.

The common factors framework is not a call to abandon theory altogether. Rather, it underscores the importance of delivering theory-based interventions within a context that fosters positive growth by mobilizing the power of the other powerful influences on client change. In particular, counselors can help clients create a supportive environment for change (e.g., by connecting to other resources in the community and fostering additional social support), develop positive expectations about their ability to change, and feel valued and supported within a strong relationship with the counselor. It is in that spirit that we move to the next section, which reviews a range of treatment approaches for addressing sexuality concerns. Before proceeding to that section, however, please read through Case Illustration 3.1, and consider the Reflection Questions to apply the general guidelines presented in this section to a client case.

CASE ILLUSTRATION 3.1

CASE STUDY: APPLICATION OF GENERAL GUIDELINES FOR SEXUALITY COUNSELING

James (age 54) and Sheila (age 53) have been married for 25 years and recently had the last of their three children move out of the home to go to college. The partners report that they are enjoying the extra time they have now that they are "empty nesters," and they've been focusing on reconnecting and re-establishing their relationship with each other. They've been in couples counseling for four months to address relationship concerns that came up during the transition to living on their own again, and they reported to their counselor that they are happy with their progress and feel closer to one another than they did when they first started counseling.

When their counselor suggested that the couple may be getting close to the point of terminating counseling, James became quiet and then said quietly, "There is one other issue that we haven't talked about yet that I want to address before we stop coming in." He went on to explain that the couple has not had vaginal intercourse for about 3 years. Sheila shared that they'd attempted intercourse a few times during that period but that James was unable to sustain an erection. Not wanting to create conflict in their relationship, both partners seemingly accepted the lack of intercourse, although James admitted in the session that he would like to be able to regain a sexual relationship with his wife. Sheila admitted that she doesn't view this as a major concern, but she's willing to talk about it if James wants to.

Reflection Questions:

1. What steps might the counselor take to maintain a supportive relationship with both clients as they move to addressing sexuality concerns?

2. How do you think the counselor can meet each client's unique needs and expectations for counseling at this point?

3. In addition to a referral for a medical evaluation, are there other community resources that you would recommend for this couple? If so, what are they?

4. How might developmental transitions be impacting the couple's sexuality concerns?

5. How do you think you would begin to address this couple's sexuality concerns? What issues might you focus on first?

6. What other concerns might arise as treatment progresses? How would you address these?

7. What do you think this couple's prognosis for sexuality counseling is, and why?

REVIEW OF APPROACHES TO SEXUALITY COUNSELING

Historically, there have been three main approaches to sex therapy (Goodwach, 2005a). First, medical approaches, such as Viagra, are used to produce physiological changes to clients' sexual functioning. Second, cognitive-behavioral therapy focuses on helping clients change their sexual behaviors and beliefs to produce the positive changes they seek. Third, a more systemic and comprehensive approach looks at clients' sexuality within a broader context of their psychological and relational functioning. In this last category, scholars have applied a number of theoretical frameworks to addressing sexuality in counseling.

In this section, we aim to familiarize readers with the range of sexuality counseling approaches and interventions that are available. First, we discuss medical treatment approaches, which may be used in conjunction with or instead of counseling. Second, we review cognitive-behavior therapy interventions, including sensate focus exercises, masturbation training, and mindfulness-based counseling. Third, we discuss integrative and other theory-based approaches to sexuality counseling. Then, we provide information about treating specific sexuality concerns and the applicability of unique treatment modalities (e.g., Internet-based treatment). The chapter concludes with a discussion of treatment outcomes in sexuality counseling.

Medical Treatment for Sexuality Concerns

The value of medications to address clients' sexual problems has been hotly debated (Althof, Rosen et al., 2005; Binik & Meana, 2009; Graham, 2007; Kleinplatz, 2003; Pacey, 2008; Rowland, 2007; Winton, 2000). The medicalization of sex therapy has been criticized by some professionals, who argue that the emphasis on medical interventions and understandings overlooks many other important influences on sexuality (Tiefer, 2012). In particular, some scholars believe that women's sexual problems are complex and contextual and therefore are more suitable for psychosocial interventions (Graham, 2007; Pacey, 2008). Overemphasizing the medical aspects of sexuality also runs the risk of devaluing diversity of sexual experiences and expressions (Tiefer, 2012). However, clients often seek, and even may prefer, medical interventions to counseling and therapy, and medical interventions can be used as an adjunct to counseling. Therefore, counselors should be familiar with basic information about medical interventions for sexual problems so that they can assist their clients in understanding all of their available treatment options, as well as be equipped to engage in interdisciplinary collaborations with medical professionals.

Goldstein (2007) proposed a five-step process for addressing sexual health problems in medical practice. First, the nature of the sexual health problem is identified and diagnosed. The second step involves educating the client (with the partner, if applicable) about the diagnosis. Third, any easily reversible causes are addressed (e.g., time-management strategies, stress reduction). Fourth, basic medical solutions, such as medication and devices, may be used. Finally, surgery is considered as a last step if other solutions have not corrected the initial concerns. Counselors can help their clients understand this process and process the possible ramifications of various treatment options.

Medical treatments for sexual dysfunctions may include medication (e.g., Sildenafil citrate or Viagra), herbal remedies (e.g., ginkgo biloba), and surgery (e.g., to repair drainage failures) (Winton, 2000). The dosage of prescribed medications may need to be adjusted to find the best dose (Sadovsky et al., 2011). One advantage of the medicalization of sexual dysfunctions is that it may reduce the stigma that people feel in seeking treatment (Rowland, 2007). However, medications may have undesirable side effects, such as diarrhea and nausea, and their benefits typically wear off once the medication is no longer taken (de Carufel & Trudel, 2006). Furthermore, medications do not offer guaranteed positive outcomes. For example, Pallas, Levine, Althof, and Risen (2000) defined four categories of "success" that men may experience from using Viagra. First, they may be *cured*, meaning that they use the drug for a limited time, and after that time, they no longer need to use it to maintain an erection for satisfying intercourse. Second, they may demonstrate *drug-dependent success,* which means that they are able to have satisfying sex while using it but not when they haven't used it. Third, they may experience *drug-dependent erections with new sexual symptoms developing*, such as pain or a desire disorder. And fourth, they may show *improvement with no intercourse,* meaning that the man has more satisfying erections but is not able to have intercourse (e.g., due to one partner's psychological blocks). In contrast, failure for Viagra to produce positive change may result from an inability to sustain improvement over time, resistance to using the drug, or failure of the medication to produce any meaningful physiological improvements.

The use of medical interventions should not preclude psychological or relational interventions, and medical interventions alone often fail to address mental or relational health concerns (Althof, Leiblum et al., 2005). Medications alone are limited in their effectiveness to treat sexual problems because sex is such an inherently relational and emotional issue (Perelman, 2002). Clients using medical interventions for sexual dysfunction should learn about realistic expectations for those treatments (Sadovsky et al., 2011). In part due to the influence of advertisements touting the seemingly quick and easy medical solution to sexual dysfunctions, clients may need information to understand the psychological and relational context for sexual concerns when they first present for treatment (Rowland, 2007).

Medication and psychotherapy can be used to complement one another in the treatment of sexual problems (Perelman, 2002). Perelman noted that although Sildenafil (i.e., Viagra) has grown increasingly common in the treatment of female sexual dysfunction, its effectiveness can be impaired by lifestyle and environmental factors, such as fatigue and relational problems. Pharmaceutical-only treatments can breed additional problems once the initial problems are resolved, including the following: adjusting to resuming sexual activity after lengthy periods of limited to no activity; the partner may resist the client's changes, such as through their behaviors and sexual desires; the partner may have sexual problems that were masked by the client's problems; a lack of self-confidence and self-esteem resulting from the sexual problems; anxiety about one's sexual performance; and the emergence of underlying relationship problems (Althof, 2010). Counseling can be useful for addressing these concerns, and it can enhance the effectiveness of medical treatment alone and play a critical role in ensuring the success in pharmaceutical interventions for sexual dysfunction (Althof, 2010; Perelman, 2002). Overall, despite the growing use of medications to treat sexual dysfunctions, professionals generally accept that the complexity of sexuality-related concerns warrants complex, multifaceted treatments (McCarthy, 2004).

Cognitive-Behavioral Therapy Interventions

Cognitive-behavioral therapy interventions are used widely in sexuality counseling and sex therapy (Althof, 2010). The main elements of this approach include providing educational information to clients, cognitive restructuring, skills training, and the use of homework between sessions, especially sensate focus exercises. In addition, recent advances have integrated mindfulness training with cognitive-behavioral approaches. In this section, we discuss each of these elements of cognitive-behavioral sexuality counseling, followed by examples of research evidence that supports the effectiveness of this approach.

Client Education

Education is a critical component of treatment for sexuality-related issues (Althof, 2010; Guldner, 1995; Hatzichristou et al., 2010; Sarwer & Durlak, 1997; Tiefer, 2001). Educational information can benefit clients and their partners (Hatzichristou et al., 2010), especially in the early treatment phases (Basson et al., 2010). Many clients enter counseling possessing limited information and/or misinformation regarding sexual functioning, often as a result of minimal sex education at home or school (Guldner, 1995). As such, many clients benefit from learning accurate information and developing new skills to enhance their sexual functioning (Guldner, 1995). As Hatzichristou et al. (2010) said,

> Each patient has the right to be fully informed concerning his or her sexual health status, as well as the evidence-based treatment options that are available, in order to participate actively in the decision-making process. (p. 344)

Topics that clients may seek information about include "What is normal when it comes to sexuality?" and "How do disabilities, health conditions, or medications impact my sexual functioning?" (Juergens et al., 2009). Counselors should be prepared to provide basic educational information to clients about these and other topics, including the following: sexual anatomy and physiology, sexual stimulation and response, sexual health skills, and suggested sexual activities (Basson et al., 2010; Guldner, 1995; Juergens et al., 2009; Public Health Agency of Canada, 2003).

Counselors can deliver educational information through verbal instruction, assigned readings, videotapes, illustrations, and anatomical models (Althof, 2010). When counselors reach the limits of their own knowledge, they should direct clients to other resources for more information (Juergens et al., 2009).

Cognitive Restructuring

Cognitive restructuring may be used to help clients create new cognitive schemas that allow for more positive sexual functioning (Althof, 2010; Basson et al., 2010; Binik & Meana, 2009). Clients may hold unrealistic expectations about sexuality and sexual functioning, so one goal of cognitive restructuring may be to help the client develop new expectations that are more realistic (Juergens et al., 2009). A more general goal of cognitive restructuring is anxiety reduction (Althof, 2010), which may be achieved by identifying cognitions that contribute to clients' sexuality-related anxieties (e.g., "I am an inadequate lover," "There is something wrong with my body that makes me unattractive," or "Everyone else is having better sex than me"). Likewise, clients may benefit from exploring thoughts about certain aspects of their sexuality that have led to feelings of guilt or shame. For example, some people have come to feel guilty or ashamed about masturbation (Coleman, 2002). A cognitive focus in sexuality counseling can help the client identify these beliefs, evaluate whether they are helping or hurting their overall functioning, and reframe or recreate new belief systems that are more conducive to positive sexual functioning.

Skills Training

An assumption of behavioral sex therapy approaches is that non-biological sexual dysfunctions stem from modifiable behavior problems that have become problematic over time (Sarwer & Durlak, 1997). Through counseling, clients can learn and implement new skills to help enhance their sexual functioning. This includes skills that are related directly to sexuality (e.g., masturbation), as well as skills that enhance their resources in other areas of their lives that reap benefits in their sexual functioning. For example, clients may benefit from learning stress reduction techniques, relaxation strategies, coping skills, and relationship-strengthening techniques. In particular, clients can learn how to communicate their sexual needs more effectively and assertively (Sarwer & Durlak, 1997; Tiefer, 2001).

Masturbation training has been used to address a range of sexual health concerns, including sexual-desire disorders and orgasm disorders, to help clients learn more about their sexual functioning and anatomy (Althof, 2010; Binik & Meana, 2009). Some of the benefits of masturbation may include improved capacity for orgasms, greater overall sexual satisfaction, and becoming more comfortable with one's body (Coleman, 2002). Clients' masturbation patterns and history are worth considering in treatment for sexual dysfunctions Lipsith, McCann, & Goldmeier, 2003). Clients who consistently have masturbated in a certain way may grow to be able to only experience orgasm in that context, inhibiting the orgasm response with a partner (Lipsith et al., 2003). In particular, orgasms through masturbation may occur more quickly and readily than those with a partner, so people who grow accustomed to this form of stimulation may not reach climax through the less-consistent stimulation that occurs during intercourse (Lipsith et al., 2003). Therefore, an exploration of clients' masturbation patterns may help to identify a need to alter or expand upon masturbation behaviors in order to help clients make progress toward their treatment goals.

Homework Assignments

Cognitive-behavioral sexuality counseling often incorporates homework assignments that clients complete outside of the session (Althof, 2010). Homework assignments are designed to help clients change non-productive behaviors or to practice new skills and techniques learned in session. For example, clients may be assigned to abstain from having intercourse at the outset of treatment (Binik & Meana, 2009). This assignment can be beneficial if clients' intercourse is adding to pressure or anxiety about performance during sexual activity. Homework assignments also may come in the form of suggested readings or keeping a log of sexual activities, along with corresponding emotions or relationship patterns.

One of the most widely used interventions in sexuality counseling and sex therapy is sensate focus exercises (Althof, 2010; Binik & Meana, 2009; Sarwer & Durlak, 1997; Stinson, 2009). Sensate focus exercises are a form of systematic desensitization, and they are designed to provide clients with gradual exposure to increasingly intense emotional and physical sensations and intimacy (Stinson, 2009). Sensate focus exercises involve nonsexual and non-demanding but intimate contact between partners (Southern & Cade, 2011). These exercises occur within a positive relational context, and they begin by creating a solid foundation of good communication, intimacy, love, support, and understanding (Southern & Cade, 2011). Clients also learn strategies for addressing their discomfort that may arise with the increasingly intense exercises (Southern & Cade, 2011). Then, partners begin by exploring their partner for their own benefit, not desiring to pleasure the partner (Southern & Cade, 2011). The exercises move through different levels of touching, starting with breasts but no genitals, then adding genitals, then full body but with self-directed stimulation (Southern & Cade, 2011; Winton, 2000). Throughout the process, the focus is on pleasure and enjoying the experience, rather than on the outcome of orgasm (Southern & Cade, 2011; Stinson, 2009). Clients aim to develop increasing awareness of the physical sensations in their bodies, a broader range of sexual behaviors, and a greater focus on foreplay (Southern & Cade, 2011; Stinson, 2009). An important assumption underlying sensate focus exercises is that every person is the expert in his or her own sexual functioning (Southern & Cade, 2011). Therefore, each person is guided to learn about their own and their partners' sexuality through the exercises with an emphasis on greater attention to the process and pleasure of the experience, rather than just focusing on the outcome of orgasm.

Mindfulness Training

Similar to sensate focus, mindfulness training focuses on helping clients be more mindful and aware of the current moment and their enjoyment of sexual experiences (Althof, 2010; Brotto, Basson, & Luria, 2008; Stinson, 2009). Clients are taught to focus on their physical and emotional sensations in the moment without judging themselves (Althof, 2010). Mindfulness-based approaches have been used with clients experiencing depression, sexual arousal and desire problems, and survivors of child sexual assault (Althof, 2010). As one example, Brotto et al. (2008) applied mindfulness training in their psycho-educational approach to address sexual desire and arousal disorders that affect women with gynecological cancer. They described mindfulness as having the client take a stance of being aware of the present moment in a nonjudgmental way. The group-based approach incorporated homework assignments, including cognitive restructuring, communication-skills practice, and reading assignments, in addition to activities to promote mindfulness. In an evaluation of the approach with a sample of 35 women between the ages of 26 and 37, participants showed positive treatment outcomes, including increased sexual desire. The researchers suggested that mindfulness is a valuable focus in sexuality counseling because it encourages clients to become more aware of their physical and emotional responses without judging them.

Evaluation of Sample Cognitive-Behavioral Sexuality Counseling Interventions

In this section, we review two examples of cognitive-behavioral interventions that have been evaluated in order to illustrate the potential effectiveness of cognitive-behavioral therapy for addressing sexual health concerns. First, Sarwer and Durlak (1997) conducted a field trial of a behavior therapy intervention for patients at a university-based sexual dysfunction clinic in the Midwestern United States. The sample included 365 patients between the ages of 20 and 65. The seven-week intervention included weekly group sessions for couples, with sessions lasting about four hours each. Participating couples were instructed to complete daily

30-minute sensate-focus homework exercises between sessions. The participants demonstrated a variety of diagnosed sexual dysfunctions at the outset of treatment. Of the 182 women with diagnosed conditions, 124 demonstrated hypoactive sexual desire disorder, 34 had inhibited female orgasm, and 24 were diagnosed with vaginismus or dyspareunia (based on DSM-III-R criteria). Among the 257 men who had been diagnosed, 100 had erectile disorder, 90 had hypoactive sexual desire disorder, and 55 were diagnosed with premature ejaculation. In only about one-fifth of the sample were both partners diagnosed with a sexual dysfunction. Sarwer and Durlak defined successful treatment outcomes to be indicated by the elimination of the original symptoms, the lack of new symptoms emerging, and the couple engaging in intercourse on at least a weekly basis during the final phase of treatment. The factors that this research demonstrated that had the greatest impact on clients' ability to achieve successful outcomes were how often participants completed the sensate-focus homework assignments and the wives' motivation for treatment. Overall, Sarwer and Durlak suggested that short-term behavioral therapy interventions for sexuality dysfunctions hold promise for promoting positive client outcomes.

Research also suggests that cognitive-behavioral therapy interventions can be integrated with other approaches to promote positive client outcomes. McCarthy (2004) outlined an integrative cognitive-behavioral therapy approach to sexuality counseling for women experiencing sexual dysfunction. In addition to the influences of cognitive-behavioral therapy, McCarthy integrates systems theory, the medical model, and known information about sexual functioning. There are four main strategies used in McCarthy's treatment approach. First, the woman develops a "sexual voice" (p. 22) and sense of responsibility for her own sexuality. This often involves addressing gender socialization issues, as female sexuality is often viewed as secondary to males' desires and control within sexual encounters. Second, the female client develops awareness of her personal preferences and desires for the types of sexual activities that she enjoys. Women may find this challenging if they have given limited previous attention to understanding their sexual desires. The third strategy focuses on increasing the woman's positive attitudes and skills to increase her ability to experience orgasms. The final strategy is relational, in that it focuses on increasing the positive relational bond with her sexual partner, especially related to her ability to communicate her sexual needs and experience emotional connection with her partner through sexual activities. When working with a couple, McCarthy encourages partners to focus less on how they are performing sexually and more on the enjoyment and satisfaction they experience within their relationship. Ultimately, a goal of McCarthy's approach is to empower women to feel that they deserve sexual pleasure and can integrate their sexuality with other areas of their lives.

Integrative and Other Theoretical Approaches

Modern sexuality counseling approaches tend to be highly integrative (Southern & Cade, 2011). In today's postmodern world, sexuality counseling and sex therapy have adopted interventions from a variety of other approaches to psychotherapy (Binik & Meana, 2009). Rather than adhering rigidly to one specific treatment approach, many sexuality counselors prefer to draw upon numerous theory-based intervention strategies. This is good news for clients, who benefit when they are able to choose from a range of potential treatment options (Pukall & Reissing, 2007). Therefore, in this section, we briefly discuss a number of different approaches that scholars and practitioners have proposed to address clients' sexuality concerns.

Psychodynamic Therapy

Sexuality was a major consideration in the early development of psychodynamic and object relations therapy (Althof, 2010; Binik & Meana, 2009), such as Freud's explanation of the Oedipus complex and penis envy. Although used less widely today, the influence of psychodynamic therapy on psychological understandings of sexuality remains significant. In particular, hypnosis may be integrated into sexuality counseling and sex therapy (Binik & Meana, 2009).

Social Constructivist and Postmodern Approaches

These approaches focus on the meaning that clients make of their sexuality (Southern & Cade, 2011). For example, Zumaya, Bridges, and Rubio (1999) outlined a systemic-constructivist approach to sexuality counseling with couples. Drawing on systems theory, Zumaya et al. suggest that sexuality issues need to be considered within the context of multiple subsystems, especially focusing on gender, eroticism, the interpersonal bond, and reproduction. At each level, counselors can explore the meanings that clients ascribe to their experiences and perceptions, especially as those meanings are influenced by the social context. Through counseling, clients aim to integrate their various meaning systems, and when necessary, they may reconstruct their meaning systems in order to promote progress toward their treatment goals. Understanding and exploring clients' perspectives toward key experiences in their sexual development and history are also central to this approach. However, the ultimate focus remains on understanding and exploring how clients make meaning of their sexuality and sexual experiences, as well as how those meaning systems have been influenced by the broader social context.

Experiential Therapy

Experiential therapy holds promise for helping clients address sexuality concerns, which often are hidden and wrapped up in an intense emotional context (Kleinplatz, 2007). Through an experiential therapy framework, an initial focus in sexuality counseling is identifying clients' strong emotional responses and then to examine those responses as a window into the client's inner world. As experiential treatment progresses, the client comes to experience a new approach to living that is more in line with their inner experiences with the world. With couple therapy, the presence of one's partner provides opportunities to identify emotional responses that arise through dialogue and experiences within the relationship. Other points of focus in experiential sexuality counseling include clients' fantasies, feelings of sexual deviance, sexuality-related memories, and sexual preferences and desires. Each of these can provide a powerful view into clients' inner experiences and meaning systems surrounding sexuality. Kleinplatz (2007) suggests that the experiential therapy approach is especially well-suited to address sexuality concerns because of the intense feelings (e.g., shame) that are attached to sexuality-related issues, especially when clients believe that sexuality problems within their relationships (e.g., sexual dysfunctions) are their fault. Experiential therapy is client-driven, and clients' unique needs drive the pace and focus of treatment.

Systemic Therapies

Systems theory allows sexuality counselors to consider multiple systemic levels that impact clients' sexuality beliefs, behaviors, and experiences (Binik & Meana, 2009; Jones et al., 2011). These systems extend from the person's biological systems to relational and broader social systems (Jones et al., 2011). The relational systems that impact clients' sexuality may include their family system, peer systems, and the intimate relationship system (Jones et al., 2011). Systemic influences can impact virtually every aspect of clients' sexuality, from their beliefs and values to their expectations within sexual encounters to their comfort with talking about sexuality in different contexts (Jones et al., 2011). Jones et al. suggested that systems theory provides a foundation for both assessment and interventions in sexuality counseling. In particular, counselors can educate clients about resources and information available about sexuality at various systemic levels. This information can facilitate discussion of the various systemic influences on each client's sexual development, which may offer insights into creating positive change.

Because sexuality is largely expressed within the context of intimate relationships, couple therapy is often used in sexuality counseling (Althof, 2010). When addressing sexuality concerns in a relationship context (i.e., couple therapy), counselors must help couples navigate the balance between respecting each partner's needs and boundaries, in that one partner's preferences may conflict with the other partner's range of perceived acceptable behaviors (Wylie, Crowe, & Boddington, 1995). Increasingly, efforts have been made to integrate sex therapy with couple therapy (Schnarch, 1997; Zumaya et al., 1999). Historically, however, these two areas have not been well connected to one another (Zumaya et al., 1999).

One conjoint treatment approach that has been applied to sexuality counseling is emotionally focused couple therapy (EFT; Johnson & Zuccarini, 2010). EFT applies attachment theory to understanding the role of sexuality within intimate relationships. Johnson and Zuccarini emphasized the influence of attachment style on clients' experiences of sexuality, in that secure attachments offer support for taking risks and fostering positive growth. In contrast, insecure attachment styles can lead to greater negative emotionality, distress, and detachment. Within EFT, the lens of attachment theory offers therapists a lens into how and why clients experience sexuality concerns the way they do. Sexuality, therefore, becomes an entree into clients' inner working models that impact how they relate to others. Clients' attachment styles can impact their sexual functioning through such factors as anxiety about body image, their emotional engagement during sexual activity, preferences for physical affection, and how partners make sexual requests of one another.

A therapist using an EFT approach in sexuality counseling would likely focus on helping clients become more aware of their emotional responses to sex- and relationship-related events, create a more supportive and responsive context between the partners, and help the clients more readily support and care for one another (Johnson & Zuccarini, 2010). Treatment begins with an assessment, which focuses on understanding the negative relationship patterns and emotional responses associated with them. Next, the clients begin to respond more calmly and thoughtfully to their emotional responses, and then partners make efforts to increase their positive relational bond. Some EFT techniques that can be applied within sexuality counseling include showing empathy, validating clients' emotional responses, tracking interactional patterns, discussing attachment theory with clients, and promoting positive communication exchanges between the partners. Although Johnson and Zuccarini (2010) did not present empirical outcomes for this specific approach, there is evidence for the effectiveness of EFT as a treatment modality for relationship concerns in general.

TREATMENT FOR SPECIFIC SEXUALITY CONCERNS AND USING UNIQUE TREATMENT MODALITIES

Moving beyond theory-based approaches, intervention strategies have been suggested for a range of specific sexuality concerns. In this section, we address some of the existing treatment guidelines for specific client populations and other specific treatment modalities.

Dysfunction-Specific Treatments

Treatments for specific sexual dysfunctions have been proposed throughout the sexuality counseling and sex therapy literature. As a context for reviewing these treatment strategies, it is important to note that most have been developed and evaluated within the context of heterosexual relationships. Therefore, there is limited information about their applicability to same-gender relationships and other relationship forms. Counselors should therefore use caution in applying this information beyond heterosexual client populations. In addition, dysfunction-specific treatments have been criticized for inadequately addressing the psychosocial context surrounding the dysfunctions. As Kleinplatz (2003) said

> We treat soft penises rather than the man or couple concerned about the erection problem. We treat the apparent vaginal spasm in "vaginismus". . . rather than the woman who has difficulty with sexual intercourse. (p. 96)

Nonetheless, it remains valuable to understand dysfunction-specific intervention strategies, as these may provide valuable treatment guidelines that may be applied to meet clients' unique needs and circumstances in counseling. Therefore, the following sexual dysfunctions are addressed in this section: male erectile dysfunction, male orgasmic disorder, premature ejaculation, female pelvic pain, hypoactive sexual desire disorder in females, hypersexual behaviors and sexual compulsions, and dysfunctions that result from medication side effects.

Male Erectile Dysfunction

The greatest amount of attention to the treatment of sexual dysfunction has been on male erectile dysfunction (Althof, 2010). Of course, much of this attention stems from medications such as Viagra, Cialis, and Levitra, which have been heavily advertised in mainstream media for many years now. Despite the focus on medication, research suggests that counseling combined with medication may produce better outcomes than medication alone. For example, Banner and Anderson (2007) pilot tested an integrative approach to treating erectile dysfunction that combined sildenafil and cognitive-behavior sex therapy. This brief (i.e., 4- to 8-week time frame) approach incorporates psychoeducation, homework assignments, and interdisciplinary treatment providers (i.e., medical and psychological), with a goal of helping men improve their erectile functioning and sexual satisfaction. Some specific homework assignments included asking clients to list positive traits about themselves and their partners, developing new ways to show their partners affection, and having partners take turns creating romantic experiences for each other. Banner and Anderson's pilot test compared the integrated treatment with treatment just using sildenafil. Both groups of men demonstrated improved erectile functioning following treatment. However, the men who received the integrative treatment, as well as their partners, had higher levels of sexual satisfaction following treatment as compared to the medication-only group. These results suggest that an integrative approach is more effective than medication alone for addressing the relational and intimacy context of erectile functioning.

Male Orgasmic Disorder

Ribner (2010) provided specific guidelines for the treatment of male orgasmic disorder (i.e., those men who do not regularly orgasm during intercourse). Ribner's approach is based on two assumptions: (a) that men who experience male orgasmic disorder face feelings that they do not meet expectations about masculinity within the larger culture and (b) that male orgasmic disorder is impacted by conflicting messages that men receive from society about the importance of self-control, yet also about the need to let go and release control during sexual activity. Therefore, an important goal of treatment is to help men become more comfortable with letting go of an intense need to be in control of oneself. The steps in Ribner's approach are as follows. First, the couple ceases from engaging in sexual intercourse for the first part of treatment. Second, when using the bathroom, the man practices starting and stopping the process of urination by contracting and releasing his PC muscle. Third, the man begins practicing using those same muscles for increasing periods of muscle tension and release, gradually increasing to tension for 10 seconds, and release for 3 seconds. Fourth, once the client has practiced these exercises for at least a week, he and his partner may resume intercourse. Fifth, during thrusting in the missionary position, the man contracts and releases the PC muscles when he feels excitement during intercourse. Ribner suggests that the release of the PC muscles during intercourse leads to orgasm. Ribner presented only anecdotal evidence for the use of this intervention. Of the four men in treatment that Ribner described, two ended treatment (one because he thought that the exercises were "annoying"; p. 10), and the other two experienced regular orgasms during intercourse. However, one of the latter two men contacted Ribner within a year after treatment to report that symptoms had come back. Therefore, there is very limited research to support the effectiveness of this approach. However, because it offers tangible steps for men experiencing male orgasmic disorder, it warrants further examination.

Premature Ejaculation

Perelman (2006) suggested that premature ejaculation occurs within a relational and psychological context. Perelman described the "Sexual Tipping Point" as "the characteristic threshold for an expression of sexual response for any individual, which may vary dynamically within and between individuals and any given sexual experience" (p. 1007). Both the male with premature ejaculation and his partner may experience distress related to the condition. Perelman suggests that treatment for premature ejaculation is most effective when it integrates pharmaceutical and sex therapy interventions. Treatment aims to help men better regulate arousal to gain control over ejaculation. It begins with a comprehensive assessment of the client's sexual history, psychological health, and sexual functioning.

Because premature ejaculation may result from physiological sources, a medical evaluation should be a precursor to therapy (Betchen, 2009; Perelman, 2006). Counseling can address intra-psychic and interpersonal contributors to premature ejaculation, such as anxiety, body image issues, poor relational skills, and fears about intimacy and sexual performance. Issues that counselors can address with clients experiencing premature ejaculation include family-of-origin dynamics, religious values, and internalized definitions of masculinity. Betchen (2009) described a systemic approach to treating premature ejaculation within couple therapy that integrates psychodynamic systems therapy with sex therapy. The first session is conjoint, followed by two individual sessions with each partner. Additional individual sessions may be added if the clinician deems necessary. The assessment process incorporates constructing a genogram to examine sexual patterns and the client's sexual history. Treatment may include sex therapy exercises (e.g., sensate focus).

The counselor may suggest that the clients use the stop-start method as they move in and out of sexual activity while the male focuses on his emotional and physical sensations (Betchen, 2009). Clients may do stop-start exercises multiple times each week to provide the opportunity for the man to increase his ejaculatory control. Through the stop-start exercises, a male client begins to notice the point at which he is aroused but still has control over his ejaculation, allowing him to choose how to respond at that point (i.e., whether to continue to orgasm or to back off to sustain the erection longer; Perelman, 2006). Male clients may view the stop-start technique as overly technical and mechanical and as an interruption to sexual activity (de Carufel & Trudel, 2006). In addition, it can detract from the intimacy and eroticism involved in sexual activity (de Carufel & Trudel, 2006).

Another technique that Betchen (2009) recommends is slow-fast penile stimulation, which involves the man's partner helping him achieve sexual arousal by stroking him, then slowing down the stroking. The other exercises that Betchen outlines gradually increase in intensity until they use varying speeds and stop-start processes during vaginal intercourse. As counseling progresses, the counselor can help the clients identify and address any interpersonal or internal challenges that arise, such as new conflicts or anxiety. Betchen suggests that counselors need to support clients in avoiding the propensity to blame one another for their problems throughout the course of treatment. The length of treatment varies, and follow-up sessions can be used to ensure gains are maintained over time. Evidence for this approach is not provided, and its applicability to same-sex couples is unclear. However, it provides an example of an integrative approach that addresses the relational context of premature ejaculation.

De Carufel and Trudel (2006) proposed a functional-sexological treatment for premature ejaculation, and they compared it to a behavioral intervention that incorporated the stop-and-start technique and the squeeze technique. The aim of the functional-sexological treatment was to help partners notice the physical states that indicate the man's level of sexual excitement, especially to notice points at which ejaculation is imminent and is still able to be controlled. During intercourse, the couple may modify their behaviors to allow the man to develop greater control over his level of sexual excitement. This may involve slowing the pace of the activity or even taking a break. The man may also use deep abdominal breathing and muscular tension control to regulate his excitement level. One important distinction that this approach makes is that while it is possible for a man to control his level of excitement, it is not possible for him to control ejaculation once a certain physical point has been reached. This approach also emphasizes the importance of enjoying the process of sexual activity, not just focusing on the orgasm. The study included 36 couples, of whom half received the functional-sexological intervention, and half received the behavioral intervention. Within each condition, half of the couples were assigned to a wait list control group. The results showed that participants in the functional-sexological intervention demonstrated longer intercourse duration, increased sexual pleasure, and greater sexual satisfaction following treatment. Participants' partners also demonstrated improvements as a result of the treatment. It's important to note that the behavioral treatment also produced treatment gains, and the researchers noted that clients may prefer the more traditional behavioral approach because the behavioral techniques are less complex to master.

Although the approaches described above have demonstrated some treatment effectiveness in research, many clients find them to be time- and energy-intensive (Perelman, 2006). Therefore, counselors should discuss the requirements of various premature ejaculation treatment options with clients so that they can understand the advantages and drawbacks of each and make an informed decision.

Female Pelvic Pain

Sexuality counseling can benefit female clients who experience chronic pelvic pain (Howard, 2012). Some conditions that can contribute to chronic pelvic pain in women include dysmenorrhea, dyspareunia, and vulvar pain, and this pain is often associated with sexual problems (Howard, 2012). Pain may be heightened during intercourse and other sexual activity. Some ways that counselors can help women facing chronic pelvic pain include validating their experiences and perceptions, educating clients about treatment options and sexual health, suggesting resources (e.g., useful books and websites), and providing options for creating change (e.g., therapy, new positions for intercourse, and medications). In some cases, intensive sex therapy may be warranted.

Vaginismus (i.e., "the involuntary spasm of the pelvic muscles surrounding the outer third of the vagina, particularly the perineal muscles and the levator ani muscles"; Jeng, Wang, Chou, Shen, & Tzeng, 2006, p. 380) can make vaginal penetration painful and/or impossible (Jeng et al., 2006). Treatment may include the use of dilators, especially combined with relaxation training (Althof, 2010). Jeng et al. described a team approach to treating vaginismus, with professionals that included gynecologists, psychologists, sexuality counselors, and psychiatrists. Treatment consisted of weekly sessions over a three-month time frame, and it included vaginal dilation exercises with one's and one's partner's fingers that progressed through systematic desensitization, Kegel exercises, the topical application of Xylocaine jelly, and the use of muscle relaxants. The client also receives educational information about female genital anatomy. Among 120 female clients seeking treatment for vaginismus at the authors' sexual health clinic, over 90% had experienced sexual intercourse 3 months following treatment. By the one-year follow-up, over 80% of the clients reported that they had regular intercourse and orgasms. Any treatments used for female vaginal pain must consider the cultural context (Kabakci & Batur, 2003), as different cultural understandings of female sexuality can impact the acceptability of treatment approaches to clients.

Hypoactive Sexual Desire Disorder

Sexual desire disorder can be complicated to treat, in that the low sexual desire may result from a host of reasons, including relationship problems, stress, physical health issues, and adjustment to major life transitions. Trudel et al. (2001) suggested that cognitive-behavior therapy is effective for women with hypoactive sexual desire disorder. They tested the efficacy of a couples' group therapy intervention for female hypoactive sexual desire disorder that was based on cognitive-behavioral therapy. A sample of 74 couples was randomly assigned to either the intervention or a wait list control group. The treatment lasted for 12 weeks, with weekly two-hour sessions with groups of four to six couples each. The groups were facilitated by two teams of mixed-gender therapists. The manualized treatment incorporated the following interventions: homework assignments, psychoeducation, sensate focus and communication skills exercises, and cognitive restructuring. These researchers found that nearly three-fourths of all of the female participants had improved or were "cured" of hypoactive sexual desire disorder at the end of the treatment, and this rate remained high (64%) at 3- and 12-month follow-up assessments. Some personal characteristics that influenced the acceptability of treatment for participants included busy schedules due to work demands, relationship problems, and a history of trauma. Therefore, the researchers suggested that the effectiveness of this treatment approach could be enhanced by adding personalized interventions (e.g., individual counseling) to the standard group format.

Bibliotherapy interventions also hold promise for addressing hypoactive sexual desire disorder. Mintz, Balzer, Zhao, and Bush (2012) tested a bibliotherapy intervention for women who experienced low sexual desire. They used Mintz's book, "A tired woman's guide to passionate sex," which is a self-help book for women in heterosexual relationships who have low levels of sexual desire. Topics covered in the book include causes of low desire, benefits people experience from sex, the impact of stress on low sexual desire, cognitive strategies for helping people have more positive thoughts about sex, sexual communication strategies, time management, adding novelty to sexual experiences, and the value of scheduling sex rather than expecting it to be consistently spontaneous. Half of the study's participants were asked to read the book in a 6-week time frame, while the other half was in a wait list control group. Pretest posttest measures showed that the participants who read the book demonstrated more positive outcomes than the control group in the following areas: increased sexual desire, arousal, and satisfaction, as well as improved overall sexual functioning. At a 7-week follow-up assessment, only the participants' gains in desire and overall sexual functioning were maintained. The authors suggested that a bibliotherapy approach to addressing low sexual desire can be effective on its own, although it may even be further enhanced by adding sessions with a therapist.

Low sexual desire disorder must always be considered in the relational context (Schnarch, 1997). Furthermore, it is important to understand the perceptions of the level of sexual desire, especially in relation to the client's partner's level of desire. Counselors can normalize the fluctuations in sexual desire that may occur over time, as well as help clients explore and address other issues that are impacting sexual desire. It is important to avoid judging or blaming clients for low sexual desire. As Schnarch (1997) said, "Low sexual desire is almost always considered a problem. I've found it often reflects good judgment: healthy people don't want sex when it's not worth wanting" (p. 127). Therefore, counselors should focus on understanding the meaning behind the low sexual desire and help the client determine how best to address it, which may go beyond the individual client to addressing patterns in their relationship and/or other areas of their lives.

Hypersexual Behaviors and Sexual Compulsions

Sexual compulsions may stem from obsessive thoughts about their preferred sexual experiences, which often are based in early negative experiences involving degradation, such as abuse (Bergner, 2002). Bergner suggests that counselors should begin by examining these clients' idealized sexual preferences (i.e., lovemaps), as well as the early experiences from which they stemmed in order to understand the meanings that the client ascribes to these. Therapy may focus on altering the client's problematic cognitions, such as this example Bergner provided: "I am a sexually abnormal, tainted, inadequate, and undesirable person" (p. 379). In addition, because clients may be especially vulnerable to engage in sexual compulsions after experiences that threaten their self-esteem, counselors can assist clients to build up coping skills and a positive sense of self-worth. Ultimately, counseling can provide these clients with corrective experiences to address their early experiences of degradation.

Hypersexual behaviors also may serve an emotional regulation function by providing a release to feelings of stress and anxiety (Reid, Carpenter, Spackman, & Willes, 2008). As such, treatment for hypersexual behaviors may focus on stress management and emotional regulation, such as by helping clients become better equipped to identify and modulate their distressing emotions. In addition, clients may benefit from learning how to better communicate their needs for comfort and support with their partners and others in their support system. Finally, counselors can help clients monitor their emotions to identify times when they may feel impulses to engage in undesirable hypersexual behaviors (Reid et al., 2008).

Dysfunctions Resulting From Medication Side Effects

Medications, such as some antidepressants, for example, selective serotonin reuptake inhibitors (SSRIs), can have sexual side effects that contribute to sexual dysfunctions (Balon & Segraves, 2008). Some medical approaches to addressing these include adding other medications (e.g., dopaminergic agents), changing the antidepressant used, and altering the dose (Balon & Segraves, 2008). Clients may be embarrassed to admit sexual side effects to their doctors, so counselors can support their clients in communicating these concerns to health care providers. Clients who experience sexual side effects to medications can benefit from learning that there are options to address these concerns, including changes to medication regimens and psychological and relational strategies. However, it is important that clients receive proper medical guidance from a physician or other qualified health care provider when addressing these changes and certainly before making any changes to their medication routines.

Treatment for Post-Menopausal Women With Sexual Problems

Treatment is complicated for post-menopausal women with sexual problems, especially when their partners also have sexual dysfunction (Goldstein, 2007). Goldstein (2007) suggested that these clients should be able to choose from a wide range of treatment options, and this often includes an educational component to teach women about physiological functioning. Counseling can be especially useful for addressing mental health and relationship concerns that are related to the sexual problems. Post-menopausal women also may benefit from medical interventions, including hormone therapy or a vacuum clitoris therapy device. In general, treatment should progress from least to most invasive options, with a high level of collaboration between the client and counselor throughout the entire process (Goldstein, 2007).

Treatment for Infidelity

Counseling to address infidelity is inherently complex, whether it involves the person who had an affair, their partner, or both. Each person may have a different goal for counseling, and clients may be unsure as to whether they wish to continue the relationship or end it. There are no simple guidelines here, and counselors can inform clients that the process of rebuilding a relationship after an affair can take a long time, especially in order to re-establish trust (Cano & O'Leary, 1997). Therapy should include early individual sessions with each client to determine if conjoint treatment is appropriate (Cano & O'Leary, 1997). In addition, through individual sessions, the therapist can discuss each partner's goals for the future of their relationship (Cano & O'Leary, 1997). Conjoint treatment may be counterproductive if partners have vastly different goals for their relationship, such as one partner wanting to continue the relationship and the other wanting to end it. Conjoint treatment, unless it is for the purpose of constructively and smoothly ending the relationship, is unlikely to be successful if either client continues to maintain a relationship with a third party. Thus, to begin conjoint treatment, the affair should be terminated.

For couples who hope to rebuild their relationship and remain together, topics to address include the emotional impacts of the affair on the partners and their relationship, what function the affair may have served in the relationship, the development of coping skills, and the role of jealousy in their interactional processes (Cano & O'Leary, 1997). Counselors can help partners develop a contract for the behaviors that they will agree are and are not acceptable (Cano & O'Leary, 1997). These behaviors may include contact with the affair partner, acceptable uses of technology, and whether any secrets may be kept between partners. The partner(s) who engaged in the affair are typically expected to engage in extra-positive behaviors that promote trust within the relationship (Cano & O'Leary, 1997). For example, this partner may seek out individual therapy, allow the partner full access to their cell phone or other electronic accounts, and agree to other situation-specific conditions (e.g., not traveling alone if the affair occurred while traveling for business).

Individual counseling may be warranted for partners who had an affair, as well as those whose partners engaged in infidelity. For clients who have had an affair or otherwise been unfaithful to a partner in a committed relationship, counselors can help these clients explore their beliefs and attitudes toward commitment in relationships. In addition, they can examine their goals for relationships and their lives in general to understand whether and how a committed relationship may or may not fit within that vision for their lives. These clients may carry a significant amount of guilt and shame that counselors can help them process. In addition, counselors can help these clients develop strategies to promote positive relationship behaviors for their current or future relationships. Clients whose partners have had affairs may have a high level of emotion attached to this experience that can be discussed in counseling. Clients may need to discuss various aspects of the affair in counseling, including when and how they learned about the affair, additional consequences of the affair on their relationship (e.g., financial and physical health concerns), and what type of relationship they would like to continue with their partner. Overall, individual counseling can be beneficial to address each partner's unique concerns and needs in the aftermath of infidelity.

Treatment for Sexual Abuse Survivors

Clients with a history of sexual abuse may seek counseling for many reasons, which may or may not be related directly to their experiences of abuse. Therefore, it is important for counselors to understand clients' goals for counseling and develop treatment plans accordingly (Wise, Florio, Benz, & Geier, 2007). When clients present for counseling with concerns related to past sexual abuse, treatment should generally progress slowly, as it may take time for clients to process the full range of their thoughts and experiences related to the abuse (Wise et al., 2007). Counselors should be careful to manage transference and countertransference, as well as to maintain clear boundaries in the relationship, including the timing of sessions, how the counseling room is arranged, and how close the counselor sits to the client (Wise et al., 2007). Some treatment approaches that may prove useful include art therapy, Rogerian therapy with a focus on validating the clients' experiences, family systems theory to address family patterns that may have contributed to the abuse (Wise et al., 2007), and mindfulness training (Brotto, Seal, & Rellini, 2012). Depending on the nature and timing of the abuse, counselors must be careful to follow any relevant legal guidelines for reporting the abuse, if applicable (Wise et al., 2007).

When clients have a history of sexual trauma, counselors should use an empowerment approach and allow the client to guide the pace of treatment (Goodwach, 2005b). Some common issues to address in treatment with survivors of sexual abuse include the following: feelings of being invalidated by others following disclosure of the abuse, shame, intimacy issues, trust, other relationship concerns, anger, a lack of trust in one's own judgment, and trauma symptoms (e.g., flashbacks or dissociation during sexual activity; Brotto et al., 2012; Rosenbaum, 2009;

Wise et al., 2007). Overall, treatment should be delivered in a way that is sensitive to the client's history of trauma in order to help the client examine how that past trauma history may be linked to current concerns.

Treatment for Sex Offenders

Many counselors are uncomfortable and lack training to be able to work competently with clients who have perpetrated sexual abuse and other sex-related crimes. Treatment for sex offenders aims to reduce the harm caused by the offense and prevent reoffending (Ho & Ross, 2012). Reoffending rates alone offer an incomplete view of the outcomes of sex offender treatment, in that sex offences are often significantly underreported. Typically, treatment combines cognitive-behavioral therapy and medications to reduce the offender's libido. The existing research provides minimal and mixed support for whether treatment for sex offenders produces actual reductions in recidivism (Ho & Ross, 2012). Counselors should seek additional specialized training before beginning to work with members of this client population.

Treatment for Former Prostitutes

Clients who have previously engaged in prostitution may have unique needs in counseling. One reason for this is the high rates of other difficult complicating factors, such as sexual assault and rape, as well as drug and alcohol use (Stebbins, 2010). Clients who have a history of prostitution should be referred for testing for STIs (Stebbins, 2010). A history of prostitution may contribute to sexual dysfunction within intimate relationships, particularly as a result of dissociating during sexual activities (Stebbins, 2010). Treatment approaches for clients with a history of prostitution may address past trauma histories, how to create a positive sense of sexuality, fostering healthy relationship intimacy, and changing problematic patterns of sexual behaviors (Stebbins, 2010). Interventions may include psychoeducation, relaxation training, building a social support network, coping skills training, and sexuality counseling to address sexual communication and behaviors (Stebbins, 2010). Although most counselors likely will not work extensively with this client population, it is useful to understand some unique concerns they may bring to sexuality counseling, especially given the sexual nature of prostitution work.

Treatment via the Internet

In recent years, there has been growing interest in delivering sex therapy and sexuality counseling interventions via the Internet (Althof, 2010; Jones & McCabe, 2011; Tiefer, 2012; van Lankveld, Leusink, van Diest, Gijs, & Slob, 2009). An advantage of these approaches is that clients can seek help anonymously and in a setting that is comfortable to them (Althof, 2010; Jones & McCabe, 2011). Internet approaches are also useful for clients who are geographically isolated, and they also can be made to be more affordable than face-to-face interventions (Jones & McCabe, 2011). However, Internet-based approaches are likely not suitable as stand-alone treatments for clients with severe sexual problems or other major problems related to the sexuality concerns (e.g., relationship or mental health problems; Jones & McCabe, 2011). Furthermore, guidelines for ethical and legal practice of Internet-based sexuality counseling are just beginning to emerge, so for now, counselors have minimal guidance as to how to do this appropriately and competently (Althof, 2010). In addition, deciphering whether Internet-based information is credible presents a challenge for counselors and clients alike, as the Internet allows virtually anyone with ideas about sexuality to share their views with the general population (Tiefer, 2012).

Two research studies by van Lankveld et al. (2009) and Jones and McCabe (2011) provide examples of Internet-based sexuality interventions. Van Lankveld et al. (2009) pilot tested an Internet-based sex therapy intervention for men in heterosexual relationships who were experiencing sexual problems. The evaluation consisted of a pretest posttest follow-up, wait list control group design. The 89 male participants who reported either erectile dysfunction or premature ejaculation were randomly assigned to either the treatment group or the wait list. The 3-month long treatment incorporated sensate focus exercises and cognitive restructuring techniques, and the therapists were eight licensed sex therapists, of whom half were male and half were female. Almost one-fourth of the participants were recommended by their therapists to seek medication in conjunction with the therapy. Among the participants who received the Internet-based intervention, 48% reported that their sexual functioning improved, 43% reported that their sexual functioning neither improved nor deteriorated, and 8% reported that their sexual functioning was worse at the end of treatment. Participants in the treatment group showed better improvement compared to those in the wait list group. Although these findings show some support for Internet-based sex therapy interventions, more research is needed to compare the effectiveness of Internet-based interventions as compared to face-to-face interventions.

Jones and McCabe (2011) evaluated an Internet-based cognitive-behavior therapy intervention for treating female sexual dysfunction. They compared a no-treatment control group with a group of women who completed a 10-week intervention. All participants had one of the following forms of female sexual dysfunction: hypoactive sexual desire disorder, sexual arousal disorder, anorgasmia, or genital pain. The intervention, called *Revive*, involved the participants and their partners engaging in communication skills and sensate focus training, along with e-mailed communications with the therapist. A unique feature of this treatment was that it involved couples engaging in guided discussions before they began their sensate focus sessions. Technological features were incorporated into the program, such that participants had to indicate that they'd met their treatment goals at each stage before they were able to access the next treatment module. The evaluation findings showed that participants who completed the treatment had better outcomes than those who didn't have treatment in the following areas: communication, emotional intimacy, sexual desire, arousal, lubrication, orgasm, satisfaction, and pain. However, about one-third of the women who completed the program reported that they still had sexual problems at the end of the treatment.

Treatment With Sex Surrogates

The use of sex surrogates has been debated (Binik & Meana, 2009; Tiefer, 2012). Today, the International Professional Surrogates Association (http://www .surrogatetherapy.org/) exists to support "a worldwide community of professionals in the field of surrogate partner therapy, which includes surrogate partners, therapists, and individuals of surrogate partner therapy" (IPSA, 2013a, para. 1). The IPSA (2013b) describes Surrogate Partner Therapy as follows:

> In this therapy, a client, a therapist and a surrogate partner form a three-person therapeutic team. The surrogate participates with the client in structured and unstructured experiences that are designed to build client self-awareness and skills in the areas of physical and emotional intimacy. These therapeutic experiences include partner work in relaxation, effective communication, sensual and sexual touching, and social skills training. (para. 1)

However, the use of surrogates is "no longer sanctioned" (Binik & Meana, 2009, p. 1021) by most sex therapy professional groups. Beyond the lack of professional support for the use of surrogates, this approach may be considered illegal prostitution in many jurisdictions (Tiefer, 2012). Therefore, we recommend that counselors not consider the use of sex surrogates as part of sexuality counseling, and counselors may need to discuss the reasons for this recommendation with clients who have heard about this treatment approach.

TREATMENT OUTCOMES IN SEXUALITY COUNSELING

Due in part to the influence of managed care, there has been an increasing emphasis on the need to demonstrate effective treatment outcomes related to sexuality counseling (Branney & Barkham, 2006). Research suggests that clients can reap benefits from counseling that addresses sexual problems. For example, Firth and Mohamad (2007) examined treatment outcomes for men at a sexual health clinic in the United Kingdom. Typically, treatment at the clinic lasts for up to 12 sessions, and it is coordinated with medical treatment when appropriate. The treatment outcomes for 70 male clients at the clinic were studied. Some of the disorders for which men were seeking treatment included erectile dysfunction, premature ejaculation, and low sexual desire. About half of the clients who participated in individual counseling demonstrated positive treatment outcomes. Other treatment approaches that the researchers identified as having good outcomes included masturbation training and sensate focus. However, clients who attended only an assessment and no subsequent treatment demonstrated poor outcomes. Interestingly, clients who had experienced some sort of significant early loss were more likely to experience negative medication side effects, although the researchers did not identify any other background characteristics that impacted treatment outcomes. This research demonstrated methodological limitations (e.g., non-random sampling and unclear measures of treatment outcomes), so its results must be considered preliminary. However, it does suggest that clients may experience positive changes through sexuality-focused interventions to address sexual dysfunctions. Future research should consider more fully the impact of client background characteristics on clients' unique needs in treatment and how these affect outcomes.

More broadly, the existing evidence base supporting the effectiveness of sex therapy interventions is limited and mixed (Binik & Meana, 2009; Guldner, 1995). There is more concrete evidence for the treatment of sexual dysfunctions through medication than there is for treatment through therapy (Rowland, 2007). A need remains for more research on the effectiveness of various treatment strategies, especially to support the ongoing need for psychological and relational interventions in combination with medical ones (Rowland, 2007). Although earlier studies, such as those by Masters and Johnson (1966; 1970), showed extremely positive results, modern critiques of these studies suggest that they were highly biased by methodological limitations, such as a lack of controls and unrepresentative samples (Binik & Meana, 2009). However, whenever possible, empirically supported treatments should be incorporated into sexuality counseling (Hatzichristou et al., 2010).

Counselors also should put in place strategies to track the effectiveness of their use of interventions in sexuality counseling (Althof, Rosen et al., 2005; Corty, Althof, & Wieder, 2011). A variety of outcome measures may be tracked to determine the effectiveness of sexuality counseling interventions, including diaries, questionnaires, physiological tests, and open-ended interviews (Rellini & Meston, 2006). As one example, Corty et al. (2011) developed an instrument to assess women's treatment satisfaction for female sexual dysfunction, called the Women's Inventory of Treatment Satisfaction-9 (WITS-9). Items were developed through focus groups with women and men. Once the final item pool was created, the researchers assessed its content validity through feedback from a panel of researchers and clinicians whose work addresses female sexual dysfunction. The final scale had three factors: (a) satisfaction with sexual activity and interest; (b) treatment satisfaction; and (c) perceived partner satisfaction. The total scale and subscales of the final nine-item scale demonstrated good internal consistency. An instrument such as the WITS-9 is useful for sexuality counseling because treatment satisfaction may impact how likely a client is to continue in treatment over time (Corty et al., 2011).

In sum, the research base supporting the effectiveness of sex therapy and sexuality counseling remains limited, especially in comparison with evidence for the effectiveness of medical treatments. However, there is a growing body of research that supports the value of sexuality counseling, especially to address the social and emotional context of sexual problems. To address a growing demand for evidence that the interventions they use work, sexuality counselors should use evidence-supported interventions when available and track treatment outcomes with the clients they serve. Before leaving this chapter, readers are encouraged to complete Exercise 3.1 to reflect upon their current level of comfort and competence to provide sexuality counseling interventions.

Exercise 3.1

GUIDED REFLECTION ACTIVITY: CURRENT COMFORT AND COMPETENCE TO PROVIDE SEXUALITY COUNSELING INTERVENTIONS

Now that you've reviewed information about several different approaches to sexuality counseling, take some time to reflect upon the following questions:

- Which treatment approaches seem to you to be most useful for working with clients to address sexuality concerns? Why do you prefer these approaches?
- How competent do you feel to conceptualize clients' sexuality concerns from a theoretical framework, as well as to use theory-based intervention strategies?
- What treatment issues (e.g., infidelity, specific dysfunctions) would you be most and least comfortable addressing in sexuality counseling, and why?
- How competent do you feel currently to create a safe, supportive, professional context for clients to discuss their sexuality-related concerns in counseling? What might you do in order to increase your level of competence?
- What are your reactions to the idea of delivering sexuality counseling over the Internet?
- How might you respond if a client sought counseling from you and asked about using a sex surrogate as part of counseling?
- What do you envision the future will hold for the treatment of sexual concerns, especially with regard to medical versus counseling approaches?

SUMMARY

In many ways, sexuality counseling is similar to counseling in general and other specialization areas. Counselors must work to establish a strong therapeutic relationship with their clients, base counseling interventions on solid, clinical-assessment data, use theoretically sound intervention strategies, and track client progress over time. However, the sensitive nature of sexuality concerns provides a unique context for sexuality counseling, as clients (and counselors!) may demonstrate a high level of discomfort throughout treatment, especially early in the process and when new challenges and issues emerge. Therefore, counselors should build a solid foundation of knowledge about sexuality, as well as a broad repertoire of skills and intervention strategies, in order to best serve clients seeking counseling to address sexuality-related concerns.

KEYSTONES

- Regardless of the treatment approach used, counselors can aim to create a supportive therapeutic environment for addressing the sensitive topics that can arise when discussing sexuality concerns.
- The earliest sessions of sexuality counseling should focus on building rapport, and therefore, they may not involve the client discussing their sexual concerns in great detail.
- Some counselor practices that foster a supportive environment for sexuality counseling include demonstrating positive communication skills, conveying a professional demeanor, showing respect for the client's autonomy, providing a physically safe and private location, using active listening skills, and using culturally competent approaches.
- Sexuality counseling treatment plans should be grounded firmly in data collected through the counselor's clinical assessment of the client.
- A physical examination should always be a precursor to clinical assessment and treatment when sexual dysfunctions are suspected.
- Given the broad range of approaches to sexuality counseling, counselors have a variety of resources at their disposal to be able to incorporate different theoretical approaches and techniques to meet each client's unique needs.
- Medication and psychotherapy can be used to complement one another in the treatment of sexual problems.
- Moving beyond theory-based approaches, intervention strategies have been suggested for a range of specific sexuality concerns.

- Due in part to the influence of managed care, there has been an increasing emphasis on the need to demonstrate effective treatment outcomes related to sexuality counseling. Research suggests that clients can reap benefits from counseling that addresses sexual problems.

ADDITIONAL RESOURCES

- American Association of Sexuality Educators, Counselors, and Therapists (AASECT): http://www.aasect.org/
- American Sexual Health Association: http://www.ashasexualhealth.org/
- U.S. Centers for Disease Control and Prevention (CDC) Sexual Health Resource: http://www.cdc.gov/sexualhealth/
- WebMD's Sexual Health Center: http://www.webmd.com/sex/

Chapter 4

Physiology and Sexual Health

The misrepresentation that everybody should be having [sex]—needs to have it, wants to have it, has a problem if they don't have it—is to change, really what sexuality IS into more of a medical thing. I think that's a terrible direction for knowledge, for understanding, for society.

—Leonore Tiefer (Stein, 2015)

Anatomy and physiology can greatly impact individuals' sexual functioning as people's health can determine their physical arousal responses and ability to fully engage in sexual activities. Many sexuality concerns arise from both a relational and emotional origin, as well as from physical and medical factors, so it can often be difficult to determine which cause is primary and which is secondary. Even for clients who present with physical issues as the primary factor, counseling can help clients address psychosocial barriers to maintaining medical treatment compliance (Althof, 2010). Most counselors do not receive training in anatomy, biology, or medicine, and thus may lack the knowledge to address the physiological aspects of clients' sexual functioning without further education. Counselors also may struggle to implement interventions that simultaneously address the physiological and psychological nature of clients' presenting issues. Having a basic understanding of the impact of physiology on sexual functioning is essential for the following reasons:

1. *First, counselors should be prepared to use correct terminology to describe sexual anatomy and functioning in communications with clients and collaborating professionals.* Without knowledge of the proper terminology, counselors may feel embarrassment or fumble to find the correct language when addressing sexual concerns with clients. Of course, counselors also should not be overly technical and

clinical when talking with clients about sexuality issues, as this can lead to client discomfort and communication barriers between counselor and client.

2. *Second, counselors must be prepared to educate their clients on the basics of sexual functioning.* Many sexual problems arise due to clients lacking information or having misinformation about sexual functioning. Therefore, counselors can help their clients learn information that will help them to enhance their sexual functioning, their views of their sexuality, and their expectations within intimate relationships. The process of education can help normalize clients' concerns and give them hope that there are strategies to improve their sexual functioning.

3. *Third, counselors without adequate knowledge about sexual physiology may overlook physiological problems or confuse them for psychological or relational ones.* Through their training, counselors learn numerous theoretical, practical, and research-based approaches to mental health treatment. Because this is what counselors know, they may assume that most of clients' sexual concerns have a psychological origin, and therefore, this may become their focus for treatment. Although psychological and relational issues often are at play when clients experience sexuality concerns, there may be a real physiological basis for these concerns. In addition, there may be physiological consequences that stem from mental health and relationship issues. Therefore, a physical examination by a qualified health care professional should be a basic step in the treatment of any sexual concerns that have a potential physiological component.

4. *Counselors should understand basic physiological issues in order to best coordinate treatment with other providers.* Counselors need to be skilled in collaborating with other health professionals and supporting clients in navigating the health system to determine the best course of treatment that will address both the physical and psychological factors that are impacting their sexual functioning. The treatment of sexuality issues is inherently multidisciplinary, and this has increasingly become the case with the increased medicalization of sex therapy. As such, clients with sexuality concerns may be working with other health care providers, such as urologists, obstetricians, gynecologists, and psychiatrists for physiological and pharmaceutical treatments for their sexual concerns, as well as other conditions that may affect sexual functioning.

5. *Finally, counselors should be aware of factors that put certain populations at risk for physiological difficulties that will impact sexual functioning, as well as work as advocates for their clients at a personal and systemic level to reduce their vulnerability to risks to their sexual health.* Counselors should be sensitive to clients' cultural backgrounds and identities, recognizing how their race, ethnicity, gender, gender identity, sexual/affectional orientation, age, mental and physical

ability, socioeconomic status, relationship status, and religion or spirituality may influence their clients' overall sexual health. Some populations are disproportionately affected by risks to their sexual health. Further, clients who experience physiological sexual difficulties may be at risk for social stigmatization as they may not be able to operate within established sexual norms. Counselors should practice multicultural competency in counseling clients about physical sexual health issues and use their skills to advocate for education, programming, and societal change that will improve the sexual health of all individuals.

The purpose of Chapter 4 is to provide readers with accurate information about physical aspects of sexual functioning and health. After reading this chapter, readers will be able to do the following:

a. Understand basic physiological functions that impact sexuality and sexual functioning
b. Describe a range of physical health issues that are related to sexuality, including sexually transmitted infections, medication side effects, illness and disability, and reproductive health
c. Understand common challenges clients may face when making decisions regarding their sexual health, infertility, and abortions

OVERVIEW OF PHYSIOLOGY AND ANATOMY RELATED TO SEXUAL FUNCTIONING

One of the most widely adopted models of physiological sexual functioning was developed by Masters and Johnson (1966), and this model categorizes sexual response in four stages: excitement, plateau, orgasm, and resolution. The Masters and Johnson model is the basis for the diagnostic criteria of sexual dysfunction in the *Diagnostic and Statistical Manual of Mental Disorders* (DSM) (American Psychiatric Association, 2013a), which are described in Chapter 6. This type of linear-based sexual response cycle is performance oriented and does not address the variability in physiological sexual response. Further, the Masters and Johnson (1966) model is genitally focused, which fragmentizes human sexuality from emotional and mental aspects of sexual pleasure outside of the physical realm (Di Giulio, 2003). This can lead to rigid expectations about sexual functioning and feeling abnormal or dysfunctional if unable to achieve a full physical response cycle, which can create anxiety and interfere with sexual functioning for individuals not able to achieve the "normal" response. The traditional model of sexual response is also problematic in that it does not emphasize the emotional connection between partners, which enhances sexual pleasure and response in relationships (Johnson &

Zuccarini, 2010). Thus, counselors should attend to physiological aspects of sexual functioning but need to consider how emotional, mental, or contextual factors may be contributing to differences in sexual functioning for clients, and allow clients to define for themselves what is satisfactory and functional sexuality.

SAFER SEX PRACTICES

Sexuality is a natural part of being a human and a vital factor in our ability to connect and develop intimate relationships with others. Engaging in sexual encounters, however, is not without risk to individuals' health, and thus, promoting responsible sexual decision-making is an integral part of helping clients develop and express their sexuality in healthy ways. In the United States, there is a tendency toward an abstinence-only focus when it comes to sexual education. This contrasts to media messages that depict spontaneous sexual activity, hookups, and sexual encounters among teens (Weiss, 2007). Thus, there is often a lack of realistic depictions and comprehensive education about sexual activity that would promote responsible sexual decision-making, thus increasing the chances of engaging in risky sexual behavior.

Current research suggests that the current efforts to prevent risky sexual behavior and the transmission of STIs and HIV are not highly effective. According to the Center for Disease Control's (CDC) Youth Risk Behavior Survey, 46.8% of high school students have had sexual intercourse within the past year, and over 70% of people report having intercourse by the time they are 20 years old (Finer & Philbin, 2013). Although many parents would like for their children to not be sexually active before adulthood and/or marriage, the data clearly show that the majority of people first engage in sexual intercourse during adolescence. Teens often do not engage in safer sexual practices, in part due to a lack of information about responsible sexual decision-making. The United States has one of the highest rates of STIs and teen pregnancy as compared to most other industrialized nations (Feijoo, 2001), with adolescents and young adults under 25 being the highest risk age group for contracting STIs or HIV and having unplanned pregnancies (Santelli et al., 2006). In a national survey by the Kaiser Family Foundation (2003), many teens reported being misinformed about safer sex practices, particularly methods that prevent STI transmission. For instance, 40.9% of teens engaging in sexual behavior did not use a condom the last time they had sex, and only 19% report using birth control pills (Centers for Disease Control, 2013a). Moreover, 75% of teens desired to learn more about sex and sexual health, including prevention of STIs, communicating effectively with partners, and condom usage (Kaiser Family Foundation, 2003).

Often, information about safer sexual practices is limited where abstinence-only education is emphasized (Weiss, 2007). Abstinence-only programs promote waiting to have sex until marriage. Abstinence-only programs have not been effective in decreasing sexual risk-taking behaviors or increasing the chances that youth will stay abstinent until married. Rates of sexual activity, STI transmission, and teen pregnancy are higher in the states that emphasize abstinence-only education (Weiss, 2007), so the goal of these programs to promote safer sex is not being met. Further, although youth who sign abstinence pledges may delay sexual activity and have fewer sexual partners, the majority of youth who take these pledges still engage in oral sex or have intercourse before marriage but are less likely to protect themselves during sexual encounters as compared to non-pledge groups (Santinelli et al., 2006; Weiss, 2007).

The limitations of abstinence-only programs do not mean that abstinence should not be promoted as a safer sex practice; however, comprehensive education that provides information about sex and safer sex practices is essential (Santinelli et al., 2006). Counselors need to be prepared to address sexual risk-taking behavior as it comes up in counseling with teenagers and their families, and they can provide psychoeducation and enhance familial communication about sexual health and behavior. Although these conversations with teens and their families may be uncomfortable and challenging to navigate, counselors need to be able to openly discuss sex and sexuality with clients. Otherwise, counselors play into the same dynamic of silence that creates a culture of sexual risk-taking in the first place. As part of the assessment process with adolescents, counselors should inquire about their sexual activity as well as their sexual behavior if they are engaging in or considering sex and not wait for clients to bring up the topic on their own. Although sexual activity may not be the focus of counseling for many adolescents, counselors should directly address sexual risk-taking behavior as a way to promote clients' overall health, just as counselors would address appetite and sleep as a part of clients' physical health. Ethically, clients have the right to complete and accurate health information, and thus, counselors have an ethical obligation to provide comprehensive education to clients (Santinelli et al., 2006).

Counselors also can work to design sexual education programs that are effective at promoting responsible sexual decision-making and reducing sexual risk-taking behavior. In a comprehensive review of sexual education programs in the United States, Kirby (2007) found that effective programs for adolescents repeated clear and consistent messages about sexual health and protective behavior, in order to challenge perceptions and social norms surrounding sex. Sexual education programs that reduced sexual risk-taking behaviors focused on multiple psychosocial factors for prevention, including knowledge, perceptions, personal values and attitudes, self-efficacy and confidence, and communication. Effective curricula set ground rules to create a safe environment, were developmentally appropriate, and employed multiple instructional techniques to target risk-taking behaviors, including lectures, games, role playing, skits, and videos (Kirby, 2007). Counselors may encounter social or community resistance to delivering sexual education outside of abstinence-only programs, yet securing support from appropriate stakeholders is necessary to effectively implement comprehensive sexual education to youth (Kirby, 2007). Thus, counselors can use their skills in creating safe environments, understanding developmental theories, facilitating group processes, and advocating for support from stakeholders to design and implement these programs.

Most sexual-education programming focuses on adolescents and youth, but comprehensive education is also important for adults throughout their lifespan. It is estimated that between one-third to one-half of HIV infections are passed on by people who know they are HIV-positive and who are not engaging in safer sex practices with their partners (Chariyeva, Golin, Earp, & Suchindran, 2012). Adults who have mental health issues and/or use substances are more at risk for contracting STIs or HIV (Schadé, van Grootheest, & Smit, 2013). Moreover, STIs and HIV infections are increasing among adults 50 and older, with some researchers estimating that the increase among older adults is higher than the increase among the general population (Johnson, 2013). The increase among older adults is in part due to involvement in sexually risky behaviors. As there is no longer a chance of pregnancy, older adults may not see themselves at risk of contracting STIs. Thus, counselors should not assume that adults are engaging in safer sex practices and assess clients' sexual behavior regardless of age. Utilizing psychoeducation to inform clients along with behavioral interventions and motivational interviewing can help to address clients' ambivalence toward practicing safer sex (Chariyeva et al., 2012). As basic sexual education resources may not be as available to adults, counselors should also advocate for and design comprehensive sexual education that is pertinent to individuals across the lifespan, implementing groups and classes within community mental health agencies, substance abuse centers, retirement communities, and assisted living facilities.

Overview of Safer Sex Practices

Counselors can provide psychoeducation to clients and communities to enhance safer sex practices. There is a range of sexual activities that are pleasurable that reduce the risk of contracting STIs, HIV, or pregnancy. The safest sexual activities include masturbation, mutual masturbation, cybersex, or phone sex, although these activities reduce physical connectivity with one's partner. Low-risk sexual activities include kissing, manual stimulation, body-to-body rubbing with genitals covered, use of sex toys, and oral sex. Oral sex is safest when a contraceptive method is used, such as a dam or a condom, as STIs can still be spread through the contact of sexual fluid with saliva. The highest-risk sexual activities include vaginal and anal intercourse. The two main strategies to prevent the spread of STIs and unwanted pregnancy while engaging in vaginal or anal intercourse are to use condoms and have intercourse within a monogamous relationship.

Birth control methods are another strategy for preventing unplanned pregnancies, but it is important for the public to be informed that only those birth control methods that create a barrier to prevent passing fluids from partner to partner (e.g., condoms) are effective against STIs. There are multiple forms of birth control, including the pill, vaginal rings, patches, shots, and intrauterine devices (IUDs). Most birth control methods have a 99% effectiveness rate at preventing pregnancy if used correctly (e.g., pill is taken at the same time each day). In the case of having unprotected sex with no method of birth control used, the morning-after pill can be taken up to five days after unprotected sex to help prevent pregnancy and is available at most drug stores or Planned Parenthood for an average cost of $30 to $60. The morning-after pill helps prevent ovulation so that there is no egg for the sperm to fertilize. There has been public controversy over the morning-after pill and so it is important to educate clients that it does not cause an abortion, which is defined as a termination of pregnancy after the egg is fertilized by sperm. If a woman has ovulated before taking the morning-after pill, the pill does not kill the fertilized egg; the pill only prevents the egg from being released if this has not already occurred.

Other methods of birth control include male withdrawal before ejaculation, which is highly effective (96%) if used correctly. Some men, however, may not have enough experience or control to effectively use the withdrawal method, and thus the risk of pregnancy increases, so this method is only suggested for partners who have a mutual trust established and where the man is in control of his ejaculation. Abstinence from vaginal intercourse is the only method that is 100% effective at preventing unplanned pregnancies and the contraction of STIs and HIV, which is why abstinence should still be encouraged within sexual education programs.

In addition to offering education on methods for practicing safer sex, addressing individual, relational, and contextual factors is important to prevent sexual risk-taking behaviors. At an individual level, promoting self-efficacy and confidence is important to help individuals communicate with their partners about safer sex practices and to make decisions about sexual behavior when partners are uncooperative (Wilkinson, Holahan, & Drane-Edmundson, 2002). Further, perceptions and normative beliefs about sexual behavior predict safer sex practices, so promotion of positive attitudes toward condom use and other forms of protection makes individuals more likely to use these methods during sexual encounters (Wilkinson et al., 2002; Kirby, 2007). At a relational level, teaching communication skills to negotiate contraceptive use can enhance self-efficacy and partner cooperation (Wilkinson et al., 2002). Counselors also can promote effective parent-child communication about sexual activity as a protective factor against risky sexual behavior in adolescents (Kirby, 2007).

Finally, at a contextual level, attending and participating in school activities, faith communities, and other community activities are protective factors against risky sexual behavior (Weiss, 2007). Thus, counselors can encourage school investment, positive activities, and social involvement for adolescent clients as an overall preventative strategy. Counselors also can promote safer sex practices by deconstructing sexual norms perpetuated by the media and by addressing clients' use of alcohol and drugs. Researchers have found correlations between the amount of sexual content viewed on television and sexual activity in teenagers, although it is unclear if the media exposure is increasing their likelihood of engaging in sex or if teens who are sexually active are more likely to watch sexual content (Grant, 2003). Sexual talk and behavior is increasingly prevalent in the media, particularly in television and movies. Sex in the media is often depicted as casual and impulsive, with most sexual encounters occurring between unmarried partners. There is little depiction of the risks involved with sex, as well as the negotiation of safe sex practices (Gruber & Grube, 2000). Sexual education is important in order to provide realistic portrayals of sexual behavior to adolescents, which include communication before and during sex and the use of protective strategies. Further, the use of alcohol and other drugs is associated with sexually risky behavior, as individuals report they are more likely to engage in casual sexual encounters and not use protection when under the influence (Weiss, 2007). Counselors need to concurrently address clients' substance use behaviors, working on reduction or elimination of substance use, as alcohol and drugs impair clients' judgment and decision-making abilities, which may hinder their practice of sexually healthy behaviors.

PHYSICAL HEALTH ISSUES

Sexually Transmitted Infections

The World Health Organization (WHO, 2014b) estimates that more than 1 million people get a STI *every day* and that one-half of all Americans will contract an STI at some point in their lives (Planned Parenthood, 2014b). As many STIs are present without the occurrence of symptoms, people may be unaware that they are infected. There are more than 30 different types of STIs, with the most common including chlamydia, gonorrhea, syphilis, genital herpes (HSV2), hepatitis B, the human papillomavirus (HPV), and trichomoniasis (World Health Organization, 2014). Chlamydia, gonorrhea, syphilis, and trichomoniasis are curable, but herpes, hepatitis B, and HPV are incurable, although the symptoms can be decreased or managed through medical care. The prevention of STIs is becoming even more important as some of the curable viral STIs, namely gonorrhea, are developing immunity to the commonly used anti-viral drugs in treatment. Most STIs are transmitted via sexual contact, including oral, vaginal, and anal intercourse, but many of the common STIs can be transmitted via blood and tissue transfers, particularly from mother to child during pregnancy.

Acquiring a STI can negatively impact clients' health, particularly for women. STIs acquired during pregnancy can contribute to adverse pregnancy outcomes, such as miscarriages, stillbirth, premature birth, or the physical-health impairment of infants. Over half a million women are diagnosed per year with cervical cancer resulting from HPV (World Health Organization, 2014). STIs can also lead to pelvic inflammatory diseases and infertility in women. For both men and women, the presence of some STIs can increase their risk of contracting HIV, so that people with certain STIs are three times more likely to get HIV than those without STIs.

Signs that a person has contracted an STI can include abnormal discharge from the vagina or penis, burning during urination or difficulty urinating, itching or sores in the genital area, abnormal vaginal bleeding, and pain in the lower abdomen or genital region, or pain during sex (Planned Parenthood, 2014b). Anyone who reports these symptoms should get tested for STIs immediately, which can include both urine and blood tests. Some STI infections may be asymptomatic, so the CDC (n.d.) recommends that individuals engaging in sexual intercourse get tested for chlamydia and gonorrhea annually. It is also recommended to get tested after unprotected sex or if one thinks their partner may have an STI. Additionally, women who become pregnant should get tested for those same STIs, along with syphilis and hepatitis B, as STIs can be harmful to the women and their babies during and after pregnancy (Centers for Disease Control and Prevention, 2013e). Most STIs have an incubation period, so there is a window in which individuals need to wait before the STI test will be accurate in detecting the infection. Another important point of education is that physicians and gynecologists typically do not regularly test for STIs (American Sexual Health Association, 2014), so clients who are concerned about their sexual health need to be direct in asking for testing. STI testing through a physician's office can be expensive and is not always covered by insurance. Cheaper testing is typically available through Planned Parenthood, local departments of public health, and alcohol and drug service agencies.

Counselors are integral in the prevention of STIs by providing sexuality education, which promotes safer sex practices, such as the reduction of partners and condom use, to decrease sexual risk-taking behaviors, as well as by providing information on the symptoms of STIs and when to get tested. Counselors can also provide pre- and posttest counseling services to clients who are concerned they have contracted an STI to help with adjustment to their diagnosis and the subsequent impact on their personal functioning and intimate relationships.

HIV/AIDS

The human immunodeficiency virus (HIV) causes acquired immunodeficiency syndrome (AIDS), a lifelong disease that impacts the ability of the immune system to function and can influence the psychological well-being of individuals with the infection. Further, there is a stigma toward HIV that is not associated with most other chronic illnesses, which can exacerbate mental health problems of persons living with HIV. Mental health problems and HIV are likely to co-occur, as individuals with mental health struggles are more at risk for contracting HIV, and those individuals infected with HIV are more likely to develop mental health issues (Schadé et al., 2013). Individuals with HIV who have mental health concerns may be less likely to follow through on treatment, which can lead to a poorer prognosis and lower quality of life and may become a public health concern as these individuals are more likely to engage in risky sexual behavior, potentially spreading HIV to others (Whetten, Reif, Whetten, & Murphy-McMillan, 2008). Individuals with HIV are more likely to develop depressive symptoms and are more at risk for suicidal ideations, attempts, and completion than the general population, including those living with other chronic illnesses (Schadé et al., 2013). Additionally, HIV-positive persons are significantly more likely to report past history of abuse and trauma and thus are more likely to exhibit symptoms of PTSD than the general population (Whetten et al., 2008). Substance abuse is also a risk factor for contracting HIV, as individuals are more likely to engage in risky sexual behavior under the influence of a substance (Schadé et al., 2013). Thus, counselors should be aware of the mental health concerns and behaviors that put clients at risk for contracting HIV, as well as the likelihood that someone who is HIV-positive may develop mental health struggles after their diagnosis.

Current data estimates that over 1 million people in the United States are living with HIV/AIDS, with approximately 50,000 new infections occurring every year (Centers for Disease Control, 2014b). Global estimates of HIV/AIDS prevalence indicate over 35 million people who are HIV-positive, with 97% of HIV-positive individuals living in low-to-middle income countries (United States Department of Health & Human Services, 2012). Ethnic minority groups are disproportionately affected by HIV in the United States, as 44% of individuals living with HIV in the United States are Black or African American and 19% are Hispanic or Latino. Men who have sex with men (MSM) are more likely to contract HIV, particularly in younger age groups. New infections in women are likely to be transmitted through heterosexual sex or injection drug use, with women accounting for 25% of the U.S. population who are HIV positive. Individuals who use injection drugs are at risk to contract the virus. Further, about 1 in 4 new infections occur among youth ages 13–24. Many youths are unaware that they have HIV, are not seeking treatment, and may unknowingly pass the infection to others. Of concern is that 1 in 6 people with HIV are unaware that they are infected (U.S. Department of Health & Human Services, 2012).

Counselors can be integral in preventing the spread of HIV through encouraging clients who report risky sexual behaviors and/or injection drug use to get tested regularly. Many public health departments or HIV treatment clinics offer free, accessible, and confidential testing. The CDC recommends that sexually active men and women who are not in a long-term monogamous relationship get tested at least annually for HIV, with more frequent testing (i.e., every 3–6 months) recommended for those who have unprotected sex with multiple partners or in higher-risk groups. Most HIV tests will check the levels of antibodies in the bloodstream to determine if one is infected. Although most people develop antibodies within 2 to 8 weeks after exposure, it can take up to 3 months to acquire a detectable level of antibodies in the bloodstream. For more accurate results, individuals should wait 3 months after exposure to get tested (Centers for Disease Control, n.d.).

For individuals who test HIV-positive, early medical intervention is essential to helping them stay healthy. The progression of HIV varies from person to person. Some individuals naturally have an immune response that slows the progression of HIV (Klimas, Koneru, & Fletcher, 2008). Co-infection with other STIs or tuberculosis can lead to health problems and compromise individuals' ability to fight the HIV virus, so screening for these other illnesses after an HIV diagnosis is important to address overall physical health. Of most relevance to counselors is an understanding of the psychosocial factors that can impact HIV disease progression. Use of tobacco, alcohol, and other substances can weaken the immune system (Centers for Disease Control, n.d.), so counselors can provide support to help HIV-positive individuals cease their substance use. Further, depression may impact individuals' motivation to seek and comply to medical treatment. Counselors working with HIV-positive clients should utilize interventions that alleviate mental health symptoms while also using motivational interviewing and behavioral strategies to address clients' compliance with medical treatment recommendations.

In cases where clients communicate that they plan to intentionally spread a STI or HIV to an identifiable third party, counselors may break confidentiality to inform the third party if counselors deem that the person may be at risk of contracting the disease (B.2.c., American Counseling Association, 2014). Before breaking confidentiality, counselors should carefully assess the intent of the client to inform their partner and possible actions the client may engage in that could spread the infection. Counselors also can provide education about responsible sexual behavior and encourage values clarification to prompt clients toward responsible decision-making (Erickson, 1990). Counselors can inform clients that knowingly or recklessly transmitting an STI and/or HIV without informing their partners and obtaining consent is a criminal offense in most U.S. states (the disadvantages of criminalizing HIV transmission are discussed below). Further, counselors should be familiar with state laws about breaking confidentiality to disclose potential harm through the spread of an infection (American Counseling Association, 2014), as these laws vary from state to state and may prohibit counselors' disclosure. Thus, counselors should consult with colleagues, supervisors, and attorneys before making the decision to disclose the potential harm to the third party to ensure that they are acting in accordance with both ethical and legal codes.

There has been significant debate as to whether laws criminalizing the transmission of HIV encourage or inhibit safer sex practices. According to the United Nations Development Programme (United Nations Development Programme, 2012), there is no evidence that these laws encourage more responsible sexual behavior. Opponents of such legislation, including many AIDS service organizations, argue that it may increase the stigma and discourage people from getting tested or participating in treatment programs for fear that they could face legal prosecution in the future, thus disempowering people living with HIV to engage in protective behavior. Further, those who are at highest risk for HIV infection (e.g., MSM, sex workers, transgender individuals, and drug users) are often stigmatized by legal policies and social norms; thus, adequately addressing prevention in these populations means promoting their basic human rights and creating climates where it is safe for people in these groups to be visible and access harm reduction services (United Nations Development Programme, 2012).

Upon diagnosis of HIV, clients may experience a range of difficult emotions from self-blame, guilt, shame, and fear. They may experience grief, as the life they were living has been altered and they likely are considering their own mortality and thus may be at risk for anxiety or depression. Counselors can provide support services for clients after diagnosis to help them process the emotional impact. Individuals who comply with medical treatment for HIV are likely to stay healthier and live longer. Counselors working with people living with HIV/AIDS need to be sensitive to not perpetuate discrimination or shame and should be aware of any beliefs or biases that may prevent them from working effectively with this population. Externalizing interventions may help clients accept their choices that led to contracting HIV and help clients define themselves outside of their disease. Counselors also can support clients in telling their loved ones about their diagnosis. Partners entering into relationships with people who have HIV may be concerned about their safety and the impact on their sexual relationship, and thus, counselors can provide education on safer sex practices to reduce the chance of spreading the virus to partners.

Counselors can advocate for clients living with HIV/AIDS in multiple ways. First, people living with HIV are protected from discrimination under the Americans with Disabilities Act (United States Department of Justice, 2012), so counselors can assist clients experiencing prejudice in their school or work settings pursue recourse for fair treatment. Counselors can also advocate at a systemic level for services that prevent the spread of HIV, such as access to sexual health checkups and clean needle distribution programs. Recognizing that individuals are going to engage in sexual and drug-use behaviors that put them at risk for HIV is essential to creating services that help people engage in these behaviors as safely as possible. Further, creating access to affordable medication, medical treatment, and mental health services for those who have contracted HIV promotes the physical and mental health of these individuals. Individuals with HIV who can remain healthy tend to engage in safer sex practices and are less likely to abuse substances, which benefits the individuals as well as the community because they are less likely to spread their infection. Counselors can be integral in providing individual and family counseling as well as programming and advocacy to prevent the spread of HIV and to enhance the lives of those living with the virus. Exercise 4.1 offers an opportunity for readers to collaborate with others to reflect upon their attitudes and beliefs about working with clients living with STIs or HIV.

Exercise 4.1

SMALL GROUP ACTIVITY FOR WORKING WITH CLIENTS LIVING WITH STIs OR HIV

Directions: Complete the following steps within a small group of colleagues:

- Step 1: As a group, generate a list of commonly held beliefs and/or biases regarding people living with STIs and/or HIV/AIDS (i.e., some of these beliefs may be specific to STIs or HIV).
  - ○ Rate these statements on a Likert scale as to how much you agree or disagree with statements (1 – completely disagree; 3 – neutral; 5 – completely agree).
- Step 2: As a group, generate a list of commonly held misconceptions about intimate relationships and sexual behavior.
- Step 3: As a group, generate a list of contextual factors that may influence peoples' vulnerability to contracting STIs and HIV.
- Step 4: Consider the statements generated in Steps 2 and 3. As a small group, discuss how these statements influence your conceptualization of the beliefs and biases produced in Step 1. How does examining the social discourses surrounding sex and contextual factors help you to personally challenge any of the beliefs and biases you agreed with in Step 1?

Medication Side Effects and Sexual Functioning

Medication management is a common treatment in psychotherapeutic services, particularly to manage acute or severe symptoms. Sexual side effects can occur with many commonly used psychotropic medications, including selective serotonin reuptake inhibitors (SSRIs) and atypical antipsychotics. SSRIs, commonly prescribed for depressive and anxiety disorders, have been studied extensively, with 20% to 80% of respondents reporting instances of sexual side effects while on SSRIs, dependent on the specific medication they were taking (Harmon, 2007; Serretti & Chiesa, 2011). Atypical antipsychotics also are prescribed often for mood disorders and have been found to significantly impact sexual functioning (Serretti & Chiesa, 2011). Sexual side effects of psychotropic medications can include lowered sexual desire, decreased arousal (decreased vaginal lubrication in women and difficulties obtaining or sustaining an erection in men), delayed or absent orgasms, and erectile or ejaculatory dysfunction in men. A less common side effect is prolonged penile or clitoral erections (Harmon, 2007). Psychotropic drugs that commonly are associated with sexual side effects are listed in Table 4.1.

There are multiple hormones and neurotransmitters that play a role in sexual functioning, many of which play a major role in mental health problems and are impacted by psychotropic medications. Dopamine, norepinephrine, and serotonin are all neurotransmitters implicated in mood disorders, schizophrenia, and substance abuse disorders. Dopamine and norepinephrine also play a role in both cognitive and physical arousal, and serotonin is related to genital arousal and sensation (Clayton & Balon, 2009). The main hormones that impact sexual functioning are testosterone and estrogen, and androgen treatment may be used for both men and women to treat low sexual desire (Segraves & Balon, 2010). Prolactin is another hormone that impacts sexual functioning. Both SSRIs and antipsychotic drugs can increase prolactin levels, which can lead to low sexual desire, erectile dysfunction, amenorrhea (absence of menstruation), and galactorrhea (spontaneous breast milk discharge unrelated to normal breast milk production) (Harmon, 2007).

Sexual side effects of medications can impact clients' quality of life and interpersonal relationships and lead to noncompliance with medication treatment regimens. Due to the amount of time spent and rapport built with clients, counselors may be in a better position than psychiatrists or physicians to detect sexual side effects (Segraves & Balon, 2010). Counselors may overlook the possibility of sexual side effects as a reason for clients' noncompliance to medication management as clients may not be forthcoming with information about their sexual behavior and relationships (Harmon, 2007; Rosenberg, Bleiberg, Koscis, & Gross, 2003). Women may be less likely to discuss sexual side effects with their counselors, psychiatrists, or physicians than men (Rosenberg et al., 2003). Counselors also may

Table 4.1 Sexual Side Effects of Commonly Prescribed Psychotropic Medications

Drug Class	*Commonly Prescribed Medications With Associated Sexual Side Effects**	*Sexual Side Effects*	*Commonly Prescribed Medications With Lower Rates of Sexual Side Effects*
Antidepressants	Anafranil (clomipramine), Celexa (citalopram), Cymbalta (duloxetine), Effexor (venlafaxine), Lexapro (escitalopram), Luvox (fluvoxamine), Paxil (paroxetine), Pristiq (desvenlafaxine), Prozac (fluoxetine), Zoloft (sertraline)	Decreased sexual desire, orgasm absent or delayed, erectile or ejaculatory dysfunction	*Minimal or no side effects:* Serzone (nefazodone), Wellbutrin (bupropion)** *Lower rates of sexual side effects:* Celexa (citalopram), Cymbalta (duloxetine), Luvox (fluvoxamine), Remeron (mitazapine)
Atypical Antipsychotics	Abilify (aripiprazole), Clozaril (clozapine), Geodon (ziprasidone), Risperdal (risperidone), Seroquel (quetiapine), Zyprexa (olanzapine)	Decreased sexual desire, ejaculatory or erectile dysfunction, orgasm absent or delayed, decreased vaginal lubrication, amenorrhea and menstrual irregularities	Abilify (aripiprazole), Geodon (ziprasidone), Seroquel (quetiapine), Zyprexa (olanzapine)
Typical/conventional antipsychotics	Haldol (haloperidol)	Ejaculatory or erectile dysfunction; orgasm absent or delayed; decreased vaginal lubrication; amenorrhea and menstrual irregularities	
Anti-anxiety agents (anxiolytics)	Xanax (alprazolam), Klonopin (clonazepam)		Buspar (busprione)**

*Brand name with generic in parentheses.
**May be used as an antidote to antidepressant-induced sexual problems.

feel uncomfortable introducing the topic of sexuality and sexual functioning and may not assess sexual side effects as a potential reason for clients not complying with their medication regimen. Counselors can overcome this barrier by introducing the topic of sexuality in initial sessions with clients through questions that assess their sexual behavior and functioning, so that clients are aware that counselors are comfortable discussing their sexual concerns. Further, counselors should be knowledgeable that sexual side effects are common with many psychotropic medications and consider these in assessments of medication management.

Detecting whether sexual side effects are related to medication can be a complicated process. Many clients will have experienced difficulties in sexual functioning prior to the start of psychotropic medication and may have other behaviors or illnesses that contribute to the sexual problems other than their mental health concerns. Many mental health diagnoses are associated with problematic sexual functioning, including mood disorders, anxiety disorders, schizophrenia and psychosis, eating disorders, and some personality disorders (Clayton & Balon, 2009; Segraves & Balon, 2010). Mental health problems frequently lead to difficulties in functioning in intimate relationships, which also can impact sexual functioning within the relationship. Further, many mental health diagnoses are comorbid with substance abuse. Although commonly viewed as a substance that enhances sexual encounters, alcohol use may interfere with arousal and orgasm in both women and men. Chronic drug use frequently leads to sexual problems, including low libido, impotence, or decreased ability to become aroused or reach orgasm (Segraves & Balon, 2010). Finally, both physical illness and medication use related to physical problems can contribute to problems in sexual functioning. Thus, assessment of the contributing factors to sexual problems can be a complex process. Counselors can help educate clients on the multiple factors that lead to sexual problems and help prepare them so that the treatments to enhance their sexual functioning may be a trial and error process.

If sexual side effects are a reason clients are not taking their medications as prescribed, counselors should encourage clients to schedule a follow-up visit with their physician or psychiatrist to discuss their concerns and for possible medication adjustments. If clients are hesitant do so, counselors can process clients' discomfort or tentativeness of broaching the topic of sexual side effects with their medication prescriber. Some clients may be more comfortable with signing a release so that the counselor can contact the prescriber directly about the clients' side effects and concerns, so that the prescriber is aware and can bring up the topic rather than putting that burden on the client (Segraves & Balon, 2010). Strategies for enhancing sexual functioning due to side effects of psychotropic medications include lowering the dosage of prescribed drugs, drug holidays (going a few days without the drug in order to engage in sexual encounters), substitution of a different drug, or antidotal drugs (e.g., Viagra) (Clayton & Balon, 2009; Segraves & Balon, 2010). If clients choose to take a lower dose or drug holidays, counselors can help prepare clients in case a relapse of symptoms occur. Drug holidays often contribute to noncompliance, as clients need to be regimented in regard to sexual engagement during those periods and they need to go back to taking the drug regularly. In terms of drug substitution, clients may be hesitant to start a new medication if their current one is working to treat their mental health symptoms, but this can be a simple fix for the sexual side effects that may be experienced. Antidotal drugs also have a good success rate but can lead to other physical side effects and may be too costly for some clients (Clayton & Balon, 2009). Along with the prescriber, counselors can help clients consider the strategy that would work best for their lifestyle.

Sexuality and Chronic Illness or Disability

People who experience chronic illness or disabilities are more likely to experience problems with sexual functioning as their overall physiological health may be impacted. Counselors should not assume, however, that clients with chronic illnesses or disabilities cannot experience a satisfying sexual life, as such an assumption is disempowering and disrespectful (Di Giulio, 2003; Richards, Miodrag, & Watson, 2006). People with disabilities can be particularly affected by societal views that tend to desexualize people with disabilities by treating them as perpetual children, leading to the assumption that these people are not interested in or have the capacity for sexual relationships (Di Giulio, 2003). Counselors also may hold these views about people with chronic illness or disabilities, which may prevent discussions of sexuality with these clients. By holding these assumptions and/or not asking clients with chronic illness or disabilities about sex, counselors do a disservice to their clients, particularly as these individuals are more likely to engage in sexually risky behaviors.

About half of all adults in the United States have chronic diseases, with the most common being heart disease, cancer, arthritis, diabetes, and obesity (Centers for Disease Control, 2014a). Cancer and heart disease are the leading causes of death in the United States. Managing a chronic illness is time-consuming, exhausting, and a life-changing process with many implications for physiological functioning. Pain and fatigue related to chronic illness and treatment can impact individuals' sexual functioning, and some chronic illnesses and/or their treatment impact fertility as well. Individuals with chronic illnesses may experience physical changes to their bodies, such as loss of musculature, scars from surgeries, loss of bodily control, or having to wear fluid bags or catheters for treatment, all of which can impact body image and the sense of oneself as a sexual being (Ussher et al., 2013). Cancer treatments in particular, including chemotherapy, radiation, and surgery, have a negative impact on sexual functioning for both men and women. Chemotherapy can impact libido and lead to erectile dysfunction in men. Chemotherapy also can trigger menopause in women, and both chemotherapy and radiation can lead to vaginal dryness. Further, prostate cancer surgery typically leads to incontinence and erectile dysfunction (Ussher et al., 2013).

Although individuals with physical disabilities will have differing needs than individuals with developmental disabilities, both populations face systemic barriers to positive sexuality, including reduced access to sexual-health information, a lack of privacy, and decreased access to sexual partners. People with developmental disabilities may be discouraged from having sexual relationships as family members or health care providers assume they do not have the capacity for sexual and emotional connection with partners (Di Giulio, 2003; Richards et al., 2006). Clients with disabilities are at increased risk for sexual exploitation and abuse and for contracting HIV/AIDS. These risks increase due to society's treatment of people with disabilities. For one, there is a lack of sexual education and preventive services provided to meet the specific needs of people with disabilities, which denies their basic human right to healthy sexuality, decreases their autonomy to engage in safe-sex practices, and results in feelings of powerlessness (Nosek, Foley, Hughes, & Howland, 2001). Further, the lack of privacy as individuals may need to always be dependent on another person for care and live-in group settings, may lead people with disabilities to seek out sexual encounters in risky places such as parks and bathrooms (Di Giulio, 2003). Finally, social marginalization and physical access issues make it difficult for people with disabilities to find partners (Taleporos & McCabe, 2002). People with disabilities report wanting intimacy and emotional connection just like non-disabled people, and supporting these individuals to establish healthy partnerships, which may include sexual activity, could serve to enhance safe-sex practices (e.g., monogamous relationships, enhanced partner communication and cooperation) to reduce their vulnerability to sexual abuse and contracting STIs.

Counselors should begin by treating *all* clients, regardless of physical or mental abilities, as sexual beings because sexuality is a normal part of the human experience. As Nicolaou (2012) states, "The reliance on spontaneous self-reporting of sexual dysfunction in clinical practice is resulting in unnecessary worsening of quality of life for clients" (p. 22). By directly inquiring about sexual and relationship issues, counselors can assess clients' needs and deficits in sexual functioning to help them build skills to create satisfying relationships for themselves. Moreover, counselors can help clients to prevent behaviors that contribute to risky sexual encounters, by providing psychoeducation about safe sex practices and prevention of sexual abuse. Counselors should provide information specific to clients' chronic illness or disability and its impact on their sexual health, including how it may affect their functioning, the suitability of contraceptive methods, and ideas for new ways to engage in and find pleasure in sexual encounters. Counselors also can educate clients and their families about inappropriate and appropriate sexual behavior, how to clearly say no to unwanted advances, promoting personal safety, and how to effectively report abuse (Di Giulio, 2003; Richards et al., 2006).

As discussed at the beginning of the chapter, traditional models of sexual response are performance oriented and focused on genital function. These models are limiting in that they do not highlight holistic or alternatives to sexuality, acknowledge that healthy sexual responses are more variable and adaptable, and may lead to misdiagnosing of sexual disorders in clients with chronic illnesses and disabilities (Di Giulio, 2003; Dune, 2012). Chronic illness and disabilities may affect clients' self-image, body esteem, and interpersonal abilities, which also can affect their intimate relationships (Taleporos & McCabe, 2002), so it is important that counselors' approaches to sexual health are multidisciplinary, focusing on the collaboration between providers and clients, as well as involving clients' families in addressing sexual well-being. Counselors can provide adjunct services to health providers as we have the ability to spend more time with clients to fully assess pre-existing factors before the illness or disability was acquired, disease-specific factors, and personal, partner, and familial response to the illness or disability, all of which may be impacting clients' sexual health and satisfaction (Bitzer et al., 2008). Counseling services should promote clients' agency in defining their sexual health needs, legitimize their concerns, and involve treatment plans with a focus on positive sexuality.

Exercise 4.2

WORKING WITH A CLIENT WITH SEXUALITY CONCERNS RELATED TO CANCER

Jack is a 54-year-old African American male who was diagnosed with prostate cancer two years ago. He has been married to his wife for 25 years and has one adult son. Jack has undergone both chemotherapy and radiation treatment that has not been successful in curing his cancer. Jack's wife made the call for them to come into counseling as a couple because Jack has been refusing to have prostate surgery to remove the tumor, which is the next step recommended by his physician. Jack says that he is concerned about being impotent after the surgery and is already frustrated by his decreased libido and erectile dysfunction he has experienced during the other treatments. Jack says, "I'd rather die than not be

(Continued)

(Continued)

able to enjoy sex again. I don't feel like a man anymore." Jack describes his sexual relationship with his wife as one of the best parts of their connection until he got cancer. Jack's wife is tearful throughout the session, saying she is trying to understand Jack's struggles, and misses having sex with him as well but that she would rather have Jack around for 30 more years and not be able to have sex with him than to have him not survive the cancer. Jack reports that his erectile functioning has been returning after stopping chemo and radiation and that he will likely live several more years given the current status of his cancer. Jack says he prefers to enjoy the rest of his life, including his sexual relationship with his wife. Although the surgery would potentially cure the cancer and prolong his life, Jack believes he will be unable to cope with and accept the impact on his sexual functioning.

Directions: Based on the information that you gathered about Jack above, develop a treatment plan for him to include the following:

- Define the presenting issue for Jack and his wife.
- Develop a treatment plan that is in line with your definition of his presenting issue to help Jack and his wife.
- Research and identify local, regional, and national services that could benefit these clients, beyond the benefits they may experience through counseling.

REPRODUCTIVE HEALTH

Promoting reproductive health is important to improve women's overall health and reduce the risk of infant and maternal mortality (Williams, Zapata, D'Angelo, Harrison, & Morrow, 2012). For women wanting to become pregnant, elimination of substance use and smoking cessation reduces the risk of spontaneous abortion, preterm delivery, restricted fetal growth, fetal alcohol syndrome, and sudden infant death syndrome (SIDS). Promoting overall physical health, including folic acid intake, is important to increase the likelihood of healthy births and children's health. There are physical health issues that also can lead to pregnancy complications. In addition to STIs and HIV, women may face other reproductive health concerns including endometriosis (when the tissue that lines the uterus grows elsewhere such as on the ovaries, bladder, or bowels), uterine fibroids (non-cancerous tumors), and gynecological cancer (Centers for Disease Control, 2014a). Thus, coordinating with physicians when counseling pregnant women about issues related to their reproductive health is essential to providing comprehensive care.

Pregnancy

Although pregnancy is a happy event for many couples, approximately half of all pregnancies in the United States are unplanned (Lee, Parisi, Akers, Borrerro, & Schwarz, 2011). While the only fail-safe way to prevent pregnancy is abstinence, the percentage of unplanned pregnancies is high given the numerous contraceptive options available. Among women with unplanned pregnancies, approximately 40% report using birth control methods inconsistently or incorrectly due to cost of contraceptives, method failure (e.g., forgetting to take birth control pills consistently or not using a condom during intercourse), and cultural norms (Frost, Darroch, & Remez, 2008). If utilizing a comprehensive-intake process, counselors assess what medications clients are taking as well as if they are sexually active. To promote the physiological and sexual health of clients, counselors need to inquire about contraceptive use. Counselors can provide psychoeducation to clients about contraceptive use and safe sex practices that are fitting for their cultural norms, help clients with medication management and communication skills to promote contraceptive use, and connect clients with services that provide low-cost contraceptives.

Women may face pregnancy complications, miscarriages, and/or neonatal loss during pregnancy. Common pregnancy complications include hypertension, gestational diabetes, and preeclampsia, which reduces blood flow to the fetus (National Institute of Health, 2013). Women experiencing depression and anxiety during pregnancy may be more at risk for complicated pregnancies and births (Alder, Fink, Bitzer, Hösli, & Holzgreve, 2007). Depression and anxiety have physiological effects on the body and can be triggered by shifts in neurotransmitter and hormone levels, which can impact maternal and fetal health. There is little research about using traditional treatments for depression and anxiety, such as CBT, with pregnant women, and some exposure techniques that initially increase anxiety may be inappropriate during pregnancy (Alder et al., 2007). Counselors working with pregnant women experiencing depression and anxiety want to consider the best treatments to relieve symptoms without creating additional distress. Strengths-based and selfsoothing strategies that focus on stress management, relaxation, mindfulness, and positivity are more appropriate for helping pregnant clients manage distress.

Approximately 10% to 25% of clinically recognized pregnancies will end in miscarriage—a pregnancy that ends on its own during the first 20 weeks (American Pregnancy Association, 2014). Miscarriages most often occur due to chromosomal abnormalities but also can be related to hormonal problems, maternal age, maternal trauma, and lifestyle choices (e.g., smoking, alcohol and drug use, malnutrition during pregnancy). In terms of neonatal deaths, approximately 4 out of every 1,000 babies die before 28 days old (The World Bank, 2014), typically due to premature birth or birth defects. Miscarriages or neonatal loss may lead to psychological distress for women, including grief, depression, anger, anxiety, guilt, self-blame, feelings of emptiness, and feeling out of control, which may be complicated by a lack of social support (Wojnar, Swanson, & Adolfsson, 2011). In subsequent pregnancies, women are likely to experience anxiety and fear of another loss. Support groups that guide participants through the grief process may help women and couples connect with others who have shared similar losses and to validate their emotional experience. Creating memories through events, rituals, and objects can help make the loss more tangible so that couples can mourn their child (Wojnar et al., 2011).

Additionally, women may experience depression during or after a successful pregnancy, which may impact their ability to care for themselves and their infant (Centers for Disease Control, 2013d). Additionally, about 4% of fathers experience depression in the year after their child's birth (Davé, Petersen, Sherr, & Nazareth, 2010). Although women with healthy births can experience postpartum depression, factors that put women at higher risk include history of infertility or miscarriages, having multiples, experiencing pregnancy complications and/or premature labor and delivery, having a baby with a disability or health complications, and having a baby as a teenager (Centers for Disease Control, 2013f). Counselors can provide a valuable service to women experiencing postpartum by coordinating with physicians for referrals. Symptoms of postpartum depression include those listed for a depressive episode in the DSM-5 (American Psychiatric Association, 2013a), along with difficulties sleeping when the baby is asleep, having negative thoughts related to one's baby, worrying about hurting one's baby, and feeling numb or guilty about not being a good mother (Centers for Disease Control, 2013f). Typical treatments for depression, such as cognitive-behavioral therapy, interpersonal therapy, and antidepressant medication are suitable for treating women with postpartum depression (National Institute of Health, n.d.). Counselors need to consider the context of the depressive symptoms and continually assess for the baby's safety during therapy.

Infertility

Infertility is defined as the inability to get pregnant or have a viable pregnancy after one year of regular, unprotected sex (Centers for Disease Control, 2013e). Couples who have never been able to have a child are experiencing primary infertility, whereas secondary infertility occurs in couples who already have a child or children but are unable to carry a viable pregnancy at the current time. Subfertility occurs when both partners have had children in previous relationships but are unable to conceive as a couple (Burnett & Panchal, 2008). Individuals and couples experiencing infertility may struggle to cope with personal distress, experience strain in their intimate relationship, and undergo financial stress and medical treatments in attempts to get pregnant. The experience of infertility is unique and complex to each client, so counselors need to have a basic understanding of the stressors that clients with infertility face in their daily lives.

As infertility affects approximately 10% to 15% of couples in the United States (Office on Women's Health, 2012), counselors are likely to encounter clients who are struggling with infertility in their practices. About one-third of infertility issues are attributed to females' health problems, one-third attributed to males, and the final third are caused by an interaction between male and female problems or due to unknown causes. The primary cause for female infertility is due to problems with ovulation, where one is not producing or releasing eggs to be fertilized (Office on Women's Health, 2012). Female infertility also may be caused by blocked or scarred fallopian tubes, which impact the ability of the egg to reach the uterus or uterine problems that affect the implantation of the egg in the uterine wall. The primary reason for men's infertility is due to problems that affect the number or quality of sperm. Factors that increase the risk of fertility issues in both men and women include age, health problems, and alcohol, tobacco, or other drug use. Stress, diet, and being over or underweight can impact women's ability to become pregnant (Office on Women's Health, 2012).

Although there are multiple psychosocial implications of infertility as explored below, researchers suggest that the majority of couples experiencing infertility may not formally seek counseling or other supportive services (Griel & McQuillan, 2004; Wischmann, 2008). This could be due to several reasons. First, individuals and couples experiencing infertility may fear being labeled or stigmatized further by counselors, or may doubt the efficacy of counseling services. However, the majority of individuals who sought counseling services for support during their infertility experience report that counseling was helpful (Wischmann, 2008). Counselors need to be aware of the barriers that prevent individuals experiencing infertility from seeking counseling services and work to address them in their practices, becoming familiar with what practices clients consider helpful. For instance, counseling interventions that emphasize education and coping skills training tend to reduce negative affect in couples experiencing infertility more than interventions that promote discussion or emotional expression (Boivin, 2003). Grief counseling when medical interventions fail or individuals decide to stop seeking treatment may foster healing (Daniluk, 2001), and group counseling can be beneficial due to the format that allows for the sharing of practical information and common experiences (Boivin, 2003; Wischmann, 2008). Counselors need to clearly link their practices to the possible positive outcomes for clients so that they can understand how counseling services can foster healthy coping responses to infertility. Clients also should be informed that pregnancy rates are unlikely to be impacted by counseling services (Boivin, 2003; Wischmann, 2008).

Secondly, medical providers may not be supportive of counseling services or referring their patients to mental health services for additional support, unless their patients are in clear distress during treatment or until medical treatment fails, so counselors need to find ways to enter the medical system and interact directly with practitioners and their patients. Counselors can create and distribute marketing materials to medical providers that clearly tie the goals of infertility counseling services to intended outcomes, in order to encourage medical providers to refer and coordinate their treatment with mental health counseling. One reason that women or couples report not accessing counseling services is due to practical concerns such as not knowing the cost or how to schedule an appointment, even when clinics where they are receiving medical treatment have materials advertising counseling services (Boivin, Scanlan, & Walker, 1999). Thus, obtaining support from medical providers in directly communicating the option for mental health services to their patients is essential to create access to counseling for infertility. Further, offering free or low-cost psychoeducational workshops to introduce fertility counseling services can educate potential clients and medical providers on the benefits of counseling.

There are multiple psychosocial challenges that individuals and couples experiencing infertility may face throughout the course of the transition. It is socially assumed in most cultures that couples will bear children and that procreation is the intended outcome of mating and sex (Burnett & Panchal, 2008). Couples may frequently be asked questions such as, "When are you going to have children?" Further, many religious traditions, including Christianity, Judaism, and Islam, promote childbearing as the highest purpose of humanity with children being a gift from God. Tribal ideologies often describe infertility as a curse, and in societies where a high value is placed on families, infertility may carry even more of a social stigma (Burnett & Panchal, 2008; Watkins & Baldo, 2004). Historically, the blame for infertility has been placed on the woman for various reasons, from her being sexually promiscuous to psychological impairment.

There is still a societal assumption that all women want to be and should be mothers and that motherhood is a fundamental component of a woman's identity. In today's modern cultures, many women delay having children until later in life in order to focus on their careers, or they may choose various methods of birth control to influence the timing of childbearing, and some women choose not to have children at all. There continue to be negative social discourses suggesting that women who do not prioritize motherhood are to be blamed for their inability to have children (Watkins & Baldo, 2004). Due to these social assumptions and historical traditions surrounding infertility, women may internalize the myth that they are to blame for infertility and thus, experience intense shame and guilt as part of their emotional experience. Both women and men experience grief and loss during their infertility journey. The loss experienced is often not tangible, except in the case of miscarriages (although early miscarriages may seem intangible as well, particularly for men who do not experience carrying the child). Couples can go through shifting identities as they define themselves outside of parenthood, creating a new life together while grieving the dream of having a child that is no longer obtainable in the way they were expecting (Daniluk, 1991; Watkins & Baldo, 2004). The grief and loss cycle may arise again as treatments fail and will be present as couples choose to stop treatment. Choosing to stop treatment, however, can provide a sense of relief for some couples and allow them to move forward in defining new goals for their life together. This forward movement can be positive and help couples heal from the experience of infertility (Daniluk, 1991).

Another common psychosocial implication of infertility is social isolation. As the experience of infertility is a "non-event transition," or an expected life event that does not occur (Daniluk, 2001), the impact of infertility may be less visible to couples' social supports. Although women and couples report primarily relying on family and friends as supports through their infertility experience (Boivin et al., 1999), family and friends may not understand a couples' experience or be confused about how to respond in a supportive manner, and some may express (often unintentionally) comments or unhelpful advice that the couple finds hurtful. Further, couples may feel angry or jealous toward others who are celebrating pregnancies and births and may choose to isolate themselves in attempt to cope with their grief and pain (Watkins & Baldo, 2004). Thus, group counseling or support groups may be a good option to connect clients to other couples who have experienced infertility to promote an understanding and normalization of their struggles and responses. The effectiveness of more informal support groups has not been empirically studied, but psychoeducational groups have been correlated to positive effects for participants, particularly in reducing negative affect (Wischmann, 2008).

Infertility also impacts couples' intimate and sexual relationships (Watkins & Baldo, 2004). Couples who have higher levels of commitment and relationship satisfaction, along with higher self-esteem and better coping skills, are likely to experience less relationship distress in facing infertility (Watkins & Baldo, 2004). For couples who are married, some may question the point of being married if they are unable to have kids, as children may have been central to their decision to get married, and they may struggle to redefine what it means to be a "family" (Daniluk, 2001). Further, each partner is likely to experience a range of difficult emotions, and they may find it hard to express these emotions or to support their partners in their experience when they are feeling emotionally drained themselves. It is common for individuals, particularly in relationships where the fertility issue is attributed to one partner, to feel they are to blame for the infertility, experiencing guilt and shame and for the other partner to experience anger or resentment toward them. Another strain on couples' relationships is the impact on sexuality.

Infertility may influence individuals' comfort with their bodies and sexuality, leaving them feeling dysphoria due to their bodies not functioning physiologically to the standard that they had expected. Medical treatments for infertility can lead to sex feeling like a procedure or chore, and this can have negative impacts on one's physical ability to have intercourse, particularly for women undergoing hormone treatments. Thus, couples may go through a shift from sex being a joyous and connective experience with their partners, to sex being a goal-oriented task that reflects their perceived inadequacies (Watkins & Baldo, 2004).

Although a full review of the medical procedures for infertility is beyond the scope of this chapter, the major treatments are briefly covered here, as counselors should familiarize themselves with the medical procedures their clients are undergoing in order to understand the implications of these procedures on clients' physical and mental health. For couples who seek medical intervention, the testing and medical treatments for infertility are often time-consuming, expensive, and invasive. The range of initial tests that couples endure to determine the cause of infertility can include ovulation testing for women, sperm count testing for men, hormone testing, and ultrasounds to check the physical condition of one's reproductive organs. Women are often asked to track their ovulation, as well as times of sexual intercourse. Postcoital tests also may be used to determine the amount of sperm in the cervical mucus, with the mucus having to be collected in a set time frame after intercourse (American Pregnancy Association, 2014).

These testing procedures can be emotionally draining and lead to sexual dysfunction, particularly as sex evolves from an act of intimate connection to a goal-oriented undertaking (Watkins & Baldo, 2004). If these less invasive tests return as normal, then more intrusive testing may be used to try to determine the cause of infertility, including hysteroscopy, laparoscopy, and an endometrial biopsy for women and a testicular biopsy in men (American Pregnancy Association, 2014). It is not uncommon for fertility tests to come back as inconclusive and have to be redone again, and for some couples, there may not be an identifiable physiological explanation for the infertility to guide medical treatment. Couples may grieve as they do not find the answers they are seeking through fertility testing and may lose trust in the medical system to help them become pregnant (Watkins & Baldo, 2004).

After a diagnosis of infertility, couples are faced with making difficult decisions about future-parenting options (Daniluk, 1991). It is important for counselors to know that 35% to 50% of couples who seek medical treatment to address fertility do not attain a pregnancy. Moreover, not all couples who experience infertility seek medical intervention (Griel & McQuillan, 2004). The main medical procedures to treat infertility include drug and hormonal therapies to stimulate ovulation, intrauterine insemination (IUI), and assisted reproductive technologies (ART), such as in vitro fertilization (IVF). Surgery may be recommended for both men and women to address structural issues or blockages that are effecting sperm production and ovulation (Office on Women's Health, 2012). Fertility medications for women may have physical side effects and risks, such as ovarian hyperstimulation syndrome (OHSS). As fertility medications affect women's hormones, they may lead to mood swings, depression, and physiological changes such as breast tenderness or vaginal dryness that may increase discomfort during sex (American Pregnancy Association, 2014), which can exacerbate distress throughout the treatment process.

IUI involves sperm (typically from their partner) being placed inside the woman's uterus to help with fertilization and is often used to treat fertility when the male factor is mild, there are problems with women's cervical mucus, or for couples with unexplained infertility. The average success rate of IUI is about 10% to 20% per cycle (American Pregnancy Association, 2014), and the average cost is $350 to $900, not accounting for medications and ultrasounds, which can increase the cost to several thousand per cycle. The most common ART utilized is IVF, in which the egg is removed from the woman's body and fertilized with sperm outside of the womb, then implanted into the woman's uterus. The average cost per cycle of IVF is approximately $12,400 (National Infertility Association, 2006), and the chance of achieving pregnancy through IVF is 40% in women under age 35 and 30% in women in their late 30s, with the effectiveness decreasing with age (Office on Women's Health, 2012). Fertility treatments, including medication therapy, increase the chance of multiple births. Thus, fertility treatments are costly, invasive, and variably effective, which can add to the distress couples experience as they invest their time and resources in treatment, become hopeful about getting pregnant, and then may experience multiple disappointments if treatments fail.

Clients experiencing infertility are likely to struggle with finding time to attend medical appointments, battling insurance companies to cover their medical procedures, and making financial decisions in regard to how much to spend on the treatments (Watkins & Baldo, 2004). Further, clients may hold ideological views that restrict their ability to undergo assisted reproductive technologies. For example, Catholic teachings often condemn masturbation, which is commonly used to obtain semen for infertility testing in men and for artificial insemination procedures. Counselors working with couples experiencing infertility should be aware of potential ideological conflicts and can help couples come up with strategies to complete medical procedures that do not violate their religious beliefs (e.g., obtaining semen samples during sexual intercourse instead of masturbation) (Burnett & Panchal, 2008).

Counselors can support couples experiencing infertility in multiple ways. Counselors should be aware that socioeconomic status can greatly affect which options couples can consider to address infertility, given that many of the treatments and the adoption process can be costly and time-consuming. Counselors can conduct an assessment of couples' resources before promoting options that may be unrealistic for the couple to pursue. Some couples may be able to define themselves as parents without a pregnancy through pursuing adoption or through taking a more active role in the lives of children of their family and friends. Moreover, helping clients express their grief is the first step to healing (Daniluk, 2001). Counselors can aid clients in redefining parenting for themselves through values clarification (e.g., "What does it mean to be a parent?"). Counselors can help promote clients' acceptance of what they cannot control and help clients focus on other life areas in which they may have more influence as they start to redefine their lives without children. A useful activity may be to have couples co-construct a five-year plan, one that includes children and one that does not. Although some clients may be resistant to considering a future without children, this activity can help couples face the reality of their situation, set limits on their pursuit of parenthood, and hopefully free them to rework their life goals and future plans together (Daniluk, 1991). Finally, the experience of infertility can feel traumatic for some partners, particularly women (Watkins & Baldo, 2004), and thus, partners may experience relationship wounds if they do not feel like their partners were emotionally supportive during the process. Counselors can support couples in healing their relationships (Daniluk, 1991); emotionally-focused couple therapy (Johnson, 2004) may be particularly suited to repair any rifts that occurred as each partner struggled to cope with the infertility experience.

Abortion

Approximately one-half of pregnancies in the United States are unintended, and 40% of unintended pregnancies are ended through abortion (Finer & Zolna, 2014). Since the Supreme Court ruled in favor of women having the right to abortion in the landmark case of *Roe v. Wade* in 1973, states across the country have passed laws to regulate the abortion procedure. At the time of this publication, 35 states mandate that women receive counseling before an abortion, with 27 of these states regulating the information given to clients during abortion counseling (Guttmacher Institute, 2014). Providing ethical services to clients seeking an abortion can be complicated by state laws that mandate content that is not relevant to a particular client or content that is skewed toward a particular outcome (Moore, Frohwirth, & Blades, 2011).

According to the American Psychological Association (American Psychological Association, Task Force on Mental Health and Abortion, 2008), women with unplanned pregnancies who have abortions are at no greater risk for mental health problems than women who carry their pregnancy to term and deliver their babies. Counselors should consider factors that can reduce one's ability to cope with the emotional effects of having an abortion, including a lack of social support, low self-esteem, strongly held religious or cultural beliefs that define abortion as immoral, poor expectations of the outcome after the abortion, reported feelings of guilt and shame, and an increased need for secrecy (Upadhyay, Cockrill, & Freedman, 2010).

Counselors working in any setting may encounter clients who are considering an abortion, who have already made the decision to abort, or who have had previous abortions. Given the stigma and controversy surrounding abortion, counselors need to be extra sensitive to engage in practices that best provide accurate information on abortion and to be respectful of clients' choices. Many counselors may hold strong personal values in regard to the morality of abortion and the rights and responsibilities of women seeking abortion as opposed to the rights of the fetus. Per the American Counseling Association Code of Ethics (2014), counselors should avoid imposing their values onto clients when counselors' values are inconsistent with clients' goals (A.4.b.). Exercise 4.3 is designed to help counselors consider their values and how they can respond ethically to clients considering abortion, as counselors need to first and foremost do no harm during these encounters. In cases in which counselors are unable to remain objective with a client due to their values on abortion, they can consider disclosing their personal views, as long as they do not attempt to coerce the client, and then refer the client to another practitioner who can be more respectful of the client's autonomy whether to choose an abortion (Millner & Hanks, 2002).

Abortion counseling typically includes three components: obtaining informed consent from the client before undergoing the abortion procedure, providing educational information about the abortion itself, and addressing clients' needs and feelings about the abortion as appropriate (Joffe, 2013). Abortion counseling differs from options counseling, which offers women information and support necessary to make a decision about their pregnancy, in that abortion counseling is for women who have already decided to have an abortion (Ely, 2007). Counselors should be aware that the majority of women, with estimates over 90%, have made up their minds to have the abortion before they set up an appointment with the clinic (Jones, Finer, & Singh, 2010; Moore et al., 2011). Thus, clients may not need help with the decision-making process and counselors should not assume this is the case. Counselors can conduct an interview with clients to determine what, if any, needs they have related to coping successfully with the abortion and can provide emotional support, skills-based interventions, and links to referral sources as necessary. The unique needs and ethical considerations for a client considering an abortion are demonstrated in the case study in Exercise 4.3.

Exercise 4.3

ETHICS DISCUSSION: COUNSELING A WOMAN CONSIDERING ABORTION

Jodie is a 21-year-old college student that you have been working with for eight sessions with the goal of reducing her binge-drinking behavior on weekends. Jodie has previously reported that she has made risky sexual decisions after a night of drinking, such as hooking up with strangers, not using condoms or other forms of protection, and forgetting to take her birth control when intoxicated. Jodie has been making progress toward her goals, reporting that she has not drunk more than 3 drinks in a night during the past 4 weeks. At your next session, Jodie arrives in tears, telling you that she found out that she is pregnant several days ago. Jodie has told her best friend, who has been supportive of her. Jodie says she does not know who the baby's father is and that she has been researching her options and is leaning toward getting an abortion and wants to use the counseling session with you to help her come to a more firm decision on whether or not to keep or terminate her pregnancy.

Directions: On your own or in a small group, reflect on the following questions:

- What are your personal values toward abortion? How would your values impact your response to Jodie?
- What are possible positive and negative psychological effects Jodie may experience if she chooses to have an abortion?
- Review the ACA Code of Ethics. What ethical standards apply to this case with Jodie, and how can you respond in a manner that is consistent with the ACA Code?
- How can the ethical principles of autonomy, fidelity, justice, beneficence, and nonmaleficence be used to choose interventions for Jodie?
- Once you have considered the four questions above, concretely detail what your next steps would be in working with Jodie if she were your client.

SUMMARY

In sum, clients' physical health is intertwined with their sexual health and overall experiences of sexuality in many ways. Counselors may lack an in-depth training in human anatomy and physiology, so they may require additional training and information to learn about physiological issues that impact their clients' sexual functioning. However, it is important for all counselors to consider ways that clients' physical health impacts their sexuality and to consider how to address physical health issues in the counseling process, such as referring clients for physical health care treatment when warranted. Given their professional background and training, counselors are in a prime position to help their clients consider ways to promote positive physical and sexual health, as well as to address the emotional and psychological impacts of physical health conditions that impact their sexuality.

KEYSTONES

- Anatomy and physiology can greatly impact individuals' sexual functioning as people's bodily health can determine their physical-arousal responses and ability to fully engage in sexual encounters with others.
- The treatment of sexuality issues is inherently a multidisciplinary process, and this has increasingly become the case with the increased medicalization of sex therapy.
- Engaging in sexual encounters, however, is not without risk to individuals' health, and thus, promoting responsible sexual-decision making is an integral part of helping clients develop and express their sexuality in healthy ways.
- Most sexual education programming focuses on adolescents and youth, but comprehensive education is also important for adults throughout their lifespan.
- Counselors are integral in the prevention of STIs by providing sexuality education, which promotes safer sex practices such as the reduction of partners and condom use, to decrease sexual risk-taking behaviors, as well as by providing information on the symptoms of STIs and when to get tested.
- Due to the amount of time spent and rapport built with clients, counselors may be in a better position than psychiatrists or physicians to detect sexual side effects.
- People who experience chronic illness or disabilities are more likely to experience problems with sexual functioning as their overall physiological health may be impacted.
- Promoting reproductive health is important to improve women's overall health and reduce the risk of infant and maternal mortality.
- Counselors need to have a basic understanding of the unique and complex stressors that clients with infertility face in their daily lives.
- Counselors working in any setting may encounter clients who are considering an abortion, who have made the decision to abort, or who have had previous abortions.

ADDITIONAL RESOURCES

- AIDS.gov (https://www.aids.gov/hiv-aids-basics/)
- American Pregnancy Association (http://americanpregnancy.org)
- American Sexual Health Association (ASHA; http://www.ashasexual health.org)
- Centers for Disease Control and Prevention (CDC; http://www.cdc.gov/sexualhealth/)
- International Association for the Study of Sexuality, Culture, and Society's (IASSCS) Archive for Sexology (http://www.iasscs.org/program/archive-sexology)
- Scarleteen: Sex Ed for the Real World (http://www.scarleteen.com)
- Planned Parenthood (http://www.plannedparenthood.org)
- World Health Organization (http://www.who.int/topics/sexual_health/en/)

Chapter 5

Lifespan Development and Sexuality

People are sexual beings. To deny our sexuality is to deny our humanity.
It should come as no surprise, therefore, that our sexuality begins the moment
of birth and lasts until our death, even if we live a long life.

—Bruce King & Pamela Regan, 2014, p. 248

How people understand and experience their sexuality develops and changes over the span of their lives. From beginning to end, people are sexual beings throughout their entire lifespan. People continue to grow and develop throughout their lives, and this chapter will provide a background of common sexuality-related developmental experiences and changes throughout the lifespan and will integrate developmental theories and research to aid in understanding the complex, integrated process and experience of living as a sexual being. As counselors, this should come as no surprise for us because development is a foundational part of our philosophy and background. In this chapter, we will explore the biopsychosocial nature of sexual development and walk through developmental stages from conception to older adulthood. After reading this chapter, readers will be able to do the following:

- Describe common sexuality-related experiences at different phases of life
- Apply developmental theories to conceptualize clients' sexuality-related concerns
- Discuss the ways that people ascribe meaning to their sexuality-related experiences across different phases of their lives

SEXUALITY ACROSS THE LIFE CYCLE: AN OVERVIEW

Sexuality is a foundational experience throughout the entire lifespan, from conception to death (DeLamater & Friedrich, 2002). Life is started by sexual activity when an egg and a sperm unite creating a zygote that forms into a human baby over approximately nine months. Even in the womb, babies' sexual organs form based on hormone levels (Hines, 2011). Interactions with and observations of parents, peers, and other people shape sexual norms through social and interpersonal interactions during childhood and adolescence. Sexual hormones become very important physiologically in adolescence (Hines, 2011), and adolescence is often when sexual experimentation and relationships commence. Young adulthood is often the period when more stable sexual relationships and practices are formed, though people are starting to form committed relationships and begin families at later ages in westernized societies than in the past (Arnett, 2000, 2011). Middle adulthood holds additional changes and transitions that impact sexuality, relationships, and family. In middle adulthood, people tend to become more committed to their self-image of whom they are sexually and how they will express that with others. Many societal expectations about sexuality change during middle and older adulthood, which tends to lead to a decline of public expressions of sexuality as age increases (King & Regan, 2014). Hormonal and physiological changes also occur throughout the lifespan and impact sexuality (Al-Azzawi & Palacios, 2009; Buvat, Maggi, Guay, & Torres, 2013).

Thus, changes throughout the lifespan contribute to an evolving sense of sexuality over time. While this can be especially true as people are transitioning from one developmental stage to another, other life changes can impact human sexuality. These changes can be internal, as in a change in how people view themselves, or they can be external, such as the beginning or ending of a significant relationship. As a context for understanding sexual development over time, this section integrates important theoretical perspectives from Erik and Joan Erikson, Carol Franz and Kathleen White, Sigmund Freud, and Jean Piaget to provide insights into each developmental stage (i.e., prenatal, childhood, adolescence, young adulthood, middle adulthood, and older adulthood) and to enhance knowledge and understanding of the biological, psychological, and sociological changes throughout the lifespan (see Table 5.1). These developmental influences are inherently intertwined with other areas of the Contextualized Sexuality Model addressed throughout the chapters of this book and are specifically described in this chapter.

Developmental stages describe experiences and developments that are commonly experienced throughout the lifespan, though they are not experienced and do not impact all people uniformly. Experiences throughout the development process, especially early in life, play a critical role in shaping sexual beliefs, experiences, satisfaction, conceptualizations, and expressions, as well as connections to oneself,

Table 5.1 Theoretical Tasks and Growth Throughout the Developmental Stages

	Erik Erikson's Psychosocial Stages and Associated Basic Strengths	Erikson's Radius of Connectedness in Significant Relations	Carol Franz & Kathleen White's Attachment Pathway Extension of Erikson's Psychosocial Stages	Sigmund Freud's Psychosexual Developmental Stages	Jean Piaget's Cognitive Developmental Stages
Childhood	1. Trust vs. Mistrust: Hope (infancy: 0–16 months)	1. Maternal Persons	1. Trust vs. Mistrust	Oral Stage (0–1 year)	Sensorimotor (0–2 years)
	2. Autonomy vs. Shame and Doubt: Will (early childhood: 17–36 months)	2. Parental Persons	2. Object & Self-Constancy vs. Loneliness and Helplessness	Anal Stage (1–3 years)	Preoperational (2–7 years)
	3. Initiative vs. Guilt: Purpose (play age: 4–5 years)	3. Basic Family	3. Playfulness vs. Passivity or Aggression	Phallic Stage (3–6 years)	Concrete operational (7–11 years)
	4. Industry vs. Inferiority: Competence (school age: 6–12 years)	4. Neighborhood, School	4. Empathy & Collaboration vs. Excessive Caution or Power	Latency Stage (6–puberty)	
Adolescence	5. Identity vs. Role Confusion: Fidelity (adolescence: 13–19 years)	5. Peer Groups and Outgroups; Models of Leadership	5. Mutually/Interdependence vs. Alienation	Genital Stage (puberty onward)	Formal operational (11+ years)
Young Adulthood	6. Intimacy vs. Isolation: Love (young adulthood: 20–40 years)	6. Partners in Friendship, Sex, Competition, and Cooperation	6. Intimacy vs. Isolation		
Middle Adulthood	7. Generativity vs. Stagnation: Care (adulthood: 40–60 years)	7. Divided Labor and Shared Household	7. Generativity vs. Self-Absorption		
Older Adulthood	8. Integrity vs. Despair and Disgust: Wisdom (old age: 60+ years)	8. "Mankind" "My Kind"	8. Integrity vs. Despair		

Sources: Erikson, 1997; Franz & White, 1985.

Exercise 5.1

Guided Reflection Activity: As we develop, we begin to form our sexual norms, expectations, and rules about what is healthy and when sexual thoughts, behaviors, and relationships should occur in different stages of life. What are your expectations about what types of experiences a person "should" have at each stage of life?

- What sexuality-related experiences do you think *should* begin during childhood?
- What do you think *should* begin to occur in adolescence?
- What do you think *should* occur in young adulthood?
- What do you think *should* occur in middle adulthood?
- What do you think *should* occur in older adulthood?
- Overall, how do you think your expectations about what *should* happen at each stage of life might impact your work with clients at each stage of life who are experiencing sexuality-related concerns?

---

significant others, family, friends, and people in general. While this chapter focuses on common sexual development, experiences, and transitions, it is important for counselors to keep in mind that they need to understand the experiences, meanings, and contexts for *each* unique client, as they are often different from client to client.

In the next section, we will progress through common stages of the lifespan to understand common sexual developmental milestones, experiences, and expressions at each stage of life. To help conceptualize and understand the complex biological, psychological, and social changes throughout the lifespan, it is helpful to think about your own development and the developmental processes of other people that you know. This may help you think about what happens in each stage, as well as what it is like to experience that stage and what meaning these experiences might have for your future clients. Readers are invited to complete Exercise 5.1 as one way to reflect on these processes.

SEXUALITY IN CHILDHOOD

Sexuality in the Prenatal Stage

Sexual development starts from very early in human physical development, and in fact, it starts when a sperm and egg meet. At that time, the genetic code for the developing zygote will come together and form 23 pairs of chromosomes, one of which contains the genetic information to determine biological sex (Feldman, 2014). The zygote will undergo the process of mitosis repeatedly to transform one circular cell into over a million cells in the shape of a human over the course of roughly 40 weeks. While you may be thinking that this development has little to do with sexuality, you may be shocked to find out that male fetuses have been discovered to have erections in utero (Calderone, 1983) and that baby girls can have vaginal lubrication shortly after birth (Langfeldt, 1981)! We are innately sexual beings, and this illustrates that we do not become sexual sometime around adolescence when sexual desires come more to the surface. Sexuality is a part of our lives from conception.

Biological sex is determined when the sperm and egg combine, and sexual development continues to occur while in the uterus of the individual's mother. The zygote makes significant physical changes to replicate itself and to form an embryo in two weeks, and the embryo continues to grow and begins to form a more human-like appearance as the embryo turns into a fetus eight weeks into development (Feldman, 2014). Around four months into development, the fetus has developed genital organs that are typically distinct enough for biological sex to be determined via ultrasound. The differentiation of genital cells into male or female genital organs is thought to be impacted by a hormone class called androgens that includes testosterone, which occurs in higher levels for males than it does for females during the 8th through 24th week following development (Feldman, 2014; Knickmeyer & Baron-Cohen, 2006). Biologically, there is significant sexual development that occurs in the prenatal stage of life.

A fetus can even begin to form, in a rudimentary way, socially, as the fetus is able to hear external sounds and feel her/his mother's movements in the third trimester of pregnancy (Gerhardt & Abrams, 2000). Shortly after birth, the infant is able to recognize his or her mother's voice and will pay her more attention than other people. The fetus can also interact with his or her mother, or some observant people, in rudimentary ways by moving around in the womb, especially as the time of the birth is approaching.

Apart from the interactions between child and mother, interactions with the child's future caregivers also impact their sexual development. The family in which a child is raised imparts numerous beliefs and norms about how the child should be, think, and act sexually and with regard to their gender. Oftentimes, the first questions asked of an expectant mother are, "When are you due?" and "Is it a girl or a boy?" Blue or pink gifts are often bought in American mainstream culture, and these reinforce the gender roles through specific colors in order to start the child off within the cultural expectations for what it is to be, a boy or a girl. Baby showers often provide gender-specific clothes, diapers and diaper accessories, books, bags, and toys that will later surround the child in her or his room and home. Beyond the material items, caregivers also talk together about how they will raise their child and develop plans for the child, even sometimes talking about possible future romantic relationships with friends' children. While this is usually said in jest, sexual orientation, gender identity, and sexual behaviors are presupposed, and these familial and cultural beliefs can have a longstanding influence on children's sexuality and gender development.

Infancy

There is widespread agreement that the relationship between parents or caregivers and the infant play a large role in the infant's development. The attachment relationship between the infant and the caregiver has a large impact on the rest of the development across the lifespan (Ainsworth, 1989; Ainsworth, Blehar, Waters, & Wall, 1978; Bowlby, 1969). John Bowlby and Mary Ainsworth focused on "attachment" relationships between the infant and mother, and many others have continued to find the significance of attachment relationships on the infant's life (Bartholomew & Horowitz, 1991; Bretherton, 1992; Coan, 2010; MacKinnon & Marcia, 2002; Mercer, 2011; Schore & Schore, 2008). Attachment styles are important in many psychological aspects, including affect and stress regulation, and researchers have even found that there are neurological differences based on different attachment styles (Coan, 2010; Mercer, 2011; Schmitt & Jonason, 2015). The benefits are associated with a type of attachment relationship called *secure attachment*, and the less positive outcomes come from the *insecure attachment* styles (dismissing, fearful, and preoccupied attachment). Chapter 8 focuses on sexuality and intimate relationships and further discusses the impact of attachment on sexual relationships.

Attachment research findings illuminate and support Sigmund Freud's and Erik Erikson's psychodynamic theoretical statements about early development. While Freud's and Erikson's theories differ significantly, they both agreed that development is significantly impacted in the first years of life through infants' relationships with primary caregiver(s). Therefore, sexual development in infancy (the oral and trust vs. mistrust stages) is heavily involved in and impacted by developing these attachment relationships with caregiver(s). Key perspectives on the development of sexuality in early childhood can be found in the work of Sigmund Freud, Erik Erikson (with updates by Carol Franz and Kathleen White), and Jean Piaget, and some of their major ideas are summarized in Boxes 5.1, 5.2, and 5.3, respectively.

If you watch a baby during the infancy stage, you are likely to notice a lot of objects going into the baby's mouth! Freud (1949; 1957) posited that babies do this because they are in the oral stage of psychosexual development where pleasure comes from the mouth. One of babies' first reflexes is the sucking reflex (Feldman, 2014), and drinking milk gives babies satisfaction from hunger, connection to mother or whomever is feeding the baby, and a good feeling. This behavior continues on for months as babies continue to put things in their mouths. They put all kinds of things, fingers and toes, keys and teethers, paper and clothes, and hair and string. Sexuality at this stage, according to Freud (Goldman & Goldman, 1982), is about receiving pleasure through the mouth and centers around oral stimulation and pleasure.

BOX 5.1   SIGMUND FREUD'S MODEL OF PSYCHOSEXUAL DEVELOPMENT

Freud (1949; 1957) postulated a model of *psychosexual development* with five overall stages, starting with the oral stage and moving through anal, phallic, and latency stages to finally arrive with the genital stage, starting in adolescence (see Table 5.1). Freud believed that sexual (and aggressive) drives (*libido* and *thanatos*, respectively) were the dominant urges that impacted people. These drives were toward receiving pleasure through specific areas of the body, which the stages are named after, and Freud thought that people could become *fixated*, or stuck, in any of these stages if they did not have their needs met in that area when they were in that developmental stage, which would have significant impact on the person's psychological symptoms and interpersonal behaviors (Freud, 1949; 1957; Goldman & Goldman, 1982). The id (following the pleasure principle), the ego (following the reality principle), and the superego would be used by people to navigate the developmental stages including developing romantic relationships in adolescence and adulthood.

BOX 5.2   ERIK ERIKSON'S MODEL OF PSYCHOSOCIAL DEVELOPMENT AND CAROL FRANZ AND KATHLEEN WHITE'S EXTENSION

While Freud's approach was focused on sexual urges and on a pathological way of looking at personality and development, Erikson shifted attention away from the body and more toward intrapersonal (internal) conceptualizations and interpersonal

(Continued)

(Continued)

(external/social) interactions. Erikson (1960) composed a model of *psychosocial development* based on the ego that instead highlighted the reality that challenges and conflicts occur as people conceptualize who they are and what their environment is like (*psycho-*) as they are living in a social and political world (-*social*). Erikson did not believe that our development was driven by sexual, bodily urges; rather, he believed that people's experiences within themselves and with others stimulated or stymied development as people navigated these common stage-oriented experiences as they move across the lifespan from birth to older adulthood.

Erikson's theory has been criticized as being overly focused on masculine development and not as applicable to feminine development and by being not as applicable for women as it is for men (Gilligan, 1987). Specifically, Erikson's psychosocial model seemed to focus more on an individual and internal development and did not take into account the impact of relational development or the differences between the biological sexes. To address these concerns and to expand the application of Erikson's model, Carol Franz and Kathleen White (1985) adapted Erikson's stages to encompass two pathways, an individuation pathway (mostly as Erikson posited) and an attachment pathway (with more focus on the interpersonal developmental aspects). Franz and White also drew from Robert Selman's work on perspective taking and Jean Piaget's work on cognitive development to describe a fuller conceptualization of psychosocial development.

BOX 5.3 JEAN PIAGET'S COGNITIVE DEVELOPMENT STAGES

Jean Piaget was a Swiss psychologist who focused on children's development and greatly added to our understanding of how children learn and think and the major ways that children think in different developmental stages (Feldman, 2014). From his observations, Piaget noted that children seem to learn through their experiences and filter what they are learning through previous experiences. He said that children form a *schema*, an internal, mental structure that recognizes and makes meaning from patterns of behaviors and said that schemas are modified and expanded with continued experiences. As Piaget continued to study how children think, he postulated that there were four distinct developmental stages, *sensorimotor, preoperational, concrete operational*, and *formal operational*, to understand how the world functions. Infants begin by thinking primarily through how they feel about a situation and by only taking into account their own perspective (sensorimotor stage), and then children move into thinking symbolically (preoperational stage), logically along with being able to take different perspectives (concrete operational), and abstractly, being able to combine, manipulate ideas (formal operational) (Feldman, 2014). Piaget's developmental model is a stage model, meaning that someone progresses from one to the next in order and without any variations and has impacted many subsequent developmental models, including Erikson's and Franz and White's models (Franz & White, 1985).

Early Childhood

Ideally, early childhood will start with a sense of trust in close relationships and with a secure attachment with significant others (parents or caregivers) that allows the child to have a secure base from which to explore the world during childhood. In early childhood, toddlers and young children explore their worlds, their bodies, and themselves to find that they are capable and that there is consistency in who they are and in the behaviors of those that they love. The successful outcome of this stage is to have a positive belief in oneself and sense that they can do things by themselves, while still being connected to significant others, particularly their parents or caregivers. Children go from being entirely dependent on caregivers in the beginning to being capable of doing all manner of tasks and relating with different people at the end of this stage.

Toddlers often want to be very independent, and many parents will tell you that their favorite word is "No!" Freud (1949; 1957) and Erikson (1968) both conceptualized this as a part of asserting themselves, and Freud focused on toilet training being a crucial focus of development and that the anal area was now the main source of pleasure. Specifically, toddlers are focused on the pleasure from excreting urine and feces and face social pressures to control those bodily functions (Goldman & Goldman, 1982). The outcome of the anal stage is important for sexual development because of how it impacts future interpersonal interactions, especially in romantic relationships. Therefore, how parents or caregivers help their children through this stage can have lasting impact. Stevenson (1996) discussed problems (such as anal expulsive or retentive characteristics) that can arise starting in this stage if the child's conflict of holding and releasing bodily excretions is not resolved well. Children face the challenge of relating with authority figures and managing the bodily sensations and functions of holding bodily excretions and releasing them at the right time and the right place. This is one of the earliest conflicts of trying to manage internal and external pressures and desires for how to best behave, and this sets a precedent for future sexual and non-sexual behaviors. How children interact with their parents or caregivers while going through the anal stage impacts how that person will continue to relate with authority figures and impacts personality characteristics including defiance, passive-aggression, meticulous care, and cooperation (Stevenson, 1996). Ideally, children will learn how to work collaboratively with people and will develop positive views of self and others that will support open and mutually affirming relationships later in life.

Erikson (1968) and Franz and White (1985) agreed with Freud that this was an important developmental period, though Erikson focused more on the child being an autonomous individual who can do things without help from others in the stage he called autonomy vs. shame and doubt. Erikson saw this early childhood stage as one full of exploration and challenges inherent in coming into contact with the environment. There are all kinds of new experiences and discoveries that can bring about problems. For example, the new ability to walk and move around brings about problems such as how to open doors to explore another room or the outside, or the ability to use hands and feet leads to wondering how to use a toy in a way to get a desired result, or even the ability to talk and use an expanding vocabulary can lead to figuring out how to com municate in ways that will lead to desired results. Through experiences and resolutions of conflicts in this early childhood stage, Erikson (1968) thought that children developed a sense of competency that would help children begin to take initiative in even more challenges and problems that arise from continued exploration in the upcoming "play age." Sexually, this sense of competency (or inadequacy) and openness (or reticence) can impact what the child later will be willing to explore and do alone or with partner(s). Further experiences also impact the sense of competence and openness to new experiences, though this early childhood stage is where this originates.

Franz and White (1985) noted that there is a new form of attachment where the young child has to be able to separate from the parent or caregiver and become more autonomous to successfully resolve the challenges in this developmental stage. Therefore, the child has to have some internal constancy of feeling connected to their parent or caregiver to be able to explore and do things separate from their parent or caregiver. This means that there is a stable internal connection and figure that allows the child to not feel alone and helpless while exploring. This forms a basis for having a relationship with a significant other in that the ability to esteem another person and to consider what another person would like is initiated during this stage (Franz & White, 1985). This process is not finished during this period, though young children are able to start to do this with some success and will continue to learn how to do this well into adolescence (McDevitt & Mahler, 1980).

As toddlers and young children are exploring and trying out new behaviors, they tend to engage in a lot of mimicry, especially of their parents or caregivers. They learn many behaviors, words, and meanings by observing their parents, with whom they have the most significant relationships at this time period (Erikson, 1997).

They will even start to display some sexual behaviors by holding hands, hugging, or kissing others during this time period. These behaviors tend to decrease as they move into elementary school and emerge again with the onset of sexual exploration and relationships. Also in the early childhood period, there are many biological changes and developments. Mobility significantly increases so that toddlers begin to walk at the beginning of this stage and, by the end, children are able to run, jump, and climb the world around them (Feldman, 2014). Toddlers and young children explore their world far more than the infants could and focus on the world around them and what they can do in it (Göncü, Mistry, & Mosier, 2000). So finding their abilities and their limits are an important part of this stage, though toddlers also explore their bodies. This includes genital exploration, and toddlers and young children have been found to stimulate their genitals and seem to experience pleasure, and it has been found that in some cultures mothers participate in stimulating male infants' genitals during some play situations (Goldman & Goldman, 1982). This exploration tends to lead into the Freud's phallic stage, where children are more interested in pleasure from their genitals than from their anal area.

Preschool Age

As early children near the age for school (typically five in Western societies), they move into another developmental stage where they begin to relate and play more with people their own age. Their most significant relationships shift from their parental figures to their basic family members (Erikson, 1997), though they develop the ability to engage in reciprocal play with their peers as well during this period (Göncü et al., 2000). How they play with their peers and family members, how they take initiative and handle guilt, and how they begin to understand and experience their genitals are important developmental aspects of the preschool ages.

Freud (1949; 1957) focused more on male psychosexual development and called this stage the phallic stage, and he has been criticized for this exclusive focus, and Neo-Freudians talk more about how it impacts both sexes (Goldman & Goldman, 1982; Hockmeyer, 1988; Weber, 1983). The Freudian concepts of penis envy, castration anxiety, and the Oedipus and Electra complexes are applicable starting in this developmental period, and the psychoanalytic concepts of womb envy and genital anxiety added by Karen Horney (1967) are also applicable. Psychoanalytic theory posits that during this stage children begin to focus more on their and others' genitals because they have found pleasure in touching themselves as they have begun to explore and discover their bodies. Because they become aware of the possibility of pleasure from their genitals, they are interested in the genitals, especially their parents or caregivers genitals, and the above Freudian and later psychoanalytic concepts emerged because of conflicts that this brings about for children and their families. Many have written on these terms and the theoretical importance that they have on people and sexuality (e.g., Grossman, 1986). The main shift here is that children notice and begin to experience pleasure from their genitals, which often leads to conflict with parents or caregivers.

In this stage, the conflict can be challenging for children and parents or caregivers to navigate. Children often are still trying to be autonomous by taking initiative, though they still have a lot to learn from their parents and need to rely on them for love, connection, wisdom, and advice for many years to come. They also are likely learning or have learned about different gender roles and identities (see Chapter 7 for a more detailed description of gender identity development and affective or sexual orientations). Exploration of these different roles and aligning with or against specific roles and identities occurs both inside and outside the family. From a psychoanalytic perspective, it is important for the child to successfully connect and identify with the same-sex parent to be able to continue to develop.

Exercise 5.2 provides readers with an opportunity to apply theoretical information about sexual development to a case study involving parents with young children.

At this stage, many children do show more interest in genitals, both their own and other people's, and some researchers have said that their exploration and touch of their genitals is enough to be called "the beginnings of masturbation" and "their earliest overt directly sexual activity" (Goldman & Goldman, 1982, p. 15).

Exercise 5.2

WORKING WITH PARENTS OF YOUNG CHILDREN

Parents or caregivers can often feel overwhelmed in their task of raising children. Children commonly push boundaries to find out what is and what is not acceptable behavior, and this leads parents and caregivers to finding appropriate education and discipline to help children to grow, learn, and behave in socially appropriate ways.

Imagine that you have a client (age 28) with a four-year-old boy in this play age period who is still not toilet trained and has pulled down his pants and peed in the play area at his preschool. The client is concerned about the boy and thinks that something needs to be done to "fix" him and his behavior.

Consider the following questions:

- How would you conceptualize the situation developmentally?
- What are some ideas for how you would work with the client and/or the boy in this situation?

Their explorations and touching of their genitals is an important part of sexual development, as this opens children up to sexual pleasure. Anything that they see or experience during this stage can strongly impact the future developmental trajectory of the person, including sexually explicit materials (Hunt & Kraus, 2009) and sexual experiences with others (Noll, Trickett, & Putnam, 2003; Tyler, Hoyt, Whitbeck, & Cauce, 2001). While those two examples commonly lead to more negative sexual outcomes and experiences, more benign experiences can also have a significant impact on sexual development. The accepted and common physical displays of affection in families during this stage can be transmitted from the parents to the children during this stage, and children can be seen to offer similar public physical displays of affection with family members and with peers (e.g. hugging, holding hands, kissing, etc.).

Psychosocially, this stage is about being able to take initiative and being able to enhance children's ability to connect and experience relationships with others (Erikson, 1968; Franz & White, 1985). Around the ages of four to six, children are in the pre-operational cognitive developmental stage and are able to think and put together more pieces of information. Children are able to start to use symbolic thinking and mental reasoning, which allows them to make connections with past experiences to understand current occurrences (Feldman, 2014). For instance, if a family member gets a coat out of the closet, the child might associate needing a coat with going to the park and ask if they are going to the park. This internalized way of thinking allows for the child to go beyond being an autonomous individual who can do things by her or himself into being someone who *starts* different actions or can set things into motion (Gibson, 2007). Specific to sexual development, this is a point in time where the child might start offering hugs or other symbols of affection.

Franz and White (1985) focused in a more attachment oriented way by talking about playfulness vs. aggression or passivity conflict in the preschool period. Because of the cognitive developments, in the play age children are also able to take on different roles with family members and with peers. By going beyond the sensorimotor stage focused on sensory input and emotional stimuli into the preoperational stage with some symbolic functioning, children can see other people as separate individuals, begin to form relationships with people who are not caregivers, and take on some different roles while playing with adults and peers. Children can begin to play together here in this stage, and in playing together, they can also start to play *with* each other (Franz & White, 1985).

If you watch children in this developmental stage, you may see that they can take on different roles in play (e.g., doctor and patient) so that both are taking initiative in their actions and both are responding to each other's actions. Ideally, the children will be able to play together, though it may be difficult to play with each other on an egalitarian basis, so aggression and/or passivity also happen while children are trying to learn to work and play *together*. This is another major developmental milestone that is important for sexual development. As sexuality is composed of both experiencing sexual bodily pleasure *and* the connection in engaging intimately *with* another person(s), this is a significant step and point where connection begins to occur (while lacking true intimacy at this stage) and a mutuality in relationships of peers can begin to develop. This is fostered and stimulated by having good role models to be able to see what mutuality, playfulness, and collaboration is like, as the work of Albert Bandura and other social learning scholars have shown us (Bandura, 1962, 1991), though parents are now sharing the function of showing children how to engage in healthy and socially appropriate behaviors as they begin to engage more with other family members and begin to engage with peers, especially as they begin to go to school.

School-Age Children

When children reach elementary school age, their experiential worlds are strongly impacted. Whereas the vast majority of their attention and connection was previously associated with their family, they often enter into a much larger world and more deeply and richly enter into a social world with many other people and more and more of a focus on the child to perform and be able to learn, to grow, and to be autonomous. Family continues to be important for the child and helps to provide some constancy as children adjust to the new conflicts, people, and places in their lives. Ideally, children have been able to develop trust, some autonomy, initiative, and playfulness and collaboration by having secure attachment relationships with parents/caregivers, seeing self in a positive way, and having some mutual and cooperative interactions and relationships with peers that will help support and stimulate continued growth.

There continues to be substantial cognitive growth during this period, and children enter into the concrete operational stage of cognitive development during school ages (6–12 years old), in which children can begin to use logical thought and can think less egocentrically (Feldman, 2014). School-aged children can start to reason and use logic to answer questions and solve problems in this stage of cognitive development and do not have to rely solely on memory and sensory information. They are also able to begin to take the perspective of others, which can lead to empathy and collaboration, a topic that we will address further later in this chapter.

Biologically, there is continued growth and development during this period, especially with gross and fine motor skills, muscle development, and overall strength (Feldman, 2014). There are both steady and relatively quick physiological changes during this stage. Children often experience growth spurts throughout this period and will continue as they enter into adolescence and puberty.

Between the phallic stage and puberty, Freud (1949, 1957) did not think that much psychosexual development occurred and named this stage the latency stage. The previous stages have introduced new bodily pleasure centers (oral, anal, and phallic/clitoral areas), though this stage does not offer a new one, and Freud saw that this was a time that those areas still brought about pleasure, though they took a backseat during the latency stage as children learned to control their sexual urges and behaved in socially appropriate ways (Goldman & Goldman, 1982). In psychoanalytic thought, the superego and ego are more fully developed, which shows a diminished interest in and expression of sexuality before puberty and the genital stage.

Psychosocially, there is much development and many changes as children enter and acclimate to school and working alone and with peers. Erikson (1968) focused on the development of industry, gaining ability, capacity, and productivity, during this developmental stage, and there certainly is a lot of ability gained during this time period! While most of the development in this period is not directly related to sexual development, the sense of self is relevant in how capable and acceptable one feels one is as that will impact how someone presents him- or herself in romantic relationships. A sense of capability is likely to lead to a sense of confidence later in life (Bandura, 1991), which will impact how that person will act based on her/his internal beliefs of self and others with more confidence leading to higher views of self and more initiative later in life. These internal working models can be modified and added to during this period of time and will serve as guides for future romantic and sexual interactions (Pietromonaco & Barrett, 2000).

Interpersonal interactions in the school age are also a relevant part of sexual development. Franz and White (1985) said that the main conflict and challenge during this developmental period is to become empathetic and collaborative or to have excessive caution or power. Because children begin to relate more with peers at school and in extracurricular activities, their experiences in peer relationships can help children learn how to take the perspectives of friends, connect with their emotional experiences, work with them together in play and school projects and experiences, and become less egocentric and self-focused. Ideally, this will lead to being able to develop empathy and the potential to work collaboratively with people, though the challenge here is similar to the previous psychosocial attachment challenge of being egalitarian in interpersonal interactions and not under or over exerting influence in those relationships (Franz & White, 1985). These relationships with peers before adolescence set the stage for how people will interact in future social and intimate relationships.

These childhood stages have a strong impact on the person's later stages of life. This is not to say that there cannot be changes to the internal working models, relationship roles and patterns, trust levels, and self-concept, as they can and do change, many times in the process of counseling. These beginning experiences, behaviors, and conceptualizations are impactful in shaping a person and set baseline expectations and beliefs for future experiences and relationships if left uncontested. Regardless, the past experiences help prepare people for what is to come, including the many sexual developmental changes that happen in adolescence. Readers are encouraged to complete Exercise 5.3 to reflect on the impact of sex education during the transition from childhood to adolescence.

Exercise 5.3

SEX EDUCATION IN CHILDHOOD AND/OR ADOLESCENCE

Depending on the state and school district, children or adolescents typically receive some form of sexual education in school. The depth, breadth, and specifics of information on sex and sexuality varies significantly and can be a hot topic for parents and students. Some parents and students want sex education to be very informative, while others do not think that sex education should be a part of what is covered in schools. When sex education is taught in schools, it most often covers information on birth control and sexually transmitted infections (STIs) and their prevention and treatment.

The age that children or adolescents become interested in knowing more about sex and sexual topics varies. Some children seem to be interested in sexuality from a young age (Klein, 1932), and many children have viewed sexually explicit material by the age of 11 (Family Safe Media, 2006; Hunt & Kraus, 2009). Sexual topics do come up in counseling children, especially when they have been exposed to sexually explicit materials and/or early childhood sexual experiences.

Consider your own views on sexuality education by reflecting on the following questions:

- When thinking about potential future sessions with clients, how comfortable do you currently feel talking with 7–10 year olds about sexual topics?
- What leads you to that level of comfort or discomfort?
- How comfortable would you feel talking with 11–13 year olds about sexual topics?
- What, if anything, would you say to the client's parents about the client's request to talk about sexual topics?
- To what extent (from none to fully) would you prefer to have the clients parent or guardian in the session when discussing sexual topics? Why?

SEXUALITY IN ADOLESCENCE

There are significant developments in sexuality during the adolescent years, including puberty, onset of romantic relationships, further sexual explorations, connection and disconnection in peer relationships, and a more developed identity in general and with regard to sexuality. This is often a turbulent time period in development because of the significant changes that happen in a few short years as adolescents turn their attention more toward peers and work to find their place in society and relationships, as well as because their bodies undergo significant physiological changes and become viable for procreation through the onset of puberty.

Biologically, puberty sends a flood of hormones through the body to help adolescents to move toward being physically, sexually mature. These hormones cause hair growth, breast development, sperm development, egg release, and hips opening along with vocal changes, growth spurts, and skin oil changes (Feldman, 2014; King & Regan, 2014). Puberty links childhood with young adulthood, and puberty has actually been occurring at younger ages in Western societies for over 100 years (Gluckman & Hanson, 2006; Marshall & Tanner, 1986; Okasha, McCarron, McEwen, & Smith, 2001) with an average range of onset in the United States currently being between 9 and 13 years old for females and between 10 and 15 for males (Centers for Disease Control, 2013b). Puberty typically begins with breast growth in females and testicular enlargement in males. Piaget's final cognitive development stage of formal operational also starts in adolescence (Gordon, 1990). In the formal operational stage, people are able to reason and use logic internally and are able to think abstractly (Inhelder & Piaget, 1958). This allows for logical experimentation and for utilization of a theory; for instance, an adolescent can try out new behaviors and use feedback to modify future behaviors.

Adolescence is a stage that brings focus back to the genitals based on the changes happening in male and female reproductive organs, as well as a stronger desire for sexual relationships and experiences, and Freud (1949; 1957) called this the genital stage. This is the last psychosexual developmental stage and results in sexual maturity from a psychoanalytic perspective. Ideally, an adolescent will have navigated the early stages, particularly the phallic stage, with little to no fixations or unresolved issues, as this will allow for greater capacity for romantic relationships. Otherwise, previous unresolved developmental challenges will reoccur in adolescence or subsequent developmental periods until they are resolved.

For Erikson (1968), adolescence was a very important developmental period and was the time frame for the identity vs. role confusion conflict. Identity development occurs on many levels, including romantic and sexual identities. To Erikson (1968), an

> optimal sense of identity . . . is experienced merely as a sense of psychological
> wellbeing. Its most obvious concomitants are a feeling of being at home in one's

body, a sense of 'knowing where one is going,' and an inner assuredness of anticipated recognition from those who count. (p. 165)

Adolescents do not achieve an optimal sense of identity, as it takes time and experiences to be able to develop an optimal sense of identity, although certainly identity development is an ongoing process during adolescence. Identity is who you are known as *personally* and *socially*, and identity includes how someone conceptualizes her- or himself as well as who others see that person as. The previous relationships with family members and peers can help support and affirm a sense of identity, though *identity formation*, Erikson's (1968) third and final developmental process of developing ego identity, has to occur by receiving feedback from others as adolescents are exploring and experimenting with different roles and/or personas.

Erikson (1968) saw identity formation as beginning in adolescence when the benefits of identification (the using and taking on roles without fully internalizing those roles into who one is) ends and by internalizing some selected previous identifications as who one is in a particular social environment. These societies or subsocieties surrounding the adolescent give feedback to the individual that will support or challenge the adolescent's sense of identity (Erikson, 1968). There is often some power struggle with adults in this process as the adolescent is in the midst of finding and asserting her- or himself as a separate, distinct person with a unique personality. This process describes the general identity developmental process, although it is applicable to the development of a sexual identity. When an adolescent was a child, there were likely ways that he or she interacted with individuals that he or she was attracted to based on ways that role models, especially parents, have done before. When in adolescence, that person can begin to develop his or her own specific styles and approaches in interactions with people that he or she is attracted to, which may be similar to or different than past ways of relating to others. When the adolescent is taking these steps, she or he is often met with some resistance, whether by parents, peers, or the romantic interest, which can lead to persistence, anxiety and/or discouragement, or looking for other ways and a new style to approach sexual and romantic relationships. This is clearly an involved process, and sexual identity often does not have a smooth developmental process. Two important factors in this process are the exploration and commitment of identities and styles (Marcia, 1964, 1966).

In the search for identity, the two most useful concepts in understanding where a person is in the process seem to be the exploration of different roles, styles, or identities and the commitment to identity (Kroger, Martinussen, & Marcia, 2010). Identity researchers have consistently drawn upon those two factors to understand where someone is in the identity development process and to identify their levels of wellness and psychological distress. This method comes from the work of James Marcia (1964, 1966) who extended Erikson's work on the identity vs. role confusion stage. These factors are especially relevant to sexual development as adolescence is a time when many people explore their sexual identity by trying out new behaviors and engaging in romantic relationships for the first time. The exploration of different sexual behaviors and different ways to interact in romantic relationships allows for the development of an understanding of who one is sexually, how to interact with a romantic and/or sexual partner, and what things are sexually pleasing and desirable. The exploration can then lead to a commitment to a sexual identity or understanding of oneself in regard to connecting with romantic or sexual partner(s) and how one prefers to behave sexually. This exploration, in adolescence or other developmental stages, typically stimulates sexual development in interpersonal, behavioral, and affective aspects.

Franz and White (1985) described the adolescence, psychosocial developmental stage as being mutuality and/or interdependence vs. alienation, as development deepens the empathic and collaboration connections from childhood to being able to depend on and have others depend on them. Adolescence typically is the onset of many sexual behaviors and for developing romantic relationships. Franz and White (1985) described that these sexual behaviors and relationships along with the cognitive development of the formal operational stage allow for the possibility of really connecting deeply with others like no preceding stage. Ideally in adolescence, there is the ability to see the self and other, as well as the relationship between the two at a complex and nuanced level that can lead to successful communication and negotiation in a mutual relationship that allows both people in the relationship to be able to be themselves. This leads to a much deeper connection than previously experienced and allows for an intimate union of the persons. This level of connection can resemble a symbiotic relationship where each organism is interdependent on the other to fully function and thrive in life. This is an ideal level of intimacy and can lead to greater satisfaction sexually through being able to deeply communicate and experience self and other. To be able to get to this depth of relationship, Franz and White (1985) said that a person would need to be able to "(a) facilitate negotiation, (b) tolerate a broad range of emotions, (c) give and take, and finally, (d) perceive accurately, understand compassionately, and take action on the feelings of self and others" (pp. 252–253). While this level of sexual and relational development is possible in adolescence, it is not often reached by the end of adolescence and is not always reached in adulthood either.

SEXUALITY IN ADULTHOOD

In all of the developmental stages, interpersonal relationships with significant others (whether parents or caregivers or romantic and sexual partners) are important, if not vital, to continued healthy sexual development. The psychosocial developmental conflicts and challenges (in both the individuation and attachment pathways) in young adulthood are both centered on deepening connection in a committed relationship. Both Erikson's (1950, 1968) original and Franz and White's (1985) extension of this developmental stage are called intimacy vs. isolation, and both focus on the importance of the connection and attachment in young adulthood. The rest of this section focuses on the developmental process for individual adults; for related aspects of couple relationships, see Chapter 8 on Sexuality and Intimate Relationships.

Young Adulthood

In the intimacy vs. isolation stage, Erikson (1963) saw intimacy as the capacity and ability to commit to another person even at considerable cost to one's self. There is a vulnerability and selflessness that is expected as one draws close to another and sacrifices a part of his or her self to enter into a deeper relationship with another person and to form a tight bond and connection with them. Erikson (1963) viewed identity as a necessary precursor for intimacy for young adults in that an individual would be able to know oneself to be able to share that with another person and to be able to know who the other person is (Pittman, Keiley, Kerpelman, & Vaughn, 2011). It also logically follows that once a person understands who she or he is that the person will be sharing that with another person. In this sharing of oneself, Erikson (1965) expected that sexual and romantic relationships would form and that there would be sexual pleasure as well as relational closeness. In healthy sexual-intimate relationships, Erikson thought that intimacy included having or working toward management of work, recreation, and other possible sexual relationships and toward mutual trust with a loved partner so that they could both experience orgasms and be open to procreation and raising offspring together. Intimacy, to Erikson, included organizing life toward joining together and forming a relationship to extend throughout the rest of the lifespan with another person that is partially supported by the partners enjoying sexual pleasure with each other.

Erikson (1968) did not discuss the exact mechanisms of how this would happen much beyond the expectation that people would look for intimacy with others after knowing oneself (successfully establishing an identity). Many others (Arseth, Kroger, Martinussen, & Marcia, 2009; Beyers & Seiffge-Krenke, 2010; Montgomery, 2005; Seginer & Noyman, 2005) have written about both of these psychosocial stages (identity and intimacy), and several have connected Bowlby's and Ainsworth's work on attachment to the intimacy stage (Cassidy, 2001; Morris, 1982; Pittman et al., 2011; Reis, 2006). The distinct nature of identity and intimacy has been questioned with a more integrated perspective of these two psychosocial developmental conflicts being offered. Some researchers have focused on the identity development process being truly a psycho*social* process that implies significant others having a strong influence on identity development and see that identity development is impacted by the intimacy with significant others (Adams & Marshall, 1996; Fitch & Adams, 1983; Kacerguis & Adams, 1980). These findings are consistent with the new term and developmental period in Western societies of emerging adulthood where identity development, search, and crisis is extended well into the twenties (Arnett, 2000, 2010; Luyckx, Soenens, Vansteenkiste, Goossens, & Berzonsky, 2007; Montgomery, 2005). So, modern young adults in Western societies are often working through the tasks of identity and intimacy, which impacts the development of their sexual relationships.

Erikson's conceptualization also did not take into account sexual and gender orientations other than heterosexual and traditional gender roles (males being masculine and females being feminine). What researchers and theorists have found out is that young adults have already had sexual attractions well before the identity and intimacy developmental periods (McClintock & Herdt, 1996) and that intimacy does not depend on being in heterosexual relationships (Josephson, 2003). Erikson (1997) somewhat recognized the later finding in saying that the significant relationships in this period are with "partners in friendship, sex, competition, and cooperation" (p. 32), though he did not see that nonheterosexual relationships have relatively similar dynamics and outcomes as heterosexual relationships (Kurdek, 1998) or that people can choose to not partner and be abstinent. Young adults can fall into many different relationship categories (celibate, committed relationship, dating, single, etc.) and sexual orientation (bisexual, heterosexual, homosexual, transsexual, etc.) typically is stable by young adulthood. Sexual orientation can fluctuate for some people in and after this stage (Diamond, 2003; Diamond & Wallen, 2011; Savin-Williams & Ream, 2007), though to whom someone is attracted does not tend to vary much (Savin-Willaims & Ream, 2007).

Often sexual relationships further develop in this stage in both intimacy and sexual behaviors. The majority of young adults have engaged in both oral and vaginal sex (Herbenick, Reece, Schick, Sanders, Dodge, & Fortenberry, 2010), and vaginal sex is very high (reported at about 99%) in heterosexual couples who have been with their partner for at least 3 months (Kaestle & Halpern, 2007). At the same time that sexual activity is increasing, young adults report that there is a desire for emotional connection with their partner (Garcia, Reiber, Massey, & Merriwether, 2012).

As sexual relationships develop, attachment plays an important role and part. Ainsworth (1989; Ainsworth et al., 1978) initially described different styles of attachment, and they have been furthered explored and defined into four current attachment styles based on the amount of anxiety and avoidance inherent in relationships with significant others. Secure attachment is considered the best attachment style that associates most closely with healthy and satisfying relationships and has low levels of attachment-related anxiety and avoidance (Ainsworth et al., 1978).

Each of these attachment styles will impact the formation and maintenance of sexual relationships. Attachment style is developed early in life, and internal working models drive conceptualizations of self, significant others, and the relationship between self and significant other(s) (Bowlby 1969; Pietromonaco & Barrett, 2000) and therefore impact sexual relationships. Internal working models and attachment styles *can* be changed; different life circumstances and new relationship interactions can challenge existing internal working models and lead to changes in attachment style and internal working models at this stage or in other developmental stages (Pietromonaco & Barrett, 2000). Counselors often help their clients to develop more secure attachments and to develop deeper intimacy with their partners.

Young adults (defined here as between the ages of 20 to 40) typically begin to have children if they are going to have any children. American women are most likely to give birth in their 20s or 30s, and American men are also most likely to father children in this age span (Centers for Disease Control, 2013c). Becoming a parent typically lowers the amount of sexual activity that is engaged in as well as sexual contentment for at least the first four and a half years (Ahlborg, Rudeblad, Linnér, & Linton, 2008), though many people experience renewed sexual satisfaction sooner than that (Boroumandfar, Rahmati, Farajzadegan, & Hoseini, 2010). Behavioral changes with a child including less sleep and free time, body and body image changes (Olsson, Lundqvist, Faxelid, & Nissen, 2005), and increased stress may require changes in couples' sexual life while their child(ren) are younger.

Middle Adulthood

For adults aged 40 to 60, defined here as middle adulthood, sexual activity tends to decrease, though middle-aged adults continue to engage in sexual behaviors (Herbenick et al., 2010). A large percentage of people continue to have sexual intercourse, and almost one third of adults aged 40 to 80 said that they engaged in sexual intercourse at least once a week (Laumann, Glasser, Neves, & Moreira, 2009). Sexual satisfaction is often high in middle adulthood, and sexual satisfaction has been found to be correlated with more frequent vaginal intercourse, especially when there is mutual orgasm between partners (Costa & Brody, 2012) and with relationship satisfaction (Byers, 2005).

Erikson (1963) and Franz and White (1985) have the same psychosocial stages for all of adulthood, and in middle adulthood, they see that the main development conflict is generativity vs. stagnation. In this stage, there is a desire to see outcomes for one's actions. This includes having children and seeing them do well, along with wanting to be productive and creative (Erikson, 1997). Because emotional intimacy and connection is often already established going into this stage, the slight decrease in sexual activity from the 20s and 30s may be due to trying to be productive and creative in non-sexual ways.

This may also lead to either solidifying a family during this stage or to leaving current relationship(s) and starting over with new committed relationships. In the United States, the divorce rate is around 45% (Amato, 2010), though the divorce rate for 50 to 64-year-olds has almost doubled recently (Brown & Lin, 2012). Of the people that divorce, most of them remarry, and often they remarry within 2 to 5 years (DeWitt, 1992). As relationship dissolution is currently easier to measure in heterosexual relationships due to published divorce rates than homosexual or bisexual relationships, it is unclear if people of different sexual orientations have similar or different stability rates in their relationships, although some researchers have suggested that nonheterosexual relationships have a somewhat lower stability rate due to having less barriers to leaving the relationship (Kurdek, 1998; Peplau & Fingerhut, 2007). Based on this information, it is common for sexual relationships to begin, continue, and/or end during middle adulthood (Amato, 2010; Brown & Lin, 2012) with productivity focused on existing romantic relationships or put into new relationships.

During this developmental period, physiological changes that impact sexual development are also likely to occur. Around 80% of women experience menopause between the ages of 44 to 55 (Al-Azzawi & Palacios, 2009), which is when women have their last menstruation cycle. There are often changes for years before and the year after menopause, including hot flashes, decreased estrogen, fatigue, and decreased vaginal lubrication (King & Regan, 2014). These can produce personal and interpersonal challenges, and medical treatment may help alleviate some of the symptoms of menopause. Despite these challenges, many women have reported no change in interest in sex due to menopause (Segraves & Segraves, 1995), and some women have reported increased interest in sex (Dillaway, 2005). Men do not have such a profound change in their hormones, though they do gradually have lower testosterone levels. Only 20% to 50% of men aged 55 have below normal testosterone levels for young-adult males (Buvat et al., 2013). Some men also experience lower penile stiffness and volume, though they can still experience and enjoy sexual activity into older adulthood (Blanker et al., 2001).

Older Adulthood

Sexuality continues in older adulthood, and though there are some sexual challenges that often occur as one ages, both sexual activities and relationships can flourish in older adulthood. Researchers have consistently found that relationship status, mental and overall health, and consistent sexual activity are linked with sexual satisfaction for older adults (Matthias, Lubben, Atchison, & Schweitzer, 1997; Lindau et al., 2007; Schick et al., 2010).

Matthias et al. (1997) found that almost 30% of older adults had engaged in sexual activity in the past month and that 67% were satisfied with their current level of sexual activity. Similarly, Schick et al. (2010) found that 20% to 30% of adults remained sexually active even into their 80s! In both studies, the researchers found that sexual activity did tend to decrease with age and that relationship satisfaction was related to frequency of sexual activity. Older adults have reported challenges for staying sexually active, including low sexual desire, decreased vaginal lubrication, and unable to orgasm for women and erectile difficulties for men (Lindau et al., 2007). Despite these difficulties, only some older adults have sought medical or other help for their sexual challenges (Lindau et al., 2007). Also, some older adults may not be aware of some of the health concerns and need for protection from STIs. Therefore, it can be very important for counselors to educate their older adult clients about how to protect themselves from STIs.

Psychosocially, older adults are in the integrity vs. despair and disgust stage where ideally integrity will help bind together one's life and a connection with others that leads to wisdom (Erikson, 1997). In the last stage of life, older adults can look back over their lives and also the lives of others that they've shared experiences with and see the interconnectedness of life. They may be able to look at their children's lives and see patterns and relevant issues because of the experiences that they or others that they know have had. There is a wholeness characterized by integrity that allows one to see self more fully as well as see the larger, global or cosmic picture (Schroots, 1996; Sneed, Whitbourne, & Culang, 2006). This includes being able to see significant others more clearly and/or fully and can enhance sexual emotional intimacy. Typically, older adults have more free time, which also allows them to spend more time with significant others and engage in sexual and non-sexual leisure activities together.

SUMMARY

Sexual development starts at the beginning of life and ends at the end of the lifespan. People undergo significant changes across developmental stages, and sexuality looks different in each of the developmental stages with different changes, challenges, experiences, and growth. It is important to understand common sexual developmental stages and to realize that each person's experiences will be different and to take that into account when working with a client regarding sexual issues and to assess the client's own perceptions, feelings, and meanings. To conclude this chapter, Exercise 5.4 provides an opportunity to apply the information covered in this chapter to your own sexual development over time.

Exercise 5.4

CASE CONCEPTUALIZATION ON SEXUAL DEVELOPMENT

It is important to think developmentally about someone's sexual history and experiences to understand what has happened in their sexual lives, what impact those experiences have had on her or him, and what meaning he or she attributes to those sexual aspects of his or her life. To help develop an understanding of someone else's sexual development, you are encouraged to think about your own sexual development and to understand and put into context your own history and experiences. When thinking back on your own sexual development, what are the major developmental experiences that you had in each of the developmental stages, and what impact have they had on you and/or meaning have they had in your life? For the stages that you have not yet experienced, write in how you think that you might be impacted in that stage(s).

Developmental Stage	Experience(s)	Impact/Meaning
Prenatal	_____	_____ _____
Childhood		
Early	_____	_____ _____
Play	_____	_____ _____
School	_____	_____ _____
Adolescence	_____ _____	_____ _____ _____
Young Adulthood	_____ _____	_____ _____ _____
Middle Adulthood	_____ _____	_____ _____ _____
Older Adulthood	_____	_____ _____

KEYSTONES

- People's experiences and understanding of their sexuality change and develop over their lifespan.
- Developmental theories provide a context for understanding the transitions that people may face related to their sexuality across their lifespans.
- Although developmental theories suggest common experiences at developmental stages, each individual is unique and may have different experiences at each stage.
- At each stage, physiological changes will interact with psychological and relational ones to impact clients' sexuality.

ADDITIONAL RESOURCES

- Center for Disease Control and Prevention Growth Charts. (http://www.cdc.gov/growthcharts/).
- Feldman, R. S. (2014). *Development across the life span* (7th ed.). Upper Saddle River, NJ: Pearson.
- King, B. M., & Regan, P. C. (2014). *Human sexuality today* (8th ed.). Upper Saddle River, NJ: Pearson.

Chapter 6

Sexuality and Mental Health

Sex is virtually all in the head anyway.

—John Cloud (2010)

Sexuality and mental health have a dynamic, bidirectional relationship, in which changes in one area directly impact the other (Bitzer et al., 2008; Levine, 2009). Because sexuality is such a central part of people's lives, there are many mental health-related factors and influences on our sexuality, including how we choose to think, feel, and behave sexually. This chapter delves deeper into the intersections between sexuality and mental health. After reading this chapter, readers will be able to do the following:

a. Understand common processes involved in sexual decision-making
b. Describe the impacts of mental health disorders and substance abuse and dependence on sexual functioning
c. Understand the diagnostic criteria for sexual dysfunctions that clients may experience
d. Identify the impact of sexual trauma on sexuality and sexual functioning

SEXUAL DECISION MAKING

Although sex is often portrayed in the American media as spontaneous, passion- and lust-driven, and without much forethought or planning, people actually engage in significant decision-making processes to help them consider their sexual behaviors, attitudes, and activities, including when to have sex and what kind of sex to have. While some of those thoughts, feelings, and behaviors act at an unconscious level, many sexuality-related decisions are made through intentional processes. In this section, we explore the processes through which people make decisions with regard to their sexual activities. These influences are important for counselors to understand because clients' confidence in their sexual decision-making abilities may impact their overall sense of satisfaction and confidence with regard to their sexual functioning. There is not one decision-making process that everyone uses in deciding whether to engage in sexual behaviors, and if so, in which sexual behaviors they want to engage (Abraham & Sheeran, 1993; Christopher & Cate, 1984; Juhasz, 1975; Oswalt, 2010). Many factors impact people's decisions about sex, and this section reviews a number of the factors that have been identified in previous research (Oswalt, 2010).

Relational Concerns

Relational concerns, including the amount of love and connection in a relationship, are an important factor in people's decisions whether to engage in a particular sexual activity (Browning, Hatfield, Kessler, & Levine, 2000; Christopher & Cate, 1984; Oswalt, 2010). How much people love and like their partners, partners' feelings toward each other, their level of relational commitment, the length of their relationship, and their thoughts of continued romantic involvement with their partners are all relevant relational concerns and impact decisions about engaging in sexual activities (Christopher & Cate, 1984; Oswalt, 2010).

Social Norms and Pressure

Peer pressure and family expectations also impact sexual decision-making. If peers are engaging in sexual activities, then adolescents may be more likely to engage in those same activities (Romer et al., 1994; Rosenthal, Lewis, & Cohen, 1996). What people think that their peers are doing, especially in adolescence, impacts which sexual activities they are more likely to consider engaging in. Also, family expectations and history impact sexual decision-making (Paul, Fitzjohn, Herbison, & Dickson, 2000). The impacts of social pressure and norms are most pronounced during adolescence but often continue to young adulthood (Regan & Dreyer, 1999).

Concerns About Risks Associated With Sexual Activity

Many sexual activities carry some risks, and concern about these risks is another factor in sexual decision-making. Sexually transmitted infections (STIs), including the human immunodeficiency virus (HIV), and pregnancy are common concerns and risks in having unprotected sex (Levinson, Jaccard, & Beamer, 1995; Oswalt & Wyatt, 2013).

Developmental Stage

Three groups of researchers (Oswalt, 2010; Randolph & Winstead, 1988; Sanderson & Cantor, 1995) have all found that people who are more focused on their own identity (i.e., during the identity vs. role confusion stage) choose to engage in sexual activities for different reasons than people who are more focused on creating intimacy (i.e., during the intimacy vs. isolation stage). In other words, sexual decisions seem to be made for different reasons dependent on the current developmental processes at play.

Amount and Quality of Previous Sexual Experience

The number of previous sexual partners someone has had also has been shown to impact sexual decision-making. Christopher and Cate (1984) found that people who have had only one sexual partner choose to engage in sexual activities most strongly because of relational reasons (e.g., out of affection and to move toward a future with their partner), while people who have had more than one sexual partner engage in sexual activities most strongly because of sexual arousal and receptivity. Other researchers have found a similar relationship between increases in the number of sexual partners and increases in the likelihood of engaging in casual sex (Mikach & Bailey, 1999; Ott, Millstein, Ofner, & Halpern-Felsher, 2006). The quality of previous sexual experiences also matter; if someone has had positive past experiences, then she or he is more likely to engage in the future and vice versa. However, there is not a perfect correlation as might logically be expected based on the quality of past sexual experiences. People who have experienced past sexual trauma would be expected to not engage or less frequently engage in sexual activities; however, there is not a uniform response for people with a history of sexual trauma (Briere & Runtz, 1987).

Expectations for Physical Pleasure

Societal norms hold that men are primarily motivated to engage in sexual activities in order to experience physical pleasure. Women are often not thought to hold physical pleasure as such a high priority, and some researchers have found that this factor is more important for males (Browning et al., 2000; Hill & Preston, 1996). However, other researchers have found that both males and females desire the physically pleasurable aspects of sex (Oswalt, 2010; Randolph & Winstead, 1988; Rosenthal et al., 1996; Traeen & Kvalem, 1996; Wyatt, 1997). While it is not clear if there are differences between the sexes, it is clear that physical gratification and pleasure of sexual activities impacts sexual decision-making. Of course, not all people believe that sex will be a pleasurable experience, and people also may hold negative expectations about the physical sensations (e.g., pain) that they may experience during sexual activities. Some people experience pain during intercourse (e.g., dyspareunia), and some females may begin to experience pain during intercourse as they go through menopause (Dennerstein, Dudley, & Burger, 2001). For these people, negative expectations about pain during sexual activities factors into their sexual decision-making.

Future Plans and Goals

Some adolescents and college students choose not to engage in some sexual activities because they would impact some of their future plans and goals for themselves and their future families (Monsen, Jackson, & Livingston, 1996; Moore & Davidson, 2006; Oswalt, 2010; Young, Denny, & Spear, 1999). Similarly, committed partners may engage in specific sexual activities (including the use and non-use of birth control methods) based on their plans to try to have or to not have children, and partners may talk about whether or not they would like to have a baby in the near future and make sexual decisions regarding type of sexual activities and whether they will use birth control means (Frost & Darroch, 2008; Zolna, Lindberg, & Frost, 2011).

Biological Sex

Biological sex has also been found to impact sexual decision-making (Browning et al., 2000; Christopher & Cate, 1984; Hill & Preston, 1996; Oswalt, 2010; Randolph & Winstead, 1988). For example, Oswalt (2010) investigated differences between males and females in the above factors of sexual decision-making and found differences between all factors except for relational concerns. Females had higher scores than males on concern about risks associated with sexual activity, future plans and goals, and developmental stage, and males had higher scores than females in social norms and pressure, expectations for physical sensation, and amount of previous sexual experience in Oswalt's sample of college students.

Celibacy and Abstinence

While most people choose some degree of sexual activity, other people make sexual choices for abstinence and celibacy (Abbott, 2000; Sobo & Bell, 2001). Approximately 1% of people choose to be celibate over the course of their lifespans, and many people experience periods of abstinence in their lives (Siegel & Schrimshaw, 2003). Celibacy is defined here as being permanently single across the lifespan, and abstinence is used for the choice of not engaging in oral, vaginal, or anal sex for a period of time. The time periods of abstinence vary depending on the person (i.e., some choose abstinence before being in a committed relationship and/or marriage and some choose abstinence during or after being in a committed relationship), and around one-sixth of 18 to 29 year olds (Laumann et al., 1994; Leigh, Temple, & Trocki, 1993) and around one-third of 60 to 69 year olds (Leigh et al., 1993; Marsiglio & Donnelly, 1991) have been sexually inactive over the past year. Donnelly (1993) found that sexual inactivity was correlated with lower quality of sexual relationship, little to no shared activities with partner, and having children; and Donnelly, Burgess, Anderson, Davis, and Dillard (2001) found that shyness, difficulty relating to others, and negative body image were related to abstaining from sexual relationships. In addition, some people have received biological or medical diagnoses (like HIV) that lead people to choose abstinence, though not all who have received such a disorder choose abstinence (Carey, Carey, Maisto, Gordon, & Vanable, 2001).

Celibate individuals, on the other hand, are not sexually inactive because of these difficulties; they purposefully choose to be single and to not engage in partnered sexual activities (Sobo & Bell, 2001). While many people might think of clergy when thinking about celibate people, many lay people are also celibate. People across history have chosen to be celibate for different reasons including sociopolitical, personal, and/or religious reasons (Abbott, 2000; Sobo & Bell, 2001). Some, such as Joan of Arc, choose celibacy to make a sociopolitical statement and to move toward societal change. Others have chosen celibacy because of personal reasons such as controlling sexual energies or not making attachments associated with sexual partnerships. Some religious orders demand celibacy as part of the vows to become a leader in the religious community, and many cultures have had shamans also practicing celibacy for spiritual reasons (Abbott, 2000; Sobo & Bell, 2001). When working with a client who is celibate or abstinent, it is important not to immediately assume a reason for celibacy or abstinence.

Summary

There are many factors that impact how people make decisions about their sexual activities and experiences, and these factors do not uniformly impact everyone's sexual decision-making. People make sexual decisions for varying reasons and are affected by their internal rationale and by their social groupings to various degrees. Age and developmental level, amount of sexual experience, love and connection in a sexual relationship, and amount of current desire for children have all been shown to directly correlate with the likelihood of engaging in sexual activities. At the same time, sexual activities require some degree of choice (except in the cases of rape and sex when inebriated) and decision-making. Another influence on sexual decision-making is found in a person's overall mental health, which may be impacted by the presence of mental health symptoms or disorders, which is addressed in the next section.

SEXUAL IMPLICATIONS OF MENTAL HEALTH DISORDERS

When people develop mental health symptoms—such as depression, anxiety, psychosis, or cognitive problems—there are often corresponding changes in their sexual functioning (Davison & Huntington, 2010; Dobkin, Leiblum, Rosen, Menza, & Marin, 2006) and their romantic relationships (Shaver, Schachner, & Mikulincer, 2005). Mental health symptoms also can have indirect impacts on sexual functioning. For example, depression is connected to self-esteem (Cheng & Furnham, 2003), which is related to sexual activities and frequency (Ethier et al., 2006). At the same time, sexual changes can impact relationships and mental health symptoms (Al-Azzawi & Palacios, 2009; Briere & Runtz, 1987). Overall, mental health and sexuality are intimately connected. This section reviews some sexuality-related implications of the major categories of mental health disorders.

Anxiety Disorders

Anxiety disorders make up the most common mental health disorder category, with about 29% of Americans expected to receive an anxiety diagnosis in their lifetime (Kessler et al., 2005). Anxiety can impact sexuality by increasing or decreasing blood flow to the vagina, relationship intimacy, and sexual satisfaction and can lead to sexual difficulties (Bodinger et al., 2002; Déttore, Pucciarelli, Santarnecchi, 2013; Norton & Jehu, 1984). On the other hand, sexual concerns often cause anxiety (Barlow, 1986; Rowland & Incrocci, 2008). Performance anxiety is common among people with sexual arousal problems and orgasm difficulties for both females and males, while low sexual desire among men and women has been connected to higher levels of anxiety (Rowland & Incrocci, 2008). Sexual dysfunctions are more likely for people with anxiety disorders than for people without a mental health disorder in that 50% of people diagnosed with obsessive-compulsive disorder and 64% of people diagnosed with generalized anxiety disorder had a sexual dysfunction compared to 30% of people without a diagnosis (Kendurkar & Kaur, 2008).

When people feel anxious, the acute stress response activates hormones that increase blood pressure and volume, slow down digestion, decrease pain, increase vigilance and awareness, and alter their cognitive processes (Charmandari, Tsigos, & Chrousos, 2005). These changes help the body to respond to the stressful stimuli. When the body continues to be anxious, it will work to maintain higher alertness, awareness, and vigilance by focusing blood toward the stressed body sites, continuing to inhibit digestion and causing hormonal challenges in the body. When we only experience acute stress for a short period of time, our bodies are able to return to a normal state with little to no problems. However, prolonged stress can lead to chronic physiological and behavioral problems (Charmandari et al., 2005).

Low levels of anxiety actually can improve sexual arousal through increased blood flow and volume in the genital areas and increased alertness. Higher levels of anxiety lead to moving the blood away from the genitals to more stressed areas of the body, which can lead to sexual problems. Physiologically, the problems can include decreases in erectile rigidity and volume or in vaginal lubrication and blood flow, which lowers sexual functioning and satisfaction. The decrease in vaginal lubrication and blood flow can even lead to pain during sex (Rowland & Incrocci, 2008). Anxiety can also decrease interpersonal intimacy by increasing emotional reactivity, which can lead to relational conflict and distress (Wei, Vogel, Ku, & Zakalik, 2005).

Sexual problems, including but not limited to sexual dysfunctions, can also lead to increased anxiety. Women who have experienced pain during sex have reported fear and anxiety about it happening again. Likewise, men with erectile problems often feel anxious about experiencing them again in the future. There can be a negative cycle between sexual problems and anxiety, and it is important for counselors to be aware of this and to work to reduce anxiety in clients with sexual problems. Systematic desensitization, sex education, relationship counseling, and specific anxiety treatments are recommended for consideration in these cases.

Mood Disorders (Depressive and Bipolar Disorders)

Making up the second most common category of mental health disorders are the mood disorders, which impact approximately 21% of people over the course of their lifetimes (Kessler et al., 2005). Mood disorders contain two different categories in the Diagnostic and Statistical Manual of Mental Disorders (DSM-5) put out by the American Psychiatric Association (American Psychiatric Association; 2013a). In the previous edition of the DSM, these categories were combined into one category of mood disorders, and researchers have not always separated depressive and bipolar diagnoses from each other. Part of why mood disorders are looked at together is because of the similarity of the disorders and the potential difficulty in differential diagnosis among mood disorders. The foundational components of mood disorders are the three mood episodes (i.e., depressive, manic, and hypomanic episodes), and the main diagnostic difference between major depressive disorder and bipolar I or II disorder is the lifetime history of a manic or hypomanic episode (American Psychiatric Association, 2013a). Because someone with a bipolar diagnosis can be experiencing a depressive episode and have very similar symptoms and experiences as someone diagnosed with major depressive disorder, it is important to understand the most recent mood episode when considering current mood implications for sexuality. Depressive and manic episodes impact sexual functioning and decision making differently, and people with either type of mood disorder commonly experience sexual problems (Dell'Osso et al., 2009; Mazza et al., 2009).

Manic episodes are typically brief (i.e., less than 2 weeks) periods of hyper-arousal and hyperactivity compared to a baseline mood state for an individual (American Psychiatric Association, 2013a). A common characteristic of mania is engaging in higher-risk behaviors, including adventurous and/or aggressive behaviors, excessive spending, and more frequent sexual activities. In a manic episode, people may engage in sexual activities more frequently or with more partners, and in fact, these behaviors are a part of the diagnostic criteria for bipolar I disorder (American Psychiatric Association, 2013a). Thus, manic episodes may increase sexual expression and activity (Dell'Osso et al., 2009; Mazza et al., 2011). There are few research studies investigating the sexual implications of being in a manic episode (Damian & Miclutia, 2013), which is possibly due to a short duration and small percentage of people who receive treatment during a manic episode. However, Mazza et al. (2011) found a difference in the desire for and frequency of sexual behaviors between people in a manic episode and people in a hypomanic episode. In another study in Turkey, women with a bipolar diagnosis reported lower usage of contraceptives when compared with women with a depressive, schizophrenic, or no diagnosis (Bursalioglu, Aydin, Yazici, & Yazici, 2013).

People who have been diagnosed with bipolar disorder may be prescribed medications to stabilize their mood, as well as antidepressants. Both mood stabilizers and antidepressants have been found to have negative side effects for sexual functioning (Clayton et al., 2002; Modell, Katholi, Modell, & DePalma, 1997; Smith, O'Keane, & Murray, 2002), and some antidepressants have been found to induce sexual dysfunction (Gregorian et al., 2002). Selective serotonin reuptake inhibitors (SSRIs) are a commonly prescribed class of antidepressants and have a strong documentation of negative sexual side effects. Modell et al. (1997) found that 73% of patients on an SSRI had at least some degree of sexual side effects including decreased desire, arousal, and frequency and duration of orgasm, while only 14% of patients on Bupropion had negative side effects (77% reported positive sexual side effects). While there are many considerations for medical doctors to prescribe an antidepressant, SSRIs have the worst prevalence and severity of antidepressants. On the other hand, mood stabilizers as a class and lithium in particular do not tend to have negative sexual side effects and may even help negate some of the sexual side effects of antipsychotics (Nagaraj, Nizamie, Akhtar, Sinha, & Goyal, 2004).

Depressive episodes can have negative sexual implications as well (Baldwin, 2001; Bancroft, Janssen, Strong, & Vudadinovic, 2003; Clayton, 2002; Kennedy, Dickens, Eisfeld, & Bagby, 1999), and 76% of people diagnosed with major depressive disorder also reported sexual dysfunction in one study (Kendurkar & Kaur, 2008). Depressive symptoms include low energy, sluggish feeling, apathy, and below their average interest level in common activities (American Psychiatric Association, 2013a). Just as people experiencing depressive symptoms have reduced energy and interest in their average activities, they also may lose interest in or desire for sexual activities. Sexual dysfunctions are commonly associated and experienced with depressive symptoms (Clayton, 2002; Dunn, Croft, & Hackett, 1999; Kennedy et al., 1999). Sexual arousal, desire, and orgasm are all negatively impacted by depressive symptoms. When antidepressants are used for treatment of depression, the sexual dysfunction can increase in severity (Clayton, 2002), and sexual dysfunction can start from use of some antidepressant medications (Kennedy et al., 1999; Montgomery, Baldwin, & Riley, 2002; Nurnberg et al., 2003; Salerian et al., 2000). Thus, people with depressive symptoms who are taking antidepressants can receive a double dose of negative sexual implications. Counselors can educate clients about the possible etiologies for their sexual difficulties when they are experiencing depressive symptoms. However, not all antidepressants cause negative side effects (Modell et al., 1997), and clients should consult with their medical doctor about any concerns with their medications. For clients who most benefit from SSRIs for their depressive symptoms, sildenafil has been found helpful for increasing arousal, orgasm, and overall sexual satisfaction (Nurnberg et al., 2003; Salerian et al., 2000).

CASE ILLUSTRATION 6.1

SHIRLEY, A CLIENT WITH DEPRESSIVE AND SEXUAL CONCERNS

Shirley is a 36-year-old female who presents to counseling with recurrent depression, a recent breakup from her partner of 10 years, and mild anxiety. She has been experiencing depressive symptoms for almost a year, though the recent breakup is what prompted her to make an appointment for counseling. On intake, she said that she experienced depression first in her early twenties and again later in her twenties. Over the past year, she has said that she has had decreased interest and pleasure, weight gain, trouble sleeping, fatigue, and difficulty concentrating. She has been able to work on a consistent basis, though she has used all of her sick days for the year on days when she felt like she could not get out of bed. Shirley feels worthless and that life does not have meaning, and some thoughts of ending her life have occurred recently, especially after her romantic relationship ended. She said that she used to enjoy the relationship and sex, though that changed roughly a year ago. The couple started to have some unresolved conflict that kept reoccurring, and Shirley stopped being sexually responsive because she did not want to have sex about 10 months ago. Shirley tried to engage in sexual activities on 3 or 4 occasions in the past 8 months, though she was not aroused or mentally engaged when they tried. She is concerned that she will never want to have sex again and will not be able to find or maintain another romantic relationship.

Questions for Reflection and Discussion:

1. What impact do you think Shirley's mental health and sexual concerns have on each other?

2. How serious do you think Shirley's sexual concerns are? What prognosis would you give for Shirley?

3. What recommendations or treatment plan would you have for Shirley?

4. How would your treatment goals address both her sexuality concerns and her mental health symptoms?

Psychotic Symptoms

Psychotic symptoms can be a part of several different diagnoses including major depressive disorder, bipolar I disorder, schizophrenia, and schizoaffective disorder. Medications are almost always a part of treatment plans when psychotic symptoms are present (Seligman & Reichenberg, 2007), though these medications often have sexual side effects (Baggaley, 2008; Smith et al., 2002), which can compound the other impacts that psychotic symptoms can have on people's sexual functioning and health. People with psychotic symptoms, especially with symptoms of schizophrenia and schizoaffective disorder, often also have relational difficulties including difficulty with emotional processing, social cues, and vocal emotional tones (Kern, Glynn, Horan, & Marder, 2009; Sergi et al., 2007). It can be difficult to clearly comprehend what people are trying to convey because of difficulty with understanding facial expressions, tone of voice, and other body language. People with psychotic symptoms also may have a hard time differentiating between hallucinations or delusions with reality when experiencing active symptoms. This can lead to relational conflict and difficulties in being intimate. In fact, many people with schizophrenia actually are more troubled by their difficulty sexually than with other problem areas (Lambert et al., 2004).

Antipsychotic medications often make sexual difficulties worse. These medications are typically sedatives to decrease the amount of hallucinations and delusions, and they also inhibit motivation and reward and decrease blood flow from the peripheral parts of the body. This means that antipsychotic medications can lead to arousal and orgasm problems, and they also may decrease libido (Baggaley, 2008). Because of the sexual side effects of antipsychotic medications and sexuality being an important concern for many people with schizophrenia, Baggaley (2008) suggested to consider not taking antipsychotic medications to improve sexual functioning and overall treatment adherence, taking a different antipsychotic that is less likely to have sexual side effects, or to add another medication to mitigate the sexual side effects.

SUBSTANCE ABUSE AND SEXUALITY

Substance abuse is another potential influence on sexuality. Substance abuse and addictions impact romantic relationships (Seligman & Reichenberg, 2007), and some of the effects of substance intoxication can impact sexual arousal and performance. When dependence on a substance develops, the addiction may become a prominent part of the person's life, thereby decreasing the importance of other areas in life, including sexual relationships. As such, it is not surprising that there is also significant comorbidity between substance abuse and dependence and sexual dysfunctions (Johnson, Phelps, & Cottler, 2004).

Rates of substance use and abuse remain high. According to the 2013 U.S. Substance Abuse and Mental Health Services Administration's (SAMHSA, 2014) national survey, approximately 24.6 million Americans, representing 9.4% of the population 12 years and older, used illicit drugs in 2013. Furthermore at the time of the survey, 60.1 million Americans (22.9%) binge drank alcohol in the past 30 days. Given these high rates, it is important for counselors to understand the intersections between substance abuse and sexuality. Substance use occurs with sexual activities in both healthy and unhealthy ways. For example, some people may report that substance use can enhance their sexual expression and satisfaction, or substance use might negatively impact sexual performance, functioning, and relationships. A thorough assessment is often needed to determine if substance use is positively or negatively impacting sexual expression, satisfaction, and relationships. It can be much easier to see the negative consequences of substance abuse and dependence upon sexuality.

Illicit drugs can impact the dopamine levels in the mesocorticolimbic system and initiate the brain's reward system, which typically leads to pleasurable feelings and other various changes, depending on the drug of use (Feltenstein, & See, 2008). With substance dependence, the brain has been so used to the dopamine and stimulation to the reward system of the brain that there is actually pain in the absence of the substance leading to changes in the brain's stress system and other changes in the brain that differ according to the substance (Feltenstein & See, 2008). When this happens, people dependent on a substance tend to have many behavioral changes that have a negative impact on their social, romantic, and vocational aspects of life (Seligman & Reichenberg, 2007). It is not uncommon for substance dependence to lead to stealing money from loved ones, skipping important family and social events, and other negative interpersonal interactions. Also with substance dependence, there often is some degree of cognitive distancing from other aspects of life other than the substance and its use (Fisher & Harrison, 2009).

In romantic relationships, there are commonly communication problems, hostility, and disapproval when a partner has substance use problems (Jacob, Ritchey, Cvitkovic, & Blane, 1981). Positive communication is a hallmark with relationship satisfaction (Litzinger & Gordon, 2005) and is connected to relationship satisfaction and sexual satisfaction (Byers, 2005; Litzinger & Gordon, 2005). Negative communication and interaction patterns and cycles in the couple are evident in couples that stay together when one or both are dependent on substances (Copello, Velleman, & Templeton, 2005; Epstein & McCrady, 1998). Overall, marital dissatisfaction is higher when there is substance dependence or abuse (Homish & Leonard, 2007), and relationship satisfaction is significantly connected with sexual activity and sexual satisfaction (Byers, 2005; Litzinger & Gordon, 2005; Santtila et al., 2007). In summary, there is typically lower relational and sexual satisfaction and decreased sexual activity with substance abuse and dependence.

Also, there is a significant correlation between sexual dysfunction and substance abuse. Depressant substances decrease awareness, blood flow, and breathing, all of which can decrease sexual experience and performance in substance intoxication. Substance abuse has been linked to higher rates of sexual dysfunction (Carnes, Murray, & Charpentier, 2005; Horvath, Calsyn, Terry, & Cotton, 2007; Johnson et al., 2004). People who use illicit drugs or alcohol have been shown to have a significantly higher amount of sexual dysfunction than people who do not use illicit drugs or alcohol (Johnson et al., 2004), and approximately 40% of people with sexual addictions also reported substance abuse (Carnes et al., 2005). Thus, there is a clear connection between sexual problems and substance abuse, both in relational and physiological aspects.

SEXUAL DYSFUNCTIONS

Male and Female Sexual Dysfunctions in the DSM-5

The *Diagnostic and Statistical Manual of Mental Disorders–Fifth Edition* (DSM-5; APA, 2013a) includes an entire category designated for sexual dysfunctions composed of ten total disorders, of which four are exclusively for males and three are exclusively for females. The sexual dysfunctions are related to sexual arousal and desire (erectile disorder, male hypoactive sexual desire disorder, and female sexual interest/arousal disorder), pain (genito-pelvic pain/penetration disorder), orgasm (delayed ejaculation, premature [early] ejaculation, and female orgasmic disorder), and not otherwise specified (substance/medication-induced sexual dysfunction, other specified sexual dysfunction, and unspecified sexual dysfunction). There are some recent changes from the *Diagnostic and Statistical Manual of Mental Disorders-4-Text Revision* (DSM-IV-TR) to the DSM-5 in the names and criteria of sexual dysfunctions, and the name changes are represented in Table 6.1 (Zucker, 2013).

Table 6.1   Recent Name Changes of Sexual Dysfunctions

DSM-IV-TR Sexual Dysfunctions	*Corresponding DSM-5 Sexual Dysfunctions*
Male orgasmic disorder	Delayed ejaculation
Male erectile disorder	Erectile disorder
Female orgasmic disorder	Female orgasmic disorder
Female sexual arousal disorder (for females)	Female sexual interest/arousal disorder (for females)
Hypoactive sexual desire disorder (for males and females)	Male hypoactive sexual desire disorder (for males)
Dyspareunia Vaginismus	Genito-pelvic pain/penetration disorder
Premature ejaculation	Premature (early) ejaculation
Sexual aversion disorder	(none)
Sexual dysfunction due to a general medical condition Substance-induced sexual dysfunction	Substance/medication-induced sexual dysfunction
Sexual dysfunction not otherwise specified	Other specified sexual dysfunction Unspecified sexual dysfunction

Sources: American Psychiatric Association, 2013a; Zucker, 2013.

For males, there are four specific sexual dysfunctions, erectile disorder, male hypoactive sexual desire disorder, delayed ejaculation, and premature (early) ejaculation. The first two are related to arousal and desire, and the latter two are related to orgasm. The criteria for all four disorders include the symptoms being present for the vast majority (75% to 100%) of partnered sexual activity for at least the past six months and causing clinically significant distress (American Psychiatric Association, 2013a). Each of these can be *lifelong* (i.e., where the symptoms have always been present) or *acquired* (i.e., having sexual dysfunction after previously experiencing significantly more sexual functioning) and can be *generalized* (i.e., in all circumstances) or *situational* (i.e., only in certain circumstances). Therefore, clients who meet the criteria for these disorders may seek counseling to help relieve the distress and/or symptoms that they are experiencing. Erectile disorder is appropriate for males who have marked difficulty obtaining or maintaining an erection or have had a marked reduction in the rigidity of erection, and male hypoactive sexual desire disorder is appropriate when males have no or low sexual or erotic thoughts, fantasies, and desires. Delayed ejaculation is appropriate when there is a marked delay, infrequency, or absence of ejaculation during partnered sexual activity, and premature (early) ejaculation is appropriate when ejaculation happens within a minute of penetration and before the male wishes.

In past research, the most common male sexual dysfunction has been premature ejaculation, which is estimated to impact around 30% of males at some point in their lives (Laumann et al., 2009; Waite, Laumann, Das, & Schumm, 2009) and can lead to relationship challenges (Graziottin & Althof, 2011; Kempeneers et al., 2012). The new diagnostic criteria that came out with the fifth edition of the DSM now specifies that premature ejaculation must occur within one minute of penetration. The APA (2013a) noted that this will drastically reduce the people diagnosed with this disorder, due to the time specifier, and they speculated that only about 1% to 3% of men will now be diagnosed with premature ejaculation. In terms of treatment, Masters and Johnson (1970) developed a behavioral technique to help treat premature ejaculation called the "squeeze technique," where the partner repeatedly stimulates the male's penis until he is close to orgasm and then squeezes the penis with thumb and fingers until the male calms down to help condition a delay in orgasm. More recently, a treatment combination of cognitive and sex therapies with medications has been recommended for premature ejaculation (Barnes & Eardley, 2007).

Erectile disorder is the most or second-most common male sexual dysfunction, with around 13% to 21% of 40- to 80-year-old males and 40% to 50% of 60- to 70-year-old men experiencing this condition (American Psychiatric Association, 2013a; Porst et al., 2013). The lifelong prevalence of erectile disorder is unknown, although the chance of experiencing erectile disorder increases with age (American Psychiatric Association, 2013a; Laumann et al., 2009; Lindau et al., 2007). Some people call the difficulty of achieving or maintaining an erection, "impotence," a term that typically carries a negative connotation for the male. Usually, there is a physiological rationale for this condition, and it is recommended that men with this condition consult with their medical doctor (King & Regan, 2014; Porst et al., 2013). The symptoms could be due to circulatory, prostate, neurological, injury, hormonal, or substance use reasons (Porst et al., 2013). It is important to assess for the possibility of substances, including medications, causing the symptoms (which would be more appropriately diagnosed as substance/medication-induced sexual dysfunction) and working with the client's physician in cases where the client wants help with erectile disorder symptoms. Medication therapy for erectile disorder is the most common form of treatment (Porst et al., 2013). In cases where it is more of a psychological cause for erectile difficulties, sensate focusing exercises are often the recommended treatment (King & Regan, 2014; Masters & Johnson, 1970). Stress, depression, and performance anxiety can impact erections, and allowing couples to not focus on performance and to explore what sexual activities and touches are pleasurable can be helpful in achieving and maintaining erection (Berry & Berry, 2013; King & Regan, 2014).

The frequency and prevalence of male hypoactive sexual desire disorder has been shown to vary across cultures and ages. Laumann et al. (2009) found that 18% of men in the United States had a lack of sexual interest over the past year and that 3.3% frequently had a lack of sexual interest. The APA (2013b) reported that 12.5% of Northern European men and 28% of Southeast Asian men have low sexual desire. In clinical populations, around half of couples experience low sexual desire, although it tends to be higher in females than males, and males with hypoactive sexual desire tend to be older than females with low sexual desire (Segraves & Segraves, 1991). While developmental history, current relationship(s), stress, and medical conditions may impact sexual desire, it seems that the main factor for most males is a lack of erotic thoughts (Carvalho & Nobre, 2011; Rubio-Aurioles & Bivalacqua, 2013). Knowing the etiology of the issue (psychological, relational, or physiological) and orienting treatment accordingly is recommended (Rubio-Aurioles & Bivalacqua, 2013).

Delayed ejaculation has a low frequency of occurrence, and it is estimated to affect less than 1% of men overall (American Psychiatric Association, 2013a). The main cause of delayed ejaculation is thought to be based on psychological factors and not physiological factors (Corona et al., 2006; Rowland, Keeney, & Slob, 2004; Rowland, 2005). Rowland et al. (2004) found that males with delayed ejaculation had very similar physiological responses to males with and without other sexual dysfunctions, though their subjective, internal arousal was reported lower than other males. Corona et al. (2006) also had similar conclusions, though they also admitted that some medications can delay ejaculation, specifically selective serotonin reuptake inhibitors (SSRIs), which are commonly prescribed anti-depressants. Because of this and increases in the prevalence in use of SSRIs, it may be that the frequency of delayed ejaculation increases (Corona et al., 2006). There are not currently any medical treatments for delayed ejaculation, and treatment can be difficult (Hartmann & Waldinger, 2007). Behavioral techniques of guided stimulation moving from solo ejaculation toward partnered, typically intravaginal, ejaculation, cognitive-behavioral focus in changing inhibitory beliefs and increasing internal sexual arousal, and systemic approaches to shifting and enhancing the couple's erotic potential and patterns are recommended approaches to treating delayed ejaculation (Hartmann & Waldinger, 2007).

While there is not a specific male sexual pain disorder, some men do experience pain during sexual activities (Davis, Binik, & Carrier, 2009). There is almost always a physiological reason for the pain, and it is important to consult a physician for possible prostate or urological problems (Davis et al., 2009).

For females, the frequencies of the three gender-specific sexual dysfunctions are not clearly determined, and the APA (2013a) openly stated the lack of evidence and the large possible differences in prevalence in different cultures. According to Laumann et al. (2009), the most common female sexual dysfunctions are lack of sexual interest (33%) and lubrication difficulties (22%), which is characterized in the DSM-5 as the sexual dysfunction of female sexual interest/arousal disorder (American Psychiatric Association, 2013a). Laumann et al. found that 33% of women experienced low sexual interest and 22% experienced lubrication difficulties in the past year, while about 10% and 6%, respectively, experience them on a regular basis. It is uncommon for couples to show comorbidity of another sexual dysfunction (notably orgasm, pain, and erectile dysfunctions) with female sexual interest/arousal disorder (Hertlein, Weeks, & Gambescia, 2007). In clinical populations, around half of couples report low sexual desire in at least one partner, and low sexual desire tends to be more common in females than males (Segraves & Segraves, 1991). Female sexual interest/arousal disorder may be treated from individualistic and systemic perspectives, and an integration of these approaches, called the intersystem approach, can be beneficial. Intersystem treatment consists of lowering response anxiety, helping the couple see the issue through a systemic lens, improving the couple's communication regarding sexual intimacy, improving overall intimacy in the relationship, working with underlying fears, and behavioral interventions such as sensate focus (Hertlein et al., 2007). This approach takes into account the intra- and interpersonal aspects of this low sexual desire.

Female orgasmic disorder is another fairly common sexual dysfunction impacting women. According to the APA (2013a), the prevalence of female orgasmic problems varies between 10% to 42% of women, based on age, culture, duration, and severity. Laumann et al. (2009) found that about 20% of American women had experienced the inability to orgasm and that 5.7% of women frequently were unable to orgasm. The statistics from the APA and Laumann et al. are only based on the inability to orgasm and do not take into account the level of distress for those symptoms, and thereby they do not mean that all of those women would meet the criteria for female orgasmic disorder. The criteria for female orgasmic disorder requires that there are few to no orgasms or a marked reduction in orgasmic sensations, experienced in the past six months (American Psychiatric Association, 2013a). The most common form of female orgasmic difficulties are in vaginal intercourse, though some females do not experience orgasms in any partnered or solo sexual activities (Spence, 1997). There are varied mental and physical stimulations that impact female sexual arousal and orgasm, and there is not one way that women experience orgasms (American Psychiatric Association, 2013a; Carnes et al., 2005; Kope, 2007).

Both physical stimuli and the female's response to the physiological changes in her body impact both arousal and orgasm. Kope stated that "(t)he brain is the primary site of orgasm for women" (2007; p. 97) to support her position on the importance of non-genital factors with this disorder. Whipple and Brash-McGreer (1997) discussed female sexual response with four factors: the capacity to experience pleasure, openness to sexual pleasure, physical capacity to respond to sexual stimulation, and the ability to experience orgasm. Counseling treatment for female orgasmic disorder should be undertaken after a physical evaluation by a medical doctor to rule out any physiological cause. Facilitating the exploration of past pleasurable and non-pleasurable sexual experiences, of what is sexually stimulating and pleasurable (both mentally and physically), and of how she experiences sexual arousal can be beneficial in treatment to aid in increasing awareness and pleasurable sexual arousal that could lead toward experiencing orgasm (Kope, 2007). Treating any comorbid sexual dysfunctions in the partner (including erectile disorder, male hypoactive sexual desire disorder, and female sexual interest/arousal disorder) is also important because of how the sexual problems are impacting both partners and impacting their sexual and non-sexual interactions.

The third sexual dysfunction for women is genito-pelvic pain/penetration disorder and includes two previous DSM-IV-TR diagnoses: dyspareunia and vaginismus. Because of the comorbidity of the two previous diagnoses and the difficulty in differential diagnosis, the two were combined into the current nomenclature (IsHak & Tobia, 2013). The APA (2013a) reported that about 15% of North American women experience pain during intercourse, and Laumann et al. (2009) found that 19.7% of women said that sex was not pleasurable (4.2% said it was frequently so) and that 12.7% of women said that they experienced pain during sex (2.8% said frequently so). There can be physiological and psychosocial reasons for genito-pelvic pain/penetration disorder, including anxiety and other psychological symptoms, gastrointestinal problems, provoked vestibulodynia, overactive muscles on the pelvic floor, previous trauma, relational problems, and sexual distress, and treatment is provided by different health care professionals including medical doctors, physical therapists, sex therapists, and mental health professionals (Rosenbaum, 2013). This disorder can be one of the most difficult of the sexual dysfunctions to treat with cultural messages, physical and/or mental pain, and relational conflict and/or distress as relevant factors to experiencing genital lubrication, pain, receptivity, and pleasure (Bley, 2007; Hertlein et al., 2007; Kope, 2007; Rosenbaum, 2013). Muscle relaxation, mindfulness techniques, anxiety-reduction techniques, systematic desensitization and other behavioral techniques, individual and couples therapy, physical exercise, and medications are possible treatments for genito-pelvic pain/penetration disorder (Bley, 2007; Rosenbaum, 2013).

Other Sexual Dysfunction Disorders

There are three other sexual dysfunctions that have not yet been mentioned: substance/medication-induced sexual dysfunction, other specified sexual dysfunction, and unspecified sexual dysfunction. Substance/medication-induced sexual dysfunction is appropriate to diagnose when a substance (i.e., alcohol, opioids, sedatives, cocaine, etc.) or medication is causing the sexual dysfunction symptoms. This is often the case with antidepressants, antipsychotics, and hormonal contraceptive medications (American Psychiatric Association, 2013a) causing decreased blood flow or lubrication. Other specified sexual dysfunction is appropriate to use when the person does not meet the full criteria for any of the sexual dysfunctions and the clinician wants to indicate another reason for the sexual dysfunction (e.g., sexual aversion or hypersexual) or can be used for sexual dysfunctions that evolve after the DSM-5 was published. Unspecified sexual dysfunction is used when the clinician does not specify the reason for not meeting the criteria for another sexual dysfunction or can be used on a provisional basis when there is not enough information to accurately diagnose the symptoms (American Psychiatric Association, 2013a).

Paraphilias and Paraphilic Disorders

There is another category of sexual concerns that the DSM-5 has categorized as paraphilias. According to the APA (2013a), "The term *paraphilia* denotes any intense and persistent sexual interest other than sexual interest in genital stimulation or preparatory fondling with phenotypically normal, physically mature, consenting human partners" (p. 685). In other words, paraphilias are atypical sexual preferences. Some people have desires for or are sexually aroused by exposing their genitals to unsuspecting others, giving or receiving pain during sexual activities, inanimate objects, or cross-dressing. Having a desire for such stimuli is not diagnosable in and of itself; the paraphilia needs to cause the individual clinically significant distress or impairment or cause harm or risk of harm to another person for an accurate diagnosis as a paraphilic disorder (American Psychiatric Association, 2013a). Richard Krueger and Meg Kaplan (2001), renowned experts in sexual therapy and paraphilias said, "Many of the paraphilias blend with consensual sexual practices that are not a source of distress or impairment of functioning but rather constitute forms of sexual expression that are chosen and practiced by significant numbers of people" (p. 391), illustrating that there are significant and important differences between paraphilias and paraphilic disorders. Some paraphilias can be healthy in sexual expression and practice for some people, and paraphilic disorders cause distress and/or impairment and can become the focus for treatment in counseling.

The DSM-5 contains eight specific paraphilic disorders, as well as two diagnoses for *other specified* and *unspecified paraphilic disorders*. Voyeuristic disorder is characterized by being aroused from watching unsuspecting person(s) disrobe, be naked, and/or engage in sexual acts. Exhibitionistic disorder is being aroused from exposing one's genitals to unsuspecting person(s). Frotteuristic disorder is characterized by arousal from touching or rubbing against nonconsenting person(s). Sexual masochism disorder is characterized by arousal from being humiliated, beaten, bound, or other forms suffering, and sexual sadism disorder is arousal from inflicting a form of suffering on another person(s). Pedophilic disorder is sexual interest and arousal in prepubescent child(ren). Fetishistic disorder is sexual arousal from nonliving or specific nongenital body part(s), and transvestic disorder is characterized by arousal from cross-dressing (American Psychiatric Association, 2013a). Experiencing the descriptors listed is not enough to be accurately diagnosed with and treated for those paraphilic disorders, there also needs to be clinically significant distress from the thoughts, desires, or experiences and/or that there have been specific sexual behaviors acted out upon nonconsenting persons.

There are two general subcategories of paraphilic disorders in terms of diagnostic criteria for the paraphilic disorders in the DSM-5. The first subcategory contains disorders that must cause clinically significant distress or impairment (including sexual masochism, fetishistic, and transvestic disorders), and the second category can cause clinically significant distress or impairment or has been acted out with nonconsenting person(s) (including voyeuristic, exhibitionistic, frotteuristic, sexual sadism, and pedophilic disorders). All paraphilic disorders can be manifested by fantasies, urges, and/or behaviors to fit the diagnostic criteria (American Psychiatric Association, 2013a).

Treatment for paraphilic disorders is relatively similar for each disorder, although treatment can be difficult (Sandat, 2014). Treatment typically aims to achieve four outcomes: (a) reducing the frequency and intensity of sexual desires and arousal, (b) increasing awareness, (c) controlling exposure of sexually arousing stimuli, and (d) treating comorbid disorders (Kaplan & Krueger, 2012; Sandat, 2014). Cognitive-behavioral therapy (CBT), along with medication, is typically recommended by researchers and clinicians in this area, though there is limited evidence for the utility of CBT with these disorders (Garcia & Thibaut, 2011; Kaplan & Kreuger, 2012; Thibaut, 2012). CBT has been recommended because it helps people with paraphilic disorders with cognitive distortions by examining and challenging their irrational beliefs, using social and assertiveness skill training, sexual education, helping with intimacy deficiencies, and addressing any trauma history (Kaplan & Krueger, 2012). Garcia and Thibaut (2011) suggested combining CBT with sexual impulse training, relapse prevention, empathy training, and biofeedback. A combination of counseling and medication is often recommended. Gonadotrophin-releasing hormone analogues (GnRH), selective serotonin reuptake inhibitors (SSRIs), and steroidal antiandrogens have been recommended based on increasing evidence for their efficacy with paraphilic disorders (Garcia & Thibaut, 2011; Thibaut, 2012).

Compulsive Sexual Behaviors and Hypersexuality

While there is currently no diagnosis for overly active sexual behaviors, there has been an ongoing debate about the inclusion of a diagnosis for when there seems to be excessive energy, focus, and behaviors on sexuality (Carnes et al., 2005; Giugliano, 2008; Goodman, 2001; Kafka, 2010; Levine & Troiden, 1988). People who overly focus on sexuality often have some qualities similar to those who have addictions to substances (e.g., cravings, intoxication, and withdrawal symptoms), which has led some experts to describe compulsive sexual behaviors as a sex addiction. Others focus more on the compulsive nature of the thoughts, feelings, and behaviors of people who seem to have an excessive focus on sex. Still, other researchers see this as an abundance of sexual energy, attention, and activity and prefer the terms *hypersexuality* (Kaplan & Krueger, 2010) or *hypersexual* (Kafka, 2010). Because of this, there are various terms used to describe these behaviors, including sex addiction, sex compulsion, sex dependence, and hypersexual that are used by different clinicians and researchers. Because of the varied terminology, a combined term of sexual compulsion/addiction/dependence (SCAD) has been created to try to unify the various terms (Burlew & Barton, 2002).

There are a lot of similarities to hypersexual or SCAD behaviors with behaviors of several mental health and substance disorders. There are compulsive, addictive, and dependence components to SCAD, and people tend to view this through a certain framework based on the name that they use for this. So while naming a phenomenon is sometimes a mundane activity, naming excessive sexual behaviors does seem to impact the lens through which compulsive sexual behaviors are viewed. For example, these behaviors are compulsive similar to obsessive-compulsive disorder, in that the behaviors may be done in an effort to decrease anxiety and pain (Goodman, 2001). With this perspective, treatment would focus on decreasing and controlling compulsive sexual behaviors and urges by increasing self-management and self-control.

Unlike compulsions, sexual behaviors often are pleasurable and enjoyable, which is more like an addiction as SCAD behaviors are driven, enjoyable, and reduce a strong impulse to partake in those behaviors (Goodman, 2001). Treatment implications from an addictions framework may lead to focusing on people ceasing all relevant behaviors (sobriety) and learning to support oneself with internal and external resources are goals within this perspective. However, there are problems applying the sobriety approach with sexual activities. Would the goal of treatment really be to cease all sexual activities? Although complete cessation of certain behaviors (i.e., any that are harmful to oneself or others) may be appropriate, it may not be possible or desirable for people to aim to cease any and all sexuality-related involvement and activities, given that sexuality is a central aspect of people's lives. Therefore, addiction-focused treatment may require modifications from typical interventions used in relations to substances when applied to compulsive sexuality-related behaviors.

Hypersexuality is a term that has been proposed by some that emphasize that "excessive" sexual activity is culturally and contextually based and that there are more problems in conceptualization and treatment when using other nomenclature. This perspective focuses more on the symptoms that a person experiences and how that is negatively impacting functioning (Kafka, 2010; Kaplan & Krueger, 2010). These are legitimate and important viewpoints to critically examine and reflect upon if planning to work with this population because of the pros and cons to each of the perspectives. For the sake of convenience, the name "hypersexuality/SCAD" will be used in the rest of this chapter to emphasize the different perspectives that can be used with this phenomenon.

Hypersexuality/SCAD can cause significant problems in functioning and relationships. People who excessively engage in sexual activities may face negative impacts in other areas of functioning (vocational, economic, social, familial, etc.) and cause significant distress (Giugliano, 2008; Goodman, 2001; Kafka, 2010; Kafka & Hennen, 1999; Kaplan & Krueger, 2010). People with hypersexuality/SCAD often engage in sexual activities without intimacy and connection to the person(s) that they are sexually active with, in risky settings, and despite recurrent negative effects in their lives. The activities that people with hypersexuality/SCAD engage in can vary from compulsive masturbation, pornography use, telephone and/or cyber sex, promiscuity, and strip club usage (Kafka, 2010; Kaplan & Kreuger, 2010), and many have other addictive behaviors with substances, work, eating, and/or spending (Carnes et al., 2005).

As mentioned before, there is a significant connection between sexuality and substance abuse, and there is also a significant connection between hypersexuality/ SCAD and other addictions. In a study of 1604 participants, Carnes et al. (2005) found that 80% of gay males, 79% of heterosexual females, and 69% of heterosexual males with hypersexuality/SCAD also met criteria for an addictive disorder. They also found that over 40% simultaneously engaged in sexual behaviors in conjunction with the substance to which they were addicted, as well as that over 50% had other family members who also were addicted to something. In reviewing the mental health literature comorbidity with hypersexuality/SCAD, Kafka (2010) reported that people with hypersexuality/SCAD are more likely to have sexual dysfunctions and eating, mood, anxiety, substance abuse, and impulse control disorders. Black, Kehrberg, Flummerfelt, and Schlosser (1997) found that 86% of a sample of 36 participants with compulsive sexual behavior also had an axis I DSM-III-R diagnosis.

Treatment for hypersexuality/SCAD often includes impulse control training, emotional-regulation skills training, some form of abstinence, referral to the 12-step Sexaholics Anonymous program, relapse prevention, examining and otherwise fulfilling underlying needs and desires, couples therapy, treatment for comorbid diagnoses, and medication (Carnes, 2000; Carnes et al., 2005; Goodman, 2001; Kaplan & Kreuger, 2010; Sugrue, 2007). There are many theoretical approaches used to work with people with hypersexuality/SCAD, and treatment is typically an integrated approach to holistically cover all of the presenting concerns and is expected to last longer than treatment for most other presenting concerns (Carnes, 2000; Sugrue, 2007).

Sexual Variations and Atypical Behaviors

Sexuality can be expressed and enjoyed in many different ways. While this chapter has covered many sexual difficulties and some things that are atypical sexual desires or concerns, sexual desires and behaviors do vary among people who are sexually health. There is no one way that healthy sexuality is expressed, as healthy sexual expression covers a broad range of activities and really is dependent on the consent, impact on functioning, and sexual, romantic, and overall satisfaction. Therefore, it is important for counselors to consider their beliefs about what is "normal" sexual behavior and to avoid imposing their sexual values on clients. Exercise 6.1 will help you to think about your sexual values and beliefs.

Exercise 6.1

GUIDED REFLECTION ABOUT HEALTHY SEXUAL BEHAVIORS

The following list of sexual activities can help you consider your thoughts on healthy sexuality. For each activity on the list, think about in what circumstances and how frequent it is healthy to engage in the following sexual activities. In terms of circumstances or frequency, you may think that it is not healthy to engage in the particular activity, and you can indicate that in your response.

Sexual Activity
Circumstances (partnered, alone, group, etc.)
Frequency

- Kissing
- Hugging
- Petting
- Hand or Manual Sex
- Oral Sex
- Genital Sex
- Anal Sex
- Group Sex
- Swinging Sex (trading partners)

SEXUAL TRAUMA

Sexual trauma also significantly impacts how an individual experiences and acts as a sexual being. Sexual trauma, including rape, childhood sexual abuse, and unwanted sexual experiences, can happen at any age and can have significant physiological, mental, and interpersonal repercussions (Planty, Langton, Krebs, Berzofsky, & Smiley-McDonald, 2013). Therefore, counselors need to be aware of the impact of sexual trauma and of recommended treatment approaches to help clients to heal. Incidents of sexual trauma are unfortunately relatively commonplace. The impact of sexual trauma can last for years, although with treatment, many survivors are able to enjoy sexual relationships and activities (Woodward & Joseph, 2003).

Sexual trauma is an umbrella term that includes rape, incest, childhood sexual abuse, molestation, sexual harassment, and unwanted sexual experiences. Sexual trauma unfortunately is a common issue today. Many researchers (e.g., Putnam, 2003) have reported on the problems that can stem from experiences with sexual trauma. However, recently, some researchers (Calhoun & Tedeschi, 2004) have also focused on the resilience and possible growth that people can have through healing from sexual trauma and from other life changes that bring about further growth. Therefore, it is important to avoid pathologizing people who have experienced sexual trauma, and counselors can help these clients identify both the challenges and strengths they have encountered as a result of the trauma they faced. In this section, the types of sexual trauma will be discussed, and then treatment considerations will be provided.

Childhood Sexual Abuse

Childhood sexual abuse (CSA) is also a broad term that covers many types of different sexual trauma. Incest (i.e., sexual activity between family members that are too closely related to marry), rape (i.e., vaginal or anal penetration by any body part or object or oral penetration by a sexual organ), childhood pornography (i.e., pornographic material of people under the age of 18), and unwanted sexual experiences (i.e., any sexual activity that was not desired) are all specific examples of CSA. To be categorized as CSA, most experts agree that sexual contact (a) needs to be between a child and someone five or more years older than the child or (b) needs to be done without the child's consent (Browne & Finkelhor, 1986; King & Regan, 2014). There may or may not be violence, forced activity, or consent given to classify as CSA. Most perpetrators of CSA are known by the child and are male (Berliner & Elliott, 1996; Finkelhor, 1991; Morison & Greene, 1992). While many think of child molesters as "dirty old men," this stereotype is not accurate (Fuselier, Durham, & Wurtele, 2002; Laumann et al., 1994).

There have been various findings for the prevalence of CSA, though in several studies, researchers have consistently reported that between 10% to 20% of children under the age of 18 experience some form of CSA by the time that they are 18 years old (Pereda, Guilera, Forns, & Gómez-Benito, 2009). The statistics differ for females and males, with females (25.3% of population) being more likely than males (7.5% of population) to experience and report CSA (Pereda et al., 2009). Researchers typically find that females are 2.5 to 3 times more likely to experience CSA than males (Putnam, 2003). Some researchers have suggested that CSA for males may actually occur at higher rates that may even approach the rates for females, but social stigmatization and conditioning may lead males to not report CSA or to not see that they have experienced CSA (Finkelhor, 2010; Pereda et al., 2009). Males are commonly seen as sexual aggressors, and even if the child is a male and the adult is a female, people often assume that it was not abusive because they think the male may have enjoyed the experience or even may have initiated the sexual activity (Finkelhor, 2010). Age is another important factor with CSA. About a quarter (26.3%) of CSA cases in the United States were made against 12- to 14-year-olds (United States Department of Health and Human Services, 2013). Almost two-thirds of people who experienced CSA were between the ages of 9 and 17, with the age ranges of 15- to 17-year-olds (20.9%) and 9- to 11-year-olds (18.4%) both having about a fifth of the substantiated CSA cases. Children under the age of 9 are also at risk of CSA, with prevalence rates of 2.6% for 0- to 2-year-olds, 14% for 3- to 5-year-olds, and 17.2% for 6- to 8-year-olds (United States Department of Health and Human Services, 2013). Overall, children between the ages of 12 and 17 are at greater risk in the United States, and children between 6 and 11 years old also face a significant risk.

The consequences of CSA are difficult to clearly measure and identify. While negative mental health, physiological, and social effects are correlated with CSA, attributing the results solely to CSA is difficult because negative familial and socioeconomic factors are commonly experienced alongside CSA (Putnam, 2003). Absent parents, the presence of stepparents, parent mental illness and/or substance use problems, and social isolation are common in the families of children who experience CSA, and each of these factors also negatively impacts mental health (Putnam, 2003). However, CSA has the potential to negatively impact people's sexual development, especially if they do not heal through treatment or other efforts. Some of the specific long-term impacts may include negative beliefs about sex and relationships, unclear boundaries, unbalanced hierarchical power structures, and difficulty identifying sexual coercion. Each of these issues may impact clients' needs in counseling.

Rape

Rape is another common form of sexual abuse, with approximately one-fifth of women experiencing rape or attempted rape at some point during their lifetimes (Black et al., 2010). Over 10% of high school females have had sex when they did not want to (Kann et al., 2014). Planty, Langton, Krebs, Berzofsky, and Smiley-McDonald (2013) found that around 270,000 females experienced rape or sexual assault in 2010. Typically, rape is perpetrated by one male against one female without a weapon (in about 90% of cases) (Planty et al., 2013). However, rape can happen to males and can be perpetrated by females. Rape also is typically perpetrated by someone known to the person who experienced rape, which is the case in about 78% of cases (Planty et al., 2013). Rape, as defined above, is the vaginal or anal penetration of any body part or object or oral penetration of a sexual organ (Federal Bureau of Investigation, 2013) and can cause substantial mental and physiological harm. Between 2005 and 2010, approximately 60% of women who were raped were injured during the assault, although only 35% of those injured women sought treatment for the injuries (Planty et al., 2013). Mental injuries also can occur, impacting mood, self-esteem, anxiety, substance abuse, and suicidal thoughts (Campbell, 2008). If untreated, symptoms could develop to the point of meeting the criteria for mental health disorders such as post-traumatic stress disorder and major depressive disorder. Communities often have physical, legal, and mental health services for people who have experienced rape, and 77% of people who were raped received assistance from a victim service agency (Planty et al., 2013).

Sexual Harassment

Sexual harassment, as defined by the United States Equal Employment Opportunity Commission (EEOC), is "unwelcome sexual advances, requests for sexual favors, and other verbal or physical conduct of a sexual nature" (n.d.). To qualify as sexual harassment, the verbal or non-verbal behaviors need to be unwanted and of a sexual nature. In 2011, there were almost 34,000 resolved cases of harassment with 20% receiving merit resolutions totaling over $100 million in monetary benefits by the EEOC, which does not count any civil lawsuits (EEOC, n.d.). While there were over 30,000 reported cases, there are many more unreported cases of sexual harassment. Das (2009) found that 41% of women and 32% of men have experienced sexual harassment at work. This can lead to negative changes, and Chan, Lam, Chow, and Cheung (2008) found that experiencing sexual harassment is related to decreased job satisfaction, commitment, and performance, physical health, and psychological wellbeing.

Treatment of Sexual Trauma

Negative short- and long-term problems can arise from sexual abuse (Chan et al., 2008; Pereda et al., 2009). The negative personal and social changes are important to take into account, and the decreases in the person's ability to function in vocational, social, and familial areas are also important to address. This is especially true for CSA, and some see CSA as one of the most serious public health problems (Pereda et al., 2009). In one study, 62.8% of children that had been sexually abused met diagnostic criteria for at least one mental health diagnosis, and 29.5% met criteria for two or more diagnoses (McLeer et al., 1998).

There are several treatment models for treating trauma and even more models for treating mental health symptoms (e.g., depression, anxiety, self-esteem, and stress) associated with sexual trauma. Trauma-focused cognitive behavioral treatment (TF-CBT), the triphasic model, eye movement desensitization and reprocessing

(EMDR), self-trauma model, and medication are all approaches that have demonstrated some efficacy of treating sexual trauma. When treating sexual trauma, it is important for counselors to consider the sexual and non-sexual symptoms of the client along with the characteristics of your client, your own theoretical orientation and client conceptualization, and the research showing the efficacy of different approaches to best select the best treatment for your client. It is also important to consider and discuss with your client the focus of treatment (which may or may not include treatment of past sexual trauma) and how much emphasis to put on working with the client on sexual trauma before assuming her or his intentions and desires and trying to put more or less focus than the client is expecting. Counselors also should remember the importance of recognizing the potential for post-traumatic growth to occur via healing after the trauma. Calhoun and Tedeschi (2004) found that nearly half of people who have experienced a traumatic event report some benefit later in life. Counselors can best support their clients in navigating the challenges associated with sexual trauma by focusing on clients' strengths and resources and by providing a non-stigmatizing, supportive context for healing to occur.

SUMMARY

In conclusion, there is a complex relationship between people's mental health and their experiences of sexuality. Counselors working with clients to address sexuality-related concerns must consider the various ways that these two dynamics intersect. From a cognitive standpoint, there are a number of possible influences on the processes that clients use to make decisions related to their sexuality, even allowing room for some of these decisions to be made spontaneously and without much forethought or planning. Other intersections between sexuality and mental health can be found in the links between sexuality and mental health disorders, substance abuse, and specific sexual dysfunctions. Furthermore, clients who have experienced sexual trauma may find that there are long-term impacts of the trauma—both positive and negative—that impact their sexual functioning and attitudes. Overall, these various influences offer counselors a wide range of opportunities to address clients' experiences with sexuality and link those experiences with their mental health functioning.

KEYSTONES

- Sexuality and mental health have a dynamic and bidirectional relationship, in which changes in one area directly impact the other.
- Many factors impact people's decisions whether, when, and how to engage in sexual activities.

- Many common mental health and substance abuse disorders—including anxiety and mood disorders—have implications for clients' sexual functioning.
- Counselors should familiarize themselves with the sexual dysfunctions outlined in the DSM-5.
- Sexual trauma can have significant short- and long-term impacts—both positive and negative—on clients' sexual attitudes, experiences, and functioning.

ADDITIONAL RESOURCES

- International Institute for Trauma and Addiction Professionals. (2015). *Sex Addiction Therapist Training.* Retrieved from http://www.iitap.com/events/sex-addiction-workshops
- Masters, W. H., & Johnson, V. E. (1970). *Human sexual inadequacy.* New York, NY: Bantam Books.
- Schnarch, D. (1998). *Passionate marriage: Keeping love and intimacy alive in committed relationships.* New York, NY: Owl Books.
- VandeCreek, L., Peterson, F. L., & Bley, J. W. (2007). *Innovations in clinical practice: Focus on sexual health.* Sarasota, FL: Professional Resource Press.

Chapter 7

Gender Identity and Affectional/Sexual Orientation

Whether I "really" am a woman, or whether I "had a choice" or not, or whether anything, no longer matters. Having an opinion about transsexuality is about as useful as having an opinion on blindness. You can think whatever you like about it, but in the end, your friend is still blind and surely deserves to see. Whether one thinks transsexuals are heroes or lunatics will not help to bring these people solace. All we can do in the face of this enormous, infinite anguish is to have compassion.

—Jennifer Finney Boylan, 2013, p. 248

Gender identity and affectional/sexual orientation are all critical components of sexuality. Before you read this chapter, we invite you to pause for a moment to reflect on how you would define yourself along these dimensions. What would your responses be? As we proceed through the chapter, we recommend that you reconsider these responses as you delve deeper into the complexity of understanding each of these aspects of human sexuality. Gender and sexual identities are extremely complex and may be much more fluid than many people believe. Identities are at least in part relational and therefore socially constructed, rather than fixed, inherent qualities (Maher & Tetreault, 1993). Although biological factors shape our identities, the roles and concepts we assign to identities are shaped by social and cultural contexts, which are always in flux and changing across time. As society evolves, so do the roles and concepts associated with being female and male, as well as homosexual and heterosexual. Grasping the idea of identities as social constructions is essential to understanding the range of possible gender and affectional/sexual orientation identities that you may encounter in counseling.

Throughout this chapter, we aimed to use a critical consciousness in our approach to the language used to describe gender and affectional/sexual orientation, although the English language remains restrictive in its use of terms in relation to sexuality. Therefore, we had to make decisions about clarity of language to enhance the reader's understanding and in order to maintain consistency of terms across the academic literature. We worked within these limitations to create what we hope is a chapter that counteracts dominant discourses and deconstructs heteronormativity. We hope that this approach to this chapter encourages readers to examine their own stance toward working with LGBTIQQA (i.e., lesbian, gay, bisexual, transgender, intersex, queer, questioning, and allies) clients and to feel open to sharing their thoughts with others, as it is this ongoing discourse that promotes the practice of a critical consciousness and the production of anti-normative knowledge. After reading this chapter, readers will be able to do the following:

a. Understand the definitions of sexual/affectional orientation and gender identity
b. Examine how cultural, historical, and societal factors impact gender norms and expression
c. Identify contextual factors that may create stress in the life of LGBTIQQA clients
d. Describe strategies to help LGBTIQQA clients cope with minority stressors

DEFINING GENDER IDENTITY AND AFFECTIONAL/ SEXUAL ORIENTATION

Language is an important component of working with LGBTIQQA clients. The terms covered below are common to LGBTIQQA communities, but language is often limiting and may not adequately capture clients' sense of self. Language is also fluid, and common terms vary by culture and context. Thus, it is important for counselors to recognize that the definitions below are not all-encompassing of the possible language clients may use to express themselves and for counselors to honor the terms that clients select for themselves.

Gender Identity

Gender and sex are often used interchangeably to refer to persons as male or female; however, these terms are non-synonymous, as sex is purely physical based on chromosomal makeup (i.e., XX, XY, or some combination thereof), while *gender* is the social, mental, and emotional state associated with sex but not always associated with anatomy (Singh, Boyd, & Whitman, 2010). Thus, *gender identity* is one's psychosocial sense of being male, female, neutral or some combination thereof, and is based in one's self-conception of their gender (Davis, 2009). Gender identity is enacted through *gender roles*, which are socially constructed expectations for appearance and behavior that often define how men and women act and interact (Killermann, 2013). Gender roles are culturally and historically bound and thus change over time and location. *Gender expression* refers to how individuals present their gender in ways that do or do not align with traditional gender norms. Typically, gender expression is described as feminine or masculine or as androgynous for someone who does not have a particular gender expression that aligns with the male or female binary (Killermann, 2013).

Gender identity, especially in Western societies, tends to be based on a binary between male and female, masculine and feminine. There are multiple possibilities, however, for defining gender, and for many people, gender expression falls outside of the dominant norms (Killermann, 2013). The various terms related to gender identity are presented in Table 7.1. Many trans individuals may take steps, such as cross-sex hormone (CSH) therapy and gender reassignment surgery (GRS), to make their outer physical self match their internal felt sense of gender identity. Some trans individuals may choose just to cross-dress or have a more androgynous expression of their gender, while others may feel that medical treatment is necessary to feel congruence between their sex and gender. Although some individuals who transition will identify as transsexual, others who transition may identify with their internal sense of being male or female and thus find the term transsexual to be unsuitable to their experience (Singh, Boyd, & Whitman, 2010). The terms *MTF* (male-to-female) and *FTM* (female-to-male) are used to refer to gender categories of transsexual individuals while they transition. The term trans also includes intersex individuals. Intersex characteristics may or may not display at birth, and some people may not know they are intersex without genetic testing. Some intersex individuals are surgically "normalized" as infants, but the chosen sex may not align with their gender expression and may affect their sexual response and emotional well-being as adults (Singh, Boyd, & Whitman, 2010).

Trans individuals may feel that conventional pronouns (she/he, her/him, hers/his) do not fit with their gendered identity and use gender-neutral pronouns for reference, such as using the plural form (them/they) of pronouns. The pronoun *hir* is the transgender equivalent to her/him and hers/his, and *ze* is the equivalent to she/he pronouns. According to Transgender Committee formed by the Association of LGBT Issues in Counseling (Association for Lesbian, Gay, Bisexual, and Transgender Issues in Counseling Transgender Committee, 2010), some clients may choose to use conventional gender pronouns, so counselors should follow clients' lead on the pronouns they wish to use. Exercise 7.1 invites you to participate in a conversation with a colleague using non-gender specific language in order to examine how entrenched gendered-laden words are in the English language.

Table 7.1 Common Terminology

Term	Definition
Gender Identity	
Gender variance	The capacity of not conforming to societal gender norms associated with physical sex is a normal part of gender expression that has been documented across cultures. Some cultures and nations (e.g., the Hijra of India) have a third gender category that normalizes expression outside of the gender binary.
Androgyny	The state of being neither particularly masculine nor feminine or a more ambiguous sense of gender expression.
Genderqueer	This is another manifestation of gender identity for persons who reject the gender binary, and genderqueer persons may identify as neither masculine nor feminine, both, or some combination thereof.
Trans	The prefix *trans-* is derived from the Latin for "across from" or "on the other side of." It is a catch-all term for individuals who cross gender or sex boundaries. The term *trans* may appear as capitalized when referring to the general community, similar to ethnic designations such as Jewish.
Transgender	This is used as an umbrella term for individuals who blur the lines of traditional gender expression. Most commonly used to refer to people who do not fit the socially prescribed gender roles associated with their biological sex, such as people who cross-dress, or people who may feel that their biological sex does not correspond with their gender identity.
Transsexual	Persons who take steps to transition to the biological sex that corresponds with their gender often utilize this term. Others who transition may identify with their internal sense of being male or female and find the term *transsexual* to be unsuitable to their experience.
Intersex	These are persons who are born with ambiguous genitalia and/or chromosomal anomalies other than the XX-female and XY-male phenotypes and thus are not born distinctly male or female.
Cisgender	The prefix *cis-* from the Latin meaning "on this side of," refers to people who feel their sense of gender identity matches their biological sex (e.g., my sex is biologically female and my felt sense of gender is also that of a female).
Sexual/Affectional Orientation	
Gay	This is a commonly used term for men with emotional, spiritual, or sexual attraction to other men but sometimes is used to refer to both men and women attracted to the same sex.
Lesbian	This refers to women with emotional, spiritual, or sexual attraction to other women.

Table 7.1 (Continued)

Bisexual	These are persons with emotional, spiritual, or sexual attraction to both men and women, although these attractions may not necessarily occur at the same time or to the same extent.
Omnisexual or pansexual	These are persons who are attracted to persons regardless of gender or gender expression.
Asexual	These are persons who lack sexual attraction to others or who have low interest in sexual activities or intimate relationships. These persons may experience emotional attraction and romantic connection to others in intimate relationships.
Demisexual	These are persons who do not feel sexual attraction until an emotional connection is established with another person in an intimate relationship.
Heterosexual/ straight	These are persons who experience emotional, spiritual, or sexual attraction to persons of the opposite sex.

Exercise 7.1

PRACTICE USING NON-GENDER SPECIFIC LANGUAGE

Directions: Working with a partner, pick a recent interaction that you had with a significant other, family member, or friend to discuss with your partner. Each person will describe their chosen interaction in non-gender specific language for approximately 2 to 3 minutes, trying not to use the following words:

- He, His, Him, She, Hers, Her
- Boy, Man, Boyfriend, Husband, Father
- Girl, Woman, Girlfriend, Wife, Mother

As a group, process the activity.

- What was it like to try to have a conversation without using the common gender-specific pronouns in the English language?
- LGB individuals may not feel comfortable discussing dating, partners, or significant others amongst peers and coworkers, particularly if they are not out in certain environments. How did this exercise help you connect to the challenges LGB individuals may face in daily conversations with others?
- How did this exercise help you to connect to the experiences of trans people who may find that current labels and pronouns do not adequately describe their gender identity?

Sexual/Affectional Orientation

Sexual orientation is used to describe a person's sense of emotional, romantic, sexual, *or* spiritual attraction toward another person. There has been movement to change the term sexual orientation to *affectional orientation*, as identified in the Association for Lesbian, Gay, Bisexual, and Transgender Issues in Counseling's (ALGBTIC; 2012) competencies for counseling LGBQQIA individuals, to capture the complexities of attraction and challenge the stereotype that those with minority sexual orientations are only invested in sexual attraction. To align with this movement by ALGBTIC, affectional orientation will be used throughout the rest of the chapter when referencing sexual orientation. The terms *homosexual* and *heterosexual* originated in language in the late 1800's (Ford, 2013), with homosexual referring to persons with emotional and sexual attraction to the same sex and heterosexual referring to attraction to the opposite sex. For many persons, sexual orientation falls along a range of possibilities; although similar to gender identity, the definition of sexual orientation is often constrained by the homosexual/heterosexual binary that is not fitting of every person's sense of attractions. The common terms related to sexual/affectional orientation are presented in Table 7.1.

Counselors working with LGBTIQQA clients should be aware of the spectrum of identities that this acronym encompasses and that the identities explored in this chapter are not all-encompassing of the possible affectional orientations or gender identities that individuals can experience. At times throughout this chapter, we use other combinations of the LGBTIQQA acronym to reference specific groups within these communities, particularly in referring to affectional orientation as distinct from gender identity. Some clients may choose to not identify as they view their identities as more fluid and that the available language does not adequately capture their own experience of their gender identity and/or affectional orientation. For competent practice with LGBTIQQA clients, counselors should never assume a label for a client and allow clients to identify themselves. Moreover, counselors should at the least be familiar with dominant terminologies, acknowledge identities as a spectrum, and be willing to educate themselves about unfamiliar terminology as it arises with clients. An effective way of learning about terminologies as related to working with LGBTIQQA clients is to engage in discussions with counselors or other professionals who are active in LGBTIQQA communities.

Allies

The term *ally* refers to a counselor, client, or other individual who provides therapeutic, personal, or social support to individuals who self-identify as LGBTIQQ (Association for Lesbian, Gay, Bisexual, Transgender Issues in Counseling, 2012). An LGBTIQQ ally is someone who increases awareness and knowledge of, or sensitivity to, important issues that LGBTIQQ individuals face (Finkel, Storaasli, Bandele, & Schaefer, 2003). Due to heterosexual and cisgender privilege, allies are integral contributors to the fight for social justice for and with individuals of minority affectional orientations and/or gender identities as they can bring their voices and resources to work with LGBTIQQ communities in resisting heteronor-mativity (Munin & Speight, 2010). In the last decade, advocacy has been described as "a professional imperative" (Myers, Sweeney, & White, 2002) for professional counselors. Professional counselors can answer the call to advocacy for LGBTIQQ communities through facilitating their own and others' development as allies.

All persons, regardless of identity, can act as LGBTIQQA allies (Waters, 2010), yet individuals will have differing needs for support in order to take action, depending on one's existing awareness, knowledge, and skills. For example, you may wish to demonstrate more empathy toward LGBTIQQ individuals through thinking or behaving differently. Some allies may not feel comfortable confronting comments that are discriminatory toward LGBTIQQ individuals; however, they may choose not to participate in conversations that are degrading toward LGBTIQQ individuals by staying silent or excusing themselves from the conversation. There is less risk involved in the latter option, yet the choice to not participate is still an act of ally-hood because they chose not to perpetuate discourses that are harmful to LGBTIQQ individuals. Reading and working through the activities in this chapter is itself an act of allyhood, as you are informing yourselves about LGBTIQQA people through these activities. We provide the exercise below as an opportunity for increasing your awareness of your own values, beliefs, and assumptions that could impact your work with LGBTIQQA clients.

Exercise 7.2

DEVELOPING AWARENESS

Directions: During this reflection activity, be as honest as possible. This activity is to help you develop your personal awareness about your own personal values, beliefs, and assumptions that may impact your work with LGBTIQQA clients.

Part 1: Write down your positionality: How do you identify as a person? Write down the top five identities that influence your way of being in the world. These could be based on your race, ethnicity, religion/spirituality, socioeconomic status, ability, family

(Continued)

(Continued)

dynamics, career choices, or whatever the first five identities are that come to your mind. If not in your top five identities, how do you identify (or choose not to identify) in terms of your gender identity and sexual orientation? Do you identify as an ally to LGBTIQQA communities?

Part 2: Take a few minutes to write down commonly held assumptions about persons who identify as LGBTIQQA. These can be statements that you have heard perpetuated in the media or other social interactions. Now for each assumption you wrote down, identify the assumption as potentially positive, negative, or neutral. Finally, rate your level of agreement with each assumption on a scale of 1 to 5 (1: Completely disagree; 2: Moderately disagree; 3: Neither agree nor disagree; 4: Moderately agree; 5: Completely agree).

Part 3: Now, in small discussion groups, discuss how your responses in Part 2 may impact your ability to counsel LGBTIQQA clients. Also, during the discussion, consider your positionality from Part 1 and how that may have impacted your statements and your view of and agreement with those statements in Part 2. If your positionality (i.e., primary identities) was different, how may that impact your view of the statements in Part 2? If you feel any of your values, beliefs, or assumptions may impair your ability to work with LGBTIQQA clients, how can you prepare and improve your competencies as a counselor to not do harm to these clients?

HISTORICAL, SOCIETAL, AND CULTURAL CONTEXT

The experience of LGBTIQQA individuals is inexorably linked to the historical, societal, and cultural context in which these individuals are located. Until the last few decades of the 20th century, homosexuality was considered abnormal, an abomination, and vilified in modern Western cultures. During the 1950s, research by Alfred Kinsey and Evelyn Hooker brought affectional/sexual orientation into the field of empirical study, with studies demonstrating sexual orientation as a continuum and that there were no significant differences between the personalities of homosexual and heterosexual men (Schreier & Lassiter, 2010). These studies began the movement within psychology that led to the depathologization of homosexuality, with homosexuality being removed from the Diagnostic and Statistical Manual of Mental Disorders (DSM) in 1973 (Chernin & Johnson, 2003). In 1975, ALGBTIC was founded as a division of the American Counseling Association (ACA). Since the 1970s, mental health organizations, including the ACA, the American Psychological Association, and the National Association of Social Workers, have taken explicit steps toward reducing homonegativity within the mental health field and improving service delivery for LGBTIQQA clients (Barret & Logan, 2002).

Even given the advances in the mental health professions toward providing competent treatment to LGBTIQQA individuals, there has been little research focused on understanding the experiences of LGBTIQQA people of color, those in lower socioeconomic status (SES) strata, and even those that identify outside of the more commonly accepted affectional/sexual orientations and gender identities (e.g., genderqueer, pansexual, asexual, or non-identifying). There is not room in this chapter to adequately capture all of the unique concerns of various populations within LGBTIQQA communities, but counselors should be aware of the impact that other intersecting identities will have for LGBTIQQA clients. For case studies relevant to various populations within LGBTIQQA communities, counselors should reference the *Casebook for Counseling LGBT Persons and Their Families* (Dworkin & Pope, 2012).

Societal discourses produce beliefs and values that impact the lives of LGBTIQQA individuals, often in a negative way. *Heteronormativity* refers to the pervasive dominant discourses and social norms that naturalize and normalize heterosexuality. One way that heteronormativity reproduces itself is through the assumption that people are heterosexual unless they tell you otherwise. Heteronormativity is based in an essentialist view of gender, assuming that gender is inherent, stable, and fixed, thus reinforcing the gender binary of male and female (Killerman, 2013; Lottes & Grollman, 2010). A heteronormative view is that men and women have natural roles in life that align their biological sex, gender identity, and sexual orientation; as such, opposite-sex relationships are the only appropriate type of intimate relationships. *Homonegativity* is a term that captures the subtle ways in which disapproval is expressed toward homosexuality or gender variance (Lottes & Grollman, 2010). Homonegativity may take place through *microaggressions*, daily verbal or behavioral acts that communicate negativity or hostility. Microaggressions are often unintentional insults but also can take the form of direct discrimination (Shelton & Delgado-Romero, 2013). For example, a parent who refers to a child's same-sex intimate partner as a "friend" is a slight that would be considered a microaggression.

Trans or gender non-conforming individuals also may experience heteronormativity and homonegativity through questioning of their gender expression or being incorrectly labeled as gay, lesbian, or bisexual, even if the transgender individuals identify as heterosexual. *Transprejudice* is a term that more specifically captures the experience of discrimination for transgender or gender non-conforming individuals, based on the lack of acceptance or fear of individuals who transgress or blur the dominant gender binary (Association for Lesbian, Gay, Bisexual, and Transgender Issues in Counseling Transgender Committee, 2010). Both homonegativity and transprejudice can occur through more subtle means, such as microaggressions toward LGBTIQQA individuals or can lead to more obvious discrimination, from verbal harassment to physical or sexual violence. This discrimination and oppression toward LGBTIQQA individuals generates a climate that can lead to *minority stress*. Minority stress occurs when external events based in prejudice, such as loss of a job or social rejection, directly impact LGBTIQQA individuals' well-being or influence their expectations of how society is going to respond to them (Meyer, 2003). Further, LGBTIQQA individuals may internalize the negative beliefs about LGBTIQQA identities that are entrenched in dominant discourses, thus affecting their self-concept and leading to a personal stigmatization. Whether operating on an external or internal level, researchers have shown that LGB individuals who experience high levels of minority stress report impaired well-being, including a higher prevalence of mental health issues and suicide (Meyer, 2003), and researchers are starting to find that trans individuals also suffer as a result of minority stress (Grant et al., 2011; Herman, 2013).

Heteronormativity, homonegativity, and transprejudice create *heterosexual* and *cisgender privilege*, an unearned and invisible benefit to those who identify or pass as heterosexual and/or cisgender. These benefits can include access to resources, credibility, or not having to worry about discrimination. For example, heterosexual individuals can freely talk about intimate relationships in their workplace or can easily hold their partners' hands in public without concern of repercussions. Cisgender individuals do not have to worry about finding a safe place to use the restroom, spaces that are typically divided based on the gender binary. It is important for heterosexual and cisgender counselors working with LGBTIQQA clients to examine the privileges, as prompted in Exercise 7.3, they have based on their affectional/sexual orientation and gender identity in order to recognize the impact of heteronormativity on LGBTIQQA clients.

Exercise 7.3

PRIVILEGE

Directions: List or discuss the other ways that heterosexual and cisgender individuals experience privilege. These may include small daily acts, the ability to live genuinely without anxiety or fear, or access to systemic or institutionalized protections or resources. It may be helpful to share your reflections with a colleague, supervisor, or classmate.

TRADITIONAL SEXUAL IDEOLOGIES

The physiological aspects of sexuality that impact sexual health were explored in Chapter 4. Fully understanding the sexuality of women and men involves an analysis of the cultural, social, and political frameworks that influence traditional gender roles and gendered interactions in intimate relationships and sexual encounters (Amaro, Raj, & Reed, 2001). Women's and men's perceptions of their sexual selves and what roles to enact in sexual relations tend to be guided by *sexual scripts*, defined as internalized messages from society that specify desirable experiences of women and men's bodies and appropriate sexual interactions between two partners, particularly in a heterosexual couple (Hill, 2006; Wiederman, 2005). Our understanding of female and male sexuality is created through social discourses, with the media having a strong impact on the dissemination of sexual scripts in Western cultures (Kunkel, Cope, & Biely, 1999). Often, the media in the United States depicts traditional sex as an intense, romantic act that spontaneously occurs when a man and a woman feel an attraction to one another. Typically, men initiate sex, and women are depicted as the object of desire in media images (Ward & Friedman, 2006), and these gendered sexual behaviors will be explored more fully in the sections below.

Schneider and Gould (1987) identified five components of sexual scripts: (a) Whom does an [individual] have sex with, that is, what are the limits and constraints of appropriate partners? (b) What acts does an [individual] engage in sexually from the whole range of possible sexual acts? (c) When is sex done, that is, at what times of the day, month, or year, and in one's life cycle? (d) Where, in setting or circumstance, does sex occur? and (e) Why do people have sex, that is, what are the culturally approved accounts for doing sexual things that people provide for themselves and others? (p. 129). Exercise 7.4 asks you to personally examine your sexual scripts by answering the above questions. Sexual scripts may be useful in decreasing anxiety around sexual behavior because they provide guidance and predictability about how to act and what to expect from one's partner in sexual encounters (Wiederman, 2005). Sexual scripts, however, can be limiting and lead to negative labeling of individuals' behavior, which can be disempowering. Given their basis in cultural norms at any given time and location, sexual scripts may vary within a culture based on individuals' race and ethnicity. For example, African American women are more often depicted in the media as asserting their sexual needs and desires or taking more pleasure in sexual experiences (Stephens & Phillips, 2005), whereas Caucasian women are more often portrayed as sexually restrained or less forward in sexual encounters.

By understanding sexual scripts, counselors can help clients challenge internalized messages that prevent them from creating healthy sexual relationships.

Exercise 7.4

INDIVIDUAL REFLECTION ACTIVITY ON SEXUAL SCRIPTS

Directions: Take a few minutes to examine your own sexual scripts by writing down your personal responses to the five questions by Schneider and Gould (1987). Reflect on your responses: Where did these beliefs and values come from? Which beliefs or values most influence your own sexual behavior? Which beliefs or values have alleviated anxiety about your sexuality or sexual behavior, and which have caused you anxiety in the past? Finally, consider if there are any of your scripts that you would like to change. How could you go about challenging and reconstructing new scripts that are more fitting with your personal beliefs and values?

Counseling approaches that focus on externalization of problems, such as solution-focused brief therapy (de Shazer, 1982) and narrative therapy (White, 2007), may be useful to deconstruct sexual scripts that negatively impact clients' sexual functioning. Cognitive interventions can help clients challenge and reconstruct existing traditional scripts that impact sexual desire and encourage clients to be more open and adaptable in their sexual interactions. Additionally, cognitive therapy can help couples emphasize desire and satisfaction in their sexual relationship (Pridal & LoPiccolo, 2000).

Female Sexuality

Traditional female sexual scripts emphasize women's passivity, agreeableness, and purity in sexual behavior, with their main role being the sexual gatekeeper (Curtin, Ward, Merriwether, & Caruthers, 2011). Women's role as the sexual gatekeeper may be inadvertently reinforced in their families, as parents may be more concerned or controlling over daughters' sexual behavior than their sons', as women are the ones who risk getting pregnant through sexual encounters (Wiederman, 2005). At the same time, women are objectified for their bodies and sexuality and also are expected to make themselves sexually available to men although they are not the ones expected to initiate sex. These sexual scripts create an environment where women, especially young women, become focused on meeting the needs of their male partners, often at the expense of their own sexual needs and desires. A core difference, however, between traditional female and male sexuality is that women do not have to reject all things masculine in order to construct their femininity. Thus, women's sexuality has space to be more flexible and fluid and remain within acceptable norms of sexual behavior, and indeed, women show more variability in affectional and sexual attraction across social contexts than do men (Peplau & Garnets, 2000).

Several factors influence women's role as the gatekeeper of sexual encounters. First, women's biology puts them more at risk for unintended consequences of sexual encounters, namely women can get pregnant and more easily contract sexually transmitted infections (STIs) (Alexander, Coleman, Deatrick, & Jemmott, 2011). Since these risks are more serious for women than for men, women are likely to be more cognizant of the potential outcomes of sexual encounters and seek to limit their number of partners or increase their use of contraception to prevent an unintended pregnancy and contraction of STIs. Secondly, gender norms influence women's role as sexual gatekeepers as women's sexual desire tends to be either ignored and/or shamed. Women who are sexually direct or openly active are seen as flawed in that they lack self-control or possess poor judgment and are often socially shamed through the use of negative labels that are attached to sexually open behavior for women (e.g., slut or whore) (Wiederman, 2005). Thus, women are taught to either deny their sexual desire and/or to control it effectively in order to align with traditional feminine gender norms of the woman as passive and pure. As explored further in the Male Sexuality section, masculine gender norms portray men as more sexually desirous and active, which in turn influences women to feel responsible for their male partners' sexual desire in addition to their own (Wiederman, 2005).

Ultimately, traditional female sexual scripts can lead to a lack of knowledge about sex and low-sexual assertiveness among women. Young women who endorse more traditional gender norms tend to experience less comfort with their bodies during sexual encounters (Curtin et al. 2011). Further, body self-consciousness can impact women's ability to experience sexual pleasure and can lead to sexual impairments if women feel disengaged or ill at ease during sexual encounters (Curtin et al., 2011). Thus, this passive approach to sexuality that is embedded in feminine gender norms can impede women's ability to feel good about their sexual selves. Counselors can help female clients take more ownership over their sexual experiences through psychoeducation, body-image work, and assertiveness training. Further, reconstructing sexual scripts may serve to reduce women's anxiety about their sexual functioning, and counselors also can incorporate interventions (e.g., systematic desensitization, mindfulness, etc.) to address the anxiety directly as needed.

Male Sexuality

Traditional male sexuality is governed by discourses that encourage boys and men to not only become masculine but to actively reject any roles associated with feminine sexuality or subordinate masculinities, often leading to men's sexuality being more rigid and constricted than that of women (Bader, 2009). Richardson (2010) referred to the discourses that set the ideal practices for male sexuality as *hegemonic masculinities*, in which men are expected to be sexually skillful, confident, strong, and even aggressive. Hegemonic masculinities may lead men to restrict their emotional experiences except through anger or aggression, and indeed, men, regardless of race, ethnicity, nationality, or age, seek mental health assistance at lower rates than women (Addis & Mahalik, 2003). Men may internalize that crying, showing sensitivity, or asking for help is a sign of weakness, associated with femininity and homosexuality (Stevens & Englar-Carson, 2010), and this rigid sense of emotional expression may impact their ability to emotionally connect with partners in intimate relationships (Elder, Brooks, & Morrow, 2012). Therapies that promote emotional engagement and attachment bonds, such as emotionally focused therapy, may be useful to help men who are experiencing struggles with sexual intimacy in their intimate relationships (Johnson & Zuccarini, 2010).

Traditional masculinity is highly regulated by interactions between men and other men. As such, men may focus on performing heterosexuality through sexual encounters with numerous women to establish credibility with other men about their masculinity, namely that they are neither feminine nor gay (Richardson, 2010). Due to the peer pressure, men are often thought to be more sexually desirous than women. As such, frequent sexual activity is viewed as more acceptable for men than for women (Wiederman, 2005; Elder et al., 2012), which may lead to men engaging in sexually risky behaviors, such as having multiple partners, in order to perform masculinity. Men may privately value emotional connection with women or waiting for the "right woman" to engage in sexual encounters, but these scripts go against hegemonic masculinity, and men may not feel comfortable discussing these non-dominant views with male friends (Richardson, 2010). To challenge the sexual scripts that endorse risky sexual activity for men, counselors can help men establish networks of male friends that encourage positive sexuality and healthy relationships in addition to addressing emotional connection in their intimate relationships. Systemic and group counseling may be useful for men to establish social connections that promote emotional intimacy and to reconstruct masculinity.

Consequently, hegemonic masculinity leads to the invisibility of males as the victims of sexual assault or violence. A common misconception for men is that since men are always interested in sex, they cannot be assaulted because men always want sexual encounters to occur. Further, the constructions of men as strong and aggressive means that men should be able to fight off any potential attackers, particularly if the perpetrator is a woman (Turchik & Edwards, 2012). These misconceptions may lead to male survival of sexual assault being minimized, and as a result, many men may be unwilling to report an assault that occurs due to feelings of humiliation and fears that others will discredit their disclosure. Male survivors of sexual assault are likely to suffer from intense feelings of self-blame, guilt, and shame, be at risk for PTSD, and experience difficulties in sexual and interpersonal functioning (Elliott, Mok, & Briere, 2004; Turchik, 2012). Further, men who experience sexual assault demonstrate risky behaviors to psychologically cope, such as increased substance use, smoking, and sexual risk taking behaviors (Turchik, 2012). As most sexual assault response programs are geared toward female survivors, men may be unable to find outlets to address their mental health needs. Thus, the current system of mental health prevention and response to sexual assault that is built upon these inaccuracies that violence only occurs by males onto females leads to services that are inadequate to meet the needs of male survivors and also LGBTIQQA individuals.

GENDER IDENTITY

There has been a slow social shift toward recognizing that gender identity can fall into many different domains outside of the male and female binary. Although gender dysphoria and gender identity disorder (GID) remain as mental health diagnoses in the DSM-5 and the ICD-10 respectively, the mental health and medical fields have shown increased understanding of trans identities. With the implementation of the DSM-5, the American Psychiatric Association (American Psychiatric Association, 2013a) took a step toward depathologizing gender variance by renaming GID as Gender Dysphoria, eliminating the language of "disorder" from the description. Further, APA made a statement to make clear that gender non-conformity is not a mental disorder (American Psychiatric Association, 2013b). Following similar arguments that led to the removal of homosexuality from the DSM, there is a movement to remove these diagnoses from the classification system altogether as they potentially lead to the stigmatization and pathologizing of gender variance (Carroll, Gilroy, & Ryan, 2002; Langer & Martin, 2004). On the other hand, some practitioners argue that the diagnosis may offer validation to trans individuals and that it provides a framework for practitioners to define and respond to clients' dissonance about their gender (Burgess, 2009).

While mental health professions have generally lagged behind in setting competent standards for working with trans clients, the World Professional Association for Transgender Health (WPATH) has led the way in setting mental health and medical standards of care for transgendered individuals. WPATH has held international symposiums dedicated to promoting transgender health since 1969, and the organization published their original Standards of Care (SOC) in 1970 (WPATH, 2014). Any counselors working with trans clients should be familiar with the WPATH SOC for the Health of Transsexual, Transgender, and Gender Non-Conforming People and ALGBTIC's competencies for working with transgender clients. Gender non-conforming individuals are at risk for mental health struggles and experiencing harassment or violence due to the lack of social acceptance. Researchers have found that up to 78% of trans individuals report harassment at their schools, and 90% report discrimination at their place of employment, with 60% having experienced physical and/or sexual assault and 41% having attempted suicide (Grant et al., 2011; Haas, Rodgers, & Herman, 2014). Many of the mental health struggles trans individuals experience can be resolved when they find a congruence between their felt sense of gender and biological sex and the ability to be able to freely express their gender identity without fear of rejection, harassment, or violence. Counselors should be aware that much of the distress trans individuals experience is due to social discrimination toward their sense of self (Mallon & DeCrescenzo, 2009).

For trans people who wish to transition, often their symptoms of depression, anxiety, or suicidal ideation recede once they begin to transition, and may fully dissipate upon achieving their desired physical state (Murad et al., 2010). Thus, medical treatment such as hormone therapy or reconstructive surgery is typically the most effective treatment for the mental health concerns of trans individuals, particularly for those who identify as transsexual. Much of the review below is focused on the counseling concerns and treatment strategies for transgender and transsexual individuals, as there is not enough space in this chapter to cover the concerns of everyone along the gender-variant spectrum. While medical treatment is a viable treatment strategy for many trans individuals, not all gender variant individuals desire to transition, and thus may not seek out medical intervention. Counselors should always respect the agency of their clients in the way they self-identify and wish to present and live as their felt gender identity.

Common Counseling Concerns

There are many specific considerations to keep in mind when working with trans clients, therefore it is impossible to capture all that a counselor needs to know to become competent in working with trans individuals in this chapter. Counselors who are beginning to work with trans clients need to seek out training and supervision from a counselor who is a trans specialist in order to maintain competent practice. First, counselors should be familiar with the diagnosis of gender dysphoria, as well as the critiques of this diagnosis. One of the criteria to diagnose gender dysphoria is that an individual is clinically distressed by their condition (American Psychiatric Association, 2013a). Often, this distress presents as anxiety or depression, with symptoms being directly associated with individuals' gender incongruence. It is important for counselors who interact with trans individuals to question the source of their distress. Helping trans clients locate this source in external factors, such as a lack of societal acceptance of trans identities, validates that there is nothing inherently wrong with an individual experiencing gender dysphoria (Coleman et al., 2011; Mallon & DeCrescenzo, 2009). Further, as discussed in depth in the ethical concerns section, "corrective" therapies are harmful to trans individuals, are not effective in changing their identities, and thus should not be employed by counselors (Langer & Martin, 2004; Coleman et al., 2011).

A major concern for trans individuals is the lack of counseling services that are trans-positive (Davis, 2009). Nationwide, there are very few mental health and other medical service providers that identify themselves as serving the trans population. The shortage of services isolates trans individuals, leading to many who may not seek out necessary health care. Further, most mental health service providers do not create options for trans identities on demographic or intake forms, which erodes the visibility of trans individuals, creating a lack of acknowledgement of their health care needs (Davis, 2009). There is a definite need to develop positive mental health services for trans individuals, and counselors can aid this development by educating themselves on health concerns of trans people. Any counselors working with trans individuals should seek out knowledge and skills that will make them competent in treating this population and should not expect their clients to be the source of that education although individual clients may need to debrief counselors on their personal concerns. Counselors who are competent in serving trans clients can get involved in their local trans communities to network and learn about the unique needs of trans individuals in their specific locations and establish visibility through directly marketing services that are trans-positive (Cole & Rosenbluth, 2012).

Transgender Youth

Many trans individuals begin experiencing gender dysphoria during childhood, often as young as three years of age (Mallon & DeCrescenzo, 2009). These children display behaviors that show a significant psychological connection with the other gender; it is important to note for trans children, these behaviors occur together and over time and are not isolated events. Trans children will typically engage in toy and role-play that is socially associated with the opposite gender and often gravitate toward playing with children of the opposite-sex. They also are likely to express a desire to and/or dress as the other gender and may display dissatisfaction with their assigned gender identity through statements about sexual anatomy or through negative reactions to parents attempting to have them dress or play in ways associated with their assigned gender (Mallon & DeCrescenzo, 2009).

Children quickly pick up on heteronormativity and may attempt to repress their desired gender expression to prevent rejection by family and peers. Trans children are often brought to mental health services not due to personal distress but because their parents are concerned about the child's gender non-conforming statements and actions (Langer & Martin, 2004). Thus, competent counseling practice with trans children will focus heavily on the parents, educating them about trans individuals, helping them to accept and respond appropriately to their child, and supporting them to make compromises that will benefit their child (e.g., when their male to female [MTF] child is at home, they will refer to her as a girl and call her by Julia instead of her given name of Joe). Counselors can support parents in learning to advocate for their child, particularly in educational settings where their child may experience discrimination by peers, teachers and administrators, and the system itself due to the lack of social acceptance of gender non-conforming behaviors.

Children who express gender dysphoria may be even less likely than trans adults to receive help due to the reluctance of helping professionals in providing treatment for gender dysphoria to children. Per the WPATH SOC (Coleman et al., 2011), children with gender dysphoria are not treated with hormone therapy due to the potential negative side effects and because many children's dysphoria may dissipate by the time they reach adolescence. In some children, gender dysphoria will intensify as they near or begin puberty; however, some trans adolescents may not have displayed gender non-conforming behaviors as a child, and thus, disclosure of gender dysphoria may come as a shock to their parents. For trans adolescents, puberty-suppressing hormones, which are a fully reversible intervention, are an option to give them more time to consider transitioning and to delay physical changes that may be more difficult to reverse after puberty (Coleman et al., 2011). Adolescents may start CSH therapy with parental consent, and typically, CSH therapy would be recommended in later adolescence as the effects of long-term hormone treatment are not fully reversible. Top surgery for female to male (FTM) adolescents may be considered before individuals turn 18 if they have been on testosterone for a year and living for a substantial amount of time as male, but bottom surgery is not suitable as an intervention until the individual reaches adulthood as it is irreversible (Coleman et al., 2011).

CSH and GRS

Within the current medical system, trans clients must go through an evaluation with a mental health provider before they can receive medical CSH or GRS services (Singh, Boyd, & Whitman, 2010). Many counselors incorrectly assume that trans individuals should attend counseling for a set period of time before seeking medical treatment via CSH or GRS to transition or have abused their power as gatekeepers by unnecessarily extending the mental health treatment of trans clients before providing them with the letter(s) necessary to enter into medical treatment. According to the WPATH SOC (Coleman et al., 2011), counseling *is not a* requirement to seek CSH, and there is no real-life experience living as the other gender or waiting period required before seeking medical treatment. In order to begin CSH, an evaluation is required by a therapist who specializes in trans issues for an appropriate referral to an endocrinologist. The evaluation is to ascertain that an individual meets the criteria for gender dysphoria, that their distress is not better explained by another mental health diagnosis and that they are familiar with the medical benefits and risks of hormone treatment (Singh, Boyd, & Whitman, 2010).

Per the WPATH SOC for GRS (Coleman et al., 2011), only one evaluation is needed from a qualified mental health professional for top surgery, and MTF clients must have been on hormone therapy for 12 months unless there was a medical contraindication. Two evaluations are needed for bottom surgery, and clients must have been on hormones and living in their desired gender role for 12 months prior to bottom surgery. Prolonged therapy, however, *is not* a requirement for CSH or GRS unless the therapist deems there are acute mental health issues that warrant treatment before proceeding to medical treatment. For example, a counselor may require that a trans client with psychosis attend therapy to reduce their symptoms before proceeding with CSH or GRS. Again, transitioning alleviates many other mental health symptoms for trans individuals (Murad et al., 2010), and therapists who think a client may need mental health treatment before being referred to medical providers should consult with other trans specialists before creating an unnecessary waiting period for a client to seek medical treatment.

Clients seeking GRS likely will need to travel out of state to find a surgeon that specializes in breast reconstruction for trans individuals and may even need to travel outside of the United States for surgeons who specialize in bottom surgery. The majority of insurance plans do not cover surgeries for trans individuals (Singh, Boyd, & Whitman, 2010) so these surgeries can be costly. Another way counselors can help trans clients is to connect them with financial advisors, health care financing companies, or help them construct a savings timeline to be able to pay for their surgeries. Trans individuals report high rates of unemployment and poverty (American Psychological Association, 2007; Grant et al., 2011; Haas et al., 2014), and economic concerns can complicate their ability to access medical treatment and create more distress.

Intersex Clients

It is estimated that approximately 1 in 1500 to 2000 individuals are intersex (Intersex Society of North America [ISNA], 2008), although rates may be higher as some individuals have subtle forms of genetic or anatomical variations that are not detected. Some individuals become aware of their intersexuality when parents or doctors notice something different about their bodies. Many intersex individuals, however, may not become aware of their status until adulthood due to withholding of medical information of intersexuality discovered in infancy, atypical development during puberty, or becoming aware of infertility as an adult. Within mental health professions, there has been little focus on the concerns of intersex individuals, leading to an erasure of their identity and potentially adding to their distress of being viewed as atypical (Singh, Boyd, & Whitman, 2010). Most intersex individuals are treated medically or surgically, which may be the source of their distress; however, current practice advocates for positive mental health support to help intersex individuals and their families make informed decisions on how to live with intersexuality (Lee, Houk, Ahmed, & Hughes, 2006).

In past decades, the accepted medical practice was to alter the genitalia of intersex children at birth, based on the idea that gender identity is fixed from birth, believing corrective surgery would allow children to develop and function "as normal" and also decrease parental distress so they could develop a better relationship with their child. There is mixed evidence about the psychosexual outcomes of early surgery, and the effects can depend on the intersex condition that is present (Lee et al., 2006), although there is no evidence that growing up with ambiguous genitalia causes significant psychological issues. Surgery performed without the permission of intersex individuals lacks sensitivity to their bodily integrity and internal sense of gender identity, which can lead to a sense of betrayal or shame (Morland, 2008). Further, corrective surgery that leads to anatomical changes that do not correspond with intersex individuals' internal gender identity can cause distress and lead to unnecessary medical procedures for gender reassignment later in life. Thus, current medical practice encourages parents to assign a gender at birth but for surgery in newborns to occur only when functioning is impaired, not for cosmetic reasons or to relieve parental distress (Lee et al., 2006). In 2004, ACA passed a resolution to protect children from unnecessary surgery for cosmetic reasons, respecting the internal identity and associated emotional life of intersex individuals (Singh, Boyd, & Whitman, 2010).

Counseling Strategies

To effectively work with trans clients, counselors need to take a practical and systemic approach, in many ways working as a case manager and consultant in addition to a counselor (Carroll et al., 2002; Singh, Boyd, & Whitman, 2010). As successful transitioning alleviates most other mental health issues that trans individuals are experiencing (Murad et al., 2010), counselors need to move beyond talk therapy to help clients connect with resources and address the everyday life activities that will ease the transitioning process. For instance, a MTF client may have never gone out in public dressed as a female, and a counselor can go with a client on a public outing to provide a reassuring presence during an anxiety-provoking event. Counselors can assist trans clients learn to pass by helping clients pick out clothes and coaching clients on how to sit, stand, or move in ways fitting their new gender (Cole & Rosenbluth, 2012). In particular, MTF clients may experience more difficulties in learning how to dress and act as females, simply due to the complexity of clothing styles, undergarments, make-up, and hairstyle options that are appropriate for females. Counselors may want to have makeup and wigs available in their office so that MTF clients can "try on" their new identities as females before committing to hormone therapy.

Counselors need to be aware of how the lack of access to public spaces that are gender segregated may impact the lives of trans individuals. Access to public spaces, such as restrooms, dressing rooms, locker rooms, homeless shelters, domestic violence shelters, and prison, may be limited due to the gender segregation of these spaces (Herman, 2013). The lack of access to safe restroom facilities can be a serious issue, as trans individuals may be denied access to restrooms or experience verbal harassment and even physical assault when trying to use a gender-segregated public restroom. These threats can lead to anxiety about using public restrooms and can affect individuals' education, employment, and participation in public and social activities. Trans individuals may not use the restroom as needed, which can lead to dehydration, urinary tract infections, and other kidney- or bowel-related problems (Herman, 2013). Counselors can work with clients on managing anxiety about using these spaces by helping them with "passing" or with identifying safe or gender neutral restrooms. Further, counselors can advocate for gender-neutral bathrooms in their workspaces and communities to create safe spaces for trans clients.

It is important for counselors to know places and businesses in their communities that are trans-friendly (Carroll et al., 2002), such as transgender support groups or LGBT organizations that are welcoming and inclusive for trans individuals. Many communities have chapters of Parents, Families, and Friends of Lesbians and Gays (PFLAG), which are also welcoming to trans individuals and their families. As clients begin to transition, they may not feel comfortable going out in public, so these groups can provide a safe and supportive environment for clients to practice dressing and interacting as their desired gender. Further, clients who are transitioning may want to find services where they will be comfortable and/or accepted, including hairstylists and/or wig shops, laser hair removal services, gyms or personal trainers, apparel stores, and for MTF individuals, stores that sell female undergarments. Counselors who have connected with business owners ahead of time can assure their clients that they are entering into a safe space. Finally, some trans individuals may need to find new employment at an employer that will be supportive of their transition or may desire to change employment once they pass as their desired gender (Pepper & Lorah, 2008). The Human Rights Campaign has an employer database, the Corporate Equality Index that is annually updated with practices and policies of companies to assist trans clients in finding employers that are protective and supportive. Some clients may choose to go "stealth" once they pass and/or transition, to move to new locations or enter into new environments where no one knows they are trans (Pepper & Lorah, 2008).

Counselors working with trans clients will also need to do legwork to connect with medical professionals on a local, regional, national, or even international scope that provide adequate and ethical care to trans individuals (Carroll et al., 2002). One way to find a trans-positive provider is through the WPATH website. Depending on your location as a counselor, there may be few to no medical professionals who are willing and able to work with trans individuals. If counselors cannot easily identify local medical professionals who are trans-friendly, particularly endocrinologists who provide CSH therapy or voice and communication therapists, counselors may want to take on the task of calling around to see which medical professionals work with trans individuals to protect clients from discriminatory or intolerant responses (Cole & Rosenbluth, 2012). In most areas, clients will be able to find an endocrinologist without having to travel too far for CSH. Insurance plans may or may not cover CSH, depending on the plan and how endocrinologists bill the treatment, but hormone therapy is typically less expensive than many clients expect. Some trans clients may have bought hormones off the street or the Internet, and counselors should be firm with clients about the risks of buying and using hormones without the care of a medical doctor (Mallon & DeCrescenzo, 2009).

Trans clients who are transitioning also experience an emotional impact during this process. Clients are likely to experience a sense of grief and loss, perhaps over their self before the transition or over missing out on growing up as male or female (Barret & Logan, 2002). Further, clients may go through a purge stage, where they rid their spaces of clothes, accessories, and hygiene products associated with their pre-transition gender. With transitioning, there is also a gain (for FTMs) and loss (for MTFs) of male privilege that may be emotionally difficult for clients to accept (Cole & Rosenbluth, 2012). Trans clients are often susceptible to body image struggles, as they also are impacted by the cultural discourses defining the ideals for male and female body types (Singh, Boyd, & Whitman, 2010). Last, many trans clients face anxieties about revealing their status as trans in intimate partnerships (and rightfully so as revealing their identity may put them at risk for sexual assault or violence), which can put these clients at risk for unsafe sexual behaviors (Carroll et al., 2002). Counselors working with trans clients' need to develop a comfort level in talking about sexual behavior in order to adequately address trans clients anxieties about safely entering into intimate partnerships and navigating sexual experiences (Singh, Boyd, & Whitman, 2010).

Finally, counselors can be a bridge between trans clients and their families. Many trans clients experience rejection after coming out to their families (Singh,

Boyd, & Whitman, 2010), and counselors can support and educate family members coming to terms with clients' identities. Family counseling is particularly important for working with trans youth, but adult clients may also desire family sessions. Some clients may not have come out as trans until later in adulthood and may have a committed intimate relationship and children that they wish to protect (Ettner, 1996). Some clients may wish to dissolve their marriages before revealing their identities to their partners, and some may choose to reveal their true gender identity to their partner in hopes that they can maintain their relationships. Counselors can support clients in revealing their gender identity to their partner. Many partners may react with shock, anxiety, or even disgust to the disclosure, and they may question their own gender identity and sexuality, so counselors need to prepare trans clients for these reactions (Ettner, 1996). Some partners may leave the relationship, and others may choose to stay with their partner and live together in a same-sex relationship or as a friendship. Either way, counselors can help couples negotiate the transition together, providing support to both partners' experiences and helping them to redefine their intimate relationship in the process. Trans clients may need to seek legal aid to help with divorce proceedings or custody hearings, and counselors can connect them to agencies that specialize in this as listed in the resource list at the end of the chapter. Case Illustration 7.1 is presented for the reader to consider how to apply counseling strategies with a client questioning their gender identity.

CASE ILLUSTRATION 7.1

CANDACE

Candace, a 20-year-old Caucasian female who identifies as a lesbian presents to your office with depressive symptoms, including low mood, loss of interest in activities, difficulty sleeping and fatigue, and mild suicidal ideation. Candace is dressed in baggier clothes and has her hair cut short. Candace is from a small town, and moved to this more urban area after she graduated from high school. As you get to know Candace, she reveals that she has struggled with feelings of discontent around her gender identity, stating that she does not feel like a female. Candace reveals that she has identified more with males since she was a child and engaged in more male-identified play activities throughout her childhood and adolescence. Candace says she has always been attracted to women and came out as a lesbian in her teens. Candace says that as she has gotten older, she has become more and more disgusted with her body, particularly her breasts, which is negatively impacting her sexual relationship with her partner of a year. Candace says that her partner believes she may be transgender, and Candace reports that what she has read online about trans individuals fits with her current struggle. Candace says that she is still confused about whether or not she is transgender, and what that may mean if she is trans. Candace also discusses concerns about her family, saying that it took her parents several years to accept her as a lesbian and that she does not know if they could handle her being transgender.

Application Exercise

Based on the information that you gathered about Candace above, develop a treatment plan for her to include the following:

- Start by considering if you are qualified to treat Candace based on the ACA Code of Ethics, WPATH SOC, and ALGBTIC's competencies for counseling transgender clients. How would you handle a referral, or what can you do if there are no qualified treatment providers for transgender clients in your area?
- What is an appropriate diagnosis for Candace? Explain your rationale.
- Develop a treatment plan that is in line with your diagnoses to help Candace. Based on what you learned about counseling trans clients in this chapter, what do you think is the most important treatment objective and why?
- What adjunct services will be useful for Candace? Research and identify local, regional, and national services and spaces that are trans-positive and would be beneficial to Candace.

LESBIAN, GAY, AND BISEXUAL AFFECTIONAL ORIENTATIONS

Common Counseling Concerns

For the purposes of brevity in this section, we use the acronym lesbian, gay, bisexual, queer, and questioning (LGBQQ) as lesbian, gay, and bisexual tend to be the most prevalent affectional orientations with which people identify. Many of the following counseling concerns and strategies may apply to clients with other affectional orientations, such as pansexual or asexual, although clients with identities other than LGB may have unique concerns that are not addressed in this chapter. We include queer and questioning orientations to highlight the spectrum of affectional orientations as to not render invisible those identities that may be less ascribed to or predominant in the general population.

As with trans individuals, social prejudice and rejection of LGBQQ identities can lead to psychological struggles for LGBQQ people. LGBQQ youth who experience high levels of family rejection due to their affectional orientation are six times as likely to report high levels of depression and eight times as likely to have attempted suicide as LGBQQ peers who did not experience or experienced low levels of family rejection (Ryan, Huebner, Diaz, & Sanchez, 2009). Approximately 64% of LGBQQ youth report feeling unsafe in their schools due to their affectional orientation (Gay, Lesbian, & Straight Education Network, 2011). Societal prejudice also contributes to LGBQQ individuals turning to substance abuse or sexual risk-taking to deal with their distress. As such, rates of substance abuse are high in LGBQQ communities, particularly among LGBQQ youth (Hughes & Eliason, 2002; Ryan et al., 2009). Sexual risk-taking behaviors also put LGBQQ individuals at a higher risk of contracting STIs or HIV and AIDS, particularly for men who have sex with men, which can be damaging to their overall health (Centers for Disease Control, 2014b).

Coming out is the process in which individuals accept their attractions for themselves and then reveal their affectional orientation to others. LGBQQ clients may experience anxiety during this process, and counselors can support clients in considering the positives and negatives of coming out to various others and how to cope with potential reactions (Barret & Logan, 2002; Chernin & Johnson, 2003). Counselors should respect clients' decisions about whether to come out and avoid persuading clients one way or the other. Coming out too early can create great distress for a client and may negatively impact significant relationships, and expressing doubts about a client coming out (unless there is a clear, direct risk involved) may be confusing and lead to self-doubt for LGBQQ individuals (Barret & Logan, 2002; Chernin & Johnson, 2003). Counselors working with LGBQQ clients should be aware that they may experience a sense of grief and loss as they come out, including losses related to their sense of self, their life as it was before coming out, heterosexual privilege, and potentially their relationships with significant family members and friends (Chernin & Johnson, 2003).

Social prejudice can lead to LGBQQ clients experiencing difficulties in multiple important areas in their lives. First, clients may experience discrimination or heterosexism at their places of employment. Counselors may need to help clients in coping with a discriminatory workplace, making decisions on whether or not to come out at work, or exploring other job options if clients find their workplace to be too hostile (Chernin & Johnson, 2003). Another area where LGBQQ clients may struggle is finding a religious or spiritual home that is accepting and affirming of their affectional orientation. Many LGBQQ clients may have grown up with religious doctrines that describe homosexuality as a sin and may have felt ostracized by their religious communities even before coming out. These religious beliefs can lead to LGBQQ clients feeling distrustful, angry, or hurt, and some individuals may choose to distance themselves from their religious communities (Chernin & Johnson, 2003). Clients may want to process their beliefs to resolve any dissonance between their religion or spirituality and affectional orientation and connect to more affirming religious communities within their chosen affiliation. Some clients may choose to remain in their religious communities but not reveal their same-sex attractions (SSAs) or affectional orientation, and counselors should respect clients' agency in making this choice. Counselors should support clients to make the choice that is most fitting at the time, preparing clients to navigate the challenges of balancing conflicting identities, whether this involves their family, place of employment, or religious and/or spiritual community (Pope, Mobley, & Myers, 2010).

In working with LGBQQ clients, counselors should always consider the impact of cultural context and developmental issues throughout the lifespan of clients' identities as LGBQQ. LGBQQ people of color may experience more alienation and societal stigma (Barret & Logan, 2002) and may fear being rejected by their cultural support systems if they come out (Pope et al., 2010) and/or experience racism within the LGBQQ community. Further, LGBQQ people often have more financial struggles than the general population, in part due to discrimination in the workplace and to the lack of societal benefits for same-sex partnerships (American Psychological Association, 2007), and LGBQQ people of color may be even more at risk for economic struggles due to the disproportionate numbers of racial minorities in lower socioeconomic status (SES) in the United States. Finally, older LGBQQ adults may face unique challenges such as social isolation, lack of social support services for aging, and financial stress (Chernin & Johnson 2003).

Bisexual Clients

There are multiple myths about bisexuality that may negatively impact bisexual individuals, with two of the main myths being that bisexual individuals are really just gay or lesbian who do not want to come out and that bisexuals must be promiscuous because they are not satisfied with just one gender (Barret & Logan, 2002). Many of these myths are perpetuated because bisexuality is a threat to heteronormative discourses, given that the presence of bisexuality destabilizes the homosexual and heterosexual binary (Barker & Langdridge, 2008). Thus, bisexuality is often rendered invisible and considered to be a made-up identity. Bisexual individuals may be affected by heteronormativity in similar ways as lesbians and gay men but also may experience *biprejudice* from LGBTIQQA communities as well, due to the view that bisexual individuals can "choose" heterosexuality. Further, given this perception of bisexuality as the ability to choose between genders, some lesbian and gay individuals may feel that bisexuality threatens their movement for civil rights, which is largely based on the promotion that lesbian and gay identities are not a choice but innate (Barret & Logan, 2002).

Biprejudice can contribute to higher rates of mental health problems in bisexual individuals than in heterosexual, lesbian, or gay individuals, and can also lead to more difficulties in accessing mental health services (Barker & Langdridge, 2008). Counselors should affirm bisexuality as a valid sexual orientation when a client identifies as bisexual or is considering bisexuality as their affectional orientation. Further, counselors should recognize that not all lesbian and gay communities may be welcoming of bisexual individuals and can aid clients in identifying welcoming communities (Barret & Logan, 2002).

Same-Sex Couples

Counselors working with same-sex couples should be knowledgeable about factors that are specific to relationship satisfaction and stability in same-sex partners (Spitalnick & McNair, 2005). Such factors include internalized homonegativity, lack of social support, and barriers to leaving the relationship, which may impair individuals' ability to connect with their partners and cope with relationship distress (Rotosky, Riggle, Gray, & Hatton, 2007). Also, same-sex partners often report low levels of social support for themselves as an individual and for their relationship (Kurdek, 2003; 2004). Thus, same-sex partners may need a counselor to help them build a "family-of-choice," which includes connecting them to gay and lesbian organizations within their area of residence (Green & Mitchell, 2002).

Further, barriers to leaving the relationship are a positive predictor of stability in same-sex partners; same-sex partners, however, report less barriers to leaving their relationship than opposite-sex partners (Kurdek, 1998). Barriers can include the following: social barriers, such as encouragement from others to remain in a relationship; institutional barriers, such as maintaining financial stability or legal implications of ending one's relationship; and moral barriers, or beliefs about remaining in a committed relationship over time (Kurdek, 1998). Same-sex partners may dissolve their relationships, even when the relationship is somewhat positive, more quickly and more often due to the lack of social and institutional support for same-sex relationships (Kurdek, 1998). Counselors may need to normalize changes in relationship satisfaction over time, and encourage partners to draw on their commitment to each other and rewards derived from the relationship to help same-sex couples try to first work through issues (excluding abuse and violence) before choosing to end their relationship (Pope, 2013).

Building families-of-choice and establishing rites can be protective factors for same-sex couples' relationships. Having an affirming social support in place may provide encouragement for partners to continue their relationship as well as lead to higher relationship satisfaction (Green & Mitchell, 2002). Counselors can support same-sex couples in establishing relationship rites, especially if same-sex partners lack role models or a support system in their place of residence. A wedding or vow ceremony may increase same-sex partners' commitment to one another as they are publicly stating their intent to remain in the relationship, creating another moral barrier to leaving the relationship (Kurdek, 1998; Green & Mitchell, 2002).

Intimate partner violence (IPV) does occur in same-sex partnerships, with approximately one-quarter to one-half of same-sex partners reporting incidences of IPV (Murray & Mobley, 2009). Gender role assumptions that suppose same-sex partners are socially and physically matched overlooks the fact that power and violence still operate in same-sex relationships (Brown, 2008). Gender role socialization can still impact power dynamics and other social dynamics (e.g., race, socioeconomic status, ability, etc.) and can also affect power construction in same-sex relationships (Brown, 2008; Green & Mitchell, 2002). Even if same-sex couples deny physically abusive situations, one partner may be using financial or emotional means to mistreat the other partner (Brown, 2008). Counselors should recognize that IPV does occur in same-sex relationships despite gender role assumptions, be knowledgeable about how IPV operates in same-sex relationships, and assess for IPV with same-sex partners accordingly.

Counseling Strategies

The first step in providing competent counseling services to LGBQQ clients is to explore your own personal beliefs and values that may impact your work with this population. Counselors should also be aware of current social and political issues that may impact their clients, including antidiscrimination employment laws, bullying and hate crimes prevention, and same-sex marriage recognition. Providing legal rights to LGBQQ individuals still remains a hotly contested political topic, and indeed with all the current momentum, there has been significant backlash that resulted in the passing of state constitutional amendments that define marriage as solely between a man and a woman and the adoption of legislation allowing counseling students to refuse services to a client based on religious beliefs. The states' amendments were recently struck down as unconstitutional in the ruling of the U.S. Supreme Court, which requires all U.S. states to license and recognize same-sex marriages (*Obergefell v. Hodges,* 2015). In regard to the latter, ACA (*Ward v. Wilbanks,* 2011) has made a clear stance against such legislation, arguing that it goes against counselors' ethical imperative of nondiscrimination and doing no harm, as refusing to treat LGBQQ clients on religious grounds could lead to clients feeling stigmatized on the basis of their affectional orientation or gender identity.

Of most benefit to LGBQQ clients are counselors' support, acceptance, and recognition of important values and concerns. The most important strategy in counseling LGBQQ clients is to respect their agency in how they want to define themselves and how they choose to live their lives in a way that is congruent with their identities. In an effort to correct the pathologization of LGBQQ identities, particularly homosexuality, the mental health field moved toward gay-affirmative therapies in the 1990s and 2000s. A concern with gay-affirmative therapy is that practitioners not familiar with the actual stance of these therapies may ineptly push clients toward identification with LGBQQ communities whenever a client expresses same-sex attraction (SSA) or gender dysphoria in an effort to showcase their acceptance of LGBQQ individuals (Beckstead & Israel, 2007). Some clients, however, who express SSA or gender dysphoria may have other identities or roles that conflict or supersede their affectional attractions or gender identity (Pope et al., 2010). Further, pushing clients to come out when they are not ready or are in a risky situation can be harmful, and so it should always be the clients' choice of when to come out and to whom (Chernin & Johnson, 2003).

Counselors can provide acceptance and support for clients' identity exploration and development. Interventions may include cognitive behavioral strategies to help clients build active coping skills, along with emotionally focused approaches that allow clients to identify and explore feelings related to their coming out process. A systemic approach also is necessary with LGBQQ clients due to the prevalence of homonegativity. As high levels of internalized homonegativity and minority stress are related to depression and anxiety (Meyer, 2003) and low levels of relationship satisfaction, counselors working with LGBQQ clients should be knowledgeable and efficient in approaches that work to counteract homonegativity (Green & Mitchell, 2002; Greene, 2007). Counselors can use constructivistic counseling approaches (e.g., feminist, solution-focused, or narrative therapy) that work to externalize homonegativity by locating negative views of homosexuality in societal institutions and discourses rather than the individual. Counselors may need to aid clients in building social support networks, including finding religious communities that are welcoming of LGBQQ individuals.

ETHICAL CONCERNS IN WORKING WITH LGBTIQQA CLIENTS

There are several clauses within the ACA (2014) Code of Ethics that are relevant to working with LGBTIQQA clients. First, the Code of Ethics promotes respect, dignity, and welfare of clients as counselors' primary responsibility (A.1.). The code also requires that counselors act in ways to avoid harming their clients (A.4.a.) and that counselors are aware of their values so they do not impose their values onto clients (A.4.b.). Ethical and competent work with LGBTIQQA clients starts with counselors developing a sense of awareness about their biases and values that may conflict with counseling LGBTIQQA individuals. The reflective activities at the beginning of this chapter were designed to enhance counselors' self-awareness, and the Heterosexual Questionnaire developed by Rochlin (1998) is another good resource.

With increased awareness, counselors can then develop the knowledge and skills necessary for competent work with LGBTIQQA clients. Finally, ACA includes gender, gender identity, and sexual orientation in their nondiscrimination clause (C.5.) and as multicultural considerations in interpreting assessments with clients (E.8.).

Reparative therapy (also termed conversion therapy) is based in behavioral attempts to convert individuals from homosexual orientations to heterosexual orientations. Reparative therapy has been deemed an unethical practice by ACA, the American School Counseling Association, the American Association for Marriage and Family Therapy, the American Psychological Association (APA), the American Psychiatric Association, the National Association of Social Workers, and the American Medical Association. A task force of the APA (2009) reviewed the existing research on reparative therapy, finding that the results of methodologically sound studies indicated that it is unlikely for individuals to reduce same-sex attractions and increase opposite-sex attractions through sexual orientation change efforts (SOCEs). The risks of reparative therapy include reinforcing a self-prejudice against LGB identities, which could lead to negative emotions such as guilt, shame, anxiety, depression, and suicidal ideation in clients (American Psychological Association, 2009). Thus, mental health and medical organizations underscore the ethical principle of nonmaleficence (first, do no harm) given the lack of evidence supporting the effectiveness of reparative therapy along with the potential psychological harm that a client may experience by undergoing SOCEs.

Further, SOCEs are based in a pathologizing stance of LGBQQ identities, assuming that a nonheterosexual orientation is a mental disorder and/or something that needs to be changed or fixed (Whitman, Glosoff, Kocet, & Tarvydas, 2013). As discussed above, not all LGBQQ clients may want to come out or identify with LGBTIQQA communities, but reparative therapies are not based in giving clients agency or choice on how they want to live congruently. Reparative therapies do not present the reality that clients can live a healthy and happy life as LGBQQ individuals, instead constructing LGBQQ people as unhappy, lonely, and dissatisfied. Many reparative therapies use religious doctrine in SOCEs, also excluding the multiple ways that clients can integrate their affectional orientation and gender identity into their religious or spiritual affiliation (American Psychological Association, 2009). Thus, reparative therapy can be considered discriminatory against LGBQQ individuals, which would be in violation of the ACA (2014) Code of Ethic's nondiscrimination clause (C.5.) that includes sexual orientation and gender identity.

Counselors can be put in a complex ethical position should a LGBTIQQ client directly ask for reparative therapy, as counselors are bound to both respect the dignity and agency of individuals (A.1.a.), while also acting to avoid harming their clients (American Counseling Association, 2014, A.4.a.). Counselors should have forthright discussions to inform clients that reparative therapy is not condoned by ACA or any major mental health or medical association, is not supported as an effective treatment by research, and indeed can be potentially harmful (Whitman et al., 2013). Further, counselors should inform clients that reparative therapy is a religious-based, not psychologically based, treatment. If the client still wants a referral to reparative therapy after the counselor provides psychoeducation to clients on reparative therapy and discusses other effective therapeutic approaches that can help clients reconcile their same-sex attractions with their religious beliefs (e.g., Pope et al., 2010), counselors should discuss clients' right to be informed on the nature of services provided by anyone practicing conversion therapy (American Counseling Association, 2014, A.2.b; Whitman et al., 2013). Thus, ethical practice dictates that counselors respect clients' request for the referral, while providing them with information so they can make an informed decision about engaging in reparative therapy and be prepared for their encounter with a referral counselor.

SUMMARY

At the outset of this chapter, we invited readers to consider their self-definition of their own gender identity, affectional orientation, and sexual orientation. We do not expect that readers' identities in these areas would have shifted dramatically based on a reading of this chapter. However, we do hope that readers' conceptualizations of these areas of life have been expanded, particularly as they reflect on the meanings that their clients may ascribe to their gender, affectional, and sexual identities. As with many other areas of sexuality, the topics addressed in this chapter involve a complex interplay of biological, psychological, relational, and social factors. The developmental and historical shifts in each of these factors can lead to an evolution in our individual and societal understandings of gender identity and affectional orientation over time. Counselors are in a prime position to support clients as they examine their unique identities and navigate the mental health, relational, and social challenges that may arise as a result of these identities. By increasing their knowledge of gender identity and affectional and sexual orientation, counselors can best serve their clients in sexuality counseling.

KEYSTONES

- Societal discourses produce beliefs and values that perpetuate heterosexism, homophobia, heteronormativity, homonegativity, and transprejudice, which impact the lives of LGBTIQQA individuals, often in a negative way.
- It is important for counselors to honor the terms that clients select for themselves in describing their gender identity and/or affectional orientation.
- Discrimination and oppression toward LGBTIQQA individuals generate a climate that can lead to minority stress.

- The first step in providing competent counseling services to LGBTIQQA clients is to explore your own beliefs and values that may impact your work with this population.
- Any counselors working with trans clients should be familiar with the WPATH SOC for the Health of Transsexual, Transgender, and Gender Non-Conforming People and ALGBTIC's competencies for working with transgender clients.
- As successful transitioning alleviates most mental health issues that trans individuals experience, counselors need to take a practical and systemic approach, connecting clients with resources and addressing activities that ease the transitioning process.
- In working with LGBQQ clients, counselors should consider the impact of cultural context and developmental issues on clients' identities as LGBQQ.
- Reparative therapy (also termed conversion therapy) is based in behavioral attempts to convert individuals from homosexual orientations to heterosexual orientations and has been deemed an unethical practice by the ACA.

ADDITIONAL RESOURCES

- Association of LGBT Issues in Counseling (http://www.algbtic.org)
- Corporate Equality Index (http://www.hrc.org/campaigns/corporate-equality-index)
- Dworkin, S. H., & Pope, M. (Eds.). (2012). *Casebook for counseling lesbian, gay, bisexual, and transgender persons and their families.* Alexandria, VA: American Counseling Association.
- Gay, Lesbian, & Straight Education Network (http://www.glsen.org)
- Human Rights Campaign (http://www.hrc.org)
- Intersex Society of North America (http://www.isna.org)
- Lambda Legal (http://www.lambdalegal.org)
- National Coalition for LGBT Health (http://lgbthealth.webolutionary.com)
- Parents, Families, & Friends of Lesbians and Gays (http://www.pflag.org)
- Transgender Law & Policy Institute (http://www.transgenderlaw.org)
- Transparentcy: Supporting Transgender Parents and their Children (http://www.transparentcy.org)
- The Trevor Project: Suicide Hotline for LGBT Youth (http://www.thetrevorproject.org; 866-488-7386)
- World Professional Association of Transgender Health (http://www.wpath.org)

Chapter 8

Sexuality and Intimate Relationships

The intimacy in sex is never only physical. In a sexual relationship
we may discover who we are in ways otherwise unavailable to us, and
at the same time, we allow our partner to see and know that individual.
As we unveil our bodies, we also disclose our persons.

—Thomas Moore, 1940

The dynamics of intimate relationships play a significant role in the types and frequency of sexual activities and in the connection that people experience as sexual beings. Romantic attraction, intimacy, attachment styles, sexual desire, and relational patterns are some of the relationship dynamics that impact relational and sexual satisfaction. Integrating sexuality counseling with couples counseling can be beneficial for clients, and counselors should be prepared to address both sexual and relational aspects that relate to clients' presenting concerns. There are also specific relationship situations (i.e., infidelity, divorce, and dating) that counselors should understand and be prepared to work with clients in the context of intimate relationships. This chapter will address relational dynamics of sexuality, the integration of couples and sexuality counseling, and some specific relationship situations that may arise in sexuality counseling. After reading this chapter, readers will be able to do the following:

a. Discuss dynamics of intimate relationships that impact sexuality
b. Understand the impact of attachment on relationship and sexual processes in couples
c. Describe the advantages of integrating sexuality counseling with couples counseling
d. Identify strategies to use to address specific relationship concerns in counseling

THE DYNAMICS OF COUPLE RELATIONSHIPS

Intimate relationships are not just the sum of their parts; what goes on inside each individual, as well as the relationship itself, creates many different patterns and dynamics that can be confusing and overwhelming when beginning to work with couples. Counseling couples is different than counseling individual clients because of the change of focus from one individual to two people's relationship with each other. Sexual concerns almost always are of importance in couples counseling, and there are several relevant layers that are important to conceptualize and address when working with couples with regard to sexuality. Ideally, partners will hold similar values and beliefs with one another in terms of important sexuality-related topics, although that is not always the case. Intimacy is about being close with another person and sharing oneself with that person. There are many ways that people can share themselves with others, involving varying degrees of engagement, attraction, closeness, and desire. One important sexual dynamic in couples' relationships is romantic attraction.

Romantic Attraction

Although many people have a clear sense of the qualities and features that are attractive to them in another person, researchers have had a difficult time pinning down the main factors that contribute to romantic attraction. Romantic attraction is the subjective evaluation and experience of being drawn to another person. While common stereotypes—and even some researchers—suggest that males are most drawn to physical attractiveness and females are most attracted to ambition and socioeconomic status, it turns out that attraction is not that simple (Eastwick & Finkel, 2008; Eastwick, Finkel, & Eagly, 2011; Graziano, Jensen-Campbell, Shebilske, & Lundgren, 1993). The "Big Five" personality characteristics (i.e., openness, contentiousness, extroversion, agreeableness, and neuroticism) (Barelds & Dijkstra, 2008; Figueredo, Sefcek, & Jones, 2006; Luo & Zhang, 2009) or other personality characteristics (Eastwick et al., 2011), physical attributes/beauty (Eastwick & Finkel, 2008; Eastwick et al., 2011; Luo & Zhang, 2009), humor (Hansen, 1977; McGee & Shevlin, 2009), and similarity or complementarity to self (Barelds & Dijkstra, 2008; Eastwick et al., 2011) have all been proposed factors influencing romantic attraction. Research findings have been mixed for all of these, although physical attributes and beauty have been among the strongest and most robust characteristics connected with romantic attraction (Fletcher, Kerr, Li, & Valentine, 2014; Graziano et al., 1993; Luo & Zhang, 2009), and personality (e.g., similarity or complementarity) has also found significant support (Barelds & Dijkstra, 2008; Luo & Zhang, 2009).

Social forces can influence our attraction to others, including the impressions of friends, family members, and others (Graziano et al., 1993). When looking at pictures and perceived ratings of peers of the physical attractiveness of the person in each picture, college students were asked to rate the attractiveness of the people in the photographs. Females were more susceptible to changing opinions based on others' feedback on a person, while males tended to focus on their own perspectives. However, this was only true when there were more negative evaluations of the pictures and not when peers' ratings were higher (Graziano et al., 1993). In a different study, Luo and Zhang (2009) found that people's attraction was also impacted by whether the potential partner was interested in them in return. After completing a round of speed-dating, participants were given information about whether the prospective partners were interested in them, and there was a significant, direct relationship ($r = .45$, $p < .01$) in which participants were more interested in people who were also interested in them.

Interestingly, what people say that they want in a romantic partner is not always what they find most attractive. Several studies have been completed with single heterosexuals who participated in speed-dating to see what people find romantically attractive (Eastwick & Finkel, 2008; Eastwick, Finkel, & Matthews, 2007; Luo & Zhang, 2009). Most people did not follow their pre-speed-dating answers about the people that they most wanted to date from their speed-dating encounters. Speed daters seemed to connect with some in ways that were not anticipated (e.g., physical attractiveness, earning potential, and personality), which led to romantic attraction and desire for further contact (Eastwick & Finkel, 2008). Along similar lines, romantic attraction has been difficult to predict. Fletcher et al. (2014) attempted to predict potential romantic interest that may arise during brief contact between single New Zealanders looking for someone to date and an observer watching brief interactions between the two singles. Only the attractiveness/vitality ratings were significantly able to be predicted, while the warmth/trustworthiness and status/resource were not. Overall, when trying to understand romantic attraction, it seems that beauty really is in the eye of the beholder. From a counseling perspective, it is useful to talk with clients about the characteristics and dynamics that led to their initial attraction to their romantic partners.

Intimacy

While romantic attraction can bring people to each other, intimacy is what keeps people together. Intimacy has been defined and explored in different ways. Affective or emotional, cognitive, intellectual, physical, recreational, romantic, sexual, social, and verbal are all different types of intimacy that have been explored by researchers (Dandurand & Lafontaine, 2013; Laurenceau, Rivera, Schaffer, & Pietromonaco, 2004; Moss & Schwebel, 1993; Schaefer & Olson, 1981; Tolstedt & Stokes, 1983). Intimacy is a critical component of sexual relationships, and it has been found to be a strong predictor of physical and mental health as well (Dandurand & Lafontaine, 2013; Steil, 1997). People with high levels of intimacy are more likely to have lower levels of illness, quicker illness recovery rates, lower levels of depression, and greater life satisfaction (Dandurand & Lafontaine, 2013). Intimacy is strongly tied to sexual satisfaction and is important for counselors to be able to conceptualize and facilitate in couples' relationships (Cooper, Shapiro, & Powers, 1998; Dandurand & Lafontaine, 2013; Greeff & Malherbe, 2001; Sanderson & Cantor, 2001; Schaefer & Olson, 1981; Tolstedt & Stokes, 1983).

Intimacy is a significant developmental part of young adulthood (see Erikson, 1950 and Chapter 5 of this book for further information) and seems to be a basic human need (Dandurand & Lafontaine, 2013; Erikson, 1950; Laurenceau et al., 2004; Prager & Roberts, 2004; Rogers, 1972; Sullivan, 1953). Intimacy connects people to their partners and impacts the relationship and each person in the relationship because of the close, powerful connection (Cooper et al., 1998; Prager & Roberts, 2004). A couple's level of intimacy is connected with their amount of sexual activity and satisfaction, which may be why intimacy is strongly correlated with life satisfaction (Cummins, 1996). Because intimacy is a complex and important concept, we will clarify what intimacy is, how it develops, and the skills needed to develop and maintain it.

Clarifying the Concept of Intimacy

Intimacy is conceptualized here as the connection and closeness experienced in sexual relationships (Sternberg, 1997) and contains emotional, cognitive, behavioral, and interpersonal components (Moss & Schwebel, 1993). Intimacy is felt and experienced in each individual and is a part of the relationship between the two individuals (Dandurand & Lafontaine, 2013). Intimacy is also the primary motive for people in committed relationships to engage in sexual activity together (Cooper et al., 1998). Therefore, intimacy is experienced individually inside a relationship with a significant other where there is emotional, cognitive, behavioral, and physical closeness shared between the partners.

Prager and colleagues (Lipert & Prager, 2001; Prager, 1995; Prager & Roberts, 2004) developed a framework to more easily conceptualize the complex concept of intimacy. For people to be intimate with each other, they proposed that three necessary and sufficient conditions must be met. These criteria help to differentiate between intimate and non-intimate interactions and relationships, and Prager and Roberts (2004) reminded readers that the presence of sexual activity does not automatically mean that nonphysical intimacy is also present. For interactions to be intimate, Prager and Roberts proposed that the necessary and sufficient conditions are *self-revealing behaviors, positive involvement with the other*, and *shared understandings*. The first condition, self-revealing behaviors, requires that people expose themselves emotionally and/or physically to their partners and invite them into their private lives. The interactions that partners have together also have to have a positive quality to them, meaning that the people are connected and that positive regard is present in their verbal and nonverbal behaviors. This requires that the intimate partners focus on each other and have a positive perspective of the other person. Therefore, defensiveness and accusatory approaches are absent in intimate interactions, as this sets people at odds with each other instead of connecting them. The last necessary and sufficient condition—shared understandings—requires that partners be in tune with one another. This develops over time as partners get to really know each other, including their inner worlds of thoughts, feelings, and beliefs, and share at least some basic meanings and/or values together. An example of this is when partners are able to understand with just a gesture or facial expression how the other person is really feeling and thinking. It can also involve much deeper understandings of core messages of feeling loved and valued when one's partner shares a word of praise for them. All three conditions are necessary for intimacy. In intimate interactions, partners will be open and share themselves with a positive perspective and regard for the other, and the partners will understand each other because they understand the meanings of the verbal and nonverbal messages that express their internal worlds.

Clearly, there are different levels and depths of intimate interactions, which Prager and Roberts (2004) acknowledged. They also believed that over time, partners can gain further knowledge of each other and can develop more accurate understandings of the other's internal world. The *extensiveness of intimate relating and accuracy of the accumulated shared personal understandings* together build the level of relational intimacy that partners can experience (Prager & Roberts, 2004). Frequent interactions of quality connection and relational depth are required to have extensive levels of intimacy. Sustained levels of deeper intimacy are dependent on regularly sharing about oneself and gaining a deeper understanding of one's partner. Therefore, deeper levels of intimacy do not randomly develop. Rather, intimacy is cultivated as intimate partners share more of themselves with each other and form a growing reservoir of shared understandings and meanings.

Precursors of Intimacy

For intimacy to develop, Erikson (1950; 1968) believed that a person needs to have a clear identity, or an understanding of who one is and "an inner assuredness of anticipated recognition from those who count" (Erikson, 1968, p. 165). This is important because it is difficult to share with another person one's own identity and inner world if that person is not sure of it him- or herself. Erikson posited that intimacy usually develops in young adulthood after one's identity takes root. In other words, one has to know who they are before they can truly share intimacy with another.

Identity is not the only prerequisite for deeper levels of intimate connection. Intimacy requires ongoing connections between partners that are characterized by openness, positive regard, and understanding. There has to be a lack of accusatory, alienating, attacking, defensive, and distancing behaviors from both parties as people draw close to one another and expose sometimes intense emotions and core beliefs about oneself, their partner, and life (Prager & Roberts, 2004). This requires a level of emotional maturity that is able to handle internal, intense emotions without engaging in behaviors that diminish connection and that is able to remain close to the partner as he or she is sharing intense emotions. This is not a task for the faint of heart!

Emotional Intelligence and Differentiation of Self

Two dynamics that influence processes in intimate relationships include emotional intelligence and differentiation. Emotional intelligence (EI) has been described by John Mayer and colleagues as "the ability to carry out accurate reasoning about emotions and the ability to use emotions and emotional knowledge to enhance thought" (Mayer, Roberts, & Barsade, 2008, p. 511). EI has been categorized into four cognitive components that are reflected in the following abilities: (a) accurately perceiving and identifying emotions, (b) using emotions to facilitate thought, (c) understanding emotions, and (d) managing emotions (Mayer & Salovey, 1997; Mayer, Salovey, Caruso, & Sitarenios, 2003). Similarly, in conceptualizing EI more generally, Daniel Goleman (2001) suggested that the four domains of self-awareness, self-management, social awareness, and relationship management highlight the important interplay of emotions in relational contexts and interactions.

The cognitive components of EI reflect the important internal processes involved in interactions between intimate partners. To be able to really share and understand one's own internal world, as well as another's internal world, it is vital to have a functional use of each component. For example, perception and identification of emotions are essential to articulate how one is feeling to a partner in a way that the partner can understand and so that the partners can share the meaning of the emotions together. Also, a functional ability to manage one's emotions after a difficult relationship injury, such as an affair, is important because intense emotions of sadness, fear, and pain are extremely likely to be present in both partners, and it would be impossible to understand and experience one's partner's emotions without being able to manage one's own emotions.

Murray Bowen (1978) focused his conceptualization of human development and interactions in intimate relationships on the concept of differentiation of self, which operates at the following two levels: first, it is the ability to separate one's emotions and thoughts from each other, and second, it is the ability to be one's self when being intimately connected with another person (Skowron, 2000). Differentiation of self and EI overlap in that both require the ability to see oneself as separate and connected to another. Titelman (2014) described lower levels of differentiation of self, leading people to being

> underresponsible for themselves and/or overresponsible for others, guided primarily by emotions or impulses with little to no reliance on thought, consumed by relationships with little energy left for self-direction, and tend to have major physical, emotional, or social symptoms and more marital disruption. (p. 121)

Low levels of EI and differentiation of self will cause difficulties in being intimate and close in sexual relationships. Skowron (2000) found that two of the four sub-categories of differentiation of self (i.e., emotional cutoff and emotional reactivity) were significantly connected to the amount of marital adjustment in married heterosexual couples, and these are the two sub-categories of differentiation of self that are most closely associated with Goleman's (2001) domains of EI. These findings suggest that intimacy is strongly connected to relational satisfaction (Cooper et al., 1998; Dandurand & Lafontaine, 2013; Greeff & Malherbe, 2001; Tolstedt & Stokes, 1983) and highlight the importance of EI and differentiation of self in determining how well partners are able to be intimately connected with each other.

Communication Skills

Intimate relationships are impacted by communication skills. Communication styles have been found to predict relationship satisfaction in dating couples (Meeks, Hendrick, & Hendrick, 1998). Even after controlling for other important variables in relationship satisfaction (i.e., attachment style and conflict resolution skills), communication skills were predictive of relationship satisfaction (Eğeci & Gençöz, 2006). Communication skills have been broadly categorized into four areas: listening and responding skills (sometimes called active listening skills in counseling), verbal communication skills, non-verbal communication skills, and conflict management skills (Beebe, Beebe, Redmond, Geerinck, & Salem-Wiseman, 2015). These skills can be taught to clients in couples counseling (Jacobson, 1984).

Active listening skills include reflecting feelings, content, and meaning; summarizing; attending behaviors; exploratory questions; and paraphrasing. These skills are commonly taught in counseling programs (Ivey, Ivey, & Zalaquett, 2014) and help connect the listener with the speaker. Active listening skills are used by the non-speaking partner after the speaking partner has finished talking, and they demonstrate understanding, tracking, and caring for the partner and his or her ideas. When partners demonstrate active listening skills, they promote positive regard within the relationship, as well as shared understanding emotionally and cognitively.

Expressive communication skills (including both verbal and non-verbal skills) include self-disclosure, body language, vocal tone, and self-involving statements (e.g., "I-statements"). These skills allow partners to share thoughts, feelings, and beliefs with their mate. Expressive communication skills also include the ability to clearly articulate what one wants and the ability to influence others (Beebe et al., 2015). Sexual partners can communicate with one another through words, gestures, touch, and tone of voice. The ability to effectively use expressive communication skills helps to establish connection and openness in intimate relationships.

Conflict management and resolution skills may be the most important in maintaining sexual relationships. Several studies verify that increasing conflict resolution skills helps to improve relationship satisfaction (Eğeci & Gençöz, 2006; Jacobson, 1984; Sierau & Herzberg, 2012; Wenzel, Graff-Dolezal, Macho, & Brendle, 2010), and unresolved conflict can lead to the termination of intimate relationships (Bray & Jouriles, 1995; Fincham, 2003; Gottman, 2014; Rodrigues, Hall, & Fincham, 2006). Thomas and Kilmann (1975) posited five categories of conflict management and resolution strategies, which are differentiated by the amount of cooperation (i.e., working to satisfy the partner's concerns) and assertiveness (i.e., working to satisfy one's own concerns) that are used to work toward a solution. The *competing* style has high levels of assertiveness and low levels of cooperation, the *collaborating* style has high levels of both assertiveness and cooperation, the *compromising* style has medium levels of both assertiveness and cooperation, the *avoiding* style has low levels of both assertiveness and cooperation, and the *accommodating* style has low levels of assertiveness and high levels of cooperation. The ideal conflict resolution style is therefore the collaborating style, as it is working toward a "win-win" outcome for both oneself and the partner.

Gottman and colleagues (Gottman, 2014; Gottman, Gottman, & DeClaire, 2006; Gottman & Levenson, 1992) have studied romantic relationships and the likelihood of staying together or separating largely based on how the couples respond to conflict. Gottman's groundbreaking work in this area involves making predictions with remarkable accuracy about whether couples will remain together based largely on how they manage conflict. Based on their work, Gottman and colleagues have identified "the Four Horsemen of the Apocalypse" for relationships that lead to relationships ending. All four Horsemen (i.e., criticism, defensiveness, contempt, and stonewalling) are negative ways to resolve conflict (Gottman et al., 2006). These negative interactions also lead to negative regard, instead of a positive regard, and therefore stop intimacy and decrease relationship satisfaction. Three of the four horsemen—criticism, defensiveness, and contempt—are competing conflict resolution strategies, and the last, stonewalling, is an avoiding conflict resolution strategy. The Four Horsemen lead to partners being pitted against one another and often shut down connection and intimacy. To avoid this and work toward reconnecting, Gottman et al. (2006) suggested that partners should respond to any of the Horsemen by turning toward the partner and demonstrating openness to listening and remaining engaged with one another. Turning toward can be a move to repairing the conversation by reducing tension and helping both partners be more relaxed with a humor, a smile, or an apology. Also, partners could reconnect by *accepting influence* of the other partner by being open to perspectives of and persuasion from the other partner. These behaviors can rebuild connection and sustain emotional bonds and friendship in the relationship (Gottman et al., 2006).

Balancing Multiple Demands

Today's couples are most likely feeling stressed, as they have many responsibilities and roles to balance. Worker, parent, social club member, citizen, daughter or son, sibling, and partner are common roles for adults today, and sometimes the last one can be pushed to be the last priority. Phyllis Moen (2003) edited a book called *It's About Time: Couples and Careers*, describing the challenges of juggling work hours, leisure activities, parenthood, overall well-being, and managing a household. Moen and other scholars cited an almost 50/50 male-to-female ratio in the workplace, and desires to balance a household and work contribute to the current challenges facing intimate partners.

With divorce rates in the United States being around 50% for first-time marriages and higher for subsequent marriages (Fine & Harvey, 2006), it is important for intimate partners to define their priorities together and discuss strategies for maintaining connection and intimacy with all of the demands facing them. Intimacy is a significant factor in intimate relationships satisfaction, including sexual satisfaction, and counselors can help couple-counseling clients to realize the importance of taking time for their relationship, build intimacy through positive involvement with the other, foster shared understandings of one another, cultivate EI and differentiation of self, and enhance their communication skills. Readers are invited to consider the application of these skills in the following case study.

CASE ILLUSTRATION 8.1

CYNTHIA AND DANE

Cynthia (age 40) and Dane (age 41) came to counseling because of some troubles they have been experiencing in their relationship. They reported that they have been arguing a lot recently and that they are concerned about whether or not that they will stay together. Cynthia and Dane are committed to their relationship and think that the past arguments have been pulling them apart. They both came from families that experienced divorce, and they said that part of why they are really trying to work this out is for their two children, who are 9 and 12 years old.

Cynthia and Dane met when they were both in college studying business. Dane studied music business, and Cynthia studied business administration and then went on to get her MBA. They started dating near the end of college and then dated for four years before getting married. Initially, Cynthia said that Dane's work ethic and sense of humor were what first attracted her, and Dane said that Cynthia's drive, body, and passion is what he liked about her. They have been married for 15 years and had their first child three years into their marriage. They were both very happy in the years that followed and feel like they adjusted to being parents pretty well. Cynthia reduced hours at work until their now 9-year-old son started going to school, and she then dove into her work again. Dane said that their sexual intimacy started getting less frequent during that time and that he also started to feel less close to Cynthia "because of work." Cynthia said that she felt like she had to prove herself at work and that she did put a lot of effort into work, though she also reported that she still did as much as she could at home during those years too, up until the past six months.

Dane reported that their fights have gotten bad in the past three months, though Cynthia said that it started about six months ago, right after she got a promotion and raise at work. She said that her job has required her to be working about five hours per week more and that she feels unsupported because Dane has not picked up some of the slack at home. Dane coaches their 12-year-old daughter's travel softball team, and their season started a couple of months after Cynthia received her promotion. Dane said that he has tried to do more at home and was able to at first though the extra work as a softball coach has left him tired at the end of the day, and he cannot prepare for the next day like he used to do to help the family.

Cynthia reported that the couple gets into arguments at night frequently. Cynthia usually comes home around 8 PM from work and spends a little time with their children before the children go to sleep. Then, Cynthia comes downstairs and is frustrated by the amount of work that needs to be done around the house and complains to Dane about the status of the house. She said that Dane usually does not respond visually or audibly, which she admits triggers her and she then explodes on him. Dane said that he tries to keep in his emotions when Cynthia has been approaching him at night, though he eventually cannot do it anymore and "loses it on her."

Dane said that their fights were getting bad when they started yelling loud enough that their children woke up one night. They reported that when their 9-year-old son came to them crying, they stopped arguing that night and try not to argue anymore when their children are home. However, they both say that about once a week they get into a big argument and say that the arguments have been getting worse and that it is harder to control themselves. Dane and Cynthia reported that they are not feeling as close as they used to and that they have not been able to be sexually intimate for the past two months, which is a long time for them, because of the pent up feelings that they are both having.

Questions:

1. What do you see are the main relational concerns in Cynthia and Dane's relationship?

2. What positive and negative communication patterns are present in their relationship?

3. What do you think is leading to the current arguments that they are having, and how do the arguments impact their current intimacy and satisfaction?

4. What are your treatment goals for couples counseling with Cynthia and Dane?

5. What prognosis would you give for Cynthia and Dane? Why?

Attachment

Many researchers have pointed to early life experiences significantly impacting romantic relationships later in life. The most researched topic in this area that adds to our understanding of intimate relationship dynamics comes from attachment theory. Researchers have found that how people interact with their caregivers early in life is predictive of how they are likely to interact in sexual relationships. Bowlby (1957; 1973; 1982; 1988) initially proposed attachment theory based on observing parent-child interactions, and Ainsworth and colleagues Ainsworth et al., 1978; Ainsworth & Wittig, 1969) expanded attachment theory by adding attachment styles that were present in children based on their connection to their caregivers. While the attachment styles that Ainsworth and colleagues proposed have shifted over time, attachment styles are thought to strongly impact sexual relationships.

Attachment behaviors are "any form of behavior that results in a person attaining or maintaining proximity to some other clearly identified individual who is conceived as better able to cope with the world" (Bowlby, 1982, p. 668). While this clearly relates to parent-child relationships, attachment behaviors are also important in adult intimate relationships. Bowlby said that "knowledge that an attachment figure is available and responsive provides a strong and pervasive sense of security . . . can be observed throughout the life cycle, especially in emergencies" and that attachment "is regarded as an integral part of human nature" (1982, p. 669). Toward the end of his career, Bowlby believed that attachment helped to form a sense of safety and trust between people, especially in times of crisis and anxiety, and that attachment impacted people at all stages in the life cycle (Bowlby, 1982). Therefore, attachment theory contends that early relationships with attachment figures lead to sustained patterns of emotional regulation, interpersonal interaction patterns, and internalized views of self and other. More recent attachment researchers have found support for Bowlby's concepts and found that attachment strongly impacts emotional regulation and some neurological processes in adulthood (Coan, 2010; Mercer, 2011; Schore & Schore, 2008). In addition, Schore and Schore (2008) described how attachment is involved in affect regulation and developing an emotional sense of self. Overall, attachment theory researchers have supported the importance of attachment for cognitive, emotional, and relational development, as well as for developing ways to manage our emotions and internalize interaction patterns in close relationships (Mercer, 2011).

Attachment Styles

Attachment styles have been reinterpreted since Ainsworth proposed them (Johnson & Zuccarini, 2010). Currently, four different attachment styles have been identified as affect regulation strategies for managing stressful situations and have been categorized based on levels of anxiety and avoidance in close relationships (Mikulincer, Shaver, & Pereg, 2003; Wei, Russell, Mallinckrodt, & Vogel, 2007) or based on positive and negative views of self and other (Bartholomew & Horowitz, 1991). The attachment styles are referred to as secure, dismissive, preoccupied, and fearful attachment.

Secure attachment is characterized by low levels of both attachment anxiety and avoidance, combined with positive views of self and other. People with secure attachments are likely to turn toward others when stressed or anxious and be able to be comforted. People with *dismissive* attachment behaviors typically move away from intimate interactions as those interactions tend to feel uncomfortable, especially when they are stressed. Dismissive attachment is characterized by low levels of attachment anxiety, high levels of attachment avoidance, a positive view of self, and a negative view of others. In contrast, preoccupied attachment is characterized by high levels of attachment anxiety, low levels of attachment avoidance, a negative view of self, and a positive view of others. People with *preoccupied* attachment behaviors want to be close with others when stressed, but they are anxious about being rejected or feeling unloved when they are with others. People with fearful attachment are characterized by having high levels of both attachment anxiety and avoidance, as well as negative views of self and others. People with *fearful* attachment behaviors want to be close to others, though they think that they will have negative interactions with them that leave them feeling scared that they will get hurt (Bartholomew & Horowitz, 1991; Mikulincer et al., 2003; Wei et al., 2007). The latter three attachment styles (dismissive, preoccupied, and fearful attachment) are often called insecure attachment because of the difficulties in intimate relationships that they encompass. Consistently, researchers have found differences in secure and insecure attachment styles, and they have determined that secure attachment style is important for higher levels of wellbeing (Izard, 2002).

Attachment and Intimate Relationships

Attachment theory is useful for understanding intimate relationships and working with intimate partners in counseling (Johnson & Zuccarini, 2010). Some relevant findings from past research include the following: secure attachment leads to more relaxed and confident engagement in sexual activities (Mikulincer & Shaver, 2007); higher levels of attachment related anxiety and avoidance are connected with less positive and more negative feelings during sexual activities (Birnbaum, Reis, Mikulincer, Gillath, & Orpaz, 2006); higher anxiety is related to sexual difficulties, including sexual arousal and pleasure (Birnbaum, 2007); and there are differences between people with more anxiety and more avoidance during sex (Davis, Shazer, Widaman, Vernon, Folette, & Beitz, 2006). In summary, secure attachment is connected with positive sexual relationships and more engagement in sexual activities, while insecure attachment styles are connected with more negative sexual experiences, less pleasure and connection, and greater rates of sexual problems.

Working with intimate partners to be able to connect in more secure ways and to navigate through insecurities and fear is important to increase connection, intimacy, and frequency of sexual activities. Emotionally focused therapy

(EFT) has been found to be effective in working with couples with general relational concerns, history of trauma, past affairs, and sexual concerns in counseling (Johnson, 2004; Johnson, Hunsley, Greenberg, & Schindler, 1999; Johnson & Wittenborn, 2012; Johnson & Zuccarini, 2010; Lebow, Chambers, Christensen, & Johnson, 2012, MacIntosh & Johnson, 2008). In general, EFT is used to help partners to increase their connection and works through three stages of therapy: assessment and de-escalation, restructuring the bond and changing interactional patterns, and consolidating and integrating changes (Johnson, 2004). EFT can help to strengthen connection and intimacy, which can lead to increased satisfaction in intimate relationships, changes in attachment styles and behaviors, and more frequent, satisfying, and pleasurable engagement in sexual activities.

Sexual Desire Between Partners

Another important interpersonal dynamic in couple relationships is sexual desire. It is not clear what specific factors lead to different levels of sexual desire, although relationship quality is related to amount and frequency of sexual activity (Greeff & Malherbe, 2001; Tolstedt & Stokes, 1983) and is likely related to sexual desire. Hormones also seem to impact sexual desire (Basson, 2007; Davis, 1998, Leiblum, 2002; van Anders, 2012; van Anders, Hamilton, & Watson, 2007). Testosterone levels in men and women can lead to different levels of solitary and partnered sexual activities (van Anders, 2012). Gender role expectations also play a role. Overall, men tend to desire to engage in sexual activities more frequently than women, although this gap seems to be shrinking (Leiblum, 2002). As described previously, level of intimacy, overall life balance and stress, and attachment styles all impact the desired amount of intimacy or closeness and engagement in sexual activities, and they may also impact sexual desire.

While partners may be compatible in many ways, they may hold different views about how much and what sexual activities they want to engage in with each other. People with avoidant attachment tend to separate connection and sex more than other attachment styles (Gillath & Schachner, 2006), and they are less likely to engage in sexual intercourse and more likely to engage in masturbation alone (Bogaert & Sadava, 2002). Again, partners need strong communication and conflict management skills to help come to satisfactory resolution of differences between them, but not all partners are able to successfully resolve these concerns.

Interaction Patterns

When both partners desire similar amounts of intimacy and sexual activity, then there can be strong ties and satisfaction for both partners. However, when one partner desires greater closeness and/or sexual activity than the other partner, problematic interaction patterns can arise. One such pattern is the *demand-withdraw pattern* (sometimes called the pursuer-distancer pattern) (Eldridge & Christensen, 2002; Weiss & Heyman, 1997). These patterns occur when one partner begins to demand something (e.g., emotional closeness or sex) from the other partner, who then begins to distance him- or herself from the demanding partner. When intimate partners develop inflexible, recurrent patterns characterized by demand and withdrawal, negative outcomes may arise. The person in the demanding role may experience hyperarousal, negative recurrent thoughts and feelings, attempts to avoid thinking about the interaction (Malis & Roloff, 2006), and increased cortisol (i.e., the main stress hormone) levels (Heffner, Loving, Kiecolt-Glaser, Himawan, Glaser, & Malarkey, 2006). The person in the withdrawing role may experience greater stress, attempts to avoid thinking about the interaction (Malis & Roloff, 2006), and increased cortisol levels (Heffner et al., 2006). If demand-withdraw patterns are left uninterrupted, they can lead to decreased intimacy and relational satisfaction, and even divorce (Heavey, Christensen, & Malamuth, 1995; Noller, Feeney, Bonnell, & Callan, 1994).

Therefore, it is important for counselors to be aware of the demand-withdraw pattern and to help partners change this negative interactional pattern. Weiss and Heyman (1997) suggested helping partners to engage in "editing" behaviors, which include devising alternate ways to attribute behaviors other than automatic thoughts that emerge, experiencing the other person's underlying emotions during the conflict, and understanding the reason for the behaviors based on previous negative interactions in close relationships. They also cautioned immediately assuming that withdrawal behaviors are negative, as they can help to limit the escalation of the conflict if they return to work to resolve it in a timely manner.

While the demand-withdraw negative interaction pattern is the most researched, it is not the only problematic relationship pattern that can lead to negative outcomes (Fincham & Beach, 2006; Weiss & Heyman, 1997). Others include blame-blame, confront-confront, confront-defend, complain-defend, complain-complain, defend-complain, and displeasure-displeasure negative escalation cycles (Weiss & Heyman, 1997). For example, a blame-blame cycle could result from each partner viewing him- or herself positively and the other negatively and having learned to dismiss the other's perspectives when in agitated emotional states. If both partners do not understand their current relational dynamics and choose to blame the other partner for relational problems, this could lead to greater levels of distress and heightened attempts at blaming the other for the greater relational problems. This difficulty in resolving distress can lead to a cycle of more intense problems that leads to even worse interpersonal interactions. Gottman (1994) found that non-distressed couples sometimes experience these negative escalation cycles, although they are able to repair the damage by spontaneously stopping the negative escalation, which distressed couples find more difficult to do.

Sexual Decision-Making in Relationships

Another important relational dynamic is how and who makes decisions regarding sexual activities within a couple. As partnered sexual activities take place as a part of a relationship, typically both partners have a choice in terms of what, when, and how often to engage in sexual activities. Unless partners are in complete agreement in all of those choices, they must engage in some negotiation and decision-making processes. Sexual decision-making has many important factors, including relational concerns, social norms and pressure, concerns about risks or consequences associated with sexual activity, developmental stage, amount and quality of previous sexual experience, expectations for physical sensation, future plans and goals, and biological sex, which are discussed in Chapter 6 on *Sexuality and Mental Health*. These decisions can become more complex within the context of a couple's relationship.

In making decisions as a couple about sexual activities, there are several different factors that can influence the decision-making process. Decisions impact the family unit, the couple's relationship, and each partner individually, and intimate partners may consider the reach of these influences in making decisions about how to express their sexuality. Family-related factors include decisions about pregnancy and the impact of the family's schedule on the amount of time and energy available for sexual activities. Couple-focused factors include how partners view sexual activities as relating to their goals for intimacy, how connected partners feel toward one another, and the impact of other stressors or relationship dynamics on couple's views about their sexual activities. Finally, sexual decision-making is made at the individual level based on levels of personal sexual desire and arousal (Ariely & Loewenstein, 2006). People will also consider their own wishes and desires in how they approach their sexual decision-making process.

There is limited research on how couples approach the sexual decision-making processes (Ariely & Loewenstein, 2006). Goodwin and Scanzoni (1989) described general decision-making processes within couples, and these have implications for their decisions about sexuality. Goodwin and Scanzoni asserted that couples make decisions in light of the following factors: their levels of affection, love, cooperativeness, and commitment to one another as well as gender role norms related to coerciveness, power, and cooperation. In particular, they believed that connection with one's partner leads to less coercive behaviors and greater sharing of power that would make it easier to come to consensus on sexual decisions (Goodwin & Scanzoni, 1989).

Decisions are also facilitated when both partners approach them with more positive communication and conflict resolution skills, as well as a desire to cooperate with one another. However, partners may enter the sexual decision-making process with differing communication and conflict resolution skills or different motivations for engaging or not engaging in sexual activities. Partners with greater persuasive skills, power, and motivation are more likely to coerce or manipulate their partners into engaging sexually in the way that the former partner desires. This is not likely to be a healthy long-term sexual decision-making strategy and can lead to violence, aggression, or hostility in the relationship (Berns, Jacobson, & Gottman, 1999), as well as the end of the relationship (Fine & Harvey, 2006), although these dynamics can even arise occasionally in egalitarian relationships. It is important to note that each partner in a relationship should have the full right to consent freely to engage in any sexual activities. Any form of forced or coerced sexual activities represent a form of sexual assault. Therefore, counselors who recognize these patterns in their clients' relationships should ensure that their clients are safe and connected with local resources for sexual trauma, as appropriate.

A common relational dynamic is that one partner is the primary initiator of sexual intimacy, and the other partner limits the frequency of sexual activity by not accepting the initiation of sexual activity (Clark & Hatfield, 1989). Typically, men initiate sex more than women in heterosexual relationships (Finkel & Eastwick, 2009), although certainly women can be primary initiators of sexual activity as well. This pattern may lead to frustration for both partners if both partners are not satisfied with the amount of sexual activity in their relationship. The initiator may become frustrated and feel rejected, and the initiator's partner may begin to feel pressured for sexual activities. In some cases, one or both partners may distance themselves from each other, physically and/or emotionally, which can contribute to additional problematic relationship patterns. Counselors can help clients facing these dynamics develop mutually agreeable ways of determining patterns of initiating sexual activity, as well as help clients develop more effective communication patterns so that each partner can more effectively convey their needs, as well as understand their partner's needs. Ideally, counselors can help clients work toward a mutually agreeable level of sexual involvement that satisfies both partners and allows for both partners' needs to be understood and met.

Monogamous and Nonmonogamous Relationships

Most of the discussion to this point focused on monogamous couple relationships, which are the most common form of romantic relationships (Conley, Moors, Matsick, & Ziegler, 2013). However, they are not the only kind of romantic relationships. There are other types of nonmonogamous relationships including bigamy, polygamy, polyamory, open relationships, swinging, and affairs. All of these terms, except for affairs, can be called consensual nonmonogamous (CNM) relationships, as the arrangements are mutually agreed upon by the people involved (Barker & Langdridge, 2010; Conley et al., 2013). There is currently a lot of stigma against nonmonogamous relationships in the United States (Conley et al., 2013), although people in CNM tend to report positive relationship qualities, such as closeness, happiness, good communication, and honesty (Barker, 2005; Klesse, 2006; Visser & MacDonald, 2007). It is important for counselors not to fall prey to stigmatizing this population of approximately 4% of the total population (as cited in Conley et al., 2013, for their unpublished data), as stigma can hinder the therapeutic relationship and clients' progress toward treatment goals.

Many of the points made above regarding romantic relationship are also applicable to CNM relationships, although there are some important differences. In monogamous relationships, intimacy and sexual activity are understood to take place between only two people, and emotional and/or physical intimacy with someone other than one committed partner is likely to result in jealousness, possessiveness, and hurt in monogamous relationships. Intimacy is expected to happen only in the context of the committed relationship, and there is only one relationship of importance. However, partners in CNM relationships typically specify and agree to boundaries, such as for allowable sexual activities with others and the number of partners, and these relationships can vary in terms of the degrees of closeness with one or more partners (Klesse, 2005). When operating within the agreed upon boundaries of the relationship, CNM partners usually report low levels of jealousy and happiness in their lives (Barker, 2005; Klesse, 2006; Visser & MacDonald, 2007).

INTEGRATING SEXUALITY COUNSELING WITH COUPLES COUNSELING

As sexual concerns typically overlap with couples' relational concerns, it is beneficial to adopt an integrated approach that combines sexuality counseling with couples counseling. Treatment for sexual concerns often entails both behavioral and/or cognitive components. For example, for female pain disorders previously called vaginismus and dyspareunia and now called genito-pelvic pain or penetration disorder, a combination of couple-based cognitive-behavioral sex therapy, communication training, sex education, confrontation and disputation of anxious expectations for painful sex, systematic desensitization, sensate focusing, and Kegel exercises is recommended in reducing symptoms (Meston & Bradford, 2007). There is significant support for combining sexuality counseling and couples counseling due to the nature of sexual activities and satisfaction. Sexual activities are often desired to be done with a partner, and interpersonal dynamics impact sexual experience, performance, pleasure, and satisfaction. Sexual problems are often related to anxiety in the relationship, performance anxiety, and relational distress. When a partner experiences anxiety, blood can move away from sexual organs, and anxious thoughts can crowd out the ability to connect with one's partner and limit sexual stimulation (Bodinger et al., 2002; Déttore et al., 2013; Norton & Jehu, 1984). A partner might be able to manage emotional states while alone or in individual counseling and yet have difficult managing anxiety and other emotions in the presence of the partner.

Integrating elements from sexuality counseling with couples counseling helps to support partners' engagement with one another and to increase bonding and decrease anxiety. As one example of the benefits of this integration, Frühauf, Gerger, Schmidt, Munder, and Barth (2013) conducted a meta-analysis to investigate the effectiveness of couples counseling alone compared to couples counseling with sexual-skills training for the treatment of sexual dysfunctions. The findings of this study suggested that couples counseling integrated with sexuality counseling had more robust benefits than couples counseling alone. Integrating sexual-skills training, sexual education, and behavioral strategies (e.g., sensate focusing techniques, start-stop and squeeze technique, and sexual enhancement techniques) of sex therapy into sessions can greatly benefit couples by increasing their sexual pleasure and satisfaction.

The integration of sexuality and couples counseling needs to include a thorough assessment of sexual and relational aspects within and between each partner. Investigating each partner's sexual history and the history of the relationship helps to identify patterns of both positive and negative relationship and sexuality-related concerns. Patterns of positive and negative interactions and experiences are important to understanding the current difficulties the couple is facing. A thorough assessment can lead to a clearer understanding and conceptualization of the presenting concerns and will aid in choosing appropriate treatment methods. Treatments can vary based on presenting concerns and include sex-therapy techniques, communication and conflict resolution-skills training, intimacy enhancement, cognitive restructuring of maladaptive beliefs, and techniques to increase eroticism and desire (e.g., the use of erotic materials, discussions of sexual desires and fantasies, and rekindling earlier desires).

SEXUALITY COUNSELING FOR SPECIFIC RELATIONSHIP CONCERNS

This section addresses three relationship challenges that may lead clients to seek counseling: (a) infidelity, (b) divorce, and (c) re-entering the dating scene after a long-term relationship ends. The focus for each of these three situations will be to briefly discuss the main relevant aspects and counseling considerations.

Infidelity

When someone learns that his or her partner has had an affair, a wide range of intense emotional reactions may arise. Partners typically experience a sense of loss at the broken trust, as well as feel a sense of emotional pain. Depressive feelings are common after infidelity, and adjustment can be very difficult, especially if there are any relationship changes such as separation or divorce (Hall & Fincham, 2006). The impact of an affair can be similar to the effects of other traumatic experiences (Janoff-Bulman, 1992; Johnson, Makinen, & Millikin, 2001). As overall intimacy is lowered, sexual intimacy also often decreases after revealing an infidelity. It is important to complete a comprehensive mental health assessment for both partners to understand their mental health symptoms and resources, as both partners can experience negative symptoms.

In the aftermath of an affair, couples may come to counselors looking for answers in terms of whether they should stay together. This is an important decision to explore in counseling in order to help each partner get a clearer picture of how they would like the relationship to proceed. It is important for counselors to put aside their own values in these situations and allow the couple to make a decision together about their future. If the couple decides to separate, individual counseling can be beneficial for each partner to process their response to the dissolution of the relationship and find new direction for their lives.

If the couple decides to stay together and work through the infidelity, couples counseling can be helpful to resolve the wound in the relationship. In this case, it is important to understand the couple's interactions and dynamics pre-infidelity (Johnson et al., 2001). The couple may have demonstrated negative interaction cycles that may re-emerge after some healing in the relationship has taken place. Before attending to the pre-infidelity relational dynamics, it is important to work toward some level of healing and forgiveness. Johnson et al. described infidelity as an "attachment injury" and explained how to use EFT to work with couples after an affair. They illustrated that after de-escalating the conflict and helping the partners to be accessible and responsive to each other, it is important to help the partners reconnect and heal through opening up and sharing their vulnerabilities, insecurities, and connection to each other. By leading the couple to reconnecting and healing after infidelity, counselors can help guide clients to better emotional regulation, relational satisfaction, greater intimacy, and a reestablished sense of trust and connection. Readers are encouraged to complete Exercise 8.1 to explore some of the ethical considerations when addressing affairs in counseling.

Exercise 8.1

ETHICAL DISCUSSION

When working with couples in counseling, one partner may reveal in an individual session that he or she has had an affair, either currently or in the past. This can present a dilemma for counselors, especially if they have not explained the limits of confidentiality during the informed consent process. Read the following vignette, and answer the subsequent questions:

> You have been seeing a couple, Andrew and Alexander, for three weeks to help them address communication problems, and in the third session, you split the session into two parts to do a thorough individual assessment with each partner, which is part of your normal work with couples. During Alexander's session, he admits that he had an affair for a month with a mutual friend of Andrew's that ended three months ago. Alexander said he does not think that it is currently a part of their relational difficulties and that it will just make things worse if Andrew finds out about it. Alexander asks you not to tell Andrew about the affair and to keep it a secret.

1. Would you honor Alexander's request?

2. What ethical principles (beneficence, nonmaleficence, fidelity, etc.) are relevant in this case?

3. What are the benefits of not telling Andrew? What are the potential problems?

4. What would you like to tell your clients in informed consent about how you will handle "secrets?"

Divorce

Couples may divorce for many reasons. Between 25% and 50% of divorcing couples have reported that infidelity was the reason for separating (Kelly & Conley, 1987), which means that the majority of divorces are not due to infidelity. Known predictors of divorce include marital dissatisfaction (Gager & Sanchez, 2003; White & Booth, 1991), differences in levels of interdependence between partners (Kurdek, 1993), negativity (Matthews, Wickrama, & Conger, 1996), and demographic characteristics, such as younger couples and couples with lower levels of income (Amato, 2010). Divorces vary in the degree of conflict present while the couple is going through the divorce process, and they can have very little to extremely high levels of conflict and stress (Amato, 2010; Fabricius & Luecken, 2007). High-conflict divorces have more problems than lower conflict divorces for partners and children (Lebow & Rekart, 2007). For the children and for the ex-partners, it is important to minimize the conflict during and after the divorce process, as increased conflict is related to several negative overall health indicators (Amato, 2010; Fabricius & Luecken, 2007; Lebow & Rekart, 2007).

It is important for counselors to complete a comprehensive clinical assessment for partners who are undergoing a divorce. Many symptoms may arise (e.g., depression, trauma, grief and loss, and anxiety; Fine & Harvey, 2006) during this process, and it is also important to ascertain and collaboratively come to specific goals for counseling. If the goals are vague, such as "help us get through the divorce," the counselor and client may be unsure how to best proceed in counseling. As there are many functional, logistical, and practical changes as people go through divorce, talking about the adjustments that the client is experiencing is likely to be beneficial to the client (Salts & Smith, Jr., 2003). Also, re-conceptualizing who the client is as an individual, outside of the relationship, is helpful for some clients because of the ways that relationships shape our identities (Roccas & Brewer, 2002). Various theoretical approaches can be utilized with clients going through divorce, and interventions vary based upon theoretical approaches to helping clients gain closure (Salts & Smith, Jr., 2003).

Dating

As people re-enter dating relationships after past relationships with significant problems or divorce, there may be some lingering impacts based on their past experiences (Lucas, 2005). It can be beneficial to help clients work through the residual beliefs, attitudes, and emotions about themselves and their partners after experiencing a significant relationship dissolution that may negatively impact future romantic relationships. There are no clear rules or guidelines for when and how people should re-enter dating relationships after the end of a previous relationship. However, some steps that may be beneficial for clients to take to prepare to re-enter dating relationships include reading self-help books, going to counseling, talking with friends and cultural leaders, and attending workshops or support groups, although people vary in what is helpful to them (Ganong & Coleman, 1989; Higginbotham, Miller, & Niehuis, 2009). Therefore, it is very important to talk with clients who are coming in to help adjust to dating again or re-engaging in sexual intimacy about what their specific goals are for counseling, as well as how they would like to change, develop, heal, or grow through their counseling sessions.

SUMMARY

Intimate relationships have a strong impact on sexual expression and intimacy. Romantic attraction, intimacy, levels of sexual desire, interaction patterns, and sexual decision-making are all important factors that impact sexual relationships. Intimacy is especially important in intimate relationships because of its strong connection with relationship and sexual satisfaction. Intimacy is characterized by self-revealing behaviors, positive involvement with one's partner, and shared understandings. It is important for counselors to understand these topics in order to conceptualize clients' sexual and relational health concerns. Understanding these topics can also lead to better integration of sexuality and couples counseling, which is often the best practice when working with clients facing relational and sexual concerns. These are especially important in some specific relational situations that were discussed, including infidelity, divorce, and dating stages of intimate relationships.

KEYSTONES

- The dynamics of intimate relationships play a significant role in the types and frequency of sexual activities and in the connection that people experience as sexual beings.
- Romantic attraction is the subjective evaluation and experience of being drawn to another person.
- Intimacy is a significant factor in sexual relationships and sexual activity for several reasons.
- Communication, conflict management, and resolution skills are important in maintaining sexual relationships.
- Other important relationship dynamics to consider in sexuality counseling include intimacy, sexual desire, interactional patterns, and sexual-decision making processes within couples.
- Integrating elements from sexuality counseling with couples counseling helps to support partners' engagement with one another and to increase bonding and decrease anxiety.
- Three relationship issues that may lead clients to seek counseling include infidelity, divorce, and re-entering dating relationships after a long-term relationship ends.

ADDITIONAL RESOURCES

- Diamond, D., Blatt, S. J., & Lichtenberg, J. D. (Eds.). (2007). *Attachment and sexuality*. New York, NY: Lawrence Erlbaum Associates.

- Gottman, J. (1994). *Why marriages succeed or fail*. New York, NY: Simon & Schuster.
- The International Centre for Excellence in Emotionally Focused Therapy. *Creating Connection*. (2007). Retrieved from http://www.iceeft.com
- Mashek, D. J., & Aron, A. (Eds.). (2008). *Handbook of closeness and intimacy*. Mahwah, NJ: Lawrence Erlbaum Associates.
- Mikulincer, M., & Goodman, G. (Eds.). (2006). *Dynamics of romantic love*. New York, NY: Guilford.

Chapter 9

Cultural and Contextual Influences on Sexuality

Imagine a female client who has been referred for counseling by her OBGYN due to the distress she is experiencing related to infertility. Now, consider that this client comes from a culture in which femininity is tied closely to a woman's ability to conceive and give birth to many children. In addition, consider that she is a recent immigrant to the United States and has limited English language proficiency. In what ways might this client's cultural background be impacting both her sexuality-related concerns and her comfort in seeking counseling to address those concerns?

In this chapter, we take a broader approach to understanding sexuality by examining the cultural and contextual influences that impact clients' sexual functioning and experiences. Within the counseling profession, there has been a longstanding interest in ensuring that counselors demonstrate multicultural competence, and this is just as important in the realm of sexuality counseling as it is in other counseling specialties. The influence of one's culture and other contextual factors (e.g., religion, socioeconomic status, geography and regional variations, and the media) begins very early in life. Therefore, these influences become inextricably intertwined with people's sense of sexuality over time. Before reading any further, please take a moment to reflect upon the questions in Exercise 9.1, which address your perspectives toward the contextual influences on sexuality.

We caution all readers against making any assumptions about clients based on their cultural and contextual backgrounds. Although research can help to identify patterns between and among groups of people, sexuality is an inherently individual part of life. Therefore, we cannot say there is any one way to define how sexuality will be experienced within a group of people. As just one example, we could not assume that every Jewish female will experience and express her sexuality in the same manner, as the definition of "Jewish female sexuality" will vary between groups and individuals. Therefore, the next section of this

---

Exercise 9.1

CONTEXTUAL INFLUENCES ON SEXUALITY

Take time to consider your reactions to the following questions. You can write in a journal about your responses or discuss them with a trusted colleague or supervisor.

1. In what ways do you think that clients' perspectives about sexuality are shaped by their cultural context? How do you think these cultural messages are shared?

2. Have you had any experiences with clients in which it seemed their cultural beliefs had a negative impact on their views about their sexuality? What were these experiences like? How did you discuss these beliefs with your clients?

3. What are the biggest challenges you face in discussing cultural issues related to sexuality with your clients?

4. How might you handle a counseling situation in which you felt that a client's cultural or religious beliefs were having a negative impact on their sexuality-related attitudes and experiences, but the client does not appear interested in discussing these influences?

5. What cultural groups do you think it would be easiest for you to work with related to sexuality issues? Why?

6. What cultural groups do you think it would be most difficult for you to work with related to sexuality issues? Why?

7. In what ways might you consider cultural and other contextual influences to be a resource or strength in counseling? How could you draw upon these resources in your work with clients?

8. What do you think it means to demonstrate multicultural competence when it comes to sexuality counseling? Are there any unique aspects of competence that would be unique to sexuality counseling as compared to counseling in general?

---

chapter discusses an intersectional approach to understanding cultural and contextual influences on sexuality. The sections that follow review existing research that demonstrates the powerful impact that various contextual influences—including religion, culture and ethnicity, socioeconomic status, geographic and regional variations, and the media—can have upon human sexuality. The chapter concludes with a discussion of counseling strategies to help clients address cultural and contextual influences that impact their sexuality. After reading this chapter, readers will be able to do the following:

a. Describe an intersectional approach to understanding sexuality and culture
b. Discuss the intersections of various contextual and cultural influences on sexuality
c. Consider how best to apply counseling strategies that aim to help clients consider the impact of their cultural backgrounds on their current sexuality-related concerns

AN INTERSECTIONAL APPROACH TO UNDERSTANDING CULTURE AND SEXUALITY

Traditional approaches to multicultural competence training have focused on providing information about cultural trends within specific groups (Sears, 2012). Although it is important to understand common cultural values and belief systems, there is so much diversity within groups that this form of training can be misleading and overlook individualistic differences within cultural groups (Sears, 2012). There is diversity within virtually every cultural or contextual group, making it impossible to create clear-cut rules about how a person will view their sexuality in light of any one given background characteristic. Furthermore, when we focus too much on one aspect of the context surrounding sexuality (e.g., gender, culture, or social class), we run the risk of failing to account for other relevant influences (Binnie, 2011).

Therefore, in this book, we advocate for an intersectional approach to understanding the cultural and contextual influences upon human sexuality.

An intersectional approach holds that we must consider the multiple contextual influences upon a person to fully understand their unique experiences (Kazyak, 2012; Nagel, 2000). An intersectional approach views each person as uniquely shaped by multiple social locations, based on such contextual characteristics as their racial and ethnic background, their sexual orientation, gender, and socioeconomic status (Sears, 2012). Sears (2012) outlined the following eight key tenets of the intersectional approach. First, the intersectional approach holds that each person encompasses multiple statuses based on contextual variables. Second, some or all of these statuses may carry advantages and disadvantages. Third, each person's various statuses interact with one another. Fourth, the influence of each status cannot be considered without consideration of the other statuses. Fifth, over time, each status's influence may change based on individual or societal changes. Sixth, above all, each client is a unique person. Seventh, professionals must be mindful of their own biases and assumptions, regardless of whether they share or do not share statuses with the clients they serve. Finally, professionals should be mindful of the intersectional statuses that they themselves possess.

To illustrate the intersectional approach, consider the diagram presented in Figure 9.1. In Figure 9.1, we begin with sexuality defined by one characteristic—gender (i.e., male sexuality). At each subsequent level, we add one additional contextual variable (e.g., age, sexual orientation, and socioeconomic status). Consider how each contextual difference might uniquely influence male sexuality. Once we have added multiple influences, we can see how their impacts intersect to create a unique contextual dynamic in the categories at the bottom level of the diagram. For example, consider the two bookends of this bottom level: high socioeconomic status, gay, 18-year-old, male sexuality and low socioeconomic status, heterosexual, 58-year-old, male sexuality. Sexuality for each of these categories likely is experienced very differently. In particular, consider which statuses within each variable would carry potential privileges and oppressions and especially the potential for multiple non-privileged statuses to intersect (Watson, Robinson, Dispenza, & Nazari, 2012). Finally, once you've considered the variables included, consider also those not yet included (e.g., religion, ethnicity, and geography). The full picture of individual sexuality encompasses a broad range of intersecting influences.

Figure 9.1 Illustration of the Intersectional Approach

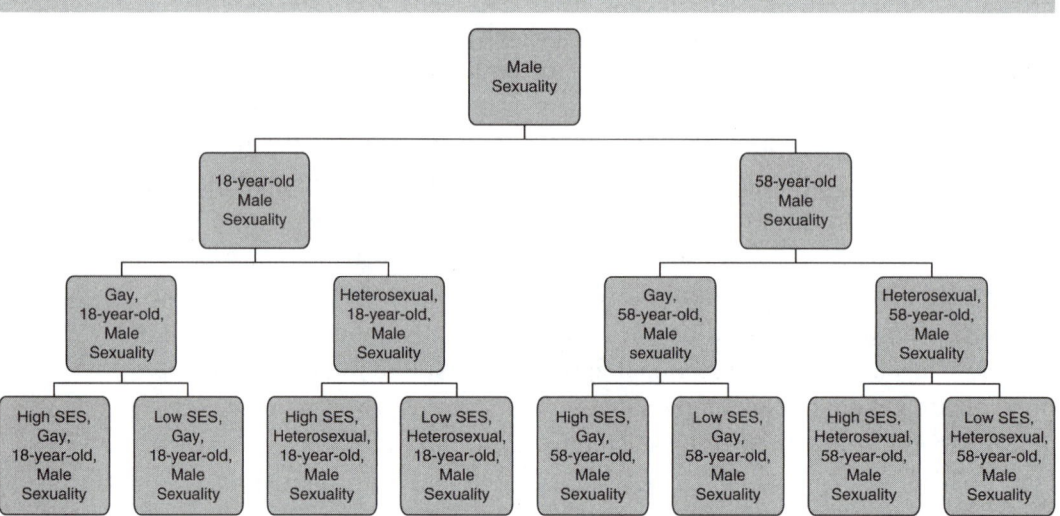

In the following sections, we examine trends in research that explore how various cultural and contextual variables impact sexuality. This research is certainly useful for counselors as they consider how their clients' background characteristics may impact their presenting concerns. However, we urge readers to review these sections with a critical eye, in that it is important to avoid oversimplifying clients' experiences or assuming that cultural and contextual trends will apply in each client's unique situation. The research we review provides some examples of how these influences might be at play, but it is always important to discuss with clients their own unique perspectives and experiences in relation to their cultural and other background influences.

RELIGION AND SEXUALITY

Many people find it challenging to integrate their spirituality and religious beliefs with their sexuality (Mahoney, 2008). Religion can be especially influential on sexuality-related values and experiences during critical developmental periods, such as adolescence (Goodson & Zhang, 2008). Religious groups may be conflicted and present contradictory messages about sexuality. For example, on the one hand they may encourage followers to "be fruitful and multiply" and yet also downplay the pleasurable and positive aspects of sexuality (Gutierrez, 2012; Hull, 2008). Throughout history, many religious traditions have emphasized the potential negative consequences of sexual behaviors that occur outside of marriage or, more restrictively, for non-reproductive purposes (De la Garza-Mercer, 2006). In addition, many religious traditions address sexuality with a lack of attention to the emotional context (Glassgold, 2008). Religious traditions may hold sexual self-control as virtuous and suggest that those who cannot control their sexual desires should feel guilt and shame (Hull, 2008). Some religious groups discourage or even forbid masturbation, viewing masturbation as overly focusing on self-pleasure (De la Garza-Mercer, 2006).

Sexual orientation has long been a challenging issue within many religious traditions. Because many religious groups denounce homosexuality, many gay, lesbian, and bisexual (GLB) individuals struggle to reconcile their religious beliefs with their sexual orientations (Roseborough, 2006). However, Roseborough suggests that people can experience personal and spiritual growth over time as they seek to reconcile, integrate, and understand their beliefs in this regard. Roseborough proposes that coming out stories can become "faith narratives" (p. 58) through which people can come to view their process of coming out as a reflection of spiritual growth and personal development over time, as they integrate these unique aspects of their lives.

Within any religion, people may differ in the extent to which they follow religious teachings, laws, and rules regarding sexuality (Keshet-Orr, 2003; Rosenau & Tan, 2002). Therefore, it is important to consider how counseling clients view their own religious beliefs and practices as a strength or hindrance to their sense of sexuality. Furthermore, some people don't ascribe to a particular religious tradition, and yet, they may view their sexuality as being very much related to their sense of spirituality in their lives. Therefore, counselors should not assume that clients who aren't part of any religious tradition have no religious or spiritual dimensions to their sexuality. In particular, people may have been influenced by religious values of their families while growing up, even if they no longer practice that same religion. The remainder of this section provides a brief introduction to sexuality within three major religious traditions: Judaism, Islam, and Christianity.

Judaism

The Jewish tradition normalizes sexuality as a natural part of life, although one that should be contained within marriage (Keshet-Orr, 2003). Orthodox Jewish tradition in particular restricts sex to occurring within heterosexual marriages (Glassgold, 2008). For gay and lesbian Jewish men and women, then, religious beliefs may contribute to feelings of guilt and distress related to their sexual orientation (Glassgold, 2008). Keshet-Orr (2003) explored the influence of Jewish law on Jewish women's sexuality. Keshet-Orr notes that there is variability in the teachings and interpretations of many aspects of Jewish law. One aspect of Jewish law is called "Onah," and it holds that women have a right to sexual enjoyment within marriage, provided by their husbands (Keshet-Orr, 2003). Some other traditional Jewish laws regarding sexuality include limiting sex to the missionary position and only having intercourse at certain points in a woman's menstrual cycle (Keshet-Orr, 2003). Therefore, although Jewish law puts forth some very specific views on sexuality, there is diversity in how these laws have been interpreted in different groups and at different times in history.

Islam

Modern Islam is diverse and evolving (Gutierrez, 2012). Traditionally, Islamic teachings have encouraged sexuality within marriage and held that homosexual activities are unacceptable (Gutierrez, 2012). In addition, traditional Islamic teachings held that women were supposed to submit to their husbands and provide sexual pleasure for them (Gutierrez, 2012). Some Islamic countries have established religiously based laws regarding sexuality and gender expression, such as public interactions between men and women and how women are permitted to dress (Gutierrez, 2012). Gutierrez noted that younger generations of Islamic people around the world are redefining what influence Islamic beliefs have on sexual identity. Therefore, it is important for counselors to consider generational influences when working with Muslim clients related to sexuality issues.

Christianity

There is no one singular way to define Christian sexuality, as different denominations and faith traditions hold different perspectives and interpretations about various aspects of sexuality (Edger, 2012). The Bible (e.g., I Corinthians 6:18) calls special attention to the harmful nature of sexual sins, in that they are committed against one's own body (Rosenau & Tan, 2002). Generally, stricter, more traditional interpretations of the Bible are associated with more conservative views on various aspects of sexuality, including homosexuality, gender roles, abortion, pornography, and sex outside of marriage (Edger, 2012). Some Christian teachings hold that engaging in same-sex sexual activities is sinful, as is heterosexual sex outside of marriage (De la Garza-Mercer, 2006).

Biblical scholars have cited different sections of the Bible to either support or oppose homosexuality (Edger, 2012). Many conservative Evangelical Christian groups stand in opposition to homosexuality (Edger, 2012), making this a major issue of internal conflict for lesbian, gay, and bisexual members of these religious groups. Some groups hold that homosexuality on its own is not a sin, but engaging in any form of homosexual activity is a sin (Edger, 2012). However, as new interpretations of Scripture have emerged that suggest that homosexuality may not inherently be sinful, some gay, lesbian, and bisexual Christians have been able to combine their religious identities with an acceptance of their sexual orientations (Edger, 2012).

Evangelical Christianity encompasses a broad, diverse population that is characterized by diversity of its traditions and interpretations of Christian doctrine (Edger, 2012). However, some common beliefs are held among most Evangelical Christian groups, such as the authority of the Bible as a guide for living, the need to be born again, and the drive to evangelize and spread the evangelical belief system to others (Edger, 2012). Typically, Evangelical Christians believe that sex should occur only within heterosexual marriage, which has given rise to a sexual-purity movement, holding that people should wait to have sex until they are married (Edger, 2012). However, there also has been growing attention to the notion of sex addiction within Evangelical Christian communities, which may result from the belief system that holds sexual thoughts to be impure unless they occur within that heterosexual, married context (Edger, 2012).

Because of Christian churches' tendency to promote sexual relationships only within the context of marriage, single individuals may feel as though they are left without sufficient guidance to make decisions about their sexual attitudes and behaviors (Rosenau & Tan, 2002). Some may question fully the prohibition of sex outside of marriage; others may struggle to know what specific behaviors are and are not appropriate (Rosenau & Tan, 2002). Many people learn through their Christian churches that they should not have sex until they are married, as well as that women should be submissive to men (Mahoney, 2008). Often, however, church leaders are relatively silent on the subject of sexuality (Mahoney, 2008). This silence, combined with the rules against sexual behaviors outside of marriage, can lead people to feelings of guilt and confusion (Mahoney, 2008; Rosenau & Tan, 2002).

Integrating Religion and Sexuality

For many people, integrating sexuality with religious and spiritual beliefs can become a lifelong process, which is often confusing and challenging (Mahoney, 2008). This integration can be especially difficult in the context of unique challenges, such as sexual abuse. Religious and spiritual variables can influence clients' experiences with sexual abuse, especially when the abuse had clear religious connections (e.g., when abused by a clergy member; Ganzevoort, 2002). However, religion also can provide survivors with a form of coping (Ganzevoort, 2002). Some of the specific religious themes that survivors of sexual abuse may struggle with include guilt and innocence, trust in God, forgiveness, and blaming God (Ganzevoort, 2002).

For many people, there is a parallel between sexual and spiritual maturity. Rosenau and Tan (2002) spoke of the notion of mature sexuality that integrates religion to govern "sexual behavior out of heart motivation, not law" (p. 190). This notion may prove useful to clients grappling with how to integrate these two aspects of their lives—in other words, making choices based on the guidance of the heart of their faith and their devotion to their religion and God, rather than based on guilt over following a set of religious-based proscribed rules (i.e., legalism). Rosenau and Tan (2002) provide an example of this through the distinction of asking "How far can I go?" (i.e., a rule-based question) versus asking, "How can I help my partner and companion produce a loving, sexual wholeness?" (i.e., a heart-based decision) (p. 190).

Overall, for many people, the integration of religion and sexuality is a challenging process. People may struggle when they feel that the teachings of their religion run counter to their sexual identities, experiences, and/or beliefs. Furthermore, they may find that the sexuality-related rules put forth by their religion do not account for the complexity of their lives. On the other hand, a person may also view their religious and spiritual beliefs, practices, and communities as a source of strength, support, and guidance for making positive sexuality-related decisions. Therefore, counselors have a unique opportunity to help clients explore and integrate these two significant aspects of life.

RACE, CULTURE, ETHNICITY, AND SEXUALITY

By culture, we are referring to "a system of shared beliefs, values, customs, and behaviors that the members of society use to cope with their world and with one another" (Fourcroy, 2006, p. 955). Some of the ways that culture impacts people's sexuality are through the religious values of the culture, social norms and customs, and cultural views about sexuality (Fourcroy, 2006). One's cultural background also can influence how they perceive the impact of their physical status—including any disabilities they have—on their sexuality (Greenwell & Hough, 2008). Research also suggests that one's cultural background can influence one's overall view of sexuality. Historically, westernized cultures tend to have held more negative views toward sexuality, while Eastern cultures have been more accepting (Goodwach, 2005a; 2005b). Therefore, cultural influences on sexuality can be significant. These influences can become especially significant through cross-cultural exchanges. For example, cross-cultural intimate relationships can highlight cultural differences (Nagel, 2000), and couples may need to navigate these differences as they build and maintain their relationships. Some of the specific areas of research that high-light the influence of culture and ethnicity on sexuality include attitudes toward homosexuality, immigration, and gender.

Attitudes Toward Homosexuality

Individuals' attitudes toward same-sex relationships and the LGBT community can be influenced by their cultural backgrounds. As one example, research suggests that gay, lesbian, and bisexual African Americans face some unique challenges, although there have been mixed findings on attitudes toward homosexuality within the African American community (Lewis, 2003). Within the LGBT community, some African Americans experience racism, and therefore, they may be less likely to get involved in their local LGBT communities (Lewis, 2003). Although African Americans may be less accepting of homosexuality compared to White Americans, they also appear to be less supportive of policies and practices that discriminate based on a same-sex orientation (Lewis, 2003). Members of the LGBT community who are from cultural backgrounds that do not sanction same-sex relationships may face particular challenges during the coming-out process. For example, they may experience pressure from family or cultural group members to hide their sexual orientation from other members of their cultural groups. In some cases, people who come out may be shunned by members of their cultural groups, adding to the com-plexity of the coming-out process. Counselors should therefore be mindful of these cultural influences on attitudes toward homosexuality when working with clients who are coming out themselves or who have family members who are doing so.

Immigration

Immigration can have a unique and profound impact on sexuality. Through immigration, people may experience major differences in the cultural norms regarding sexuality and intimate relationships between their home countries and their new countries (Huang & Akhtar, 2005). First, immigrants may experience differences in the extent to which sexuality is visibly expressed in the different countries. For example, this could be reflected in ways of dressing, such as non-sexualizing clothing in some countries and sexually revealing clothing in others. Second, gender-role norms may be very different between immigrants' countries, including the division of household labor, the participation of women in the economy, and views on the meaning of masculinity and femininity.

Third, countries may hold different levels of acceptance toward homosexuality. Relatedly, definitions of what constitutes "homosexual" activity can vary between cultures. For example, in some countries, kissing between men is considered normal and not sexual, but in others, it would be viewed as homosexual behavior. Fourth, immigrants' cultures may differ in their views toward arranged marriage and whether marriage should be based on love or social status. Fifth, the stress of immigration itself can impact immigrants' sexuality, such as by making them less expressive of their sexuality or by impacting the extent to which they make safe and healthy choices regarding their sexuality. Sixth, immigrants may experience new opportunities for cross-cultural sexual and romantic relationships, which can bring both pleasure and stress related to cross-cultural differences.

Okazaki (2002) provided an example of the impact of immigration on sexuality in an exploration of the influence of Asian American culture on sexuality. Okazaki first noted that Asian American cultures are diverse, although certain common experiences and cultural values may be found within this population. Some trends that Okazaki notes have been identified in research on sexuality among Asian Americans include conservative values about sexual activities being restricted to marriage, modesty, and reluctance to seek sexuality-related health care. Two significant factors that can influence Asian Americans' sexuality are acculturation (i.e., the extent to which individuals have adopted mainstream American perspectives toward sexuality) and religion, as religious-belief systems can vary widely among Asian Americans. Overall, Huang and Akhtar (2005) suggest that immigration can present opportunities for sexual growth and/or stress.

Culture and Gender

The intersections between culture, gender, and sexuality have been explored in previous research. For example, researchers have suggested that African American women have historically been sexually objectified within American culture, particularly dating back to slavery (Watson et al., 2012). This objectification can become internalized and contribute to distress as African American women develop their sexual identities. In addition, many cultures around the world hold clear rules as to what types of sexual behaviors are permitted and not permitted based on gender, especially for women (Fourcroy, 2006). Women's sexuality may be impacted in an especially negative way in cultures that sanction human trafficking, violence, and male infidelity (Fourcroy, 2006). Other forms of cultural oppression of women in cultures around the world include honor killings, dowries for brides, war-related rape (Fourcroy, 2006), and genital circumcision.

Female genital circumcision is an issue that has gained greater attention in recent years (Fourcroy, 2006). According to Fourcroy, female genital circumcision "is practiced by both Muslims and non-Muslims alike residing in sub-Saharan African countries that include, but are not limited to, Egypt, Sudan, Somalia, Ethiopia, Kenya, and Chad" (p. 955). There are different forms of female genital circumcision, ranging from minor to severe (i.e., full removal of the clitoris), and it is not considered a religious custom (Fourcroy, 2006). Proponents of female genital circumcision view it as a way to reduce a woman's sexuality in order to uphold her family's honor and prevent her from engaging in immoral or promiscuous behaviors (Fourcroy, 2006). Physical risks of undergoing female genital circumcision may include infection, shock, hemorrhaging, and death (Fourcroy, 2006). In addition, the procedure can remove the woman's physical sexual sensitivity, which can contribute to sexual dysfunction (Fourcroy, 2006). However, the effect can vary (Fourcroy, 2006).

Summary

Sexuality and culture intersect in complex ways. Cultural-group norms can influence values and attitudes toward sexuality. Some culturally sanctioned practices (e.g., female genital circumcision and human sex trafficking) can have an extremely negative impact on sexual and emotional health. However, positive sexuality-related cultural norms also can provide a source of support and motivation, such as when cultural messages promote positive, loving, respectful sexual relationships. People do not necessarily automatically accept the sexuality-related beliefs and norms within their ethnic and cultural groups; therefore, counselors can discuss each client's perceptions about the unique impact of these factors on their own lives.

SOCIOECONOMIC STATUS AND SEXUALITY

To date, there has been a minimal focus on social class within research on sexuality (Binnie, 2011). Therefore, we have limited information about how socioeconomic variables—such as education and income levels—impact clients' sexuality. Some possible reasons it has not been addressed include the discomfort and embarrassment surrounding social class and political pressure to avoid the issue (Binnie, 2011). Socioeconomic status has not only been ignored in sexuality-focused research. Media representations of sexuality also often ignore issues of poverty and socioeconomic status and their impact on sexuality (Ashcraft, 2003). It seems that discussions of sexuality within professional and general populations often pay minimal attention to how socioeconomic status influences sexual practices, beliefs, and identity.

Existing research suggests that socioeconomic status impacts sexual health. For example, Gonzales and Rolison (2005) used data from the 1992 National Health and Social Life Survey to examine socioeconomic differences in sexuality. They found that higher socioeconomic status was associated with more frequent masturbation, more frequently thinking about sex, and being more sexually adventurous. Gonzales and Rolison suggested based on these findings that people who have a higher level of socioeconomic status enjoy a higher level of sexual capital than those with lower socioeconomic statuses. More recently, Eisenberg, Shindel, Smith, Breyer, and Lipshultz (2010) found that lower levels of education (i.e., less than high school) have been associated with more frequent sex among men. These findings, therefore, paint a complicated picture of the impact of socioeconomic status on sexuality.

However, socioeconomic characteristics likely exert a powerful influence on sexuality and sexual health. Let's consider two major aspects of socioeconomic status—income and education—and how they may influence one's sexual health. Higher levels of income can provide access to a broader range and higher number of sexual health resources, such as medical care, contraception, mental health counseling, and medical treatments for sexual health problems (e.g., sexual dysfunctions or sexually transmitted infections). In addition, with greater income may come more time and resources for leisure and relaxation, which can support relational intimacy and reduced stress. In contrast, people who have lower incomes may have difficulty accessing the resources that are readily available to people with more financial resources. Many readers have probably heard the saying, "It's much less expensive to buy condoms than it is to have a baby." However, people on extremely limited budgets may face the decision of whether to purchase condoms or buy food for their families. If they do not have access to other forms of contraception (e.g., free condoms through a health clinic), they may forgo contraception altogether or use less reliable forms of birth control (e.g., the withdrawal method, which is free but much less effective than, for example, birth control pills). It is also important to consider how the economic stressors that people with fewer financial resources face can carry over to people's sex lives. For example, someone who needs to work two or more jobs to make ends meet likely has very limited time and energy to devote to fostering positive sexuality and intimacy within a sexual relationship.

Higher levels of education also can provide access to more resources to promote positive sexuality. The more time that someone spends in formal educational environments (e.g., high school, colleges, and universities), the more opportunities they are likely to have for sex education. This education may occur through official coursework, as well as extracurricular experiences, such as school-sponsored speakers and clubs (e.g., clubs for LGBT students). In addition, many colleges and universities offer students access to a broad range of useful resources to support sexual health, including informational workshops, physical health care, mental health counseling, treatment for sexual health concerns, sexual assault prevention and response resources, and even free condoms. Furthermore, the critical thinking skills that are promoted through higher levels of education can be applied to support people in making positive sexual health-related decisions.

Although there is a need for a lot more research to study the links between socioeconomic status and sexuality, this is an important variable for counselors to consider when working with clients around sexuality issues. In particular, counselors can seek to understand how clients' access to sexual health resources is impacted by their current socioeconomic situation.

SEXUALITY AND GEOGRAPHIC AND REGIONAL VARIATIONS

Geography is perhaps one of the contextual variables that counselors consider least often in discussions of multicultural competence. However, consider the different places you've lived and visited throughout your own life, and think about how those different environments affected your life in many ways. Have you experienced life in a suburban, urban, and/or rural area? What about different regions of the country or different countries altogether? Think back on those experiences, and consider all the various ways that these geographical places differed from one another—such as the distance you had to drive to get places, how close you lived to your neighbors, how clean your surroundings were, how easy it was to access "the great outdoors," the availability of services and resources in each area, social customs and norms, how predominant a role religion played in the community, gender norms (e.g., the level of accepted patriarchy, Kazyak, 2012), and how conservative and/or liberal members of the population were. Think even about such other details about how people dressed, what people ate, and the way they talked. Any of these geographic and regional differences can impact people's sexuality in direct and subtle ways.

Similar to our discussion above about socioeconomic status, regional differences can especially impact the availability of sexual health resources within a community. Rural areas in particular may experience a significant lack of resources compared to urban and suburban areas. Sexual health-related service agencies may be a far distance away for people in rural areas, and often there is no or limited public transportation to help people get around in rural communities. This can be especially problematic for sexual health concerns that people feel ashamed or embarrassed about (e.g., sexual abuse, sexually transmitted infections, or unintended pregnancies). Someone who lacks access to their own transportation may not feel comfortable asking friends or family members for help getting to a sexual health clinic or counseling to address these issues, which can present a barrier to service access.

In addition, regional differences can be significant for members of the LGBT population in terms of the visibility of the population in different communities, access to social or supportive resources, and the level of discrimination they experience in different areas. Because gay and lesbian populations are more concentrated in urban areas, rural gay and lesbian individuals may face unique challenges (Kazyak, 2012). Definitions of femininity and masculinity for women may be different in rural areas, especially those based on agricultural economies, in that women working in agricultural jobs may present in more masculine ways (e.g., through their clothing) regardless of their sexual orientation (Kazyak, 2012). Kazyak suggests that geographic (i.e., rural versus urban) influences can have a major impact on how gay and lesbian individuals express their gender and sexuality.

Another regional difference that can impact people's sexuality is the impact of public policies, which can vary based on geography. At a societal level, there is a real benefit for the prevention of the harmful consequences of sexual activity, such as infections and unwanted pregnancies, as the cost of these outcomes can be great (Hull, 2008). However, public policies related to sexuality and sexual dissatisfaction may not rise to the level of social importance as other issues because, as Hull (2008) said, "lack of orgasms is not fatal, and they [i.e., social leaders] regard failure to achieve a deep spiritual connection with a sexual partner as a private inconvenience rather than a tragedy" (p. 137). Therefore, the level and type of attention that local and state politicians pay to sexuality-related matters can vary widely between geographic locations. One major political issue that currently varies significantly between states in the United States is the legalization of gay marriage. See, for example, the list of state laws provided by the organization, Freedom to Marry (2015). These laws are likely to continue to change in coming years. Beyond the same-sex marriage issue, several other sexuality-related issues are often debated and vary based on local and regional politics, including but not limited to abortion laws, sexuality education in schools (i.e., abstinence-only versus comprehensive sexuality education), and laws regarding prosecution of sexual abuse.

Overall, counselors must consider the various levels at which geographic and regional variations can impact clients' sexuality, including through social norms, access to resources, and relevant laws and public policies related to sexual health.

SEXUALITY AND THE MEDIA

The impact of media on sexuality has been the focus of much research, practical interventions, and debate in recent years. Media is a pervasive source of information and messages about sexuality in today's society, and sexuality is found in virtually every form of media, including television, movies, the Internet, music videos, and magazines (Brown, 2002). In this section, we address the intersections of sexuality and the media, with a particular focus on the following areas: how adolescents' sexual identities are particularly impacted by the media; the messages about sexuality that are conveyed through the media; unique considerations for the Internet and social media; the idealized images of sex and sexuality that are put forth by advertisers; and the potential value of the media for sex education.

Adolescent Sexuality and the Media

The media has become one of the major sources of sex education for today's youth (Ballam & Granello, 2011), for better or for worse. Pop culture and various forms of media have a major impact on teenagers' understanding of sexuality (Ashcraft, 2003). Wright (2009) wrote that adolescents today are so heavily influenced in their views on sexuality by the media because of the large amount of time that adolescents spend engaging with sexuality-related content via the media. Of course, adolescence is a critical time for sexuality development, as it's often a time for identity development and early experiences with relationships and intimacy. Because adolescents typically have had limited relationship and sexuality-related experiences, the norms that they perceive in the media about sexuality can have a major impact on what they view as normal and acceptable in their own lives and among their peer groups.

Media Messages About Sexuality

Messages about sexuality in pop culture are often contradictory and confusing (Ashcraft, 2003; Ballam & Granello, 2011). Bitzer et al. (2008) noted that some of the messages about sexuality put forth by the media include the following: women should be "good girls" who are timid and in control of their sexual desires; women do not have sexual fantasies; sex should be reserved for marriage; sex should not be engaged in simply for pleasure; and sex is focused only on intercourse.

Of course, for every one of these messages that can be found in the media, an opposing message can be found elsewhere in the media. For example, Ballam and Granello (2011) suggested that a different set of messages that people often receive about sexuality from the media include that sex is recreational, it does not involve contraception, there are no negative consequences from sex, and it often occurs spontaneously without any preparation and planning. Sorting through all of these messages can become very complicated, as the media does not present one singular view of sexuality, and in fact, it can portray conflicting messages at once. In addition, these messages are often in direct contrast to the messages about safer sex that are communicated by sexuality educators and counselors (Ballam & Granello, 2011).

Further, different forms of media may emphasize different messages or themes related to sexuality. For example, Wright (2009) found the following trends in a content analysis study: prime-time television shows often depict stereotypical roles for men and women and convey the message that sex carries minimal, if any risks; soap operas often normalize extramarital affairs; music videos often depict highly sexualized behaviors and perpetuate a focus on sex as being for physical pleasure only; feature films often depict non-committed sexual activity as normal and carrying few risks; and women's and teen magazines emphasize the importance of physical attractiveness as the defining aspect of sexual appeal.

Gender, sexual orientation, and race are important considerations for understanding media messages about sexuality. In general, predominant views of sexuality within the media are much more reflective of heterosexual-male sexuality (Bitzer et al., 2008). Therefore, media messages may be especially difficult for female, transgender, and LGBT people to integrate into their personal sense of sexuality. Regarding race, the media may depict women differently based on their racial backgrounds. For example, Baker (2005) used content analysis procedures to compare representations of White and Black females in advertisements in eight popular magazines, including two magazines that targeted each of the following audiences: White women, Black women, White men, and Black men. Baker's research demonstrated that magazines targeting White audiences were more likely to depict women as appearing dependent on and submissive to men. In contrast, the magazines targeting Black audiences were more likely to depict women as nurturing, athletic, and independent. We still need a lot more research to really understand how these different images put forth by media impact clients experiencing sexuality-related concerns.

The exact impact of the media's messages about sexuality is only recently beginning to be understood by researchers, although research suggests that gender and other demographic characteristics can impact the manner in which people interpret media messages about sexuality (Brown, 2002). Common social messages about sexuality put forth in the media may contribute to sexual anxiety and dissatisfaction among women (Bitzer et al., 2008). Men also can develop anxiety as a result of the common messages about sexuality in the media. In particular, they may experience feelings of inadequacy if they feel they do not measure up to the norms they perceive about their sexual functioning as compared to others (Bitzer et al., 2008). Together, the findings reviewed in this section suggest that media messages can have a powerful impact on clients' lives, especially when those messages are internalized into clients' own sexual self-concept.

The Internet and Social Media

The Internet and social media bring both potential challenges and benefits regarding sexual information. These forms of media can bring exposure to unwanted pornography and solicitations for sexual activities (Brown, 2002). However, on the positive side, these forms of technology can provide access to accurate sexual health information, including sexual communication and safe-sex methods (Brown, 2002). The credibility and accuracy of sexuality-related information that is available online can vary (Keller & Brown, 2002). In addition, people must be mindful of possible privacy limitations when seeking sexuality-related information on-line (Keller & Brown, 2002). Further, populations that need sexual health information may not always have access to the Internet, such as lower-income populations (Keller & Brown, 2002). As Internet use continues to expand in the coming years, it is likely that its impact on sexuality will be expanded as well. In particular, some future directions for research and practice in this area include how technology can promote or hinder sexuality within intimate relationships (e.g., Murray & Campbell, in press) and how counselors can mobilize technology to connect clients to resources to support their positive sexual health.

Advertising and Idealized Images of Sex and Sexuality

Sex-related messages are often used in advertising to sell products (Keller & Brown, 2002). Advertisements are so pervasive in our society that people in the United States typically see thousands of advertisements every day (Baker, 2005). The media may reflect social norms that already exist, and they also may reinforce norms that those in power (e.g., corporations, advertisers) aim to promote (Baker, 2005). Commonly, advertisements present an idealized version of reality, such as how people should look and act (Baker, 2005). Of course, people are also influenced in the idealized physical characteristics of prospective partners by the images that they see in the media (Schooler & Ward, 2006). There is an extensive body of research showing that these idealized images of sex and sexuality can impact people's body image. Although most research on the impact of the media on body image has focused on women, there is growing recognition that men are influenced by media messages about masculinity and body image as well (Schooler & Ward, 2006). Increasingly, media images have idealized male bodies that are muscular, fit, and toned (Schooler & Ward, 2006). In addition, the media often conveys the message that men are sexually confident and competent (Schooler & Ward, 2006), which can lead to additional insecurities for men who adopt these perspectives. Thus, idealized images in advertising have a powerful impact, even though most people understand that what they see in the media often doesn't match up with life in the real world (Baker, 2005; Ballam & Granello, 2011).

The Potential Value of the Media for Sex Education

The impact of the media on sexuality need not be all negative, and in fact, the media can be used by sexuality educators to promote positive sexual health. Because of the amount of time that people, and especially youth, today spend interacting with various forms of media, it offers a potentially powerful avenue for sexual health education (Keller & Brown, 2002). In some countries, soap operas are used to transmit sexual health information via storylines on the shows (Keller & Brown, 2002). There are numerous ways that sexuality-health educators can use the media to disseminate sexual health information, including via social media, public awareness campaigns, Internet-based programs, and messages embedded within media-based programs (e.g., television shows) (Keller & Brown, 2002). Keller and Brown describe "entertainment education" as putting "educational content into entertaining formats to increase knowledge, create favorable attitudes, and change overt behavior" (p. 67). For example, a teenage-drama television show might create a storyline in which characters negotiate safer sex practices or deal with the consequences of unprotected sex. Research internationally has shown some promise for these strategies for changing behaviors (Keller & Brown, 2002). Overall, although most research has focused on the negative impacts of the media on sexuality, there are potential opportunities that can come from harnessing the power of the media to promote positive sexuality-related information and resources.

COUNSELING STRATEGIES FOR ADDRESSING CULTURAL AND CONTEXTUAL INFLUENCES ON SEXUALITY

As with all areas of counseling practice, it is important for counselors to provide services that are appropriate to clients' unique background characteristics and delivered in a culturally competent manner. In light of the information discussed throughout this chapter, we suggest four major sexuality-counseling strategies when working with clients whose presenting concerns are intersecting with contextual influences. These include (a) accounting for contextual variables in treatment planning, (b) promoting clients' media literacy, (c) addressing religion with LGBT clients, when appropriate, and (d) deconstructing contextual messages about sexuality.

Accounting for Contextual Variables in Treatment Planning

Counselors must consider unique cultural factors when developing treatment plans for sexuality-related concerns (Yasan, Essizoglu, & Yildirim, 2009). For example, Yasan, Essizoglu, and Yildirim (2009) described a Muslim Turkish woman who initially received inappropriate professional treatment for vaginismus because it did not account for the influence of traditional Islamic culture. Once culturally appropriate treatment was provided, the client was in a better position to address the cultural ramifications of the treatment approach, as well as to carry out the requirements of treatment within her family context. Therefore, counselors should design treatment plans and interventions that take into account unique traditions, customs, and worldviews of clients based on their intersecting contextual backgrounds.

Interventions should not only avoid violating cultural norms, but they also can be developed to incorporate unique cultural strengths and resources. For example, clients may draw upon cultural traditions and support networks as appropriate to address sexuality-related concerns. In particular, clients may benefit from being connected to other members of their cultural groups who have had similar experiences as them (e.g., a culture-specific support group and/or mentor). In addition, as psychoeducational approaches are often an important part of sexuality counseling, counselors can provide culturally relevant sexual health information to clients and discuss how this accurate information relates to messages conveyed in the broader culture (Ballam & Granello, 2011). To this end, counselors can provide culturally relevant educational information to clients about sexuality, such as through brochures and pamphlets (Keller & Brown, 2002), which may need to be translated into the appropriate language for the target population. Counselors need not make treatment-planning decisions on their own, and the treatment-planning process can involve a collaborative dialogue that allows both the counselor and client to consider how unique, contextual variables can be addressed through counseling.

Promoting Media Literacy

Messages about sexuality in the media and pop culture should be discussed in sexuality education and counseling (Ashcraft, 2003). Conversations can promote media literacy (i.e., the ability to think critically about the media), including by helping clients examine the messages in the media about sexuality and the messages that are lacking (Ballam & Granello, 2011). Counselors can help clients develop media literacy by promoting their ability to think critically about the messages they receive in the media about sexuality (Keller & Brown, 2002). People will interpret the same messages they receive from the media in different ways (Ballam & Granello, 2011), so counselors can support clients in considering how their unique backgrounds influence how they perceive media messages about sexuality. One specific area where media literacy can be applied is to examining media messages about physical and sexual attractiveness. Counselors can help clients who fall outside of mainstream images of sexual attractiveness to examine the impact of those images on their own self-image and self-define what sexual attractiveness means to them (Watson et al., 2012).

Counselors working with young people and in schools should be sure to follow any organizational or legal requirements related to discussing sexuality with youth (Ballam & Granello, 2011). In addition to direct interventions with youth, counselors can support parents in talking with their children about sexuality and the media (Ballam & Granello, 2011). One approach is for parents to offer their opinions about representations of sexuality in the media as a way to open these conversations, while allowing the opportunity for teenagers to share their thoughts as well (Ballam & Granello, 2011). Counselors may need to initiate conversations about sexuality and the media with their client—both young and old—as clients may be hesitant to do so on their own (Ballam & Granello, 2011). Although there is growing recognition of the need for media literacy, there currently is minimal research evidence to support the effectiveness of media literacy interventions (Keller & Brown, 2002). Therefore, there is a need for future development of effective interventions to help children and adults examine the impact of the media messages on sexuality.

Addressing Religion With LGBT Clients

When clients are facing conflicts between their sexuality and cultural norms (e.g., in the case of someone with an LGBT orientation who has religious beliefs that say homosexuality is a sin), counselors can assist them in examining whether there are alternate ways to integrate their multiple identities (Glassgold, 2008). Some religious clients with a same-sex orientation may be interested in reparative therapies with the hopes of changing their sexual orientation so it is in line with their religious beliefs. Clients who ask for reparative therapies can be informed of the lack of evidence for these approaches, as well as the ethical issues that have been discussed in the field regarding these therapies (Glassgold, 2008). Further, counselors can support clients requesting these treatments in addressing the emotions that surround such a request (Glassgold, 2008). However, counselors also can support these clients in researching and evaluating their options for themselves (Glassgold, 2008).

As discussed earlier in this chapter, LGBT clients may experience a significant internal conflict between their religious beliefs and their sexual orientation and/or gender identity. In addition to this internal struggle, these clients may be judged and isolated or feel condemned by members of their religious community on the basis of their sexual orientation or gender identity. Some religious clients may be able to achieve a sense of relative comfort in remaining in a religious community that does not fully support their sexuality (Glassgold, 2008), and counselors can help clients evaluate their options in this regard. Clients also may wish to explore other faith communities to determine if they can find one that is a good fit for them, in that it aligns with their religious beliefs and accepts their sexual and gender identity as well. Local LGBT organizations (e.g., PFLAG or an LGBT center) may even be able to provide recommendations of faith communities that are welcoming to members of the LGBT population. Finding the right fit in a faith community may take some time, especially if the client does not want to disclose their sexual or gender orientation immediately (e.g., by asking the religious group's leaders about their stance on sexuality), so counselors can support clients in taking the time they need to find a community that they view as safe, comfortable, and supportive.

Deconstructing Contextual Messages About Sexuality

The ultimate challenge implied throughout this chapter is how to help clients foster positive sexuality within the unique contexts of their cultural and contextual backgrounds. Sometimes, these contextual influences help to support this positive sexuality development, but others times, these influences can create challenges and even distress. Therefore, it is fitting that we will conclude this chapter by addressing counselors' opportunities to help clients deconstruct the cultural and contextual messages they have received about sexuality. This deconstruction process can help clients evaluate whether and how they wish to continue to ascribe to these messages. As a result of this process, clients may be able to identify new opportunities for a more integrated, positive framework for understanding and expressing their own sexuality.

As we have discussed, the contextual influences on clients' sexuality are numerous, and with so many layers of influences at work in clients' lives, there is great potential for clients to experience conflicting values. Consider the following examples:

- A client who identifies as gay but also holds to religious beliefs that condemn homosexuality
- A client with physical features that are valued within her cultural community but whose same physical features are devalued and labeled as unattractive by the advertising industry

- An adolescent client who lives in an rural area where "abstinence only" sexuality education is the only message received through school, church, and home, yet has begun having intercourse with a boyfriend or girlfriend and wants to access contraception
- An immigrant who moved from a culture with strict, conservative gender roles into a culture with egalitarian gender norms

In any of the above situations, clients may feel confused and distressed when trying to resolve internal and external conflicts that these situations can produce. Clients can be encouraged to explore their naturally ambivalent feelings toward sexuality as related to the cultural messages they receive (Ashcraft, 2003). Counselors must not assume that a client has fully adopted cultural values and beliefs but rather should ask the client to describe his or her perspectives toward those values and how they impact their life (Keshet-Orr, 2003). By applying a narrative lens, counselors can help clients reconsider the stories of their various cultural and sexuality stories and beliefs, in an effort to identify new possibilities and identities (Glassgold, 2008). Overall, the intersections of sexuality with cultural and contextual influences can produce both conflicts and challenges for clients. Counselors have a unique opportunity to assist clients in sorting through the myriad variables in order to identify a positive, integrated view of their sexuality and its role in their lives.

KEYSTONES

- Although research can help to identify patterns between and among groups of people, sexuality is an inherently individual part of life. Therefore, we cannot say there is any one way to define how sexuality will be experienced within a group of people.
- There is diversity within virtually every cultural or contextual group, making it impossible to create clear-cut rules about how a person will view their sexuality in light of any one given background characteristic.
- An intersectional approach views each person as uniquely shaped by multiple social locations, based on such contextual characteristics as their racial and ethnic background, their sexual orientation, gender, and socioeconomic status.
- Many people find it challenging to integrate their spirituality and religious beliefs with their sexuality. Religion can be especially influential on sexuality-related values and experiences during critical developmental periods, such as adolescence.
- Some of the ways that culture impacts people's sexuality are through the religious values of the culture, social norms and customs, and cultural views about sexuality.

- To date, we have limited information about how socioeconomic variables—such as education and income levels—impact clients' sexuality.
- Regional differences can especially impact the availability of sexual health resources within a community. Rural areas in particular may experience a significant lack of resources compared to urban and suburban areas.
- Media is a pervasive source of information and messages about sexuality in today's society, and sexuality is found in virtually every form of media, including television, movies, the Internet, music videos, and magazines. Counselors should consider the influence of media messages on clients' sexuality-related concerns.
- Four major sexuality-counseling strategies when working with clients whose presenting concerns are intersecting with contextual influences include (a) accounting for contextual variables in treatment planning, (b) promoting clients' media literacy, (c) addressing religion with LGBT clients, when appropriate, and (d) deconstructing contextual messages about sexuality.

ADDITIONAL RESOURCES

- Peer-reviewed journal, *Sexuality and Culture* (http://link.springer.com/journal/12119)
- The Center for the Study of Sexual Culture at the University of California, Berkeley (http://cssc.berkeley.edu/)

Chapter 10

Positive Sexuality
A New Paradigm for Sexuality Counseling

*I am definitely sure that safe, frequent, and satisfactory sexual activity
is not only fun, but also a powerful booster of health!*

—Jannini, Fisher, Bitzer, & McMahon, 2009, p. 2642

It should go without saying that sex is, or at least can be, a fun, satisfying, and plea-surable aspect of life and intimate relationships. Except, of course, sometimes it isn't. Therein lies the challenge for counselors and, more broadly, for nearly everyone in modern society. We live in a society in which people are bombarded with messages about both the pleasurable aspects of sex and sexuality (e.g., "Have amazing orgasms today!" and "Please your partner, improve your relationship.") and the problems and risks associated with them (e.g., "prevent rape" or "unprotected sex could lead to unin-tended pregnancy and STIs"). Even the messages about the pleasure of sex have a possible negative undertone—such as "Your orgasms aren't as good as they could be, are they?" and "You're not doing enough to satisfy your partner." Because sexuality is a private domain in most people's lives, many of us are left with insecurities about how our own sexual attitudes, experiences, and behaviors match up to others.

In this final chapter, we explore the possibility that sex and sexuality can be powerful channels for positive personal and relational growth. In recent years, a new perspective has been emerging that suggests that sex can provide more than just fleeting physical pleasure but also key opportunities for people to learn about themselves and their partners. Developing sexuality as a positive area of one's life is about far more than just getting rid of problems. Sexuality is an important dimension of people's overall health and well-being. Ongoing growth and development in this area can be part of a broader picture of physical and mental health that can enrich a person's life across time. Counselors have the opportunity to help their clients move toward a more positive view and experience of their sexuality and its expression in their relationships. After reading this chapter, readers will be able to do the following:

a. Understand the positive sexuality framework as it relates to the Contextualized Sexuality Model
b. Identify factors within each dimension of the Contextualized Sexuality Model that facilitate positive sexuality
c. Describe benefits of positive sexuality that have been described in research
d. Understand counseling strategies that help promote positive sexuality in clients

Before we can move to addressing those topics, we must acknowledge that there are many forces at work that may lead us to focus on negative aspects of sexuality and the problems associated with it. For counselors, a major barrier to being able to help clients work toward positive sexuality is a lack of training, as we've discussed in previous chapters. As minimal as the training is that most counselors receive in sexuality, it appears that most of the training that occurs focuses primarily on sexual problems and dysfunctions, rather than providing trainees with an understanding of positive-sexuality frameworks (Miller & Byers, 2010). There has historically been an over-emphasis on problems in sexuality research and practice to the exclusion of more positive frameworks (Chillman, 1990; Diamond & Huebner, 2012; Fahs & Swank, 2011; Galinsky & Sonenstein, 2011; Hull, 2008). Diamond and Huebner (2012) even asserted that "if researchers studied the health-related sequelae of sexuality with the same rigor that they apply to exercise, diet, and alcohol use, we might be in a position to make more nuanced and effective recommendations about sexual health" (pp. 54–55). Failing to acknowledge sexual pleasure in research and practice ignores one of the major motivating factors that drives people to pursue sexual activities (De la Garza-Mercer, 2006; Hull, 2008).

Of course, counselors are also the product of the negativity that surrounds sexuality in the broader society. American society has been called "negative about sexuality" and "sexually silent" (Harris & Hays, 2008, p. 240). Much of the available information about sexuality is problem-focused, and the topic of sexual pleasure is often excluded from sexuality education programming (deFur, 2012; Fine, 1988). It should be no surprise, then, that typically, people have a broader language to describe sexual problems than they do sexual pleasure and enjoyment (Hirst, 2008). Therefore, counselors themselves may struggle to help clients find the most useful language to describe their needs and desires that would help them develop a more positive sense of sexuality in their lives. Before we discuss existing definitions of positive sexuality, we invite readers to complete Exercise 10.1 and reflect on their own personal definitions of it.

Exercise 10.1

WHAT DOES POSITIVE SEXUALITY MEAN TO YOU?

Before you move ahead to reading "official" definitions of positive sexuality and the factors contributing to it, take some time to consider the following questions:

- What does *positive sexuality* mean to you on a personal level? If you were to achieve a sense of positive sexuality in your personal life, what would that look like?
- What would a *positive sexuality* framework for counseling look like to you? How would sexuality be addressed in a counseling setting in a way that supports clients in their development in this area?
- What do you think are the most important strategies that counselors can use to support their clients in developing a more positive sense of sexuality in their lives?
- How equipped do you feel currently to assist your clients in working toward a more positive sense of sexuality in a professional and ethical manner?

DEFINING POSITIVE SEXUALITY

To formulate our definition of *positive sexuality*, we drew from existing definitions of *sexual health* and *sexual satisfaction*. First, the World Health Organization (2010) defined *sexual health* as follows:

> Sexual health is a state of physical, emotional, mental and social well-being in relation to sexuality; it is not merely the absence of disease, dysfunction or infirmity. Sexual health requires a positive and respectful approach to sexuality and sexual relationships, as well as the possibility of having pleasurable and safe sexual experiences, free of coercion, discrimination and violence. For sexual health to be attained and maintained, the sexual rights of all persons must be respected, protected and fulfilled. (p. 3)

Second, sexual satisfaction is an important component of overall positive sexuality. However, definitions of sexual satisfaction have varied in existing research, as researchers have struggled to determine how best to conceptualize this concept (Dundon & Rellini, 2009; Fahs & Swank, 2011). For example, some researchers have defined sexual satisfaction as being indicated by a high level of sexual activity, the frequency of orgasm, and basic sexual functioning (Fahs & Swank, 2011). Therefore, sexual satisfaction is a complex topic that is impacted by numerous contextual influences. Our own definition of *sexual satisfaction* as a component of positive sexuality is as follows: Sexual satisfaction describes the extent to which a person is pleased with the amount of physical, emotional, and sexual pleasure they derive from the frequency, quality, and range of sexual activities in which they are currently engaged, individually and relationally.

Defining positive sexuality is more complex than defining the symptoms of sexual problems (Maddock, 1989). In part, this is because sexuality is inherently a value-laden topic (Maddock, 1989). Therefore, any adequate definition of positive sexuality must contain the flexibility to include individuals' values, beliefs, and experiences. In light of this mandate, we define *positive sexuality* as the integration of *sexual health* and *sexual satisfaction* that encompasses a lifelong process of positive growth and development of one's sense of sexuality within his or her sexual identity, emotional and mental health, intimate relationships, and broader social contexts. The key aspects of this definition include the following: it acknowledges the importance of sexual health, including the reduction of health-related risks associated with sexual activity; its inclusion of sexual satisfaction reflects the pleasurable aspects of sexuality; it holds positive sexuality to be a lifelong process, rather than a static state that one either achieves or does not achieve; this definition underscores the connections between sexuality and mental and relational health; and it emphasizes the importance of understanding the social contexts in which one's sexuality is experienced. Therefore, positive sexuality encompasses more than just the lack of problems but rather also involves opportunities for personal satisfaction and fulfillment derived from sexuality that occurs through a developmental process within many intersecting aspects of people's lives (Southern & Cade, 2011).

FACTORS SUPPORTING POSITIVE SEXUALITY: REVISITING THE CONTEXTUALIZED SEXUALITY MODEL

The Contextualized Sexuality Model first presented in Chapter 1 provides a useful framework for identifying factors that support people in developing a positive sense of sexuality. Each of the contextual influences in this model plays an important role in either fostering or hindering positive sexuality. Therefore, in this section we review existing research that describes some of the important factors that can contribute to positive sexuality within each domain.

Physiology

To promote optimal sexual functioning, people need knowledge about how their bodies work (Hull, 2008). Therefore, accurate information about the physical dimensions of sexual functioning is an important component of positive sexuality.

People benefit when they know about the general anatomy and physiology of sexual functioning, as well as individual knowledge about unique aspects of one's own body. In other words, people's individual experiences of their physiology may differ from general trends among the broader population. Although there is much focus on the genitals as a source of physical sexual pleasure, people can experience pleasure from various other erogenous zones throughout their bodies, including their necks and ears (De la Garza-Mercer, 2006). Therefore, knowledge about one's own and one's partner's sex-related physical functioning can promote positive sexual health.

A healthy body also contributes to positive sexual functioning. People can promote sexual health through general health-promoting behaviors, such as good nutrition, adequate rest and sleep, and regular exercise. Healthier lifestyles contribute to positive sexual health by providing more energy, endurance, strength, and flexibility to enhance sexual activities. However, although physical health can contribute to positive sexual functioning, it is also important to note that conditions such as chronic health problems and physical disabilities need not signify the end of sexual activities. For example, Hull (2008) wrote that people can experience sexual pleasure even when they have significant physical disabilities. When people have physical conditions that impact their sexual health, they may be able to adapt their behaviors to devise alternative means of promoting sexual satisfaction.

Another important physiological aspect of positive sexuality is a proactive approach to minimizing health-related risks associated with sexual activity. Sex can carry physical risks—including the possibility of unintended pregnancies, physical injury, and sexually transmitted infections (STIs; De la Garza-Mercer, 2006). Therefore, people can foster positive sexuality by proactively taking steps to protect themselves against these risks, such as by using contraception and communicating with their partners if something physically hurts during sexual activity.

Recognition of the importance of physical pleasure during sexual activity is another important aspect of the physical dimension of positive sexuality. Physical pleasure is a major reason that many people pursue sexual activities, although pleasure is very self-defined (De la Garza-Mercer, 2006; deFur, 2012). Pleasure may be experienced on one's own through masturbation or with a partner, and it can be found in many different types of experiences (deFur, 2012). De la Garza-Mercer (2006) defined sexual pleasure as "the positive physical and subjective sensation and emotional experience resulting from stimulation of the genitals, breasts, and other erogenous zones" (p. 108). When people understand what gives them feelings of sexual pleasure, they can learn more about their personal preferences and dislikes (De la Garza-Mercer, 2006).

And, we cannot end a section on the physical dimension of positive sexuality without mentioning orgasms. Galinsky and Sonenstein (2011) wrote that, "Although orgasm represents only one kind of sexual pleasure, it is highly valued in American culture" (p. 613). For many people, orgasm represents the ultimate goal of sexual activity, although for others, orgasm may only be the beginning of the potential for sexual exploration and pleasure (Schnarch, 1997). There is research evidence that heterosexual couples who experience simultaneous penile-vaginal orgasms during intercourse demonstrate higher levels of sexual satisfaction (Brody & Weiss, 2012). However, simultaneous orgasms may not be possible for some couples, and they are not a requirement for sexual satisfaction. Nonetheless, the physical sensations that accompany orgasm are a significant component of sexual functioning for many people.

Developmental Influences

Sexuality and the pursuit of sexual pleasure are life-long processes (Elders, 2010; Hull, 2008; Lamb & Peterson, 2012). The development of positive sexuality occurs within broader-lifespan developmental processes. Each developmental phase of an individual's lifespan lays an important foundation for subsequent development at later phases, and this is especially true with regard to human sexuality. Chapter 5 provided a thorough review of a lifespan approach to the process of sexuality development. Here, we integrate the points made in that chapter to provide an overview of the developmental factors that contribute to positive sexuality.

An adaptive family context supports positive sexuality throughout the lifespan. Maddock (1989) defined healthy family sexuality as "the balanced expression of sexuality in the structures and functions of the family, in ways that enhance the personal identities and sexual health of individual members and the coherence of the family as a system" (p. 135). Families can model positive, open communication about sexuality (Braeken & Cardinal, 2008; Maddock, 1989), and they can help children establish healthy sexuality (Elders, 2010). Other family characteristics that have been linked to positive sexuality include gender role flexibility, warmth, intimacy, clearly defined and developmentally appropriate boundaries around sexual behavior, and shared value systems that are flexible over time (Maddock, 1989). Of course, there is not a single way to define a sexually healthy family, as families vary and need to be able to adapt to the changing society around them, as well as their own unique family cultural background (Maddock, 1989).

People need access to accurate sexual health information throughout their lives (Braeken & Cardinal, 2008; Elders, 2010). Sexuality education must be delivered through age-appropriate messages (Braeken & Cardinal, 2008), and information should be tailored to the unique needs and concerns of each phase of life. Very young children can learn appropriate language for describing their bodies, and the caregivers in their lives can provide developmentally appropriate answers to the questions that they ask. These questions reflect a natural cognitive maturational process. Although answering those questions can be difficult, parents can strive to provide sexual health information gradually over time in developmentally appropriate ways to ensure that children are exposed to information that addresses their questions but does not provide them with information that they can't yet comprehend (Maddock, 1989).

As children move into adolescence, the information that they receive, as well as the emotional context in which they receive it, can influence their sexuality development. Chillman (1990) reviewed several aspects of positive sexuality in adolescence, which included the following: self-esteem, respect for oneself and others, effective communication and decision-making skills, a growing acceptance that sexuality is a normal part of people's lives, recognition of the potential consequences of sexuality, and understanding of what consent means. Chillman also emphasized the importance of adolescents making positive decisions about whether to engage in sexual relationships, and if so, the contraception they will use (Chillman, 1990).

Of course, the topic of adolescents engaging in sexual activity is shrouded in controversy. Depending on their age, adolescents may not be able to legally consent to sexual activity, although this may depend on state laws and the age of the partner (Lamb & Peterson, 2012). Beyond whether sexual activity is legal, the maturity levels of adolescents call into question the notion of being empowered sexually during this stage of life. Particularly as a teenager, just because someone *feels* empowered sexually does not necessarily mean that they *are* empowered in the broader context of their lives and society (Gavey, 2012; Lamb & Peterson, 2012). For example, female adolescents may engage in activities that they feel makes them more mature or advanced sexually (e.g., privately stripping for a partner or a group), and yet there may be an element of exploitation by males that is involved in these activities (Gavey, 2012).

These dynamics are played out in the daily lives of American adolescents, with current research suggesting relatively high levels of sexual activity among American teenagers. According to the CDC (2013a), nearly half of American high school students have engaged in sexual intercourse. Similar findings indicate that adolescent sexual activities do not always occur within a context of safe, informed decisions. For example, among the one-third of high school students who had sex in the past three months, nearly 40% did not use a condom and nearly 77% did not use oral contraceptives during their most recent sexual intercourse (Centers for Disease Control, 2013a). These findings support the ongoing need for efforts to ensure that adolescents are supported in the positive development of their sexuality. In particular, adolescents are very inclined to copy what they see in the media, and therefore, it is important for them to be able to critically evaluate what they see, hear, and read (Lamb & Peterson, 2012). As they grow older, young people can continue to develop their critical thinking skills to examine various sexuality-related issues they face (Braeken & Cardinal, 2008).

Beyond adolescence, people's sexuality continues to develop over time, although certainly there has been less public and research attention to sexuality development in adulthood than in adolescence. Throughout adulthood, people continue to solidify their sense of sexuality, although people can experience significant changes over time that may alter the trajectory of their sexuality development. For example, consider an adult who was sexually abused as a child, but who in adulthood through counseling and other personal growth channels worked to overcome the lingering effects of that abuse in order to achieve a positive, fulfilling sense of sexuality, personally and within an intimate relationship. As another example, consider an adult who comes out as gay or lesbian in mid-life, perhaps even after having been in a long-term heterosexual marriage. Both of these examples underscore how people's positive growth related to their sexuality can be significantly altered at virtually any phase of life, so it is important for counselors to be prepared to assist clients with these transitions.

In addition, with development over the lifespan, people's physical functioning can change over time, and awareness of these changes and their impact is important. For example, at mid-life, menopause may lead some women to experience lower sexual desire, as well as reduced arousal and orgasms (Dundon & Rellini, 2009). Other physical changes that may occur over time include childbirth and lactation, hormonal changes, changes to one's physical appearance, illnesses, disabilities, and side effects from new medication regimens. These physical functioning changes need not result in negative outcomes for individuals' sexuality development. Rather, people can increasingly develop greater awareness of and comfort with their bodies and use these growth processes to facilitate continued positive sexuality development throughout their lives.

Individual Mental Health

Sexuality involves a complex integration of behaviors, attitudes, values, thoughts, and emotions. As such, an individual's overall mental health significantly impacts his or her sense of sexuality. Of course, mental health challenges can be linked to sexuality-related challenges, but the converse is also true: Positive overall characteristics of mental health can promote a positive sense of sexuality, along with an adaptive ability to manage sexuality-related challenges that arise. Existing research supports the links between mental health and sexuality, with the following mental health characteristics being especially relevant to positive sexuality.

Maturity

David Schnarch's (1997) book, *Passionate Marriage*, emphasized the importance of differentiation of self (drawing from Bowen Family Systems Theory) in the process of sexuality development, and ultimately, differentiation is a process of growing increasingly mature. Personal maturity is a signature component of one's increasing capacity for positive sexuality (Maddock, 1989). As applied to sexuality development, scholars have described maturity as integrating all aspects of oneself (Southern & Cade, 2011) and building personal character (Galinsky & Sonenstein, 2011).

Problem-Solving and Decision-Making

Positive sexuality implies that people are free from worries about negative outcomes from sexual activities, such as STIs and unwanted pregnancies (Hirst, 2008). Therefore, positive mental health supports positive sexuality in part by helping people make positive and informed decisions (Southern & Cade, 2011) and exercise good judgment with regard to sexual behaviors (Maddock, 1989).

Receptive to Pleasure

Positive mental health can increase people's ability to receive pleasure and enjoy sexual activity (Lamb & Peterson, 2012; Maddock, 1989). This includes acceptance of one's body (Southern & Cade, 2011) and the capacity to view sexuality as a positive, satisfying aspect of one's life (Hirst, 2008; Jannini et al., 2009).

Relational Skills and Capacity

The ability to be caring and connected to others promotes positive sexuality (Hirst, 2008; Galinsky & Sonenstein, 2011). Although these are relational abilities that also relate to the intimate relationships category of the Contextualized Sexuality Model, individual mental health certainly figures into one's ability to have positive intimate relationships with others. Indeed, one key element of a sex-positive approach is that people have free choice (Hirst, 2008). Through nurturing the growth of positive relational capacities, partners are able to support one another in creating this context of free choice and non-coercion that is essential to healthy sexuality. Relational skills, particularly related to communication, are also essential for promoting positive sexuality. For example, sexual assertiveness is defined as "a person's ability to communicate sexual needs and initiate sexual behavior with a partner" (Menard & Offman, 2009, p. 35). The ability to communicate assertively about one's personal desires, safety issues (e.g., safer sex practices), and personal preferences and dislikes is an important mental health ingredient in promoting positive sexuality (Hirst, 2008; Lamb & Peterson, 2012; Menard & Offman, 2009).

Self-Awareness

The same physical experiences can evoke very different reactions in different people depending on the emotions they bring up, such as guilt, freedom, release, and joy (De la Garza-Mercer, 2006). Therefore, greater self-awareness can help people understand their responses to sexual experiences. It is healthy for people to be able to acknowledge when they have ambivalent feelings toward sexuality and certain sexual activities (Lamb & Peterson, 2012), as ambivalence can be a normal reaction and an opportunity for continued self-awareness. Another important component of self-awareness related to positive sexuality is awareness of one's values, especially so people can determine whether their sexual behaviors are consistent with their values (Maddock, 1989; Southern & Cade, 2011).

Sexual Self-Esteem

Sexual self-esteem describes "one's affective reactions to the subjective appraisals of one's sexual thoughts, feelings, and behavior" (Menard & Offman, 2009, p. 35). Some of the core components of sexual self-esteem include a sense of competence, confidence, self-determination, and personal control (Galinsky & Sonenstein, 2011; Jannini et al., 2009). Sexual self-esteem is a critical component of positive sexuality, in that higher sexual self-esteem is linked to greater satisfaction with one's sexual relationship with his or her partner (Menard & Offman, 2009).

Stress Management and Relaxation

Stressors are a normal part of daily life, and more acute stressors also may arise when people face major life transitions. The ability to manage stress is linked to positive sexuality because anxiety can create major problems in people's sexual functioning and relationships (Schnarch, 1997). Therefore, other important individual mental health-related characteristics for promoting positive sexuality include the ability to manage stress, cope with challenges, relax, and remain mindful of the present moment.

Gender Identity and Sexual Orientation

A solid sense of one's gender identity and sexual orientation supports positive sexuality. However, both gender identity and sexual orientation may reflect a lifelong process of self-examination and considering the meanings one ascribes to both within the context of cultural and social norms. Therefore, periods of self-reflection and rethinking the meaning of gender and sexual orientation can reflect positive growth with regard to one's overall sense of sexuality.

People whose gender identities and sexual orientations fall outside societal norms may especially struggle with these identities. Modern approaches to sexuality education are typically grounded in heterosexual paradigms and focus predominantly on vaginal intercourse (Fine, 1988; Hirst, 2008), thereby potentially excluding a broad range of sexual orientations and activities. As such, people who have sexual identities other than heterosexual may struggle to relate to or benefit from the traditional forms of sexuality education they receive. Likewise, sexuality education can shape people's views of gender norms. In sex education curricula, women have historically been framed as being victims or defenders against male sexual advances (Fine, 1988). This type of information may set up cultural expectations regarding the expected sexual behaviors of men and women, such as men being more comfortable communicating assertively about their sexual needs and preferences compared to women (Diamond & Huebner, 2012). Thus, one aspect of positive sexuality is to be able to critically examine societal messages about sexual orientation and gender to determine one's own meaning system in these areas.

Therefore, part of people's positive sexuality development involves developing self-awareness of their gender identity and sexual orientation. These are both multidimensional constructs (Holden & Holden, 1995), so this awareness can develop over time and with consideration to the implications of these identities for different areas of their lives. This self-awareness then influences people's behaviors toward themselves and others, in that positive sexuality is enhanced when people act in ways that are consistent with their gender identity and sexual orientation (Maddock, 1989), as well as in ways that are respectful to others regardless of gender and sexual orientation (Southern & Cade, 2011; Maddock, 1989).

Intimate Relationships

Intimate relationships are perhaps the most significant domain in which people express their sexuality, and a positive relationship context supports positive sexuality for people who are partnered (Diamond & Huebner, 2012). For example, based on research with people who self-identified as having great sex with their partners of at least 25 years, Kleinplatz (2010) suggested that there are eight components of optimal sexuality. First, people are able to be fully focused on the current moment while engaged in sexual activity with their partners. Second, people experience a sense of being fully connected to their partners. Third, optimal sexuality occurs in a context of respect and caring for one's partner. Fourth, people who experience optimal sexuality have highly effective verbal and nonverbal communication. Fifth, optimal sexuality is characterized by a sense of adventure, fun, and exploration.

The sixth component is that people feel that they can be fully authentic and do not need to hide aspects of themselves. Seventh, partners experience a sense of getting lost and swept up in the moment. Finally, optimal sex produces an experience of transcendence and pure bliss. Because relationship dynamics are so critical to couples' sexuality, the remainder of this section provides an overview of the relational factors that research suggests are most likely to support positive sexuality.

Freedom From Coercion

At the most basic level, positive sexuality can only exist in intimate relationships when they are consensual, free from coercion, and non-exploitative (Hull, 2008; Jannini et al., 2009). In healthy intimate relationships, partners do not exploit one another for their own sexual gratification (Southern & Cade, 2011). Such relationships support the individual desires of each partner, although this is balanced by ensuring that each partner's individual desires do not harm or hinder the other's rights (Hull, 2008).

Fun and Playfulness

Positive sexuality is characterized by fun and playfulness between the partners (Diamond & Huebner, 2012). Partners can be relaxed and enjoy their time together, smile at one another, and laugh together. Within and beyond their sexual intimacy, there is a balance between comfort or familiarity and exploration or risk (Kleinplatz, 2010).

Intimacy

Jannini et al. (2009) said, "Intimacy and sexual activity are interdependent elements which act on each other in mutual enhancement and a positive feedback manner" (p. 2644). Sexual intimacy can play a key role in fostering positive relationship development (Diamond & Huebner, 2012; Southern & Cade, 2011), and likewise, a positive relationship context fosters positive sexuality. Some features of intimacy that promote positive sexuality include open expression of oneself, love, warmth, positive regard, and honesty (Hull, 2008; Diamond & Huebner, 2012; Southern & Cade, 2011). Overall, great sexuality occurs in a relationship that deepens and continues to grow over time (Kleinplatz, 2010).

Respectfulness and Responsiveness

Partners in healthy intimate relationships foster positive sexuality through a shared sense of mutual respect for one another (Southern & Cade, 2011). One of the ways that partners express this respect is by being responsive to each other's needs and desires (Diamond & Huebner, 2012).

Physical Dynamics

Of course, physical contact is an important component of positive sexuality within intimate relationships. However, positive sexuality does not require genital intercourse (Southern & Cade, 2011), and great sex is possible even with what most people would consider to be limitations (e.g., physical ability, older age; Kleinplatz, 2010). Just having full physical functioning doesn't guarantee great sex (Kleinplatz, 2010). Rather, positive sexuality as expressed through physical contact occurs when partners have opportunities to give to and receive from one another (Jannini et al., 2009), seek mutual satisfaction, and practice safe, responsible decision-making for positive sexual health (Hull, 2008).

Sexual Self-Disclosure

Sexual self-disclosure is the "degree to which a participant has disclosed his or her preferences regarding sexual techniques (e.g., kissing, oral sex, intercourse) to his or her partner" (Menard & Offman, 2009, p. 36). Positive sexuality is fostered when such disclosures are received with openness and respect. Self-disclosure and related communications can extend beyond sexual communications in helping couples establish boundaries and agreements about the nature of their relationship and physical intimacy. For example, in both heterosexual and same-sex relationships, some partners may agree to have open relationships in which partners may pursue sexual relations with other people, although this relationship arrangement may be more common among gay male relationships (De la Garza-Mercer, 2006). However, for many couples, such an arrangement would be unacceptable. Therefore, it is important within intimate relationships for partners to be able to disclose their values, preferences, and limitations so that these may be discussed openly.

Taking Time

It takes time to develop optimal sexuality. This isn't natural and doesn't happen quickly. To help this process, people have to challenge what they think initially or what they were taught and strive to increase their self-awareness (Kleinplatz, 2010). Further, to achieve optimal sexuality, people have to become less willing to settle for just any sex (Kleinplatz, 2010). People need to be intentional and devote time and energy to creating great sex within intimate relationships. It has to be a priority, and the priority has to translate to action (Diamond & Huebner, 2012; Kleinplatz, 2010).

Cultural and Contextual Influences

Increasingly, sexuality is being recognized as an important social justice issue, in that certain segments of the population have more negative health outcomes and less access to accurate health information and other community-based sexuality-related resources (Fahs & Swank, 2011). Therefore, there is much to be done in order to promote positive sexuality at the societal level. In this section, we consider some of the social factors that can promote positive sexuality within communities and the broader population.

Access to Quality Sexuality Education

Former U.S. Surgeon General Jocelyn Elders (2010) said that "We have a sexually dysfunctional society because of our limited views of sexuality and our lack of knowledge and understanding concerning the complexities and joys of humanity" (p. 896). As such, societies can support positive sexuality by providing access to comprehensive, accurate sexuality education (Lamb & Peterson, 2012). Communities and society must support families in promoting the sexual health of children (Elders, 2010), and access to accurate information about sexuality is critical to the development of positive sexuality (Braeken & Cardinal, 2008). A "sex-positive" (Hirst, 2008, p. 402) approach to sexuality education promotes sexual competence and holds that people have a right to sexual pleasure and wellbeing. Sexuality education cannot be value-free (Braeken & Cardinal, 2008). Therefore, it is important for educators to be transparent about the values that underlie their programs (Braeken & Cardinal, 2008). Typically, the values encompassed in comprehensive sexuality education include equality, respect, dignity, and nonviolence (Braeken & Cardinal, 2008).

Equal Access to Sexual Health Resources and Information

Education is especially critical for people who are vulnerable and whose rights may be threatened (Braeken & Cardinal, 2008). Research indicates that certain groups of people (e.g., those in marginalized groups) may have high levels of sexual activity but low levels of sexual satisfaction, and lower levels of activity also may be linked to higher levels of sexual satisfaction in other groups (Fahs & Swank, 2011). This suggests that cultural values impact the types of sexual behaviors that are viewed as acceptable and desirable (De la Garza-Mercer, 2006), and certain segments of the population may face institutional and community barriers to achieving positive sexuality. Because of the diversity of cultural values, sexuality should be addressed in a non-judgmental manner to reflect the diversity of opinions and values in U.S. society (Hull, 2008), and information should be presented through a range of avenues so that populations' unique needs can be addressed (deFur, 2012). Furthermore, supportive communities can promote the availability to all populations of community resources, such as sexual health clinics (Braeken & Cardinal, 2008).

Positive Representations of Sexuality in the Media

The way that sex and sexuality are depicted in the media contributes to perceived social norms that influence people's individual decisions about sexuality in their own lives (Lamb & Peterson, 2012). Depending on what type of media people view, they can develop a skewed perception as to what is normal. Without thinking critically about these media messages, people may make decisions that can lead to unhealthy outcomes for their sexual wellbeing. The media also holds the potential for promoting positive sexuality in that it can raise awareness about important sexual health issues, promote healthy sexual norms, and expand people's ideas about the range of sexual behaviors and choices they can make (Lamb & Peterson, 2012).

Promotion of Positive Economic Decisions Related to Sexuality

Sex is, in many ways, a commodity, and entire industries surround it. In particular, the sale of sexual pleasure can be found in the media (e.g., magazines offering tips on how to have a better orgasm), lingerie stores, and the sale of sex toys in stores and private parties. Certainly all of these things can be linked to positive sexuality if people make informed choices about them and view their use of them as consistent with their personal value system (McCaughey & French, 2001). However, McCaughey and French (2001) also pointed out the importance of individuals thinking critically about the marketing of sexual pleasure by profit-based companies. Although these products can indeed promote open dialogue about sexuality and sexual exploration, the marketing of them also can be framed in ways that make people feel insecure about their bodies, sexual functioning, or relationships. Therefore, it is useful for people to acknowledge when sex, sexuality, and sexual pleasure are being presented to them in ways that are grounded in economic transactions so that they can critically evaluate these and ensure that their decisions are personally satisfying and supportive (deFur, 2012; McCaughey & French, 2001).

Promotion of the Pleasurable Aspects of Sexuality

Jocelyn Elders (2010) also wrote that "Sex is for more than procreation once or twice in life; sex is also for a lifetime of pleasure. While this is not news to anyone, it is not part of our national conversation" (p. 896). On a related note, Diamond and Huebner (2012) stated that, "No public health outcry has ever been raised over the mental and physical health implications of population-level sexual boredom" (p. 55). Clearly, cultural messages and norms surrounding sexuality impact the way that people interpret the physical sensations associated with sexual activities (De la Garza-Mercer, 2006). As such, without normalizing the pleasurable aspects of sexuality, people may feel negative emotions (e.g., shame, embarrassment, and guilt) about their sexual experiences and desires. Typically, the topic of pleasure is not discussed in sex education programs (deFur, 2012). Rather, the emphasis in many sex education programs, especially those focused on reducing risks of problems such as STIs suggests that less sex is desirable (Diamond & Huebner, 2012). However, we are learning more from research of the potential health benefits of regular sexual activities, and so it may be that a more positive recommendation for improved overall health would be to have more sex under the right conditions (Diamond & Huebner, 2012). What those optimal conditions are, however, remains undetermined by current research, so further research in this area is needed (Diamond & Huebner, 2012).

Public Policies That Promote Positive Sexuality

Most politicians would surely recoil at the thoughts of campaigning on a platform of promoting sexual pleasure (Hull, 2008). However, political leaders can help to promote positive sexuality by advocating for policies that promote positive sexual health and decision-making about sexuality. Although governmental agencies and organizations are often hesitant to provide the comprehensive sexuality education that is essential for sexual health, a need remains for a range of public policies to promote positive sexuality (Braeken & Cardinal, 2008). These may include supporting resources for reproductive and sexual health, encouraging the competent training of health care and mental health professionals who work with patients and clients experiencing sexual health concerns, and ensuring access to credible, research-based sexual health information for the general population.

Positive Sexuality

This section has reviewed the influences at each level of the Contextualized Sexuality Model that foster positive sexuality. We conclude this section by emphasizing the importance of assuming a positive sexuality framework and viewing the potential of sexuality for personal and relational growth. Within many segments of society and in counseling training programs, there is an inherent focus on the negative potential consequences and risks associated with sexuality. Therefore, counselors must be intentional in making the positive sexuality framework a priority in their work. Professionals can work to recognize positive sexuality as a goal for many clients and to promote positive sexuality within clients' relationships and the broader society.

BENEFITS OF POSITIVE SEXUALITY

Beyond creating opportunities for people to experience physical pleasure through sex, what is the value of promoting positive sexuality at each level of the Contextualized Sexuality Model? Research suggests that positive sexuality promotes many beneficial outcomes that cross different aspects of people's lives, although to date the existing research has provided few definitive findings about the exact benefits that can be derived from positive sexuality (Diamond & Huebner, 2012). Researching this subject is inherently complex, as the principles of research ethics and integrity would make it difficult to conduct experimental research in this area. Thus, most of the existing research is correlational and therefore does not tell us whether these benefits are outcomes or consequences of positive sexuality (Diamond & Huebner, 2012; Jannini et al., 2009). In fact, it's likely that the relationships described herein are cyclical, in that positive conditions that foster positive sexuality also are further enhanced through the benefits of sexuality. For example, closeness with one's partner can promote positive sexual activities within the couple's relationship, which in turn leads to even greater relational intimacy. The benefits of positive sexuality and positive sexual health that are addressed in the existing literature fall into three categories: mental health, relational, and physical health benefits.

Mental Health Benefits

A positive sense of one's sexuality can be an avenue for positive mental health outcomes, including the following. First, sexuality provides an avenue for an individual to understand his or her values and make choices to live in accordance with those values (Braeken & Cardinal, 2008). Second, people may engage in sexual behaviors in order to regulate their emotions and moods (Diamond & Huebner, 2012; Jannini et al., 2009), so when this is done in a healthy way, sexual activities can serve as a release for stress and tension (De la Garza-Mercer, 2006). Third, by applying critical thinking skills to sexuality-related decisions, people are able to develop effective decision-making skills that incorporate accurate information (Braeken & Cardinal, 2008). Fourth, positive sexuality has been linked to positive body image (Jannini et al., 2009). Fifth, sexuality can provide a sense of fun and exploration in people's lives (De la Garza-Mercer, 2006). Finally, some people experience a state of transcendence through their sexual experiences (De la Garza-Mercer, 2006).

Relational Benefits

There are a number of relational outcomes that are linked to positive sexuality. These include the following: increased relationship satisfaction and happiness (De la Garza-Mercer, 2006; Menard & Offman, 2009); greater relational intimacy, closeness, and affection (Braeken & Cardinal, 2008; De la Garza-Mercer, 2006; Diamond & Huebner, 2012); enhanced respect for others' choices (Braeken & Cardinal, 2008); and a buffer for problems in a relationship (Diamond & Huebner, 2012).

Physical Health Benefits

Positive sexual health is linked to better overall health (Braeken & Cardinal, 2008; Diamond & Huebner, 2012). De la Garza-Mercer (2006) even said that "An orgasm a day keeps the doctor away!" (p. 114). Beyond the physical pleasure that can be found in sexual activities (Braeken & Cardinal, 2008; deFur, 2012; De la Garza-Mercer, 2006; Diamond & Huebner, 2012; Elders, 2010), the following physical health benefits can result from healthy, regular sexual activity: improved healthy functioning of the vagina in females (Jannini et al., 2009); lower cholesterol (De la Garza-Mercer, 2006); more energy (De la Garza-Mercer, 2006); release of positive hormones (De la Garza-Mercer, 2006), including oxytocin and dopamine (Jannini et al., 2009); increased testosterone production (Jannini et al., 2009); and reduced mortality (Diamond & Huebner, 2012). In addition, sexual activities can serve as a form of physical exercise (De la Garza-Mercer, 2006).

In sum, positive sexuality promotes greater health individually and within relationships and offers numerous benefits beyond the mere physical pleasure that people can experience through sexual activities. According to Diamond and Huebner (2012), "Sexual activity is, in fact, a bona fide health behavior with wide-ranging implications for mental and physical well-being" (p. 57). Therefore, counselors who help clients achieve a greater sense of positive sexuality also help to promote their overall health and wellbeing across many areas of their lives.

COUNSELING STRATEGIES TO HELP CLIENTS FOSTER POSITIVE SEXUALITY

Sexuality counseling approaches have been discussed throughout this book, so to conclude this chapter, we focus more broadly on strategies that counselors can use to work with clients in their progress toward an increasingly positive sense of sexuality in their lives.

1. *Engage in system-level advocacy.* Mental health professionals can be involved in advocacy to promote more positive views of sexuality within the broader society. Such initiatives may focus on more comprehensive and effective sex education and a prevention focus for mitigating sexual problems at a population level (Tiefer, 2009). Mental health professionals can advocate for these issues in partnership with their professional associations and through local efforts, such as by meeting with elected officials to inform them of the need for these resources.

2. *Equip clients with accurate sexual health information.* Mental health professionals can help ensure that all people, and especially youth, have access to accurate sexual health information to help them make decisions (Elders, 2010). For example, counselors can provide links to credible sources of information on their organizational websites. They also can have informational brochures and other resources available through their practice settings and help direct clients to other useful resources when new concerns arise.

3. *Promote training for counselors on positive sexuality.* We need more mental health professionals to receive training to work with clients impacted by sexuality concerns. Training methods should be diverse, such as basic instruction, modeling, and practical experiences (Miller & Byers, 2010; Southern & Cade, 2011). Professionals in training roles (e.g., faculty members and continuing education workshop providers) can work to ensure that training approaches address positive sexuality in addition to strategies for addressing sexuality-related problems.

4. *Help clients make positive sexuality-related decisions.* There are many sexuality-related decisions that clients may be facing when they seek counseling. For example, counselors can help clients decide whether and when to initiate sexual activity, overall and with new partners, and make positive decisions to reduce the risks of that activity (Elders, 2010). Counselors can help clients think through the potential consequences of the decisional options and assist them in considering options that are most aligned with their value systems.

5. *Provide a safe context for clients to explore sexuality-related issues.* Sexuality is a private and sensitive issue to discuss, and talking about sex can be scary for many people, even in a professional counseling setting. Therefore, counselors can make extra efforts to show clients that it is safe to discuss sexuality concerns and questions and that the counseling environment will be nonjudgmental and supportive for this exploration. In particular, counselors should ensure that they have proper confidentiality procedures in place to protect clients' privacy related to the sexuality topics they discuss (Elders, 2010). Additionally, counselors can help clients think critically about sexuality so that they can consider new possibilities for understanding their sexuality. For example, through counseling, people can free themselves from rigid gender-based expectations as to what is and is not acceptable regarding sexual activities (Hull, 2008). This safe context also can help clients consider more complex solutions to their concerns. As Hull (2008) said, "It is much easier to prescribe a blue pill to dilate some blood vessels than it is to explore the

expectations of physical intimacy that may be unrealistic in any given social context" (p. 139). Although these issues may be threatening for clients to address, a supportive counseling environment can help them think through the challenging concerns they face.

6. *Help clients develop effective communication skills related to sexuality.* Many people do not feel comfortable talking about sex and sexuality with others in their lives, even in the context of close relationships. However, effective communication is critical to being able to foster positive sexuality within an intimate relationship. Therefore, counselors can help their clients both express their sexual desires and preferences to their partners and ask their partners to meet these needs (Menard & Offman, 2009). Counseling sessions can provide opportunities for learning and practicing new communication skills so that difficult conversations are not perceived as so threatening outside of the sessions.

7. *Make positive sexuality a focus in counseling.* Counselors can work with clients not only to mitigate problems but also to promote positive sexuality in their lives and relationships. Based on her study of people reporting on having great sex within long-lasting relationships, Kleinplatz (2010) offered several important suggestions for counseling to promote positive sexuality. First, counselors can offer clients a more comprehensive, positive view of sexuality, such as by conveying that more fulfilling sexual experiences are possible and that sexuality is broader than mere genital intercourse. Second, clients should be encouraged to stop settling for low-quality sexual activities and instead to pursue fulfilling, satisfying sexual activities. Third, counselors can help clients foster greater emotional intimacy to further their physical connections. Fourth, counselors can ask clients to describe past fulfilling sexual experiences to provide clues to what they can strive to create again now. Fifth, counselors can emphasize the importance of quality of sex, rather than quantity. Sixth, through counseling, clients can learn how to intentionally set the context for fulfilling sex and overcome expectations that great sex must be spontaneous. Finally, Kleinplatz suggested that great sex can be achieved through the following four steps: (1) setting the intention to have fulfilling sex; (2) purposefully seeking out the contexts for having great sex; (3) practicing over time; and (4) continuing with ongoing development of one's sexuality-related skills, knowledge, and abilities. Readers are encouraged to complete Exercise 10.2 to identify steps they can take to make positive sexuality a focus in their counseling practice.

Exercise 10.2

MAKING POSITIVE SEXUALITY A FOCUS IN YOUR PRACTICE

Consider the following questions as a way to get started thinking about steps you can take in your work to ensure that you incorporate a positive sexuality focus in your work with clients.

1. Identify at least three resources in your local community that promote positive sexual health where you could send clients for information, resources, or services:

_____

_____

_____

_____

2. Identify at least three credible sources of sexuality-related information online that you would feel comfortable sharing with clients: _____

_____

_____

_____

_____

3. Identify at least three changes you could make to your counseling office environment that would foster a safe context for clients to discuss sexuality-related concerns (e.g., displaying sexual health information in your office): _____

_____

_____

_____

_____

4. Think of at least three ways you could introduce the topic of sexuality to clients in a non-threatening, supportive manner: _____

_____

_____

_____

_____

SUMMARY

Throughout this book, we addressed a range of sexuality-related concerns that clients may address in counseling. Unfortunately, many mental health professionals remain underprepared to discuss sexuality concerns with clients, including a lack of training on the topic and a lack of comfort with discussing such a sensitive topic. It is our hope that this book has equipped you, the reader, with the knowledge to address sexuality-related issues in your practice competently and in a way that honors your clients' unique needs and experiences. It is important for counselors to both be able to help their clients address the sexuality-related problems in their lives and be able to support their clients through the personal and relational growth that can develop through ongoing development of one's sexuality. We urge you to continue with your own professional development so that you will remain current on future emerging trends in the field. Overall, we encourage counselors to pursue an ongoing path toward ever-increasing competence and skills to help their clients achieve a more positive sense of sexuality that benefits them across multiple areas of their lives.

KEYSTONES

- Because sexuality is such a private domain in most people's lives, many of us are left with a lot of insecurities about how our own sexual attitudes, experiences, and behaviors match up to others.
- In recent years, a new perspective has been emerging that suggests that sex can provide more than just fleeting physical pleasure but also key opportunities for people to learn about themselves and their partners.

- As minimal as the training is that most counselors receive in sexuality, it appears that most of the training that occurs focuses primarily on sexual problems and dysfunctions, rather than providing trainees with an understanding of positive-sexuality frameworks.
- Sexual satisfaction describes the extent to which a person is pleased with the amount of physical, emotional, and sexual pleasure they derive from the frequency, quality, and range of sexual activities in which they are currently engaged, individually and relationally.
- We define *positive sexuality* as the integration of *sexual health* and *sexual satisfaction* that encompasses a lifelong process of positive growth and development of one's sense of sexuality within his or her sexual identity, emotional and mental health, intimate relationships, and broader social contexts.
- The Contextualized Sexuality Model provides a useful framework for considering the factors that can support people in the process of developing a positive sense of sexuality: physiology, developmental influences, mental health, gender identity and sexual orientation, intimate relationships, and cultural and contextual influences.
- The benefits of positive sexuality and positive sexual health that are addressed in the existing literature fall into three broad categories: mental health benefits, relational benefits, and physical health benefits.
- Counselors can use a range of practice strategies to help their clients move toward enhanced positive sexuality in their lives and relationships.

From the Author's Chair

Writing a textbook is part research—part experience—but mostly the articulation of the author's unique perspective on practice and profession. Each author has made personal decisions on how to organize the book and what, from the mass of information available, should be included. These decisions reflect the author's bias—personal interest—values and professional identity. We, as editors of the series, have invited each author to respond to the following questions as a way of providing the reader a glimpse into the "person" and not just the product of the author.

It is our hope that these brief reflections will provide a little more insight into our view of our profession—and ourselves as professionals.

—*Richard Parsons and Naijian Zhang*

Question: There is certainly an abundance of insightful points found within this text. But if you were asked to identify a single point or theme from all that is presented that you would hope would stand out and stick with the reader, what would that point or theme be?

Christine: The most important point that I hope readers take from this book is simply the importance of becoming more comfortable with talking about sexuality-related concerns in a counseling context. Every counselor has had a unique set of life experiences, so it's likely that every reader will have different aspects of sexuality that are more or less difficult to discuss with clients. However, by committing to self-reflection and growth in our understanding of sexuality and our ability to discuss sexuality with clients, we open a lot more doors to being able to support our clients in this important area of their lives.

Amber: What I hope sticks with readers is that sexuality is a normal, healthy, and integral part of the human experience. I have encountered many clients who experience feelings of guilt or shame linked with their sexuality, labeling their natural desires for who they were attracted to, the type of sex they wanted to have, or their sexual fantasies as "bad" or "abnormal." Many clients have had difficulty talking to their parents, friends, or intimate partners about sex. Avoiding these conversations creates more sexual anxiety and shame and continues the stigmatization of an essential part of our humanity and how we connect intimately with others. So, I also hope readers walk away with more ways to open these conversations about sex not only with clients but in their personal lives and larger communities as well, eroding sexual stigma through creating new discourses.

Ben: I hope that readers will really take away how sexuality is not just about sexual activities or within relationships, but it is something that impacts people's lives in many ways and throughout the entire lifespan. As counselors, development, wellness, and prevention are our cornerstones, and it is very important to keep in mind how sexuality (even when sexual concerns are not voiced as a part of a client's presenting concerns) are important to consider in conceptualizing the client's presentation, strengths, developmental stage, relationships, desires, and satisfaction in life. People are sexual beings, and sexuality is important to take into account in order to understand and work with clients holistically.

Question: In the text there is a great deal of research-cited theories presented. Could you share from your own experience how the information presented within the text may actually look or take form in practice?

Christine: I believe that a lot of counselors are not comfortable talking about sexuality, and this discomfort can lead them to avoid the topic altogether with clients. Even worse, when a client brings up the subject, they may subtly turn the discussion to other topics that they're more comfortable discussing. This is potentially damaging, in that it can add to clients' shame around their sexuality concerns, as well as take away valuable opportunities to provide clients with support. Therefore, what the information presented in the text would look like to me is the counselor opening the discussion to see if clients have any concerns related to their sexuality and being open to the topic if and when it does arise.

Amber: Human sexuality is a complex experience, influenced by multiple factors as outlined in the contextual framework that we present in the text. Thus, in practice, when clients present with a sexuality-related concern, there is rarely a clear delineation as to what may be causing their issue. Counselors have to challenge clients' commonly held conceptions of sexuality that are physiologically and genitally focused. Part of our jobs as counselors becomes educating clients on the various aspects of sexuality and encouraging patience during the exploratory and change process while engendering hopefulness that clients can achieve positive and fulfilling sexual functioning. Counselors working in the area of sexuality counseling need to be okay with the ambiguity, committed to staying current with the social discourses and medical advances related to sexuality and open to consultation with medical and other mental health professionals in order to effectively address clients' needs.

Ben: The therapeutic relationship is crucial in counseling, and as Christine pointed out, we have to be comfortable in talking about sexual topics to allow clients to be open about their sexuality so that they can grow, develop, heal, and flourish. I think that being open and accepting of people is crucial and that the theories and research that we presented in this book can sit in the back of your mind to help you conceptualize, understand, normalize, and reflect while you are with the client. I firmly believe that it is important to take time to think about and meditate on how you will not just understand the theories and research but how you will use that information to impact yourself and your clients. It is important that you reflect on how it impacts you, as that is important in understanding ourselves and allowing us to help others to engage in the work. It is also important to think about how it impacts other people, as there are many diverse experiences and perspectives that different individuals have, and this is especially true for sexuality. Reviewing this book (and other counseling books) again is important to be able to have the information presented along with your reflections and meditations on how to implement the material with our clients.

Question: As author(s) of this text, what might this book reveal about your own professional identity?

Christine: I have a strong professional identity as a counselor and counselor educator. I think counselors have a valuable role to play in helping people address the sexuality-related concerns in their lives. At the same time, I also believe we as counselors can't simply understand sexuality from our own counseling lens. Rather, we need to be open to interdisciplinary partnerships and collaborations to ensure that our clients' sexuality-related concerns are addressed in a comprehensive manner. This may include working with other such professionals as medical health care providers, sexual health educators, and public health specialists. As a counselor, I value these interdisciplinary relationships, because we can't view clients' sexuality—or any other concerns—in a vacuum!

Amber: I am drawn to the constructivistic and postpostivist philosophies and counseling approaches. I believe we create knowledge through the meaning we tie to our experiences and that human identity and our social relationships, including our sexuality and sexual relationships, are complex, fluid, and subjective. I believe these approaches are reflected throughout this text as we continually ask readers to engage in reflexive exercises on how they interpret and understand human sexuality and to critically examine their own comfort and discomfort with sexuality-related topics. Further, we strove to highlight the complex and ambiguous nature of sexuality throughout the text, as well as how social and environmental dimensions impact our conceptualizations of sex, which are continually evolving over time.

Ben: I am firmly a developmentalist and see that our prior experiences, the cultures that we have been immersed in and are a part of, and our current circumstances and situations play a strong role in shaping our lives, perspectives, and decisions. Our past led us to our present, and our present choices, experiences, and desires help lead us to our future. Sex and sexuality is not something that only happens in a bedroom; it is something that is contextually understood, individually and socially expressed and experienced, and it changes across the lifespan. The counseling philosophies of looking holistically, taking wellness and strengths approaches to people, and conceptualizing developmentally are among our strongest contributions that we counselors add to the mental health field, and I believe that is reflected in this book and in my identities as a counselor and counselor educator.

Question: What final prescription—direction—might you offer your readers as they continue in their journey toward becoming professional counselors?

Christine: Embrace the challenges that come with addressing difficult topics like sexuality! Over the many semesters I've taught a course on sexuality counseling, I've seen the many ways that challenges can arise, whether it's through value conflicts, moral dilemmas, difficulty understanding the complexity of human intimacy in relationships, and working through one's own personal history or limited knowledge about the subject. My advice is to embrace these challenges, rather than fear them. Each one presents an opportunity for both personal and professional growth, which are essential ingredients for a meaningful journey toward becoming a professional counselor!

Amber: Continuously build a critical consciousness through leaning into your areas of discomfort. Actively engage in conversations about sexuality (or any topic that makes you uncomfortable), ask questions, and stay open to learning from your clients, other professionals, and current research. Discussing topics of sexuality is a vulnerable spot for both counselors and clients. As counselors, it is okay to ask for help as you develop new areas of competency. You will make mistakes but that is part of the growth process along the way, so own your missteps and be willing to learn from them. Developing this critical consciousness will increase your awareness about self and others, making you a better counselor and advocate for your clients.

Ben: Continue to learn! There is so much out there, and this book is a good introduction to conceptualizing sexuality and working with our clients' sexuality. Development and learning is something that should never end, so continue to explore the glorious and diverse world out there and expand, expand, expand upon your strengths and knowledge to enrich your life and the lives of those that you touch!!!

References

Abbott, E. (2000). *A history of celibacy: From Athena to Elizabeth I, Leonardo di Vinci, Florence Nightingale, Gandhi, & Cher*. New York, NY: Scribner.

Abraham, C., & Sheeran, P. (1993). In search of a psychology of safer-sex promotion: Beyond beliefs and texts. *Health Education Research, 8*(2), 245–254.

Adams, G. R., & Marshall, S. K. (1996). A developmental social psychology of identity: Understanding the person-in-context. *Journal of Adolescence, 19*(5), 429–442.

Addis, M., & Mahalik, J. (2003). Men, masculinity, and the contexts of help-seeking. *American Psychologist, 58,* 5–14.

Ahlborg, T., Rudeblad, K., Linnér, S., & Linton, S. (2008). Sensual and sexual marital contentment in parents of small children—A follow-up study when the first child is four years old. *Journal of Sex Research, 45*(3), 295–304.

Ainsworth, M. D. S. (1989). Attachments beyond infancy. *American Psychologist, 44,* 709–716.

Ainsworth, M. D. S., Blehar, M. C., Waters, E., & Wall, S. (1978). *Patterns of attachment: A psychological study of the strange situation*. Hillsdale, NJ: Erlbaum.

Ainsworth, M. D. S., & Wittig, B. A. (1969). Attachment and the exploratory behaviour of one-year-olds in a strange situation. In B. M. Foss (Ed.), *Determinants of infant behaviour* (Vol. 4, pp. 113–136). London, England: Methuen.

Al-Azzawi, F., & Palacios, S. (2009). Hormonal changes during menopause. *Maturitas, 63*(2), 135–137.

Alder, J., Fink, N., Bitzer, J., Hösli, I., & Holzgreve, W. (2007). Depression and anxiety during pregnancy: A risk factor for obstetric, fetal and neonatal outcome? A critical review of the literature. *Journal of Maternal-Fetal & Neonatal Medicine, 20,* 189–209.

Alexander, K., Coleman, C., Deatrick, J., & Jemmott, L. (2011). Moving beyond safe sex to women-controlled safe sex: A concept analysis. *Journal of Advanced Nursing, 68,* 1858–1869.

Althof, S. E. (2010). What's new in sex therapy? *Journal of Sexual Medicine, 7,* 5–13.

Althof, S. E., Leiblum, S. R., Chevret-Measson, M., Hartmann, U., Levine, S. B., McCabe, M., Plaut, M., Rodrigues, O., & Wylie, K. (2005). Psychological and interpersonal dimension of sexual function and dysfunction. *Journal of Sexual Medicine, 2*(6), 793–800.

Althof, S. E., Rosen, R. C., DeRogatis, L., Corty, E., Quirk, F., & Symonds, T. (2005). Outcome measurement in female sexual dysfunction clinical trials: Review and recommendations. *Journal of Sex & Marital Therapy, 31*(2), 153–166.

Amaro, H., Raj, A., & Reed, E. (2001). Women's sexual health: The need for feminist analysis in public health in the decade of behavior. *Psychology of Women Quarterly, 25,* 324–334.

Amato, P. R. (2010). Research on divorce: Continuing and new developments. *Journal of Marriage and Family, 72,* 650–666.

American Association of Sexuality Educators, Counselors, and Therapists. (2004). *Code of ethics*. Retrieved September 12, 2013, from http://aasect.org/codeofethics.asp

American Association of Sexuality Educators, Counselors, and Therapists. (2013). *Certification types: Distinguishing sexuality educators, counselors, and therapists*. Retrieved September 9, 2013, from http://aasect.org/cert_types.asp

American Counseling Association. (2014). *ACA Code of Ethics*. Retrieved from http://www.counseling.org/resources/aca-code-of-ethics.pdf

American Pregnancy Association. (2014). *Miscarriages.* Retrieved from http://americanpregnancy .org/pregnancy-complications/miscarriage/

American Psychiatric Association. (2013a). *Diagnostic and Statistical Manual of Mental Disorders: DSM-5* (5th ed.). Arlington, VA: Author.

American Psychiatric Association. (2013b). *Gender dysphoria.* Arlington, VA: Author. Retrieved from http://www.dsm5.org/documents/gender%20dysphoria%20fact%20sheet.pdf

American Psychological Association. (2007). *Report of the APA task force on socioeconomic status.* Washington, DC: Author. Retrieved from http://www.apa.org/pi/ses/resources/publications/task-force-2006.pdf

American Psychological Association, Task Force on Mental Health and Abortion. (2008). *Report of the task force on mental health and abortion.* Washington, DC: Author. Retrieved from http:// www.apa.org/pi/women/programs/abortion/mental-health.pdf

American Psychological Association. (2009). *Appropriate therapeutic responses to sexual orientation.* Washington, DC: Author. Retrieved from http://www.apa.org/pi/lgbt/resources/therapeutic-response.pdf

American Sexual Health Association. (2014). *STDs/STIs.* Retrieved from http://www.iwannaknow .org/teens/sti/testing.html

Ariely, D., & Loewenstein, G. (2006). The heat of the moment: The effect of sexual arousal on sexual decision making. *Journal of Behavioral Decision Making, 19*, 87–98.

Arnett, J. J. (2000). Emerging adulthood: A theory of development from the late teens through the twenties. *American Psychologist, 55*(5), 469–480.

Arnett, J. J. (2010). *Adolescence and emerging adulthood* (4th ed.). Upper Saddle River, NJ: Prentice Hall.

Arnett, J. J. (2011). Emerging adulthood(s): The cultural psychology of a new life stage. In L. A. Jensen (Ed.), *Bridging cultural and developmental approaches to psychology: New syntheses in theory, research, and policy.* New York, NY: Oxford University Press.

Arseth, A. K., Kroger, J., Martinussen, M., & Marcia, J. E. (2009). Meta-analytic studies of identity status and the relational issues of attachment and intimacy. *Identity: An International Journal of Theory and Research, 9*(1), 1–32.

Ashcraft, C. (2003). Adolescent ambiguities in American Pie: Popular culture as a resource for sex education. *Youth & Society, 31,* 37–70.

Association for Lesbian, Gay, Bisexual, and Transgender Issues in Counseling Transgender Committee. (2010). American Counseling Association competencies for counseling with transgender clients. *Journal of LGBT Issues in Counseling, 4*, 135–159.

Association for Lesbian, Gay, Bisexual, and Transgender Issues in Counseling. (2012). *Association for Lesbian, Gay, Bisexual, and Transgender Issues in Counseling (ALGBTIC) competencies for counseling with lesbian, gay, bisexual, queer, questioning, intersex and ally individuals.* Retrieved from http://www.algbtic/resources/competencies

Aubrey, M., & Dougher, M. J. (1990). Ethical issues in outpatient group therapy with sex offenders. *Journal For Specialists In Group Work, 15*(2), 75–82. doi:10.1080/01933929008411915

Avery, L. D., & Gressard, C. F. (2000). Counseling regulations regarding sexual misconduct: A comparison across states. *Counseling and Values, 45*(1), 67–77. doi:10.1002/j.2161–007X.2000. tb00184.x

Baber, K. M., & Tucker, C. J. (2006). The Social Roles Questionnaire: A new approach to measuring attitudes toward gender. *Sex Roles, 54*, 459–467.

Bader, M. (2009). *Men's sexuality: Why women don't understand it–and men don't either.* Lanham, MD: Rowman & Littlefield.

Baggaley, M. (2008). Sexual dysfunction in schizophrenia: Focus on recent evidence. *Human Psychopharmacology: Clinical and Experimental, 23*(3), 201–209.

Baker, C. N. (2005). Images of women's sexuality in advertisements: A content analysis of Black- and White-oriented women's and men's magazines. *Sex Roles, 52,* 13–27.

Baldwin, D. S. (2001). Depression and sexual dysfunction. *British Medical Bulletin, 57*, 81–99.

Ballam, S. M., & Granello, P. F. (2011). Confronting sex in the media: Implications and counseling recommendations. *The Family Journal, 19,* 421–426.

Balon, R., & Segraves, R. T. (2008). Survey of treatment practices for sexual dysfunction(s) associated with antidepressants. *Journal of Sex & Marital Therapy, 34*(4), 353–365.

Bancroft, J., Janssen, E., Strong, D., & Vudadinovic, Z. (2003). The relation between mood and sexuality in gay men. *Archives of Sexual Behavior, 32*(3), 231–242.

Bandura, A. (1962). Social learning through imitation. In M. R. Jones (Ed.), *Nebraska symposium on motivation* (pp. 211–269). Lincoln: University of Nebraska Press.

Bandura, A. (1991). Social cognitive theory of self-regulation. *Organizational Behavior and Human Decision Processes, 50*, 248–287.

Banner, L. L., & Anderson, R. U. (2007). Integrated sildenafil and cognitive-behavior sex therapy for psychogenic erectile dysfunction: A pilot study. *Journal of Sexual Medicine, 4*(4ii), 1117–1125.

Barelds, D. P. H., & Dijkstra, P. (2008). Do people know what they want: A similar or complementary partner? *Evolutionary Psychology, 6*(4), 595–602.

Barker, M. (2005). This is my partner, and this is my . . . partner's partner: Constructing a polyamorous identity in a monogamous world. *Journal of Constructivist Psychology, 18*(1), 75–88.

Barker, M., & Langdridge, D. (2008). Bisexuality: Working with a silenced sexuality. *Feminism & Psychology, 18,* 389–394.

Barker, M., & Langdridge, D. (2010). Whatever happened to non-monogamies? Critical reflections on recent research and theory. *Sexualities, 13*(6), 748–772.

Barlow, D. H. (1986). Causes of sexual dysfunction: The role of anxiety and cognitive interference. *Journal of Consulting and Clinical Psychology, 54*(2), 140–148.

Barnes, T., & Eardley, I. (2007). Premature ejaculation: The scope of the problem. *Journal of Sex & Marital Therapy, 33*(2), 151–170.

Barratt, B. B., & Rand, M. A. (2009). "Sexual health assessment" for mental health and medical practitioners: Teaching notes. *American Journal of Sexuality Education, 4*, 16–27.

Barret, B., & Logan, C. (2002). *Counseling gay men & lesbians: A practice primer.* Pacific Grove, CA: Brooks/Cole.

Bartholomew, K., & Horowitz, L. M. (1991). Attachment styles among young adults: A test of a four-category model. *Journal of Personality and Social Psychology, 61*, 226–244.

Bartlik, B. D., Rosenfeld, S., & Beaton, C. (2005). Assessment of sexual functioning: Sexual history taking for health care practitioners. *Epilepsy & Behavior, 7*(Suppl. 2), S12–S21.

Basson, R. (2007). Sexual desire/arousal disorders in women. In S. Leiblum (Ed.), *Principles and practice of sex therapy* (4th ed., pp. 25–53). New York, NY: Guilford Press.

Basson, R., Wierman, M. E., van Lankveld, J., & Brotto, L. (2010). Summary of the recommendations on sexual dysfunctions in women. *Journal of Sexual Medicine, 7*(1, Pt. 2), 314–326.

Beckstead, L., & Israel, T. (2007). Affirmative counseling and psychotherapy focused on issues related to sexual orientation conflicts. In K. J. Bieschke, R. M. Perez, & K. A. Debord (Eds.), *Handbook of counseling and psychotherapy with lesbian, gay, bisexual, and transgender clients* (2nd ed., pp. 221–244). Washington, DC: American Psychological Association.

Beebe, S. A., Beebe, S. J., Redmond, M. V., Geerinck, T. M., & Salem-Wiseman, L. (2015). *Interpersonal communication: Relating to others* (6th Canadian ed.). Toronto, Canada: Pearson.

Bergner, R. M. (2002). Sexual compulsion as attempted recovery from degradation: Theory and therapy. *Journal of Sex & Marital Therapy, 28*(5), 373–387.

Berliner, L., & Elliott, D. M. (1996). Sexual abuse of children. In J. N. Briere, L. Berliner, J. A. Bulkley, C. Jenny, & T. Reid (Eds.), *The APSAC handbook on child maltreatment* (pp. 51–71). Thousand Oaks, CA: Sage Publications.

Berns, S. B., Jacobson, N. S., & Gottman, J. M. (1999). Demand-withdraw interaction in couples with a violent husband. *Journal of Consulting and Clinical Psychology, 67*(5), 666–674.

Berry, M. D., & Berry, P. D. (2013). Contemporary treatment of sexual dysfunction: Reexamining the biopsychosocial model. *The Journal of Sexual Medicine, 10*(11), 2627–2643.

Betchen, S. J. (2009). Premature ejaculation: An integrative, intersystem approach for couples. *Journal of Family Psychotherapy, 20*(2–3), 241–260.

Beyers, W., & Seiffge-Krenke, I. (2010). Does identity precede intimacy? Testing Erikson's theory on romantic development in emerging adults of the 21st century. *Journal of Adolescent Research, 25*(3), 387–415.

Binik, Y. M., & Meana, M. (2009). The future of sex therapy: Specialization or marginalization? *Archives of Sexual Behavior, 38,* 1016–1027.

Binnie, J. (2011). Class, sexuality, and space: A comment. *Sexualities, 14,* 21–26.

Birnbaum, G. E. (2007). Attachment orientations, sexual functioning and relationship satisfaction in a community sample of women. *Journal of Social and Personal Research, 24,* 21–35.

Birnbaum, G. E., Reis, H. T., Mikulincer, M., Gillath, O., & Orpaz, A. (2006). When sex is more than just sex: Attachment orientations, sexual experiences and relationship quality. *Journal of Personality and Social Psychology, 91,* 929–943.

Bitzer, J., Platano, G., Tschudin, S., & Alder, J. (2008). Sexual counseling in elderly couples. *Journal of Sexual Medicine, 5*(9), 2027–2043. doi:10.1111/j.1743-6109.2008.00926.x

Black, D. W., Kehrberg, L. L. D., Flummerfelt, D. L., & Schlosser, S. S. (1997). Characteristics of 36 subjects reporting compulsive sexual behavior. *American Journal of Psychiatry, 154*(2), 243–249.

Black, M. C., Basile, K. C., Breiding, M. J., Smith, S. G., Walters, M. L., Merrick, M. T., . . . & Stevens, M. R. (2010). *National intimate partner and sexual violence survey (NISVS): 2010 summary report.* Atlanta, GA: National Center for Injury Prevention and Control, Centers for Disease Control and Prevention.

Blanker, M. H., Rudd Bosch, J. L. H., Groeneveld, F. P. M. J., Bohnen, A. M., Prins, A., Thomas, S., & Hop, W. C. J. (2001). Erectile and ejaculatory dysfunction in a community-based sample of men 50 to 78 years old: Prevalence, concern, and relation to sexual activity. *Urology, 57*(4), 763–768.

Bley, J. W. (2007). Female genital pain: Vaginismus and dyspareunia. In L. VandeCreek, F. L. Peterson, Jr., & J. W. Bley (Eds.), *Innovations in clinical practice: Focus on sexual health* (pp. 107–117). Sarasota, FL: Professional Resource Press.

Bodinger, L., Hermesh, H., Aizenberg, D., Valevski, A., Marom, S., Shiloh, R., … & Weizman, A. (2002). Sexual function and behavior in social phobia. *Journal of Clinical Psychiatry, 63*(10), 874–879.

Bogaert, A. F., & Sadava, S. (2002). Adult attachment and sexual behavior. *Personal Relationships, 9,* 191–204.

Boivin, J. (2003). A review of psychosocial interventions in infertility. *Social Science & Medicine, 57,* 2325–2341.

Boivin, J., Scanlan, L., & Walker, S. (1999). Why are infertile patients not using psychosocial counseling? *Human Reproduction, 14,* 1384–1391.

Boroumandfar, K., Rahmati, M. G., Farajzadegan, Z., & Hoseini, H. (2010). Reviewing sexual function after delivery and its association with some of the reproductive factors. *Iranian Journal of Nursing and Midwifery Research, 15*(4), 220–223.

Bowen, M. (1978). *Family therapy in clinical practice.* New York, NY: Jason Aronson.

Bowlby, J. (1957). An ethological approach to research in child development. *British Journal of Medical Psychology, 30,* 230–240.

Bowlby, J. (1969). *Attachment and loss: Volume I: Attachment.* New York, NY: Basic Books.

Bowlby, J. (1973). *Attachment and loss: Volume II: Separation, anxiety, and anger.* New York, NY: Basic Books.

Bowlby, J. (1982). *Attachment* (2nd ed.). New York, NY: Basic Books.

Bowlby, J. (1988). *A secure base: Parent-child attachment and healthy human development.* New York, NY: Basic Books.

Boylan, J. F. (2013). *She's not there: A life in two genders.* New York, NY: Random House.

Bradford, A., & Meston, C. M. (2011). Behavior and symptom change among women treated with placebo for sexual dysfunction. *Journal of Sexual Medicine, 8*(1), 191–201.

Braeken, D., & Cardinal, M. (2008). Comprehensive sexuality education as a means of promoting sexual health. *International Journal of Sexual Health, 20,* 50–62.

Branney, P., & Barkham, M. (2006). Core outcomes in psychosexual therapy: A feasibility study of the CORE-OM. *Sexual and Relationship Therapy, 21*(1), 15–26.

Bray, J. H., & Jouriles, E. N. (1995). Treatment of marital conflict and prevention of divorce. *Journal of Marital and Family Therapy, 21*(4), 461–473.

Bretherton, I. (1992). The origins of attachment theory: John Bowlby and Mary Ainsworth. *Developmental Psychology, 28*(5), 759–775.

Briere, J., & Runtz, M. (1987). Post sexual abuse trauma: Data and implications for clinical practice. *Journal of Interpersonal Violence, 2*(4), 367–379.

Brody, J. (1984). 30 years of pioneering in sex therapy. *New York Times.* Retrieved from http://www.nytimes.com/1984/10/29/style/30-years-of-pioneering-in-sex-therapy.html

Brody, S., & Weiss, P. (2012). Letter to the editor: Simultaneous penile-vaginal orgasm is associated with sexual satisfaction. *Journal of Sexual Medicine, 9,* 2475–2477.

Brotto, L. A., Basson, R., & Luria, M. (2008). A mindfulness-based group psychoeducational intervention targeting sexual arousal disorder in women. *Journal of Sexual Medicine, 5*(7), 1646–1659.

Brotto, L. A., Seal, B. N., & Rellini, A. (2012). Pilot study of a brief cognitive behavioral versus mindfulness-based intervention for women with sexual distress and a history of childhood sexual abuse. *Journal of Sex & Marital Therapy, 38*(1), 1–27.

Brown, C. (2008). Gender-role implications on same-sex intimate partner abuse. *Journal of Family Violence, 23,* 457–462.

Brown, J. D. (2002). Mass media influences on sexuality. *The Journal of Sex Research, 39,* 42–45.

Brown, S. L., & Lin, I. F. (2012). The gray divorce revolution: Rising divorce among middle-aged and older adults, 1990–2010. *Journal of Gerontology Series B: Psychological Sciences and Social Sciences, 67*(6), 731–741.

Browne, A., & Finkelhor, D. (1986). Impact of child sexual abuse: A review of the research. *Psychological Bulletin, 99*(1), 66–77.

Browning, J. R., Hatfield, E., Kessler, D., & Levine, T. (2000). Sexual motives, gender, and sexual behavior. *Archives of Sexual Behavior, 29*(2), 135–153.

Burgess, W. C. (2009). Internal and external stress factors associated with the identity development of transgender and gender variant youth. In G. P. Mallon (Ed.), *Social work practice with transgender and gender variant youth* (2nd ed., pp. 53–64). New York, NY: Routledge.

Burlew, L. D., & Barton, A. (2002). Counseling for sexual compulsion/addiction/dependence (SCAD). In L. D. Burlew & D. Capuzzi (Eds.), *Sexuality counseling* (pp. 257–282). New York, NY: Nova Science.

Burnett, J. A., & Panchal, K. (2008). Incorporating ideological context in counseling couples experiencing infertility. *Journal of Humanistic Counseling, Education & Development, 47,* 187–199.

Bursalioglu, F. S., Aydin, N., Yazici, E., & Yazici, A. B. (2013). The correlation between psychiatric disorders and women's lives. *Journal of Clinical and Diagnostic Research, 7*(4), 695–699.

Buvat, J., Maggi, M., Guay, A., & Torres, L. O. (2013). Testosterone deficiency in men: Systematic review and standard operation procedures for diagnosis and treatment. *The Journal of Sexual Medicine, 10*(1), 245–284.

Byers, E. S. (2005). Relationship satisfaction and sexual satisfaction: A longitudinal study of individuals in long-term relationships. *Journal of Sex Research, 42*(2), 113–118.

Byers, E. S., & Macneil, S. (2006). Further validation of the interpersonal exchange model of sexual satisfaction. *Journal of Sex & Marital Therapy, 32*(1), 53–69.

Calderone, M. (1983). Fetal erection and its message to us. *Sex Information and Education Council of the United States (SIECUS) Report, 11*(5–6, 9–10).

Calhoun, L. G., & Tedeschi, R. G. (2004). The foundations of posttraumatic growth: New considerations. *Psychological Inquiry: An International Journal for the Advancement of Psychological Theory, 15*(1), 93–102.

Campbell, R. (2008). The psychological impact of rape victims' experiences with the legal, medical, and mental health systems. *American Psychologist, 63*(8), 702–717.

Cano, A., & O'Leary, K. D. (1997). Romantic jealousy and affairs: Research and implications for couple therapy. *Journal of Sex & Marital Therapy, 23*(4), 249–275.

Carey, M. P., Carey, K. B., Maisto, S. A., Gordon, C. M., & Vanable, P. A. (2001). Prevalence and correlates of sexual activity and HIV-related risk behavior among psychiatric outpatients. *Journal of Consulting and Clinical Psychiatry, 69*(5), 846–850.

Carnes, P. J. (2000). Sexual addiction and compulsion: Recognition, treatment, & recovery. *CNS Spectrums, 5*(10), 63–72.

Carnes, P., Green, B., & Carnes, S. (2010). The same yet different: Refocusing the Sexual Addiction Screening Test (SAST) to reflect orientation and gender. *Sexual Addiction & Compulsivity, 17,* 7–30.

Carnes, P. J., Murray, R. E., & Charpentier, L. (2005). Bargains with chaos: Sex addicts and addiction interaction disorder. *Sexual Addiction & Compulsivity, 12,* 79–120.

Carroll, L., Gilroy, P., & Ryan, J. (2002). Counseling transgendered, transsexual, and gender-variant clients. *Journal of Counseling & Development, 80,* 131–139.

Carvalho, J., & Nobre, P. (2011). Biopsychosocial determinants of men's sexual desire: Testing an integrative model. *The Journal of Sexual Medicine, 8*(3), 754–763.

Cassidy, J. (2001). Truth, lies, and intimacy: An attachment perspective. *Attachment and Human Development, 3*(2), 121–155.

Centers for Disease Control. (n.d.). *National HIV and STD testing resources: Frequently asked questions.* Retrieved from http://hivtest.cdc.gov/faq.aspx

Centers for Disease Control. (2013a). *Adolescent and school health.* Retrieved October 3, 2013, from http://www.cdc.gov/HealthyYouth/sexualbehaviors/

Centers for Disease Control. (2013b). *BAM! Body and mind: Questions answered.* Retrieved from http://www.cdc.gov/bam/body/body-qa.html#3

Centers for Disease Control. (2013c). Births: Final data for 2011. *National vital statistics reports, 62*(1). Hyattsville, MD: National Center for Health Statistics.

Centers for Disease Control. (2013d). *Depression among women of reproductive age.* Retrieved from http://www.cdc.gov/reproductivehealth/depression/

Centers for Disease Control. (2013e). *Infertility FAQs.* Retrieved from http://www.cdc.gov/reproductivehealth/Infertility/index.htm#aa

Centers for Disease Control. (2013f). *STDs and pregnancy: CDC fact sheet.* Retrieved from http://www.cdc.gov/std/pregnancy/stdfact-pregnancy.htm

Centers for Disease Control. (2014a). *Chronic diseases and health promotion.* Retrieved from http://www.cdc.gov/chronicdisease/overview/index.htm

Centers for Disease Control. (2014b). *HIV/AIDS.* Retrieved from http://www.cdc.gov/hiv/default.html

Chan, D. K. S., Lam, C. B., Chow, S. K., & Cheung, S. F. (2008). Examining the job-related, psychological, and physical outcomes of workplace sexual harassment: A meta-analysis. *Psychology of Women Quarterly, 32,* 362–376.

Chariyeva, Z., Golin, C. E., Earp, J. A., & Suchindran, C. (2012). Does motivational interviewing counseling time influence HIV-positive persons' self-efficacy to practice safer sex? *Patient Education & Counseling, 87,* 101–107.

Charmandari, E., Tsigos, C., & Chrousos, G. (2005). Endocrinology of the stress response. *Annual Review of Physiology, 67,* 259–284.

Cheng, H., & Furnham, A. (2003). Personality, self-esteem, and demographic predictions of happiness and depression. *Personality and Individual Differences, 34*(6), 921–942.

Chernin, J., & Johnson, M. (2003). *Affirmative psychotherapy and counseling for lesbians and gay men.* Thousand Oaks, CA: Sage.

Chillman, C. S. (1990). Promoting healthy adolescent sexuality. *Family Relations, 39,* 123–131.

Christopher, F. S., & Cate, R. M. (1984). Factors involved in premarital sexual decision-making. *Journal of Sex Research, 20*(4), 363–376.

Clark, R. D., III, & Hatfield, E. (1989). Gender differences in receptivity to sexual offers. *Journal of Psychology & Human Sexuality, 2*(1), 39–55.

Clayton, A. H. (2002). Female sexual dysfunction related to depression and antidepressant medications. *Current Women's Health Reports, 2*(3), 182–187.

Clayton, A. H., & Balon, R. (2009). The impact of mental illness and psychotropic medications on sexual functioning: The evidence and management. *Journal of Sexual Medicine, 6*, 1200–1211.

Clayton, A. H., Pradko, J. F., Croft, H. A., Montano, C. B., Leadbetter, R. A., Bolden-Watson, C., . . . Metz, A. (2002). Prevalence of sexual dysfunction among newer antidepressants. *The Journal of Clinical Psychiatry, 63*(4), 357–366.

Cloud, J. (2010). Not faking it: Why a placebo can improve sex life. Retrieved from http://healthland. time.com/2010/09/17/not-faking-it-why-a-placebo-can-improve-sex-life/

Coan, J. A. (2010). Adult attachment and the brain. *Journal of Social and Personal Relationships, 27*(2), 210–217.

Cole, S., & Rosenbluth, J. (2012, October). *Transgender specialist vs. friendly: How do you self identify?* Presentation at the annual meeting of the Licensed Professional Counselors Association of North Carolina, Greensboro, NC.

Coleman, E. (2002). Masturbation as a means of achieving sexual health. *Journal of Psychology & Human Sexuality, 14*(2–3), 5–16.

Coleman, E., Bockting, W., Botzer, M., Cohen-Kettenis, P., DeCuypere, G., Feldman, J., . . . Zucker, K. (2011). Standards of care for the health of transsexual, transgender, and gender non-conforming people. *International Journal of Transgenderism, 13*, 165–232.

Conley, T. D., Moors, A. C., Matsick, J. L., & Ziegler, A. (2013). The fewer the merrier?: Assessing stigma surrounding consensually non-monogamous romantic relationships. *Analyses of Social Issues and Public Policy, 13*(1), 1–30.

Cooper, M. L., Shapiro, C. M., & Powers, A. M. (1998). Motivations for sex and risky sexual behavior among adolescents and young adults: A functional perspective. *Journal of Personality and Social Psychology, 75*(6), 1528–1558.

Copello, A. G., Velleman, R. D. B., & Templeton, L. J. (2005). Family interventions in the treatment of alcohol and drug problems. *Drug and Alcohol Review, 24*(4), 369–385.

Corley, M., & Schneider, J. P. (2002). Disclosing secrets: Guidelines for therapists working with sex addicts and co-addicts. *Sexual Addiction & Compulsivity, 9*(1), 43–67. doi:10.1080/107201602317346638

Corona, G., Mannucci, E., Petrone, L., Fisher, A. D., Balercia, G., de Sisciolo, G., . . . Maggi, M. (2006). Psychobiological correlates of delayed ejaculation in male patients with sexual dysfunctions. *Journal of Andrology, 27*(3), 453–458.

Corty, E. W., Althof, S. E., & Wieder, M. (2011). Measuring women's satisfaction with treatment for sexual dysfunction: Developmental and initial validation of the Women's Inventory of Treatment Satisfaction (WITS-9). *Journal of Sexual Medicine, 8*(1), 148–157.

Costa, R. M., & Brody, S. (2012). Sexual satisfaction, relationship satisfaction, and health are associated with greater frequency of penile-vaginal intercourse. *Archives of Sexual Behavior, 41*(1), 9–10.

Cummings, N. A., & Sobel, S. B. (1985). Malpractice insurance: Update on sex claims. *Psychotherapy: Theory, Research, Practice, Training, 22*(2), 186–188. doi:10.1037/h0085492

Cummins, R. A. (1996). The domains of life satisfaction: An attempt to order chaos. *Social Indicators Research, 38*(3), 303–328.

Curtin, N., Ward, L. M., Merriwether, A., & Caruthers, A. (2011). Femininity ideology and sexual health in young women: A focus on sexual knowledge, embodiment, and agency. *International Journal of Sexual Health, 23*, 48–62.

Damian, L., & Miclutia, I. (2013). Bipolar female inpatients and their sexuality. *Romanian Journal of Psychopharmacology, 13*(3), 129–135.

Dandurand, C., & Lafontaine, M. (2013). Intimacy and couple satisfaction: The moderating role of romantic attachment. *International Journal of Psychological Studies, 5*(1), 74–90.

Daniluk, J. C. (1991). Strategies for counseling infertile couples. *Journal of Counseling & Development, 69,* 317–320.

Daniluk, J. C., (2001). Reconstructing their lives: A longitudinal, qualitative analysis of the transition to biological childlessness for infertile couples. *Journal of Counseling & Development, 79,* 439–449.

Darling, C. A., & Mabe, A. R. (1989). Analyzing ethical issues in sexual relationships. *Journal of Sex Education & Therapy, 15*(4), 234–246.

Das, A. (2009). Sexual harassment at work in the United States. *Archives of Sexual Behavior, 38*(6), 909–921.

Davé, S., Petersen, I., Sherr, L., & Nazareth, I. (2010). Incidence of maternal and paternal depression in primary care: A cohort study using a primary care database. *Archive of Pediatric and Adolescent Medicine, 164,* 1038–1044.

Davis, C. (2009). Introduction to practice with transgender and gender variant youth. In G. P. Mallon (Ed.), *Social work practice with transgender and gender variant youth* (2nd ed., pp.1–21). New York, NY: Routledge.

Davis, D., Shaver, P. R., Widaman, K. F., Vernon, M., Folette, W. C., & Beitz, K. (2006). "I can't get no satisfaction": Insecure attachment, inhibited sexual communication, and sexual dissatisfaction. *Personal Relationships, 13,* 465–483.

Davis, S. N. P., Binik, Y. M., & Carrier, S. (2009). Sexual dysfunction and pelvic pain in men: A male sexual pain disorder? *Journal of Sex & Marital Therapy, 35*(3), 182–205.

Davis, S. R. (1998). The clinical use of androgens in female sexual disorders. *Journal of Sex & Marital Therapy, 24*(3), 153–163.

Davison, J., & Huntington, A. (2010). "Out of sight": Sexuality and women with enduring mental illness. *International Journal of Mental Health Nursing, 19,* 240–249.

de Carufel, F., & Trudel, G. (2006). Effects of new functional-sexological treatment for premature ejaculation. *Journal of Sex & Marital Therapy, 32*(2), 97–114.

DeFronzo Dobkin, R., Leiblum, S. R., Rosen, R. C., Menza, M., & Marin, H. (2006). Depression and sexual functioning in minority women: Current status and future directions. *Journal of Sex & Marital Therapy, 32,* 23–36.

deFur, K. M. (2012). Don't forget the good stuff! Incorporating positive messages of sexual pleasure into sexuality education. *American Journal of Sexuality Education, 7,* 160–169.

De la Garza-Mercer, F. (2006). The evolution of sexual pleasure. *Journal of Psychology & Human Sexuality, 18,* 107–124.

DeLamater, J., & Friedrich, W. N. (2002). Human sexual development. *The Journal of Sex Research, 39*(1), 10–14.

Dell'Osso, L., Carmassi, C., Carlini, M., Rucci, P., Torri, P., Cesari, D., . . . Maggi, M. (2009). Sexual dysfunctions and suicidality in patients with bipolar disorder and unipolar depression. *The Journal of Sexual Medicine, 6*(11), 3063–3070.

Denehy, J. (2007). Education about sexuality: Are we preparing our youth for today's realities? *The Journal of School Nursing, 23,* 245–246.

Dennerstein, L., Dudley, E., & Burger, H. (2001). Are changes in sexual functioning during midlife due to aging or menopause? *Fertility and Sterility, 76*(3), 456–460.

Deogracias, J., Johnson, L., Meyer-Bahlburg, H., Kessler, S., Schober, J., & Zucker, K. (2007). The gender identity/gender dysphoria questionnaire for adolescents and adults. *The Journal of Sex Research, 44,* 370–379.

Derogatis, L. R. (1997). The Derogatis Interview for Sexual Functioning (DISF/DISF-SR): An introductory report. *Journal of Sex & Marital Therapy, 23,* 291–304.

de Shazer, S. (1982). Patterns of brief family therapy: An ecosystemic approach. New York, NY: Guilford Press.

Déttore, D., Pucciarelli, M., & Santarnecchi, E. (2013). Anxiety and female sexual functioning: An empirical study. *Journal of Sex & Marital Therapy, 39*(3), 216–240.

DeWitt, P. M. (1992). Breaking up is hard to do. *American Demographics, 14,* 52–58.

Diamond, L. M. (2003). Was it a phase? Young women's relinquishment of lesbian/bisexual identities over a 5-year period. *Journal of Personality and Social Psychology, 84,* 352–364.

Diamond, L. M., & Huebner, D. M. (2012). Is good sex good for you? Rethinking sexuality and health. *Social and Personality Psychology Compass, 6,* 54–69.

Diamond, L. M., & Wallen, K. (2011). Sexual minority women's sexual motivation around the time of ovulation. *Archives of Sexual Behavior, 40,* 237–246.

Di Giulio, G. (2003). Sexuality and people living with physical or developmental disabilities: A review of key issues. *The Canadian Journal of Human Sexuality, 12,* 53–68.

Dillaway, H. E. (2005). Menopause is the "good old": Women's thoughts about reproductive aging. *Gender and Society, 19*(3), 398–417.

Dobkin, R. D., Leiblum, S. R., Rosen, R. C., Menza, M., & Marin, H. (2006). Depression and sexual function in minority women: Current status and future directions. *Journal of Sex & Marital Therapy, 32,* 23–36.

Donahey, K. M., & Miller, S. D. (2000). Applying a common factors perspective to sex therapy. *Journal of Sex Education & Therapy, 25*(4), 221–230.

Donnelly, D. A. (1993). Sexually inactive marriages. *Journal of Sex Research, 30*(2), 171–179.

Donnelly, D., Burgess, E., Anderson, S., Davis, R., & Dillard, J. (2001). Involuntary celibacy: A life course analysis. *Journal of Sex Research, 38*(2), 159–169.

Drach, K. M., Wientzen, J., & Ricci, L. R. (2001). The diagnostic utility of sexual behavior problems in diagnosing sexual abuse in a forensic child abuse evaluation clinic. *Child Abuse & Neglect, 25,* 489–503.

Drescher, J. (2001). Ethical concerns raised when patients seek to change same-sex attractions. *Journal of Gay & Lesbian Psychotherapy, 5*(3–4), 181–210. doi:10.1300/J236v05n03_11

Drescher, J. (2002). Ethical issues in treating gay and lesbian patients. *Psychiatric Clinics of North America, 25*(3), 605–621. doi:10.1016/S0193–953X(02)00004–7

Dundon, C. M., & Rellini, A. H. (2009). More than sexual function: Predictors of sexual satisfaction in a sample of women age 40–70. *Journal of Sexual Medicine, 7,* 896–904.

Dune, T. M. (2012). Sexuality and physical disability: Exploring the barriers and solutions in healthcare. *Sexuality & Disability, 30,* 247–255.

Dunn, K. M., Croft, P. R., & Hackett, G. I. (1999). Association of sexual problems with social, psychological, and physical problems in men and women: A cross sectional population survey. *Journal of Epidemiology & Community Health, 53,* 144–148.

Dworkin, S. H., & Pope, M. (Eds.). (2012). *Casebook for counseling lesbian, gay, bisexual, and transgender persons and their families.* Alexandria, VA: American Counseling Association.

Eastwick, P. W., & Finkel, E. J. (2008). Sex differences in mate preferences revisited: Do people know what they initially desire in a romantic partner? *Journal of Personality and Social Psychology, 94*(2), 245–264.

Eastwick, P. W., Finkel, E. J., & Eagly, A. H. (2011). When and why do ideal partner preferences affect the process of initiating and maintaining romantic relationships? *Journal of Personality and Social Psychology, 101*(5), 1012–1032.

Eastwick, P. W., Finkel, E. J., & Matthews, J. (2007). Speed-dating as an invaluable tool for studying romantic attraction: A methodological primer. *Personal Relationships, 14*(1), 149–166.

Edelwich, J., & Brodsky, A. (1984). Sexual dynamics of the client–counselor relationship. *Alcoholism Treatment Quarterly, 1*(3), 99–117. doi:10.1300/J020V01N03_08

Edger, K. (2012). Evangelicalism, sexual morality, and sexual addiction: Opposing views and continued conflicts. *Journal of Religion and Health, 51,* 162–178.

Eğeci, I. S., & Gençöz, T. (2006). Factors associated with relationship satisfaction: Importance of communication skills. *Contemporary Family Therapy, 28*(3), 383–391.

Eisenberg, M. L., Shindel, A. W., Smith, J. F., Breyer, B. N., & Lipshultz, L. I. (2010). Socioeconomic, anthropomorphic, and demographic predictors of adult sexual activity in the United States: Data from the national survey of family growth. *Journal of Sexual Medicine, 7,* 50–58.

Elder, W. B., Brooks, G. R., & Morrow, S. L. (2012). Sexual self-schemas of heterosexual men. *Psychology of Men & Masculinity, 13*, 166–179.

Elders, M. J. (2010). Sex for health and pleasure throughout a lifetime. *Journal of Sexual Medicine, 7(Suppl.* 5), 248–249.

Eldridge, K. A., & Christensen, A. (2002). Demand-withdraw communication during couple conflict: A review and analysis. In P. Noller & J. A. Feeney (Eds.), *Understanding marriage: Developments in the study of couple interaction* (pp. 289–322). Cambridge, MA: Cambridge University Press.

Eldridge, N. S., & Gilbert, L. A. (1990). Correlates of relationship satisfaction in lesbian couples. *Psychology of Women Quarterly, 14*, 43–62.

Elliott, D. M., Mok, D. S., & Briere, J. (2004). Adult sexual assault: Prevalence, symptomatology, and sex differences in the general population. *Journal of Traumatic Stress, 17,* 203–211.

Ely, G. E. (2007). The abortion counseling experience: A discussion of patient narratives and recommendations for best practices. *Best Practices in Mental Health, 3*(2), 62–74.

Epstein, E. E., & McCrady, B. S. (1998). Behavioral couples treatment of alcohol and drug use disorders: Current status and innovations. *Clinical Psychology Review, 18*(6), 689–711.

Erickson, S. H. (1990). Counseling the irresponsible AIDS client: Guidelines for decision making. *Journal of Counseling & Development, 68,* 454–455.

Erikson, E. H. (1950). *Childhood and society.* New York, NY: W. W. Norton.

Erikson, E. H. (1960). Youth and the life cycle. *Children, 7,* 43–49.

Erikson, E. H. (1963). *Childhood and society.* (2nd ed.). New York, NY: W. W. Norton.

Erikson, E. H. (1965). *The challenge of youth.* Garden City, NY: Doubleday.

Erikson, E. H. (1968). *Identity, youth, and crisis.* New York, NY: W. W. Norton.

Erikson, E. H. (1997). *The life cycle completed.* New York, NY: W. W. Norton.

Ethier, K. A., Kershaw, T. S., Lewis, J. B., Milan, S., Niccolai, L. M., & Ickovics, J. R. (2006). Self-esteem, emotional distress and sexual behavior among adolescent females: Inter-relationships and temporal effects. *Journal of Adolescent Health, 38*(3), 268–274.

Ettner, R. (1996). *Confessions of a gender defender: A psychologist's reflections on life among the transgendered.* Louisville, KY: Chicago Spectrum Press.

Fabricius, W. V., & Luecken, L. J. (2007). Postdivorce living arrangements, parent conflict, and long-term physical health correlates for children of divorce. *Journal of Family Psychology, 21*(2), 195–205.

Fahs, B., & Swank, E. (2011). Social identities as predictors of women's sexual satisfaction and sexual activity. *Archives of Sexual Behavior, 40,* 903–914.

Family Safe Media. (2006). Pornography statistics. Retrieved from http://familysafemedia.com/pornography_statistics.html#anchor4

Federal Bureau of Investigation. (2013). Rape. *Crime in the United States, 2013.* Washington, D.C.: U.S. Department of Justice.

Feijoo, A. (2001) *Adolescent sexual health in Europe and the U.S.–Why the difference?* Washington, DC: Advocates for Youth.

Feldman, R. S. (2014). *Development across the life span* (7th ed.). Upper Saddle River, NJ: Pearson.

Feltenstein, M. W., & See, R. E. (2008). The neurocircuitry of addiction: An overview. *British Journal of Pharmacology, 154*, 261–274.

Figueredo, A. J., Sefcek, J. A., & Jones, D. N. (2006). The ideal romantic partner personality. *Personality and Individual Differences, 41*(3), 431–441.

Fincham, F. D. (2003). Marital conflict: Correlates, structure, and context. *Current Directions in Psychological Science, 12*(1), 23–27.

Fincham, F. D., & Beach, S. R. H. (2006). Relationship satisfaction. In D. Perlman & A. Vangelisti (Eds.), *The Cambridge handbook of personal relationships* (pp. 579–594). New York, NY: Cambridge University Press.

Fine, M. (1988). Sexuality, schooling, and adolescent females: The missing discourse of desire. *Harvard Educational Review, 58,* 29–53.

Fine, M. A., & Harvey, J. H. (Eds.). (2006). *Handbook of divorce and relationship dissolution.* New York, NY: Routledge.

Finer, L. B., & Philbin, J. M. (2013). Sexual initiation, contraceptive use, and pregnancy among young adolescents. *Pediatrics, 131*(5), 1–6.

Finer, L. B., & Zolna, M. R. (2014). Shifts in intended and unintended pregnancies in the United States, 2001–2008. *American Journal of Public Health.* doi:10.2105/AJPH.2013.301416

Finkel, E. J., & Eastwick, P. W. (2009). Arbitrary social norms influence sex differences in romantic selectivity. *Psychological Science, 20*(10), 1290–1295.

Finkel, M., Storaasli, R., Bandele, A., & Schaefer, V. (2003). Diversity training in graduate school: An exploratory evaluation of the safe zone project. *Professional Psychology: Research & Practice, 5,* 555–561.

Finkelhor, D. (1991). Child sexual abuse. In M. L. Rosenberg & M. A. Fenley (Eds.), *Violence in America: A public health approach* (pp. 79–94). New York, NY: Oxford University Press.

Finkelhor, D. (2010). *Sexually victimized children.* New York, NY: The Free Press.

Firth, M. T., & Mohamad, H. (2007). Men, sex and context in psychosexual therapy: Finding a suitable frame. *Sexual and Relationship Therapy, 22*(2), 221–235.

Fisher, C. D. (2004). Ethical issues in therapy: Therapist self-disclosure of sexual feelings. *Ethics & Behavior, 14*(2), 105–121. doi:10.1207/s15327019eb1402_2

Fisher, G. L., & Harrison, T. C. (2009). *Substance abuse: Information for school counselors, social workers, therapists, and counselors* (4th ed.). Needham Heights, MA: Allyn & Bacon.

Fisher, T. D., Davis, C. M., Yarber, W. L., & Davis, S. L. (2010). *Handbook of sexuality-related measures* (3rd ed.). New York, NY: Routledge.

Fitch, S. A., & Adams, G. R. (1983). Ego identity and intimacy status: Replication and extension. *Developmental Psychology, 19*(6), 839–845.

Fletcher, G. J. O., Kerr, P. S. G., Li, N. P., & Valentine, K. A. (2014). Predicting romantic interest and decisions in the very early stages of mate selection: Standards, accuracy, and sex differences. *Personality and Social Psychology Bulletin, 40*(4), 540–550.

Ford, M. (2013, May). *A brief history of homosexuality in America.* Retrieved from http://www.gvsu .edu/allies/a-brief-history-of-homosexuality-in-america-30.htm

Forstein, M. (2001). Overview of ethical and research issues in sexual orientation therapy. *Journal of Gay & Lesbian Psychotherapy, 5*(3–4), 167–179. doi:10.1300/J236v05n03_10

Fourcroy, J. L. (2006). Customs, culture, and tradition: What role do they play in a woman's sexuality? *Journal of Sexual Medicine, 3,* 954–959.

Franz, C. E., & White, K. M. (1985). Individuation and attachment in personality development: Extending Erikson's theory. *Journal of Personality, 53*(2), 224–256.

Freedom to Marry. (2015). *States.* Retrieved September 4, 2015, from http://www.freedomtomarry .org/states

Freud, S. (1949). *An outline of psycho-analysis.* (J. Strachey, trans.). London, England: Hogarth Press. (Original work published 1940).

Freud, S. (1957). *On narcissism: An introduction.* (J. Rickman, trans.). London, England: Hogarth Press. (Original work published 1914).

Friedrich, W. N., Fisher, J. L., Ditter, C. A., Acton, R., Berliner, L., Butler, J., . . . Wright, J. (2001). Child Sexual Behavior Inventory: Normative, psychiatric, and sexual abuse comparisons. *Child Maltreatment, 6,* 37–49.

Friedrich, W. N., Grambsch, P., Damon, L., Hewitt, S. K., Koverola, C., Lang, R., . . . Broughton, D. (1992). Child Sexual Behavior Inventory: Normative and clinical comparisons. *Psychological Assessment, 4,* 303–311.

Friedrich, W. N., Lysne, M., Sim, L., & Shamos, S. (2004). Assessing sexual behavior in high-risk adolescents with the Adolescent Clinical Sexual Behavior Inventory. *Child Maltreatment, 9,* 239–250.

Frost, J. J., & Darroch, J. E. (2008). Factors associated with contraceptive choice and inconsistent method use, United States, 2004. *Perspectives on Sexual and Reproductive Health, 40*(2), 94–104.

Frost, J., Darroch, J., & Remez, L. (2008). Improving contraceptive use in the United States. *In Brief.* New York, NY: Guttmacher Institute.

Frühauf, S., Gerger, H., Schmidt, H. M., Munder, T., & Barth, J. (2013). Efficacy of psychological interventions for sexual dysfunction: A systematic review and meta-analysis. *Archives of Sexual Behavior, 42*(6), 915–933.

Fuselier, D. A., Durham, R. L., & Wurtele, S. K. (2002). The child sexual abuser: Perceptions of college students and professionals. *Sexual Abuse, 14*(3), 271–280.

Gager, C. T., & Sanchez, L. (2003). Two as one?: Couples perceptions of time spent together, marital quality, and the risk of divorce. *Journal of Family Issues, 24*(1), 21–50.

Galinsky, A. M., & Sonenstein, F. L. (2011). The association between developmental assets and sexual enjoyment among emerging adults. *Journal of Adolescent Sexual Health, 48,* 610–615.

Ganong, L. H., & Coleman, M. (1989). Preparing for remarriage: Anticipating the issues, seeking solutions. *Family Relations, 38*(1), 28–33.

Ganzevoort, R. R. (2002). Common themes and structure in male victims' stories of religion and sexual abuse. *Mental Health, Religion, & Culture, 5,* 313–325.

Garcia, F. D., & Thibaut, F. (2011). Current concepts in the pharmacotherapy of paraphilias. *Drugs, 71*(6), 771–790.

Garcia, J. R., Reiber, C., Massey, S. G., & Merriwether, A. M. (2012). Sexual hookup culture: A review. *Review of General Psychology, 16*(2), 161–176.

Garos, S. (2009). *Garos Sexual Behavior Inventory test manual.* Los Angeles, CA: Western Psychological Services.

Gavey, N. (2012). Beyond 'empowerment'? Sexuality in a sexist world. *Sex Roles, 66,* 718–724.

Gay, Lesbian, & Straight Education Network. (2011). *The 2011 national school climate survey: The experience of lesbian, gay, bisexual, and transgender youth in our nation's schools.* New York, NY: Author.

Gerhardt, K. J., & Abrams, R. M. (2000). Fetal exposures to sound and vibroacoustic stimulation. *Journal of Perinatology, 20*(8), S21–S30.

Gibson, A. (2007). Erikson's life cycle approach to development. In J. Lishman (Ed.), *Handbook for practice learning in social work and social care* (2nd ed., pp. 74–85). London, England: Jessica Kingsley.

Gillath, O., & Schachner, D. A. (2006). How do sexuality and attachment interrelate? Goals, motives and strategies. In M. Mikulincer & G. Goodman (Eds.), *The dynamics of romantic love: Attachment, caregiving and sex* (pp. 337–355). New York, NY: Guilford.

Gilligan, C. (1987). *Feminism & methodology.* S. G. Harding (Ed.). Bloomington, IN: Indiana University Press.

Giugliano, J. R. (2008). Sexual impulsivity, compulsivity or dependence: An investigative inquiry. *Sexual Addiction & Compulsivity, 15,* 139–157.

Glassgold, J. M. (2008). Bridging the divide: Integrating lesbian identity and Orthodox Judaism. *Women & Therapy, 31,* 59–73.

Gluckman, P. D., & Hanson, M. A. (2006). Evolution, development and timing of puberty. *Trends in Endocrinology & Metabolism, 17*(1), 7–12.

Goldman, R., & Goldman, J. (1982). *Children's sexual thinking: A comparative study of children aged 5 to 15 years in Australia, North America, Britain, and Sweden.* Lawrence, MA: Routledge & Kegan Paul.

Goldstein, I. (2007). Current management strategies of the postmenopausal patient with sexual health problems, *Journal of Sexual Medicine, 4*(Suppl. 3), 235–253.

Goleman, D. (2001). An EI-based theory of performance. In C. Cherniss & D. Goleman (Eds.), *The emotionally intelligent workplace: How to select for, measure, and improve emotional intelligence in individuals, groups, and organizations* (pp. 27–44). San Francisco, CA: Jossey-Bass.

Göncü, A., Mistry, J., & Mosier, C. (2000). Cultural variations in the play of toddlers. *International Journal of Behavioral Development, 24*(3), 321–329.

Gonzales, A. M., & Rolison, G. (2005). Social oppression and attitudes toward sexual practices. *Journal of Black Studies, 35,* 715–729.

Goodman, A. (2001). What's in a name? Terminology for designating a syndrome of driven sexual behavior. *Sexual Addiction & Compulsivity, 8,* 191–213.

Goodreads. (2015). *Quote by Albert Einstein.* Retrieved August 16, 2015, from http://www.goodreads.com/quotes/387336-problems-cannot-be-solved-with-the-same-mind-set-that

Goodson, P., & Zhang, J. (2008). Peering through stained glass windows: How religion colors US adolescents' sexuality. *Journal of Sex Research, 45,* 83–36.

Goodwach, R. (2005a). Sex therapy: Historical evolution, current practice. Part I. *Australian and New Zealand Journal of Family Therapy*, 26(3), 155–164.

Goodwach, R. (2005b). Sex therapy: Historical evolution, current practice. Part 2. *Australian and New Zealand Journal of Family Therapy*, 26(4), 178–183.

Goodwin, D. D., & Scanzoni, J. (1989). Couple consensus during marital joint decision-making: A context, process, outcome model. *Journal of Marriage and the Family, 51,* 943–956.

Gordon, D. E. (1990). Formal operational thinking: The role of cognitive-developmental processes in adolescent decision-making about pregnancy and contraception. *American Journal of Orthopsychiatry, 60*(3), 346–356.

Gottman, J. M. (1994). *What predicts divorce?* Hillsdale, NJ: Erlbaum.

Gottman, J. M. (2014). *What predicts divorce?: The relationship between marital processes and marital outcomes* (2nd ed.). New York, NY: Lawrence Erlbaum Associates.

Gottman, J. M., Gottman, J. S., & DeClaire, J. (2006). *10 lessons to transform your marriage: America's love lab experts share their strategies for strengthening your relationship.* New York, NY: Crown.

Gottman, J. M., & Levenson, R. W. (1992). Marital processes predictive of later dissolution: Behavior, physiology, and health. *Journal of Personality and Social Psychology, 63*(2), 221–233.

Graham, C. A. (2007). Medicalization of women's sexual problems: A different story? *Journal of Sex & Marital Therapy, 33*(5), 443–447.

Graham, J. G., Liu, Y. J., & Jeziorski, J. L. (2006). The Dyadic Adjustment Scale: A reliability generalization meta-analysis. *Journal of Marriage and the Family, 68,* 701–717.

Grant, C. (2003). Teens, sex, and the media: Is there a connection? *Paediatrics & Child Health, 8,* 285–286.

Grant, J., Mottet, L., Tanis, J., Harrison, J., Herman, J., & Keisling, M. (2011). *Injustice at every turn: A report of the National Transgender Discrimination Survey.* Washington, DC: National Center for Transgender Equality and National Gay and Lesbian Task Force.

Graziano, W. G., Jensen-Campbell, L. A., Shebilske, L. J., & Lundgren, S. R. (1993). Social influence, sex differences, and judgments of beauty: Putting the *interpersonal* back in interpersonal attraction. *Journal of Personality and Social Psychology, 65*(3), 522–531.

Graziottin, A., & Althof, S. (2011). What does premature ejaculation mean to the man, the woman, and the couple? *The Journal of Sexual Medicine, 8*(*Suppl.* 4), 304–309.

Greeff, A. P., & Malherbe, H. L. (2001). Intimacy and marital satisfaction in spouses. *Journal of Sex and Marital Therapy*, 27, 247–257.

Green, R. J., & Mitchell, V. (2002). Gay and lesbian couples in therapy: Homophobia, relational ambiguity, and social support. In A. S. Gurman & N. S. Jacobson (Eds.), *Clinical handbook of couple therapy* (3rd ed., pp. 546–568). New York, NY: Guilford.

Greene, B. (2007). Delivering ethical psychological services to lesbian, gay, and bisexual clients. In K. J. Bieschke, R. M. Perez, & K. A. Debord (Eds.), *Handbook of counseling and psychotherapy with lesbian, gay, bisexual, and transgender clients* (2nd ed., pp. 181–199). Washington, DC: American Psychological Association.

Greenwell, A., & Hough, S. (2008). Culture and disability in sexuality studies: A methodological and content review of literature. *Sexuality and Disabilities, 26,* 189–196.

Gregorian, R. S., Golden, K. A., Bahce, A., Goodman, C., Kwong, W. J., & Khan, A. M. (2002). Antidepressant-induced sexual dysfunction. *Annuals of Pharmacotherapy, 36*(10), 1577–1589.

Griel, A., & McQuillan, J. (2004). Help-seeking patterns among subfecund women. *Journal of Reproductive & Infant Psychology, 22,* 305–319.

Griffin-Shelley, E. (2009). Ethical issues in sex and love addiction treatment. *Sexual Addiction & Compulsivity, 16*(1), 32–54. doi:10.1080/10720160802710798

Grossman, W. I. (1986). Freud and Horney: A study of psychoanalytic models via the analysis of controversy. In A. D. Richards & M. S. Villick (Eds.), *Psychoanalysis: The science of mental conflict* (pp. 65–87). Hillsdale, NJ: The Analytic Press.

Gruber, E., & Grube, J. (2000). Adolescent sexuality and the media: A review of current knowledge and implications. *Western Journal of Medicine, 172,* 210–214.

Guldner, C. A. (1995). Sexual health education and sex therapy: Reflections on the Canadian guidelines for sexual health education. *The Canadian Journal of Human Sexuality, 4,* 31–35.

Gutierrez, R. A. (2012). Islam and sexuality. *Social Identities, 18,* 155–159.

Guttmacher Institute. (2014). *State policies in brief: Counseling & waiting periods for abortion.* Retrieved from http://www.guttmacher.org/statecenter/spibs/spib_MWPA.pdf

Haas, A. P., Rodgers, P. L., & Herman J. L. (2014). *Suicide attempts among transgender and gender non-conforming adults: Findings of the national transgender discrimination survey.* New York, NY: American Foundation for Suicide Prevention.

Hall, J. H., & Fincham, F. D. (2006). Relationship dissolution following infidelity. In M. A. Fine & J. H. Harvey (Eds.), *Handbook of divorce and relationship dissolution* (pp. 153–168). New York, NY: Routledge.

Hansen, S. L. (1977). Dating choices of high school students. *The Family Coordinator, 26*(2), 133–138.

Harmon, A. (2007). Talking about sexual side effects: Countering don't ask, don't tell. *Adolescent Psychiatry, 30,* 147–155.

Harris, S. M., & Hays, K. W. (2008). Family therapist comfort with and willingness to discuss client sexuality. *Journal of Marital and Family Therapy, 34,* 239–250.

Hartmann, U., & Waldinger, M. D. (2007). Treatment of delayed ejaculation. In S. R. Leiblum (Ed.), *Principles and practice of sex therapy* (4th ed., pp. 241–276). New York, NY: Guilford.

Hatzichristou, D., Rosen, R. C., Derogatis, L. R., Low, W. Y., Meuleman, E. J. H., Sadovsky, R., & Symonds, T. (2010). Recommendations for the clinical evaluation of men and women with sexual dysfunction. *Journal of Sexual Medicine, 7*(1, 2), 337–348.

Heavey, C. L., Christensen, A., & Malamuth, N. M. (1995). The longitudinal impact of demand and withdrawal during marital conflict. *Journal of Consulting and Clinical Psychology, 63*(5), 797–801.

Heffner, K. L., Loving, T. J., Kiecolt-Glaser, J. K., Himawan, L. K., Glaser, R., & Malarkey, W. B. (2006). Older spouses' cortisol responses to marital conflict: Associations with demand/withdraw communication patterns. *Journal of Behavioral Medicine, 29*(4), 317–325.

Heiden, J. M. (1993). Preview-prevent: A training strategy to prevent counselor-client sexual relationships. *Counselor Education and Supervision, 33*(1), 53–60. doi:10.1002/j.1556-6978.1993.tb00268.x

Hendrick, C., Hendrick, S. S., & Reich, D. A. (2006). The Brief Sexual Attitudes Scale. *Journal of Sex Research, 43,* 76–86.

Hendrick, S., & Hendrick, C. (1987). Multidimensionality of sexual attitudes. *Journal of Sex Research, 23,* 502–526.

Herbenick, D., Reece, M., Schick, V., Sanders, S. A., Dodge, B., & Fortenberry, J. D. (2010). Sexual behavior in the United States: Results from a national probability sample of men and women ages 14–94. *The Journal of Sexual Medicine, 7,* 255–265.

Herman, J. L. (2013). Gendered restrooms and minority stress: The public regulation of gender and its impact on transgender people's lives. *Journal of Public Management & Social Policy, 19*(1), 65–80.

Hertlein, K. M., Weeks, G. R., & Gambescia, N. (2007). In L. VandeCreek, F. L. Peterson, Jr., & J. W. Bley (Eds.), *Innovations in clinical practice: Focus on sexual health* (pp. 75–92). Sarasota, FL: Professional Resource Press.

Higginbotham, B. J., Miller, J. J., & Niehuis, S. (2009). Remarriage preparation: Usage, perceived helpfulness, and dyadic adjustment. *Family Relations: Interdisciplinary Journal of Applied Family Studies, 58*(3), 316–329.

Hill, C. A., & Preston, L. K. (1996). Individual differences in the experience of sexual motivation: Theory and measurement of dispositional sexual motives. *Journal of Sex Research, 33*(1), 27–45.

Hill, D. B. (2006). "Feminine" heterosexual men: Subverting heteropatriarchal sexual scripts? *The Journal of Men's Studies, 42,* 145–159.

Hines, M. (2011). Gender development and the human brain. *Annual Review of Neuroscience, 34,* 69–88.

Hirst, J. (2008). Developing sexual competence? Exploring strategies for the provision of effective sexualities and relationships education. *Sex Education, 8,* 399–413.

Ho, D. K., & Ross, C. C. (2012). Cognitive behaviour therapy for sex offenders: Too good to be true? *Criminal Behaviour and Mental Health, 22,* 1–6.

Hockmeyer, A. (1988). Object relations theory and feminism: Strange bedfellows. *Frontiers: A Journal of Women Studies, 10*(1), 20–28.

Hoffman, R. (1995). Sexual dual relationships in counseling: Confronting the issues. *Counseling and Values, 40*(1), 15–23. doi:10.1002/j.2161-007X.1995.tb00383.x

Holden, J. M., & Holden, G. S. (1995). The sexual identity profile: A multidimensional bipolar model. *Individual Psychology, 51,* 102–113.

Homish, G. G., & Leonard, K. E. (2007). The drinking partnership and marital satisfaction: The longitudinal influence of discrepant drinking. *Journal of Consulting and Clinical Psychology, 75*(1), 43–51.

Horney, K. (1967). *Feminine psychology.* New York, NY: Norton.

Horvath, K. J., Calsyn, D. A., Terry, C., & Cotton, A. (2007). Erectile dysfunction medication use among men seeking substance abuse treatment. *Journal of Addictive Diseases, 26*(4), 7–13.

Howard, H. S. (2012). Sexual adjustment counseling for women with chronic pelvic pain. *Journal of Obstetric, Gynecological, and Neonatal Nursing, 41,* 692–702.

Huang, F. Y., & Akhtar, S. (2005). Immigrant sex: The transport of affection and sensuality across cultures. *The American Journal of Psychoanalysis, 65,* 179–188.

Hughes, T. L., & Eliason, M. (2002). Substance use and abuse in lesbian, gay, bisexual, and transgender populations. *Journal of Primary Prevention, 22,* 263–298.

Hull, T. H. (2008). Sexual pleasure and wellbeing. *International Journal of Sexual Health, 20,* 133–145.

Hunt, S. A., & Kraus, S. W. (2009). Exploring the relationship between erotic disruption during the latency period and the use of sexually explicit material, online sexual behaviors, and sexual dysfunctions in young adulthood. *Sexual Addiction & Compulsivity: The Journal of Treatment & Prevention, 16*(1), 79–100.

Inhelder, B., & Piaget, J. (1958). *The growth of logical thinking from childhood to adolescence: An essay on the construction of formal operational structures.* New York, NY: Basic Books.

International Professional Surrogates Association. (2013a). Statement of purpose and mission. Retrieved August 26, 2013 from http://www.surrogatetherapy.org/mission/

International Professional Surrogates Association. (2013b). Surrogate partner therapy. Retrieved August 26, 2013 from http://www.surrogatetherapy.org/what-is-surrogate-partner-therapy/

Intersex Society of North America. (2008). *Frequently asked questions.* Retrieved from http://www.isna.org/faq

IsHak, W. W., & Tobia, G. (2013). DSM-5 changes in diagnostic criteria of sexual dysfunctions. *Reproductive System & Sexual Disorders, 2*(2), 122–124.

Ivey, A. E., Ivey, M. B., & Zalaquett, C. P. (2014). *Intentional interviewing and counseling: Facilitating client development in a multicultural society* (8th ed.). Belmont, CA: Brooks/Cole.

Izard, C. E. (2002). Translating emotion theory and research into preventive interventions. *Psychological Bulletin, 128,* 796–824.

Jacob, T., Ritchey, D., Cvitkovic, J. F., & Blane, H. T. (1981). Communication styles of alcoholic and nonalcoholic families when drinking and not drinking. *Journal of Studies on Alcohol and Drugs, 42*(5), 466–482.

Jacobson, N. S. (1984). A component analysis of behavioral marital therapy: The relative effectiveness of behavior exchange and communication/problem-solving training. *Journal of Consulting and Clinical Psychology, 52*(2), 295–305.

Jannini, E. A., Fisher, W. A., Bitzer, J., & McMahon, C. G. (2009). Is sex just fun? How sexual activity improves health. *Journal of Sexual Medicine, 6,* 2640–2648.

Janoff-Bulman, R. (1992). *Shattered assumptions: Towards a new psychology of trauma.* New York, NY: Free Press.

Jeng, C., Wang, L., Chou, C., Shen, J., & Tzeng, C. (2006). Management and outcome for primary vaginismus. *Journal of Sex & Marital Therapy, 32*(5), 379–387.

Joffe, C. (2013). The politicization of abortion and the evolution of abortion counseling. *American Journal of Public Health, 103,* 57–65.

Johnson, B. (2013). Sexually transmitted infections and older adults. *Journal of Gerontological Nursing, 39,* 53–60.

Johnson, S. (2004). *Creating connection: The practice of emotionally focused marital therapy* (2nd ed.). New York, NY: Brunner/Routledge.

Johnson, S. M., Hunsley, J., Greenberg, L., & Schindler, D. (1999). Emotionally focused couples therapy: Status and challenges. *Clinical Psychology: Science and Practice, 6,* 67–79.

Johnson, S. M., Makinen, J. A., & Millikin, J. W. (2001). Attachment injuries in couple relationships: A new perspective on impasses in couples therapy. *Journal of Marital and Family Therapy, 27*(2), 145–155.

Johnson, S. D., Phelps, D. L., & Cottler, L. B. (2004). The association of sexual dysfunction and substance use among a community epidemiological sample. *Archives of Sexual Behavior, 33*(1), 55–63.

Johnson, S. M., & Wittenborn, A. K. (2012). New research findings on emotionally focused therapy: Introduction to special section. *Journal of Marital and Family Therapy, 38*(Suppl. 1), 18–22.

Johnson, S., & Zuccarini, D. (2010). Integrating sex and attachment in emotionally focused couple therapy. *Journal of Marital and Family Therapy, 36*(4), 431–445.

Jones, K. E., Meneses da Silva, A. M., & Soloski, K. L. (2011). Sexological Systems Theory: An ecological model and assessment approach for sex therapy. *Sexual and Relationship Therapy, 26*(2), 127–144.

Jones, L. M., & McCabe, M. P. (2011). The effectiveness of an Internet-based psychological treatment program for female sexual dysfunction. *Journal of Sexual Medicine, 8*(10), 2781–2792.

Jones, R. K., Finer, L. B., & Singh, S. (2010). *Characteristics of U.S. Abortion Patients, 2008.* New York, NY: Guttmacher Institute.

Josephson, G. J. (2003). Using an attachment-based intervention with same-sex couples. In S. M. Johnson & V. E. Whiffen (Eds.), *Attachment processes in couple and family therapy* (pp. 300–317). New York, NY: The Guilford Press.

Juergens, M. H., Smedema, S. M., & Berven, N. L. (2009). Willingness of graduate students in rehabilitation counseling to discuss sexuality with clients. *Rehabilitation Counseling Bulletin, 53,* 34–43.

Juhasz, A. M. (1975). A chain of sexual decision-making. *The Family Coordinator, 24*(1), 43–49.

Just the Facts Coalition. (2008). *Just the facts about sexual orientation and youth: A primer for principals, educators, and school personnel.* Washington, DC: American Psychological Association. Retrieved September 12, 2013, from http://www.apa.org/pi/lgbt/resources/just-the-facts.pdf

Kabakci, E., & Batur, S. (2003). Who benefits from cognitive behavioral therapy for vaginismus. *Journal of Sex & Marital Therapy, 29*(4), 277–288.

Kacerguis, M. A., & Adams, G. R. (1980). Erikson stage resolution: The relationship between identity and intimacy. *Journal of Youth and Adolescence, 9*(2), 117–126.

Kaestle, C. E., & Halpern, C. T. (2007). What's love got to do with it? Sexual behaviors of opposite sex couples through emerging adulthood. *Perspectives on Sexual and Reproductive Health, 39*(3), 134–140.

Kafka, M. P. (2010). Hypersexual disorder: A proposed diagnosis for DSM-V. *Archives of Sexual Behavior, 39*, 377–400.

Kafka, M. P., & Hennen, J. (1999). The paraphilia-related disorders: An empirical investigation of nonparaphilic hypersexuality disorders in 206 outpatient males. *Journal of Sex and Marital Therapy, 25*, 305–319.

Kaiser Family Foundation. (2003). *National survey on sexual health knowledge, attitudes, and experiences of adolescents and young adults.* Washington, DC: Henry J. Kaiser Family Foundation.

Kann, L., Kinchen, S., Shanklin, S. L., Flint, K. H., Hawkins, J., Harris, W. A., . . . Zaza, S. (2014). Youth risk behavior surveillance–United States, 2013. *Morbidity and Mortality Weekly Report, 63*(SS-4), 1–168.

Kaplan, M. S., & Krueger, R. B. (2010). Diagnosis, assessment, and treatment of hypersexuality. *Journal of Sex Research, 47*(2), 181–198.

Kaplan, M. S., & Krueger, R. B. (2012). Cognitive-behavioral treatment of the paraphilias. *Israel Journal of Psychiatry and Related Sciences, 49*(4), 291–296.

Kazer, M. W., Grossman, S., Kerins, G., Kris, A., & Tocchi, C. (2013). Validity and reliability of the geriatric sexuality inventory. *Journal of Gerontological Nursing, 39*, 38–45.

Kazukauskas, K. A., & Lam, C. S. (2009). Importance of addressing sexuality in certified rehabilitation counselor practice. *Rehabilitation Education, 23*, 127–140.

Kazyak, E. (2012). Midwest or lesbian? Gender, rurality, and sexuality. *Gender & Society, 26*, 825–848.

Keller, A., McGarvey, E., & Clayton, A. (2006). Reliability and construct validity of the Changes in Sexual Functioning Questionnaire Short-Form (CSFQ-14). *Journal of Sex & Marital Therapy, 32*, 43–52.

Keller, S. N., & Brown, J. D. (2002). Media interventions to promote responsible sexual behavior. *The Journal of Sex Research, 39*, 67–72.

Kelly, E. L., & Conley, J. J. (1987). Personality and compatibility: A prospective analysis of marital stability and marital satisfaction. *Journal of Personality and Social Psychology, 52*(1), 27–40.

Kempeneers, P., Andrianne, R., Bauwens, S., Georis, I., Pairoux, J. F., & Blairy, S. (2012). Clinical outcomes of a new self-help booklet for premature ejaculation. *The Journal of Sexual Medicine, 9*(9), 2417–2428.

Kendurkar, A., & Kaur, B. (2008). Major depressive disorder, obsessive-compulsive disorder, and generalized anxiety disorder: Do the sexual dysfunctions differ? *The Primary Care Companion to the Journal of Clinical Psychiatry, 10*(4), 299–305.

Kennedy, S. H., Dickens, S. E., Eisfeld, B. S., & Bagby, R. M. (1999). Sexual dysfunction before antidepressant therapy in major depression. *Journal of Affective Disorders, 56*(2–3), 201–208.

Kern, R. S., Glynn, S. M., Horan, W. P., & Marder, S. R. (2009). Psychosocial treatments to promote functional recovery in schizophrenia. *Schizophrenia Bulletin, 35*(2), 347–361.

Keshet-Orr, J. (2003). Jewish women and sexuality. *Sexual and Relationship Therapy, 18*, 215–224.

Kessler, R. C., Berglund, P., Demler, O., Jin, R., Mertkangas, K. R., & Walters, E. E. (2005). Lifetime prevalence and age-of-onset distributions of DSM-IV disorders in the national comorbidity survey replication. *Archives of General Psychiatry, 62*, 593–603.

Killermann, S. (2013). *The social justice advocate's handbook: A guide to gender.* Austin, TX: Impetus Books.

King, B. M., & Regan, P. C. (2014). *Human sexuality today* (8th ed.). Upper Saddle River, NJ: Pearson.

Kirby, D. (2007). *Emerging Answers 2007: Research findings on programs to reduce teen pregnancy and sexually transmitted diseases.* Washington, DC: National Campaign to Prevent Teen and Unplanned Pregnancy.

Klein, M. (1932). The effects of early anxiety-situations on the sexual development of the girl. In D. Bassin (Ed.), *Female sexuality: Contemporary engagements* (pp. 287–334). North Bergen, NJ: Book-mart Press.

Kleinplatz, P. J. (2003). What's new in sex therapy? From stagnation to fragmentation. *Sexual and Relationship Therapy, 18*(1), 95–106.

Kleinplatz, P. J. (2007). Coming out of the sex therapy closet: Using experiential psychotherapy with sexual problems and concerns. *American Journal of Psychotherapy, 61*(3), 333–348.

Kleinplatz, P. J. (2009). Consumer protection is the major purpose of sex therapy certification. *Archives of Sexual Behavior, 38,* 1031–1032.

Kleinplatz, P. J. (2010). Lessons from great lovers. In S. B. Levine, C. B. Risen, & S. E. Althof (Eds.), *Handbook of clinical sexuality for mental health professionals* (2nd ed.). New York, NY: Routledge.

Klesse, C. (2005). Bisexual women, non-monogamy and differentialist anti-promiscuity discourses. *Sexualities, 8*(4), 445–464.

Klesse, C. (2006). Polyamory and its "others": Contesting the terms of non-monogamy. *Sexualities, 9*(5), 565–583.

Klimas, N., Koneru, A. O., & Fletcher, M. A. (2008). Overview of HIV. *Psychosomatic Medicine, 70,* 523–530.

Knickmeyer, R. C., & Baron-Cohen, S. (2006). Fetal testosterone and sex differences in typical social development and in autism. *Journal of Child Neurology, 21*(10), 825–845.

Knudson, G., De Cuypere, G., & Bockting, W. (2010). Recommendations for revision of the DSM diagnoses of gender identity disorders: Consensus statement of the World Professional Association for Transgender Health. *International Journal of Transgenderism, 12*(2), 115–118. doi:10.1080/15532739.2010.509215

Kope, S. A. (2007). Female sexual arousal and orgasm: Pleasures and problems. In L. VandeCreek, F. L. Peterson, Jr., & J. W. Bley (Eds.), *Innovations in clinical practice: Focus on sexual health* (pp. 93–106). Sarasota, FL: Professional Resource Press.

Kroger, J., Martinussen, M., & Marcia, J. E. (2010). Identity status change during adolescence and young adulthood: A meta-analysis. *Journal of Adolescence, 33*(5), 683–698.

Krueger, R. B., & Kaplan, M. S. (2001). The paraphilic and hypersexual disorder: An overview. *Journal of Psychiatric Practice, 7*(6), 391–403.

Kunkel, D., Cope, K., & Biely, E. (1999). Sexual messages on television: Comparing findings from three studies. *Journal of Sex Research, 36*(3), 230–236.

Kurdek, L. A. (1993). Predicting marital dissolution: A 5-year prospective longitudinal study of newlywed couples. *Journal of Personality and Social Psychology, 64*(2), 221–242.

Kurdek, L. A. (1998). Relationship outcomes and their predictors: Longitudinal evidence from heterosexual married, gay cohabiting, and lesbian cohabiting couples. *Journal of Marriage and the Family, 60,* 553–586.

Kurdek, L. A. (2003). Differences between gay and lesbian cohabiting couples. *Journal of Social and Personal Relationships, 20,* 411–436.

Kurdek, L. A. (2004). Are gay and lesbian cohabiting couples really different from heterosexual married couples? *Journal of Marriage and Family, 66,* 880–900.

Lamb, S., & Peterson, Z. D. (2012). Adolescent girls' sexual empowerment: Two feminists explore the concept. *Sex Roles, 66,* 703–712.

Lambert, M., Conus, P., Eide, P., Mass, R., Karow, A., Moritz, S., . . . Naber, D. (2004). Impact of present and past antipsychotic side effects on attitude toward typical antipsychotic treatment and adherence. *European Psychiatry, 19*(7), 415–422.

Langer, S. J., & Martin, J. I. (2004). How dresses can make you mentally ill: Examining gender identity disorder in children. *Child & Adolescent Social Work Journal, 21,* 5–23.

Langfeldt, T. (1981). Sexual development in children. In M. Cook & K. Howells (Eds.), *Adult sexual interest in children*. London, England: Academic Press.

Larrabee, M. J., & Miller, G. M. (1993). An examination of sexual intimacy in supervision. *The Clinical Supervisor, 11*(2), 103–126. doi:10.1300/J001v11n02_09

Laumann, E. O., Glasser, D. B., Neves, R. C. S., & Moreira, E. D. (2009). A population-based survey of sexual activity, sexual problems and associated help-seeking behavior patterns in mature adults in the United States of America. *International Journal of Impotence Research, 21*, 171–178.

Laumann, M., Conus, P., Eide, P., Mass, R., Karow, A., Moritz, S., . . . Naber, D. (1994). Impact of present and past antipsychotic side effects on attitude toward typical antipsychotic treatment and adherence. *European Psychiatry, 19*(7), 415–422.

Laurenceau. J. P., Rivera, L. M., Schaffer, A. R., & Pietromonaco, P. R. (2004). Intimacy as an interpersonal process: Current status and future directions. In D. J. Mashek & A. Aron (Eds.), *Handbook of closeness and intimacy* (pp. 61–78). London, England: Lawrence Erlbaum Associates.

Lebow, J. L., Chambers, A. L., Christensen, A., & Johnson, S. M. (2012). Research on the treatment of couple distress. *Journal of Marital and Family Therapy, 38*(1), 145–168.

Lebow, J., & Rekart, K. N. (2007). Integrative family therapy for high-conflict divorce with disputes over child custody and visitation. *Family Process, 46*(1), 79–91.

Lee, J., Parisi, S., Akers, A., Borrerro, S., & Schwarz, E. (2011). The impact of contraceptive counseling in primary care on contraceptive use. *Journal of General Internal Medicine, 26*, 731–736.

Lee, P., Houk, C., Ahmed, S. F., & Hughes, I. (2006). Consensus statement on management of intersex disorders. *Pediatrics, 118*, e488–e500.

Leiblum, S. R. (2002). Reconsidering gender differences in sexual desire: An update. *Sexual and Relationship Therapy, 17*(1), 57–68.

Leigh, B. C., Temple, M. T., & Trocki, K. F. (1993). The sexual behavior of US adults: Results from a national survey. *American Journal of Public Health, 83*(10), 1400-1408.

Levine, M. P., & Troiden, R. R. (1988). The myth of sexual compulsivity. *Journal of Sex Research, 25*(3), 347–363.

Levine, S. B. (2009). I am not a sex therapist! *Archives of Sexual Behavior, 38*(6), 1033–1034. doi:10.1007/s10508-009-9474-x

Levinson, R. A., Jaccard, J., & Beamer, L. (1995). Older adolescents' engagement in casual sex: Impact of risk perception and psychosocial motivations. *Journal of Youth and Adolescents, 24*(3), 349–364.

Lewis, G. B. (2003). Black-White differences in attitudes toward homosexuality and gay rights. *Public Opinion Quarterly, 67,* 59–78.

Lindau, S. T., Schumm, L. P., Laumann, E. O., Levinson, W., O'Muircheartaigh, C. A., & Waite, L. J. (2007). *The New England Journal of Medicine, 357*(8), 762–774.

Lipert, T., & Prager, K. J. (2001). Daily experiences of intimacy: A study of couples. *Journal of Personality and Social Psychology, 98*, 224–253.

Lipsith, J., McCann, D., & Goldmeier, D. (2003). Male psychogenic sexual dysfunction: The role of masturbation. *Sexual and Relationship Therapy, 18*(4), 448–471.

Litzinger, A., & Gordon, K. C. (2005). Exploring relationships among communication, sexual satisfaction, and marital satisfaction. *Journal of Sex & Marital Therapy, 31*(5), 409–424.

Lobitz, W. C., & Lobitz, G. K. (1996). Resolving the sexual intimacy paradox: A developmental model for the treatment of sexual desire disorders. *Journal of Sex & Marital Therapy, 22*(2), 71–84.

Lottes, I. L., & Grollman, E. A. (2010). Conceptualization and assessment of homonegativity. *International Journal of Sexual Health, 22*, 219–233.

Lucas, R. E. (2005). Time does not heal all wounds: A longitudinal study of reaction and adaptation to divorce. *Psychological Science, 16*(12), 945–950.

Luo, S., & Zhang, G. (2009). What leads to romantic attraction: Similarity, reciprocity, security, or beauty? Evidence from a speed-dating study. *Journal of Personality, 77*(4), 933–964.

Luyckx, K., Soenens, B., Vansteenkiste, M., Goossens, L., & Berzonsky, M. D. (2007). Parental psychological control and dimensions of identity formation in emerging adulthood. *Journal of Family Psychology, 21*(3), 546–550.

MacIntosh, H. B., & Johnson, S. (2008). Emotionally focused therapy for couples and childhood sexual abuse survivors. *Journal of Marital and Family Therapy, 34*(3), 298–315.

MacKinnon, J. L., & Marcia, J. E. (2002). Concurring patterns of women's identity status, attachment styles, and understanding of children's development. *International Journal of Behavioral Development, 26,* 70–80.

Maddock, J. W. (1989). Healthy family sexuality: Positive principles for educators and clinicians. *Family Relations, 38,* 130–136.

Maher, F. A., & Tetreault, M. K. (1993). Frames of positionality: Constructing meaningful dialogues about gender and race. *Anthropological Quarterly, 66* (3), 118–126.

Mahoney, A. (2008). Is it possible for Christian women to be sexual? *Women & Therapy, 31,* 89–106.

Malis, R. S., & Roloff, M. E. (2006). Demand/withdraw patterns in serial arguments: Implications for well-being. *Human Communication Research, 32*(2), 198–216.

Mallon, G. P., & DeCrescenzo, T. (2009). Social work practice with transgender and gender variant children and youth. In G. P. Mallon (Ed.), *Social work practice with transgender and gender variant youth* (2nd ed., pp. 65–86). New York, NY: Routledge.

Marcia, J. E. (1964). Determination and construct validity of ego identity status (Unpublished doctoral dissertation). Ohio State University, Columbus, Ohio.

Marcia, J. E. (1966). Development and validation of ego-identity status. *Journal of Personality and Social Psychology, 3*(5), 551–558.

Marshall, B. L. (2002). 'Hard science': Gendered constructions of sexual dysfunction in the 'Viagra age'. *Sexualities, 5*(2), 131–158. doi:10.1177/1363460702005002001

Marshall, W. A., & Tanner, J. M. (1986). Puberty. In F. Falkner & J. M. Tanner (Eds.), *Human growth: A comprehensive treatise: Volume 2: Postnatal Growth Neurobiology* (pp. 171–209). New York, NY: Plenum.

Marsiglio, W., & Donnelly, D. (1991). Sexual relations in later life: A national study of married persons. *Journal of Gerontology, 46*(6), S338–S344.

Masters, W. H., & Johnson, V. E. (1966). *Human sexual response.* Boston, MA: Little, Brown & Co.

Masters, W. H., & Johnson, V. E. (1970). *Human sexual inadequacy.* Boston, MA: Little, Brown.

Matthews, L. S., Wickrama, K. A. S., & Conger, R. D. (1996). Predicting marital instability from spouse and observer reports of marital interaction. *Journal of Marriage and the Family, 58*(3), 641–655.

Matthias, R. E., Lubben, J. E., Atchison, K. A., & Schweitzer, S. O. (1997). Sexual activity and satisfaction among very old adults: Results from a community-dwelling medicare population survey. *The Gerontologist, 37*(1), 6–14.

Mayer, J. D., Roberts, R. D., & Barsade, S. G. (2008). Human abilities: Emotional intelligence. *Annual Review of Psychology, 59,* 507–536.

Mayer, J. D., & Salovey, P. (1997). What is emotional intelligence? In P. Salovey & D. Sluyter (Eds.), *Emotional development and emotional intelligence: Educational implications* (pp. 3–31). New York, NY: Basic Books.

Mayer, J. D., Salovey, P., Caruso, D. R., & Sitarenios, G. (2003). Measuring emotional intelligence with the MSCEI V2.0. *Emotion, 3*(1), 97–105.

Mazza, M., Harnic, D., Catalano, V., Di Nicola, M., Bruschi, A., Bria, P., . . . Mazza, S. (2011). Sexual behavior in women with bipolar disorder. *Journal of Affective Disorders, 131,* 364–367.

Mazza, M., Mazza, O., Pomponi, M., Di Nicola, M., Padua, L., Vicini, M., . . . Mazza, S. (2009). What is the effect of selective serotonin reuptake inhibitors on temperament and character in patients with fibromyalgia? *Comprehensive Psychiatry, 50*(3), 240–244.

McCarthy, B. W. (2003). Marital sex as it ought to be. *Journal of Family Psychotherapy, 14*(2), 1–12.

McCarthy, B. W. (2004). An integrative cognitive-behavioral approach to understanding, assessing, and treating female sexual dysfunction. *Journal of Family Psychotherapy, 15*(3), 19–35.

McCaughey, M., & French, C. (2001). Women's sex-toy parties: Technology, orgasm, and commodification. *Sexuality and Culture, 5*, 77–96.

McClintock, M. K., & Herdt, G. (1996). Rethinking puberty: The development of sexual attraction. *Current Directions in Psychological Science, 5*(6), 178–183.

McDevitt, J. B., & Mahler, M. S. (1980). Object constancy, individuality, and internalization. In S. I. Greenspan & G. H. Pollack (Eds.), *The course of life: Psychoanalytic contributions toward understanding personality development: Volume I Infancy and early childhood* (pp. 407–423). Rockville, MD: National Institute of Mental Health.

McGee, E., & Shevlin, M. (2009). Effect of humor on interpersonal attraction and mate selection. *The Journal of Psychology: Interdisciplinary and Applied, 143*(1), 67–77.

McLeer, S. V., Dixon, J. F., Henry, D., Ruggiero, K., Escovitz, K., Niedda, T., & Scholle, R. (1998). Psychopathology in non-clinically referred sexually abused children. *Journal of the American Academy of Child & Adolescent Psychiatry, 37*(12), 1326–1333.

Meeks, B. S., Hendrick, S. S., & Hendrick, C. (1998). Communication, love and relationship satisfaction. *Journal of Social and Personal Relationships, 15*(6), 755–773.

Menard, A. D., & Offman, A. (2009). The interrelationships between sexual self-esteem, sexual assertiveness, and sexual satisfaction. *The Canadian Journal of Human Sexuality, 18,* 35–45.

Mercer, J. (2011). Attachment theory and its vicissitudes: Toward an updated theory. *Theory & Psychology, 21*(1), 25–45.

Meston, C. M., & Bradford, A. (2007). Sexual dysfunctions in women. *Annual Review of Clinical Psychology, 3*, 233–256.

Metz, M. E. (2007). *Relationship Intimacy Assessment*. Retrieved from http://www.michaelmetzphd .com/20071112/INCLUDES/!!RIA-ORIG-rev%2008.pdf

Meyer, I. H. (2003). Prejudice, social stress, and mental health in lesbian, gay, and bisexual populations: Conceptual issues and research evidence. *Psychological Bulletin, 129*, 674–697.

Mikach, S. M., & Bailey, J. M. (1999). What distinguishes women with unusually high numbers of sex partners? *Evolution and Human Behavior, 20*(3), 141–150.

Mikulincer, M., & Shaver, P. (2007). A behavioral systems perspective on the psychodynamics of attachment and sexuality. In D. Diamond, S. Blatt, & J. Lichtenburg (Eds.), *Attachment and sexuality* (pp. 51–78). New York, NY: Analytic Press.

Mikulincer, M., Shaver, P. R., & Pereg, D. (2003). Attachment theory and affect regulation: The dynamics, development, and cognitive consequences of attachment-related strategies. *Motivation and Emotion, 27*(2), 77–102.

Miller, R. S., Johnson, J. A., & Johnson, J. K. (1991). Assessing the prevalence of unwanted childhood sexual experiences. *Journal of Psychology & Human Sexuality, 4*, 43–54.

Miller, S. A., & Byers, E. S. (2010). Psychologists' sexual education and training in graduate school. *Canadian Journal of Behavioral Science, 42,* 93–100.

Millner, V. S., & Hanks, R. B. (2002). Induced abortion: An ethical conundrum for counselors. *Journal of Counseling & Development, 80*, 57–63.

Mintz, L. B., Balzer, A. M., Zhao, X., & Bush, H. E. (2012). Bibliotherapy for low sexual desire: Evidence for effectiveness. *Journal of Counseling Psychology, 59*(3), 471–478.

Modell, J. G., Katholi, C. R., Modell, J. D., & DePalma, R. L. (1997). Comparative sexual side effects of bupropion, fluoxetine, paroxetine, and sertraline. *Clinical Pharmacology & Therapeutics, 61*(4), 476–487.

Moen, P. (Ed.). (2003). *It's about time: Couples and careers.* Ithaca, NY: Cornell University.

Mohr, J. J., & Kendra, M. S. (2011). Revision and extension of a multidimensional measure of sexual minority identity: The Lesbian, Gay, and Bisexual Identity Scale. *Journal of Counseling Psychology, 58,* 234–245.

Monsen, R. B., Jackson, C. P., & Livingston, M. (1996). Having a future: Sexual decision making in early adolescence. *Journal of Pediatric Nursing, 11*(3), 183–188.

Montgomery, M. J. (2005). Psychosocial intimacy and identity from early adolescence to emerging adulthood. *Journal of Adolescent Research, 20*(3), 346–374.

Montgomery, S. A., Baldwin, D. S., & Riley, A. (2002). Antidepressant medications: A review of the evidence for drug-induced sexual dysfunction. *Journal of Affective Disorders, 69*(1–3), 119–140.

Moore, A. M., Frohwirth, L., & Blades, N. (2011). What women want from abortion counseling in the United States: A qualitative study of abortion patients in 2008. *Social Work in Health Care, 50,* 424–442. doi:10.1080/00981389.2011.575538

Moore, K. A., McCabe, M. P., & Stockdale, J. E. (1998). Factor analysis of the Personal Assessment in Relationships Scale (PAIR): Engagement, communication, and shared friendships. *Sexual & Marital Therapy, 13,* 361–368.

Moore, N. B., & Davidson, Sr., J. K. (2006). College women and personal goals: Cognitive dimensions that differentiate risk-reduction sexual decisions. *Journal of Youth and Adolescence, 35*(4), 577–589.

Moore, T. (1940). *Soul mates: Honoring the mysteries of love and relationship.* New York: HarperCollins Publishers.

Morison, S., & Greene, E. (1992). Juror and expert knowledge of child sexual abuse. *Child Abuse & Neglect, 16*(4), 595–613.

Morland, I. (2008). Intimate violations: Intersex and the ethics of bodily integrity. *Feminism & Psychology, 18,* 425–430.

Morris, D. (1982). Attachment and intimacy. In M. Fischer & G. Stricker (Eds.), *Intimacy* (pp. 305–323). New York, NY: Plenum.

Morrow, S. L., & Beckstead, A. (2004). Conversion therapies for same-sex attracted clients in religious conflict: Context, predisposing factors, experiences, and implications for therapy. *The Counseling Psychologist, 32*(5), 641–650. doi:10.1177/0011000004268877

Moss, B. F., & Schwebel, A. I. (1993). Defining intimacy in romantic relationships. *Family Relations, 42*(1), 31–37.

Munin, A., & Speight, S. (2010). Factors influencing the ally development of college students. *Equity & Excellence in Education, 43,* 249–264.

Murad, M. H., Elamin, M. B., Garcia, M. Z., Mullan, R. J., Murad, A., Erwin, P. J., & Montori, V. M. (2010). Hormonal therapy and sex reassignment: A systemic review and meta-analysis of quality of life and psychosocial outcomes. *Clinical Endocrinology, 72,* 214–231.

Murray, C. E., & Campbell, E. C. (in press). The pleasures and perils of technology in intimate relationships. *Journal of Couple and Relationship Therapy.*

Murray, C. E., & Mobley, A., K. (2009). Empirical research about same-sex intimate partner violence: A methodological review. *Journal of Homosexuality, 56,* 361–386.

Myers, J. E., Sweeney, T. J., & White, V. E. (2002). Advocacy for counseling and counselors: A professional imperative. *Journal of Counseling and Development, 80,* 394–402.

Nagaraj, A. K. M., Nizamie, S. H., Akhtar, S., Sinha, B. N. P., & Goyal, N. (2004). A comparative study of sexual dysfunction due to typical and atypical antipsychotics in remitted bipolar-I disorder. *Indian Journal of Psychiatry, 46*(3), 261–267.

Nagel, J. (2000). Ethnicity and sexuality. *Annual Review of Sociology, 26,* 107–133.

Nasserzadeh, S. (2009). "Sex therapy": A marginalized specialization. *Archives Of Sexual Behavior, 38*(6), 1037–1038. doi:10.1007/s10508-009-9537-z

National Infertility Association. (2006). *The costs of infertility.* Retrieved from http://www.resolve.org/family-building-options/making-treatment-affordable/the-costs-of-infertility-treatment.html

National Institutes of Health. (n.d.). *Postpartum depression facts.* National Institutes of Health NIH Publication No. 13-8000. Retrieved from http://www.nimh.nih.gov/health/publications/postpartum-depression-facts/postpartum-depression-brochure_146657.pdf

National Institutes of Health. (2013). *What are some common complications of pregnancy?* Retrieved from https://www.nichd.nih.gov/health/topics/pregnancy/conditioninfo/Pages/complications.aspx

Nicholls, L. (2008). Putting the New View classification scheme to an empirical test. *Feminism & Psychology, 18,* 515–526.

Nicolaou, L. (2012). Sexual dysfunction in people with schizophrenia. *Mental Health Practice, 15,* 20–24.

Nijs, P. (2006). Mental health of sex counsellors and of sex therapists: Some guidelines. *Sexual and Relationship Therapy*, *21*(1), 123–129. doi:10.1080/14681990500445373

Noll, J. G., Trickett, P. K., & Putnam, F. W. (2003). A prospective investigation of the impact of childhood sexual abuse on the development of sexuality. *Journal of Consulting and Clinical Psychology, 71*(3), 575–586.

Noller, P., Feeney, J. A., Bonnell, D., & Callan, V. J. (1994). A longitudinal study of conflict in early marriage. *Journal of Social and Personal Relationships, 11*(2), 233–252.

Norton, G. R., & Jehu, D. (1984). The role of anxiety in sexual dysfunctions: A review. *Archives of Sexual Behavior, 13*(2), 165–183.

Nosek, M. A., Foley, C. C., Hughes, R. B., & Howland, C. A. (2001). Vulnerabilities for abuse among women with disabilities. *Sexuality & Disability, 19,* 177–189.

Nurnberg, H. G., Hensely, P. L., Gelenberg, A. J., Fava, M., Lauriello, J., & Paine, S. (2003). Treatment of antidepressant-associated sexual dysfunction with sildenafil: A randomized controlled trial. *The Journal of the American Medical Association, 289*(1), 56–64.

Obergefell v. Hodges, 576 U. S. (2015).

Office on Women's Health. (2012). *Infertility Fact Sheet.* Retrieved from http://www.womenshealth.gov/publications/our-publications/fact-sheet/infertility.html

Okasha, M., McCarron, P., McEwen, J., & Smith, G. D. (2001). Changes in blood pressure among students attending Glasgow University between 1948 and 1968: Analyses of cross sectional surveys. *British Medical Journal, 322,* 885–889.

Okazaki, S. (2002). Influences of culture on Asian Americans' sexuality. *The Journal of Sex Research, 39,* 34–41.

Olsson, A., Lundqvist, M., Faxelid, E., & Nissen, E. (2005). Women's thoughts about sexual life after childbirth: Focus group discussions with women after childbirth. *Scandinavian Journal of Caring Sciences, 19*(4), 381–387.

Oswalt, S. B. (2010). Beyond risk: Examining college students' sexual decision making. *American Journal of Sexuality Education, 5,* 217–239.

Oswalt, S. B., & Wyatt, T. J. (2013). Sexual health behaviors and sexual orientation in a U.S. national sample of college students. *Archives of Sexual Behavior, 42*(8), 1561–1572.

Ott, M. A., Millstein, S. G., Ofner, S., & Halpern-Felsher, B. L. (2006). Greater expectations: Adolescents' positive motivations for sex. *Perspectives on Sexual and Reproductive Health, 38*(2), 84–89.

Pacey, S. (2008). The medicalization of sex: A barrier to intercourse? *Sexual and Relationship Therapy, 23*(3), 183–187.

Pallas, J., Levine, S. B., Althof, S. E., & Risen, C. B. (2000). A study using Viagra in a mental health practice. *Journal of Sex & Marital Therapy, 26*(1), 41–50.

Paul, C., Fitzjohn, J., Herbison, P., & Dickson, N. (2000). The determinants of sexual intercourse before age 16. *Journal of Adolescent Health, 27*(2), 136–147.

Peplau, L. A., & Fingerhut, A. W. (2007). The close relationships of lesbians and gay men. *Annual Review of Psychology*, 58, 405–424.

Peplau, L. A., & Garnets, L. D. (2000). A new paradigm for understanding women's sexuality and sexual orientation. *Journal of Social Issues, 56,* 329–350.

Pepper, S., & Lorah, P. (2008). Career issues and workplace considerations for the transsexual community: Bridging a gap of knowledge for career counselors and mental health providers. *The Career Development Quarterly, 56,* 330–343.

Pereda, N., Guilera, G., Forns, M., & Gómez-Benito, J. (2009). The prevalence of child sexual abuse in community and student samples: A meta-analysis. *Clinical Psychology Review, 29*(4), 328–338.

Perelman, M. A. (2002). FSD partner issues: Expanding sex therapy with sildenafil. *Journal of Sex & Marital Therapy, 28*(*Suppl.* 1), 195–204.

Perelman, M. A. (2006). A new combination treatment for premature ejaculation: A sex therapist's perspective. *Journal of Sexual Medicine, 3*(6), 1004–1012.

Pietromonaco, P. R., & Barrett, L. F. (2000). The internal working models concept: What do we really know about the self in relation to others? *Review of General Psychology, 4*(2), 155–175.

Pittman, J. F., Keiley, M. K., Kerpelman, J. L., & Vaughn, B. E. (2011). Attachment, identity, and intimacy: Parallels between Bowlby's and Erikson's paradigms. *Journal of Family Theory & Review, 3,* 32–46.

Planned Parenthood (2014a). *The check.* Retrieved from http://www.plannedparenthood.org/health-info/stds-hiv-safer-sex/check

Planned Parenthood. (2014b). *STDs.* Retrieved from http://www.plannedparenthood.org/health-info/stds-hiv-safer-sex

Planty, M., Langton, L., Krebs, C., Berzofsky, M., & Smiley-McDonald, H. (2013). *Female victims of sexual violence, 1994–2010.* (NCJ Publication No. 240655). Washington, DC: Bureau of Justice Statistics.

Plaut, S. (2008). Sexual and nonsexual boundaries in professional relationships: Principles and teaching guidelines. *Sexual and Relationship Therapy, 23*(1), 85–94. doi:10.1080/14681990701616624

Pope, A. L. (2013). Intimate relationship commitment: An integrated conceptual model. *Journal of Couple & Relationship Therapy, 12,* 270–289.

Pope, A., Mobley, A. K., & Myers, J. (2010). Integrating identities in same-sex attracted clients: Using developmental counseling and therapy to address sexual orientation conflicts. *Journal of LGBT Issues in Counseling, 4,* 32–47.

Porst, H., Burnett, A., Brock, G., Ghanem, H., Giuliano, F., Glina, S., . . . Sharlip, I. (2013). SOP conservative (medication and mechanical) treatment of erectile dysfunction. *The Journal of Sexual Medicine, 10*(1), 130–171.

Prager, K. J. (1995). *The psychology of intimacy.* New York, NY: Guilford.

Prager, K. J., & Roberts, L. J. (2004). Deep intimate connection: Self and intimacy in couple relationships. In D. J. Mashek & A. Aron (Eds.), *Handbook of closeness and intimacy* (pp. 43–60). London, England: Lawrence Erlbaum Associates.

Pridal, C. G., & LoPiccolo, J. (2000). Multielement treatment of desire disorders: Integration of cognitive, behavioral, and systemic therapy. In S. R. Leiblum & R. C. Rosen (Eds.), *Principles and practice of sex therapy* (3rd ed., pp. 57–84). New York, NY: Guilford.

Priest, J. B., & Wickel, K. (2011). Religious therapists and clients in same-sex relationships: Lessons from the court case of Bruff v. North Mississippi Health Service, Inc. *American Journal of Family Therapy, 39*(2), 139–148. doi:10.1080/01926187.2010.530196

Priest, R., & Wilcox, S. (1988). Confidentiality and the child sexual offender: Unique challenges and dilemmas. *Family Therapy, 15*(2), 107–113.

Public Health Agency of Canada. (2003). *Canadian Guidelines for Sexual Health Education.* Retrieved August 26, 2013 from http://www.phac-aspc.gc.ca/publicat/cgshe-ldnemss/pdf/guidelines-eng.pdf

Pukall, C. F., & Reissing, E. D. (2007). The demise of sexological science is not imminent in the face of sexual medicine: Commentary on "Will medical solutions to sexual problems make sexological care and science obsolete?" *Journal of Sex and Marital Therapy, 33,* 455–459.

Putnam, F. W. (2003). Ten-year research update review: Child sexual abuse. *Journal of the American Academy of Child & Adolescent Psychiatry, 42*(3), 269–278.

Quinn, C., & Browne, G. (2009). Sexuality of people living with a mental illness: A collaborative challenge for mental health nurses. *International Journal of Mental Health Nursing, 18,* 195–203.

Randolph, B. J., & Winstead, B. (1988). Sexual decision making and object relations theory. *Archives of Sexual Behavior, 17*(5), 389–409.

Regan, P. C., & Dreyer, C. S. (1999). Lust? Love? Status?: Young adults' motives for engaging in casual sex. *Journal of Psychology & Human Sexuality, 11*(1), 1–24.

Reid, R. C., Carpenter, B. N., Spackman, M., & Willes, D. L. (2008). Alexithymia, emotional instability, and vulnerability to stress proneness in patients seeking help for hypersexual behavior. *Journal of Sex & Marital Therapy, 34*(2), 133–149.

Reis, H. T. (2006). Implications of attachment theory for research on intimacy. In M. Mikulincer & G. S. Goodman (Eds.), *Dynamics of romantic love: Attachment, caregiving, and sex* (pp. 383–403). New York, NY: Guilford.

Rellini, A., & Meston, C. (2006). The sensitivity of event logs, self-administered questionnaires and photoplethysmography to detect treatment-induced changes in female sexual arousal disorder (FSAD) diagnosis. *Journal of Sexual Medicine, 3*(2), 283–291.

Ribner, D. S. (2010). Male orgasmic disorder: A new look at an old problem. *Sexual and Relationship Therapy, 25*(1), 6–11.

Richards, D., Miodrag, N., & Watson, S. (2006). Sexuality and developmental disability: Obstacles to human sexuality throughout the lifespan. *Developmental Disabilities Bulletin, 1–2*, 137–155.

Richardson, D. (2010). Youth masculinities: Compelling male heterosexuality. *The British Journal of Sociology, 61*, 737–756.

Riemersma, J., & Sytsma, M. (2013). A new generation of sexual addiction. *Sexual Addiction & Compulsivity, The Journal of Treatment & Prevention, 20*, 306–322.

Risen, C. B. (2010). Listening to sexual stories. In S. Levine, C. Risen, & S. Althof (Eds.), *Handbook of Clinical Sexuality for Mental Health Professionals* (2nd ed., pp. 3–20). New York, NY: Taylor & Francis.

Roccas, S., & Brewer, M. B. (2002). Social identity complexity. *Personality and Social Psychology Review, 6*(2), 88–106.

Rochlin, M. (1998). The heterosexual questionnaire. In M. S. Kimmel & M. A. Messner (Eds.), *Men's lives* (4th ed., p. 472). Boston, MA: Allyn and Bacon.

Rodgers, N. (2011). Intimate boundaries: Therapists' perception and experience of erotic transference within the therapeutic relationship. *Counselling & Psychotherapy Research, 11*(4), 266–274. doi :10.1080/14733145.2011.557437

Rodrigues, A. E., Hall, J. H., & Fincham, F. D. (2006). What predicts divorce and relationship dissolution? In M. A. Fine & J. H. Harvey (Eds.), *Handbook of divorce and relationship dissolution* (pp. 85–112). New York, NY: Routledge.

Rogers, C. R. (1972). *On becoming a person.* Boston, MA: Houghton Mifflin.

Romer, D., Black, M., Ricardo, I., Feigelman, S., Kaljee, L., Galbraith, J., . . . Stanton, B. (1994). Social influence on the sexual behavior of youth at risk for HIV exposure. *American Journal of Public Health, 84*(6), 977–985.

Roseborough, D. J. (2006). Coming out stories framed as faith narratives, or stories of spiritual growth. *Pastoral Psychology, 55*, 47–59.

Rosenau, D. E., & Tan, E. S. N. (2002). Single and sexual: The church's neglected dilemma. *Journal of Psychology and Theology, 30*, 185–194.

Rosenbaum, T. Y. (2009). Applying theories of social exchange and symbolic interaction in the treatment of unconsummated marriage/relationship. *Sexual and Relationship Therapy, 24*(1), 38–46.

Rosenbaum, T. Y. (2011). How well is the multidisciplinary model working? *Journal of Sexual Medicine, 8*(11), 2957–2958.

Rosenbaum, T. Y. (2013). An integrated mindfulness-based approach to the treatment of women with sexual pain and anxiety: Promoting autonomy and mind/body connection. *Sexual and Relationship Therapy, 28*(1–2), 20–28.

Rosenberg, K., Bleiberg, K., Koscis, J., & Gross, C. (2003). A survey of sexual side effects among severely mentally ill patients taking psychotropic medications: Impact on compliance. *Journal of Sex & Marital Therapy, 29*, 289–296. doi:10.1080/00926230390195524

Rosenthal, S. L., Lewis, L. M., & Cohen, S. S. (1996). Issues related to the sexual decision-making of inner-city adolescent girls. *Adolescence, 31*, 731–739.

Rotosky, S., Riggle, E., Gray, B., & Hatton, R. (2007). Minority stress experiences in committed same-sex couple relationship. *Professional Psychology: Research & Practice, 38*, 392–400.

Rowland, D. L. (2005). Psychophysiology of ejaculatory function and dysfunction. *World Journal of Urology, 23*, 82–88.

Rowland, D. L. (2007). Will medical solutions to sexual problems make sexological care and science obsolete? *Journal of Sex & Marital Therapy, 33*(5), 385–397.

Rowland, D. L., & Incrocci, L. (Eds.). (2008). *Handbook of sexual and gender identity disorders.* Hoboken, NJ: John Wiley & Sons.

Rowland, D. L., Keeney, C., & Slob, A. K. (2004). Sexual response in men with inhibited or retarded ejaculation. *International Journal of Impotence Research, 16*, 270–274.

Rubio-Aurioles, E., & Bivalacqua, T. J. (2013). Standard operational procedures for low sexual desire in men. *The Journal of Sexual Medicine, 10*(1), 94–107.

Rudow, H. (2012). Judge throws out counseling student's suit against Augusta State. *Counseling Today.* Retrieved September 9, 2013, from http://ct.counseling.org/2012/06/judge-throws-out-counseling-students-suit-against-augusta-state/

Rudow, H. (2013). Resolution of EMU case confirms ACA Code of Ethics, counseling profession's stance against client discrimination. *Counseling Today.* Retrieved September 9, 2013, from http://ct.counseling.org/2013/01/resolution-of-emu-case-confirms-aca-code-of-ethics-counseling-professions-stance-against-client-discrimination/

Ryan, C., Huebner, D., Diaz, R., & Sanchez, J. (2009). Family rejection as a predictor of negative outcomes in White and Latino lesbian, gay, & bisexual young adults. *Pediatrics, 123*, 346–352.

Sadovsky, R., Brock, G. G., Gray, M., Jensen, P. K., Gutkin, S. W., & Sorsaburu, S. (2011). Optimizing treatment outcomes with phosphodiesterase type 5 inhibitors for erectile dysfunction: Opening windows to enhanced sexual function and overall health. *Journal of the American Academy of Nurse Practitioners, 23*(6), 320–330.

Safren, S. A. (2005). Affirmative, evidence-based, and ethically sound psychotherapy with lesbian, gay, and bisexual clients. *Clinical Psychology: Science and Practice, 12*(1), 29–32. doi:10.1093/clipsy/bpi003

Salerian, A. J., Deibler, W. E., Vittone, B. J., Geyer, S. P., Drell, L., Mirmirani, N., . . . Fleisher, S. (2000). Sildenafil for psychotropic-induced sexual dysfunction in 31 women and 61 men. *Journal of Sex & Marital Therapy, 26*(2), 133–140.

Salts, C. J., & Smith, Jr., T. A. (2003). Special topics in family therapy. In L. L. Hecker & J. L. Wetchler (Eds.), *An introduction to marriage and family therapy* (pp. 449–492). Binghamton, NY: Haworth Clinical Practice Press.

Sandat, S. H. (2014). A review on paraphilias. *International Journal of Medical Reviews, 1*(4), 157–161.

Sanderson, C. A., & Cantor, N. (1995). Social dating goals in late adolescence: Implications for safer sexual activity. *Journal of Personality and Social Psychology, 68*(6), 1121–1134.

Sanderson, C. A., & Cantor, N. (2001). The association of intimacy goals and marital satisfaction: A test of four mediational models hypotheses. *Personality and Social Psychology Bulletin, 27*, 1567–1577.

Santelli, J., Ott, M. A., Lyon, M., Rogers, J., Summers, D., & Schleifer, R. (2006). Abstinence and abstinence-only education: A review of U.S. policies and programs. *Journal of Adolescent Health, 38*, 72–81. doi:10.1016/j.jadohealth.2005.10.006

Santtila, P., Wager, I., Witting, K., Harlaar, N., Jern, P., Johnsson, A., . . . Sandnabba, N. S. (2007). Discrepancy between sexual desire and sexual activity: Gender differences and associations with relationship satisfaction. *Journal of Sex & Marital Therapy, 34*(1), 31–44.

Sarwer, D. B., & Durlak, J. A. (1997). A field trial of the effectiveness of behavioral treatment for sexual dysfunctions. *Journal of Sex & Marital Therapy, 23*(2), 87–97.

Savin-Williams, R. C., & Ream, G. L. (2007). Prevalence and stability of sexual orientation components during adolescence and young adulthood. *Archives of Sexual Behavior*, 36, 385–394.

Schadé, A., van Grootheest, G., & Smit, J. (2013). HIV-infected mental health patients: Characteristics and comparison with HIV-infected patients from the general population and non-infected mental health patients. *BioMed Central Psychiatry, 13*(35). Retrieved from http://link.springer.com/article/10.1186/1471-244X-13-35#

Schaefer, M. T., & Olson, D. H. (1981). Assessing intimacy: The PAIR Inventory. *Journal of Marital & Family Therapy, 1*, 47–60.

Schick, V., Herbenick, D., Reece, M., Sanders, S. A., Dodge, B., Middlestadt, S. E., & Fortenberry, J. D. (2010). Sexual behaviors, condom use, and sexual health of Americans over 50: Implications for sexual health promotion for older adults. *The Journal of Sexual Medicine, 7*, 315–329.

Schmitt, D. P., & Jonason, P. K. (2015). Attachment and sexual permissiveness: Exploring differential associations across genders, cultures, and facets of short-term mating. *Journal of Cross Cultural Psychology, 46*, 119–133.

Schnarch, D. (1997). *Passionate marriage: Keeping love and intimacy alive in committed relationships.* New York, NY: Owl Books.

Schneider, B., & Gould, M. (1987). Female sexuality: Looking back into the future. In B. B. Hess & M. M. Ferre (Eds.), *Analyzing gender: A handbook of social science research* (pp. 120–153). Newbury Park: Sage.

Schoener, G., Milgrom, J. H., & Gonsiorek, J. (1984). Sexual exploitation of clients by therapists. *Women & Therapy, 3*(3–4), 63–69. doi:10.1300/J015V03N03_09

Schooler, D., & Ward, L. M. (2006). Average Joes: Men's relationships with media, real bodies, and sexuality. *Psychology of Men & Masculinity, 7*, 27–41.

Schore, J. R., & Schore, A. N. (2008). Modern attachment theory: The central role of affect regulation in development and treatment. *Clinical Social Work Journal, 36*(1), 9–20.

Schreier, B. A., & Lassiter, K. D. (2010). Competencies for working with sexual orientation and multiple cultural identities. In J. A. Erickson Cornish, B. A. Schreier, L. I. Nadkarni, L. Henderson Metzger, & E. R. Rodolfa (Eds.), *Handbook of Multicultural Counseling Competencies* (pp. 291–316). Hoboken, NJ: Wiley & Sons.

Schroeder, M., & Shidlo, A. (2001). Ethical issues in sexual orientation conversion therapies: An empirical study of consumers. *Journal of Gay & Lesbian Psychotherapy, 5*(3–4), 131–166. doi:10.1300/J236v05n03_09

Schroots, J. J. F. (1996). Theoretical developments in the psychology of aging. *The Gerontologist, 36*(6), 742–748.

Sears, K. P. (2012). Improving cultural competence education: The utility of an intersectional framework. *Medical Education, 46*, 545–551.

Seeber, J. J. (2001). Pastoral support for late-life sexuality. *Journal of Religious Gerontology, 12*(3–4), 101–109.

Seginer, R., & Noyman, M. S. (2005). Future orientation, identity and intimacy: Their relations in emerging adulthood. *European Journal of Developmental Psychology, 2*(1), 17–37.

Segraves, K. B., & Segraves, R. T. (1991). Hypoactive sexual desire disorder: Prevalence and comorbidity in 906 subjects. *Journal of Sex & Marital Therapy, 17*(1), 55–58.

Segraves, R. T., & Balon, R. (2010). Recognizing and reversing sexual side effects of medications. In S. B. Levine, C. B. Risen, & S. E. Althof (Eds.), *Handbook of Clinical Sexuality for Mental Health Professionals* (2nd ed., pp. 311–328). New York, NY: Taylor & Francis.

Segraves, R. T., & Segraves, K. B. (1995). Human sexuality and aging. *Journal of Sex Education & Therapy, 21*(2), 88–102.

Seligman, L., & Reichenberg, L. W. (2007). Selecting effective treatments: A comprehensive guide to treating mental disorders (3rd ed.). San Francisco, CA: John Wiley & Sons.

Sergi, M. J., Rassovsky, Y., Widmark, C., Reist, C., Erhart, S., Braff, D. L., . . . Green, M. F. (2007). Social cognition in schizophrenia: Relationships with neurocognition and negative symptoms. *Schizophrenia Research, 90*, 316–324.

Serretti, A., & Chiesa, A. (2011). Sexual side effects of pharmacological treatment of psychiatric diseases. *Clinical Pharmacology & Therapeutics, 89*, 142–147. doi:10.1038/clpt.2010.70

Seto, M. C. (1995). Sex with therapy clients: Its prevalence, potential consequences, and implications for psychology training. *Canadian Psychology/Psychologie Canadienne, 36*(1), 70–86. doi:10.1037/0708–5591.36.1.70

Shaver, P. R., Schachner, D. A., & Mikulincer, M. (2005). Attachment style, excessive reassurance seeking, relationship processes, and depression. *Personality and Social Psychology Bulletin, 31*(3), 343–359.

Shelton, K., & Delgado-Romero, E. (2013). Sexual orientation microaggressions: The experience of lesbian, gay, bisexual, and queer clients in psychotherapy. *Psychology of Sexual Orientation & Gender Diversity, 1*(S), 59–70.

Siegel, K., & Schrimshaw, E. W. (2003). Reasons for the adoption of celibacy among older men and women living with HIV/AIDS. *Journal of Sex Research, 40*(2), 189–200.

Sierau, S., & Herzberg, P. Y. (2012). Conflict resolution as a dyadic mediator: Considering the partner perspective on conflict resolution. *European Journal of Personality, 26*(3), 221–232.

Singh, A., Boyd, C., & Whitman, S. (2010). Counseling competency with transgender and intersex persons. In J. A. Erickson Cornish, B. A. Schreier, L. I. Nadkarni, L. Henderson Metzger, & E. R. Rodolfa (Eds.), *Handbook of multicultural counseling competencies* (pp. 415–441). New York, NY: Wiley.

Singh, D., Deogracias, J., Johnson, L., Bradley, S., Kibblewhite, S., Owen-Anderson, A., . . . Zucker, K. (2010). The Gender Identity/Gender Dysphoria Questionnaire for adolescents and adults: Further validity evidence. *The Journal of Sex Research, 47*, 49–58, doi:10.1080/00224490902898728

Skowron, E. A. (2000). The role of differentiation of self in marital adjustment. *Journal of Counseling Psychology, 47*, 229–237.

Smith, S. M., O'Keane, V., & Murray, R. (2002). Sexual dysfunction in patients taking conventional antipsychotic medication. *British Journal of Psychiatry, 181*, 49–55.

Sneed, J. R., Whitbourne, S. K., Culang, M. E. (2006). Trust, identity, and ego integrity: Modeling Erikson's core stages over 34 years. *Journal of Adult Development, 13*(3–4), 148–157.

Sobo, E. J., & Bell, S. (Eds.). (2001). *Celibacy, culture, and society: The anthropology of sexual abstinence*. Madison, WI: University of Wisconsin Press.

Sobocinski, M. R. (1990). Ethical principles in the counseling of gay and lesbian adolescents: Issues of autonomy, competence, and confidentiality. *Professional Psychology: Research and Practice, 21*(4), 240–247. doi:10.1037/0735–7028.21.4.240

South, S. C., Krueger, R. F., & Iacono, W. G. (2009). Factorial invariance of the Dyadic Adjustment Scale across gender. *Psychological Assessment, 21*, 622–628.

Southern, S. (1999). Facilitating sexual health: Intimacy enhancement techniques for sexual dysfunction. *Journal of Mental Health Counseling, 21*, 15–32.

Southern, S., & Cade, R. (2011). Sexuality counseling: A professional specialization comes of age. *The Family Journal, 19*, 246–262.

Spanier, G. B. (1976). Measuring dyadic adjustment: New scales for assessing the quality of marriage and similar dyads. *Journal of Marriage and the Family, 38*, 15–28.

Spence, S. H. (1997). Sex and relationships. In W. K. Halford & H. J. Markman (Eds.), *Clinical handbook of marriage and couples interventions* (pp. 73–105). Hoboken, NJ: John Wiley & Sons.

Spitalnick, J., & McNair, L. (2005). Couples therapy with gay and lesbian clients: An analysis of important clinical issues. *Journal of Sex & Marital Therapy, 31,* 43–56.

Stebbins, J. P. (2010). Implications of sexuality counseling with women who have a history of prostitution. *The Family Journal, 18*(1), 79–83.

Steil, J. M. (1997). *Marital equality: Its relationship to well-being of husbands and wives.* Thousand Oaks, CA: Sage.

Stein, R. (2015). Female libido pill fires up debate about women and sex. *National Public Radio.* Retrieved from http://www.npr.org/blogs/health/2015/02/16/384043661/female-libido-pill-fires-up-debate-about-women-and-sex.

Stephens, D., & Phillips, L. (2005). Integrating Black feminist thought into conceptual frameworks of African American adolescent women's sexual scripting processes. *Sexualities, Evolution, & Gender, 7,* 37–55.

Stephenson, K. R., & Meston, C. M. (2010). Differentiating components of sexual well-being in women: Are sexual satisfaction and sexual distress independent constructs? *Journal of Sexual Medicine, 7*(7), 2458–2468.

Sternberg, R. J. (1997). Construct validation of a triangular love scale. *European Journal of Social Psychology, 27,* 313–335.

Stevens, M. A., & Englar-Carson, M. (2010). Counseling men. In J. A. Erickson-Cornish, B. A. Schreier, L. I. Nadkarni, L. H. Metzger, & E. R. Rodolfa (Eds.), *Handbook of multicultural counseling competencies* (pp. 195–230). New York, NY: Wiley.

Stevenson, D. B. (1996). Freud's psychosocial stages of development. *Psychosocial Development.* Retrieved from http://www.victorianweb.org/science/freud/

Stinson, R. D. (2009). The behavioral and cognitive-behavioral treatment of female sexual dysfunction: How far we have come and the path left to go. *Sexual and Relationship Therapy, 24*(3–4), 271–285.

Sugrue, D. P. (2007). Sexual addiction/compulsion: Diagnosis and treatment. In L. VandeCreek, F. L. Peterson, Jr., & J. W. Bley (Eds.), *Innovations in clinical practice: Focus on sexual health* (pp. 177–196). Sarasota, FL: Professional Resource Press.

Sullivan, H. S. (1953). *The interpersonal theory of psychiatry.* New York, NY: Norton.

Taleporos, G., & McCabe, M. P. (2002). Body image and physical disability–personal perspectives. *Social Science & Medicine, 54,* 971–980.

The World Bank. (2014). *Mortality rate, neonatal (per 1,000 live births).* Retrieved from http://data.worldbank.org/indicator/SH.DYN.NMRT

Thibaut, F. (2012). Pharmacological treatment of paraphilias. *Israel Journal of Psychiatry and Related Sciences, 49*(4), 297–305.

Thomas, K. W., & Kilmann, R. H. (1975). The social desirability variable in organizational research: An alternative explanation for reported findings. *The Academy of Management Journal, 18*(4), 741–752.

Throckmorton, W. (1998). Efforts to modify sexual orientation: A review of outcome literature and ethical issues. *Journal of Mental Health Counseling, 20*(4), 283–304.

Tiefer, L., (2001). The selling of 'female sexual dysfunction.' *Journal of Sex and Marital Therapy, 27,* 625–628.

Tiefer, L. (2006). Sex therapy as a humanistic enterprise. *Sexual and Relationship Therapy, 21*(3), 359–375. doi:10.1080/14681990600740723

Tiefer, L. (2009). Misconstruing sex therapy's dilemmas: The need for *sexualwissenschaft,* sex education, and primary prevention. *Archives of Sexual Behavior, 38,* 1046–1047.

Tiefer, L. (2012). Medicalizations and demedicalizations of sexuality therapies. *Journal of Sex Research, 49*(4), 311–318.

Tiefer, L., Hall, M., & Tavris, C. (2002). Beyond dysfunction: A new view of women's sexual problems. *Journal of Sex & Marital Therapy, 28*(Suppl. 1), 225–232.

Titelman, P. (Ed.). (2014). *Clinical applications of Bowen family systems theory.* New York, NY: Routledge.

Toledano, R., & Pfaus, J. (2006). The Sexual Arousal and Desire Inventory (SADI): A multidimensional scale to assess subjective sexual arousal and desire. *International Society for Sexual Medicine, 3,* 853–877.

Tolstedt, B. E., & Stokes, J. P. (1983). Relation of verbal, affective, and physical intimacy to marital satisfaction. *Journal of Counseling and Psychology, 4,* 573–580.

Traeen, B., & Kvalem, I. L. (1996). Sexual socialization and motives for intercourse among Norwegian adolescents. *Archives of Sexual Behavior, 25*(3), 289–302.

Trice-Black, S., & Foster, V. A. (2011). Sexuality of women with young children: A feminist model of mental health counseling. *Journal of Mental Health Counseling, 33*(2), 95–111.

Trudel, G., Marchand, A., Ravart, M., Aubin, S., Turgeon, L., & Fortier, P. (2001). The effect of a cognitive-behavioral group treatment program on hypoactive sexual desire in women. *Sexual and Relationship Therapy, 16*(2), 145–164.

Turchik, J. A. (2012). Sexual victimization among male college students: Assault severity, sexual functioning, and health risk behaviors. *Psychology of Men & Masculinity, 13,* 243–255.

Turchik, J. A., & Edwards, K. E. (2012). Myths about male rape: A literature review. *Psychology of Men & Masculinity, 13,* 211–226.

Tyler, K., Hoyt, D. R., Whitbeck, L. B., & Cauce, A. M. (2001). The impact of childhood sexual abuse on later sexual victimization among runaway youth. *Journal of Research on Adolescence, 11*(2), 151–176.

United Nations Development Programme. (2012). *Global commission on HIV and the law: Risks, rights, and health.* New York, NY: Author.

United States Department of Health & Human Services. (2012). *U.S. statistics.* Retrieved from https://www.aids.gov/hiv-aids-basics/hiv-aids-101/statistics/

United States Department of Health & Human Services. (2013). Child maltreatment 2012. Retrieved from http://www.acf.hhs.gov/programs/cb/research-data-technology/statistics-research/child-maltreatment

United States Department of Justice. (2012). *Questions and answers: The Americans with Disabilities Act and persons with HIV/AIDS.* Washington, DC: Author.

United States Equal Employment Opportunity Commission. (2002). *Facts about sexual harassment.* Retrieved from http://www.eeoc.gov/facts/fs-sex.html

United States Equal Employment Opportunity Commission. (n.d.). *Sexual harassment.* Retrieved from http://www.eeoc.gov/laws/types/sexual_harassment.cfm

United States Substance Abuse and Mental Health Services Administration (SAMHSA). (2014). *Results from the 2013 national survey on drug use and health: Summary of national findings.* (NSDUH Series H-48, DHHS Publication No. [SMA] 14–4863). Rockville, MD: Substance Abuse and Mental Health Services Administration.

Upadhyay, U. D., Cockrill, K., & Freedman, L. R. (2010). Informing abortion counseling: An examination of evidence-based practices used in emotional care for other stigmatized and sensitive health issues. *Patient Education and Counseling.* doi:10.1016/j.pec.2010.08.026

Ussher, J., Perz, J., Gilbert, E., Tim Wong, W. K., Mason, C., Hobbs, K., & Kirsten, L. (2013). Talking about sex after cancer: A discourse analytic study of health care professional accounts of sexual communication with patients. *Psychology & Health, 28,* 1370–1390.

van Anders, S. M. (2012). Testosterone and sexual desire in healthy women and men. *Archives of Sexual Behavior, 41*(6), 1471–1484.

van Anders, S. M., Hamilton, L. D., & Watson, N. V. (2007). Multiple partners are associated with higher testosterone in North American men and women. *Hormones and Behavior, 51,* 454–459.

van der Kwaak, A., Ferris, K., van Kats, J., & Dieleman, M. (2010). Performance of sexuality counselling: A framework for provider-client encounters. *Patient Education and Counseling, 81*(3), 338–342.

van Lankveld, J. J. D. M., Leusink, P., van Diest, S., Gijs, L., & Slob, A. K. (2009). Internet-based brief sex therapy for heterosexual men with sexual dysfunctions: A randomized controlled pilot trial. *Journal of Sexual Medicine, 6*(8), 2224–2236.

Visser, R., & MacDonald, D. (2007). Swings and roundabouts: Management of jealousy in heterosexual "swinging" couples. *British Journal of Social Psychology, 46*(2), 459–476.

Waite, L. J., Laumann, E. O., Das, A., & Schumm, L. P. (2009). Sexuality: Measures of partnerships, practices, attitudes, and problems in the national social life, health, and aging study. *The Journal of Gerontology Series B: Psychological Sciences and Social Sciences.* Retrieved from http://psychsocgerontology.oxfordjournals.org/content/early/2009/01/01/geronb.gbp038.short

Ward, L. M., & Friedman, K. (2006). Using TV as a guide: Associations between television viewing and adolescent's sexual attitudes and behavior. *Journal of Research on Adolescence, 16*, 133–156.

Ward v. Wilbanks, 6th Cir. R. 26.1. (2011). Retrieved from http://www.counseling.org/resources/pdfs/EMUamicusbrief.pdf

Waters, R. (2010). Understanding allyhood as a developmental process. *About Campus, 15*(5), 2–8. doi:10.1002/abc.20035

Watkins, K. J., & Baldo, T. D. (2004). The infertility experience: Biopsychosocial effects and suggestions for counselors. *Journal of Counseling & Development, 82,* 394–402.

Watson, L. B., Robinson, D., Dispenza, F., & Nazari, N. (2012). African American women's sexual objectification experiences: A qualitative study. *Psychology of Women Quarterly, 36,* 458–475.

Weber, S. B. (1983). Some perspectives on women in therapy and women as therapists. *Clinical Social Work Journal, 11*(1), 33–51.

Wei, M., Russell, D. W., Mallinckrodt, B., & Vogel, D. L. (2007). The experiences in close relationship scale (ECR)-short form: Reliability, validity, and factor structure. *Journal of Personality Assessment, 88,* 187–204.

Wei, M., Vogel, D. L., Ku, T. Y., & Zakalik, R. A. (2005). Adult attachment, affect regulation, negative mood, and interpersonal problems: The mediating roles of emotion reactivity and emotional cutoff. *Journal of Counseling Psychology, 52*(1), 14–24.

Weiss, J. A. (2007). Let us talk about it: Safe adolescent sexual decision making. *Journal of the American Academy of Nurse Practitioners, 19,* 450–458.

Weiss, R. L., & Heyman, R. E. (1997). A clinical-research overview of couple interactions. In W. K. Halford & H. J. Markman (Eds.), *The clinical handbook of marriage and couples interventions* (pp. 13–42). New York, NY: Wiley.

Wenzel, A., Graff-Dolezal, J., Macho, M., & Brendle, J. R. (2010). Communication and social skills in socially anxious and nonanxious individuals in the context of romantic relationships. *Behaviour Research and Therapy, 43*(4), 505–519.

Whetten, K., Reif, S., Whetten, R., & Murphy-McMillan, L. K. (2008). Trauma, mental health, distrust, and stigma among HIV-positive persons: Implications for effective care. *Psychosomatic Medicine, 70,* 531–538.

Whipple, B., & Brash-McGreer, K. (1997). Management of female sexual dysfunction. In M. L. Sipski & C. J. Alexander, (Eds.), *Sexual function in people with disability and chronic illness: A health professional's guide* (pp. 509–534). Gaithersburg, MD: Aspen.

White, L. K., & Booth, A. (1991). Divorce over the life course: The role of marital happiness. *Journal of Family Issues, 12*(1), 5–21.

White, M. (2007). *Maps of narrative practice.* New York, NY: W. W. Norton & Company.

Whitman, J. S., Glosoff, H. L., Kocet, M. M., & Tarvydas, V. (2013, January). *Ethical issues related to conversion or reparative therapy.* Retrieved from http://www.counseling.org/news/updates/2013/01/16/ethical-issues-related-to-conversion-or-therapy.

Wiederman, M. W. (2005). The gendered nature of sexual scripts. *The Family Journal, 13,* 496–502.

Wilkinson, A. V., Holahan, C. J., & Drane-Edmundson, E. W. (2002). Predicting safer sex practices: The interactive role of partner cooperation and cognitive factors. *Psychology & Health, 17,* 697–709.

Williams, L., Zapata, L., D'Angelo, D., Harrison, L., & Morrow, B. (2012). Associations between preconception counseling and maternal behaviors before and during pregnancy. *Maternal & Child Health Journal, 16*, 1854–1861.

Winton, M. A. (2000). The medicalization of male sexual dysfunctions: An analysis of sex therapy journals. *Journal of Sex Education & Therapy, 25*(4), 231–239.

Wischmann, T. (2008). Implications of psychosocial support in infertility—a critical appraisal. *Journal of Psychosomatic Obstetrics & Gynecology, 29*, 83–90.

Wise, S., Florio, D., Benz, D. R., & Geier, P. (2007). Ask the experts: Counseling sexual abuse survivors. *Annals of the American Psychotherapy Association, 10*(2), 18–20.

Wojnar, D., Swanson, K., & Adolfsson, A. (2011). Confronting the inevitable: A conceptual model of miscarriage for use in clinical practice and research. *Death Studies, 35*, 536–558.

Woodward, C., & Joseph, S. (2003). Positive change processes and post-traumatic growth in people who have experienced childhood abuse: Understanding vehicles of change. *Psychology and Psychotherapy: Theory, Research and Practice, 76*, 267–283.

World Health Organization. (2010). *Developing sexual health programmes: A framework for action.* Retrieved September 3, 2013 from http://www.who.int/reproductivehealth/publications/sexual_health/rhr_hrp_10_22/en/index.html

World Health Organization (2014). *Sexually transmitted infections.* Retrieved from http://www.who.int/topics/sexually_transmitted_infections/en/

World Professional Association for Transgender Health. (2014). *International symposia.* Retrieved from http://wpath.org

Wright, P. J. (2009). Sexual socialization messages in mainstream entertainment mass media: A review and synthesis. *Sexuality & Culture, 13,* 181–200.

Wyatt, G. E. (1997). *Stolen women: Reclaiming our sexuality, taking back our lives.* New York, NY: Wiley.

Wylie, K. R., Crowe, M. J., & Boddington, D. (1995). How can the therapist deal with a couple with male demands for anal sex? *Sexual & Marital Therapy, 10*(1), 95–98. doi:10.1080/02674659508405541

Yarhouse, M. A., & Throckmorton, W. (2002). Ethical issues in attempts to ban reorientation therapies. *Psychotherapy: Theory, Research, Practice, Training, 39*(1), 66–75. doi:10.1037/0033-3204.39.1.66

Yasan, A., Essizoglu, A., & Yildirim, E. A. (2009). Inappropriate treatment of a woman with vaginismus and social and psychiatric consequences in a traditional culture. *Sexual and Relationship Therapy, 24,* 286–291.

Young, M., Denny, G., & Spear, C. (1999). Area specific self-esteem and adolescent sexual behavior. *American Journal of Health Studies, 15*(4), 181–188.

Zolna, M. R., Lindberg, L. D., & Frost, J. J. (2011). *Couple-focused services in publicly funded family planning clinics: Identifying the need, 2009.* New York, NY: Guttmacher Institute.

Zucker, K. J. (2013). DSM-5: Call for commentaries on gender dysphoria, sexual dysfunctions, and paraphilic disorders. *Archives of Sexual Behavior, 42*(5), 669–674.

Zumaya, M., Bridges, S. K., & Rubio, E. (1999). A constructivist approach to sex therapy with couples. *Journal of Constructivist Psychology, 12,* 185–201.

Index